P9-DZY-033

Kayaks You Can Build

Kayaks You Can Build

An illustrated guide to plywood construction

Ted Moores & Greg Rössel

Firefly Books

A Firefly Book

Published by Firefly Books Ltd. 2004

First printing

Publisher Cataloging-in-Publication Data (U.S.)

Moores, Ted.
Kayaks you can build : an illustrated guide to plywood construction / Ted Moores and Greg Rössel.
[256] p. : col. photos. ; cm.
Includes index.
Summary: Step-by-step guide to the construction of a plywood kayak from a stitch and glue kayak kit.
ISBN 1-55297-861-3 (pbk.)
1. Kayaks – Design and construction. 2. Boatbuilding. I. Rössel, Greg. II. Title.
623.8/29 21 VM353.M66 2004

National Library of Canada Cataloguing in Publication Data

Moores, Ted
Kayaks you can build : an illustrated guide to plywood construction / Ted Moores and Greg Rössel.
Includes index.
ISBN 1-55297-861-3
1. Kayaks–Design and construction. I. Rössel, Greg, 1951- II. Title.
VM353.M67 2004 623.82'9 C2004-902570-8

Cover and interior design by Lind Design
All photos by Ted Moores except:
John de Visser: cover, 2, 6, 8, 16, 20, 28, 48, 54, 142, 144, 177, 178, 207, 208, 244
Hudson's Bay Company Archives, Archives of Manitoba: 10
Royal Canoe Club: 12
The Adirondack Museum: 13
Michael Cullen: 14

The Publisher acknowledges the financial support of the Government of Canada through the Book Publishing Industry Development Program for its publishing activities.

Published in the United States in 2004 by
Firefly Books (U.S.) Inc.
P.O. Box 1338, Ellicott Station
Buffalo, New York 14205

Published in Canada in 2004 by
Firefly Books Ltd.
66 Leek Crescent
Richmond Hill, Ontario L4B 1H1

Printed in Singapore

To my mother, Dorothy Moores, 1920–2003,
who was always ready to hold up her end of the board.

To my father, Fred Moores, 1917–1953,
who gave me my own bag of nails when I was four.

And to my grandfather, Eugene Moores, 1893–1976,
who showed me that working effectively was a system.

– T.M.

CONTENTS

INTRODUCTION

THE DRAMATIC GROWTH in the popularity of kayaks is perhaps not surprising in a world of pricey, obnoxiously loud personal watercraft. As a low-impact way to explore wilderness or to paddle through cottage country, these elegant, easy-to-transport craft are hard to beat.

The availability of kits with precut plywood components has given a growing number of paddlers the freedom to build a strong, lightweight kayak to their specifications and at a reasonable price. The common building methods used are "stitch and glue" or "tack and tape." A typical stitch-and-glue kayak kit contains precut plywood planks, epoxy and hardware. To assemble the hull, holes are drilled along each plank's edge and the plank is temporarily wired, or stitched, to the adjoining plank. The seams are then glued and covered with epoxy and fiberglass cloth. This simple construction process demands neither special skills nor a woodworking shop. All that is necessary is the desire to build it right.

Since its roots can be traced to backyard boatbuilding, it's not surprising that using plywood to build a kayak encourages experimentation and innovation. There are many good ways to use the material, and *Kayaks You Can Build* is intended to be a resource for all builders, regardless of the method they have chosen to build their boat. Much of the book is dedicated to showing you how to perform each of the construction steps in an efficient and safe manner. The three featured kayaks illustrate the many different possibilities for combining the basic building techniques. Following these instructions will enable you to build a beautiful, professional-quality kayak in your first attempt.

As professional boatbuilders and teachers, we understand the challenges faced by the first-time builder and have tried to address these by demonstrating that professional quality combines a state of mind and a few shortcuts applied in the right places; by introducing simple boatbuilding controls that will make the shape of your craft predictable; by reducing exposure time to epoxy and dust to a minimum by finding the shortest route to the best results; and by exploring enough of the "why" behind what we are doing to make the instructions valuable to anyone building a plywood boat, regardless of the method.

Some independent-minded builders feel restricted by the prosaic constraints of working with a manufacturer's manual. There is always a temptation to skip steps, to do them out of order or to give more tedious tasks a lick and a promise so that you can get to the good parts. This is bad news in boatbuilding because the process is a continuum, with each new piece dependent on the placement and quality of the previous one. We'll tell you the reasons why certain steps are important and which steps in the process can be streamlined.

That said, you will make mistakes. The trick is to keep those miscues to a minimum and ensure that any repairs are top quality. Unfortunately, few stock manuals have the space to help novices correct mistakes or, better yet, avoid them. Well, mistakes do happen and we document some common ones, how they were remedied and how they could have been avoided in the first place.

The techniques and tools suggested in this book are tried and true and a great place to start, but they are not the only way. A big part of boatbuilding is problem-solving, invention, borrowing technology from one application and using it in another, and utilizing the tools and solutions you are familiar with. So sharpen up that block plane and you'll be out on the water before you know it.

CHAPTER ONE

A Short History of the Kayak

The kayak is one of the earliest "homebuilt" boats. Its ancestry can be traced back thousands of years to the hunters of the Aleutian Islands, Siberia and Greenland. The light, sinew-lashed frame of this nimble craft was fashioned of driftwood and bone and covered with sewn hides, usually oiled sealskin. Even the construction tools were homebuilt – carved from bone or antler, chipped from stone, or hammered out of local metals.

Despite the simplicity of the raw materials used in the craft, the construction techniques and skill required to actually build one are quite sophisticated. Built by eye, experience and tradition, the Inuit (Eskimo) kayak is as much art as it is working boat and transportation.

The Pioneers of Recreational Kayaking

It is easy to forget that recreational boating is a fairly recent phenomenon. Until the nineteenth century, most watercraft (including kayaks) were used to make a living. But some individuals had the time, money or inclination to get out on the water for the sheer enjoyment of it. Some accounts credit the German doctor Georg von Langsdorf as the pioneer of recreational kayaking. Beginning in the early 1800s, Langsdorf used a traditional Aleut baidarka to explore the northern Pacific waters of Alaska, British Columbia, Washington state and California.

For sportsmen of the day without ready access to sealskin and bone, the wooden-hulled kayak seemed a more practical option. One of the earliest accounts of recreational use of a wooden kayak-like vessel was written by London barrister John MacGregor. In the mid-1800s MacGregor decided to explore the bays and waterways of Europe and beyond in a 15-foot lapstrake wooden-decked canoe he called the Rob Roy. Reminiscent of the traditional skin-covered Arctic kayak, this decked canoe design was ideal for river running and inshore cruising. MacGregor had a series of these "kayaks" built, and his published accounts of his adventures with them from the Baltic to the Nile were avidly devoured by the outdoor-loving public.

By the 1880s, boatbuilders on our side of the Atlantic had begun to take note. John Henry Rushton of Canton, New York, started building elegant decked canoes. His catalog contained a stock model canoe based on the Rob Roy as well as other models. Farther south, Staten Island-based builder

Opposite: Two men build the frame of a flat-bottomed East Hudson Bay kayak.

In 1868–69 John MacGregor, with Rob Roy Number Five in tow, toured the Eastern Mediterranean. His exploits, such as his capture by the Arabs of Hooleh, shown here, contributed to the popularity of his fourth Rob Roy adventure book, *Rob Roy on the Jordan*.

W.P. Stephens was also manufacturing decked cruising canoes that no doubt were inspired by the writings of John MacGregor.

While not truly kayaks of the seal-hunting, iceberg-dodging variety, these shorter, wider boats introduced the public to solo cruising with style. The only downside was that their complexity made them expensive and difficult to build for the novice. Nearly a century would go by before technology made wooden kayak construction a truly economical and egalitarian option.

The Folding Kayak

By the twentieth century, the notion of being able to transport a kayak easily to a suitable body of water began to appeal. If you had to assemble the boat on-site, so be it. Alfred Heurich of Munich designed a folding boat with a lace-type cover. In 1907 Johann Klepper, a tailor, acquired the rights and built a boat that could be transported as baggage on a train. The craft was constructed with a bamboo skeleton and a coated canvas hull covering.

The Klepper Company saw almost immediate success with its prodigy. The end of the First World War brought a surge of public interest in the diminutive folding boat. Klepper vessels were even employed on expeditions such as Roald Amundsen's 1926 North Pole expedition and Admiral Byrd's 1928 South Pole expedition. Thirty years later, Dr. Hannes Lindemann crossed the Atlantic in a stock Klepper double.

Inevitably, competition appeared in the marketplace. Folbot started off as an English firm in 1933, moving to New York City in 1935 and to South Carolina in 1955. The company produced both folding and rigid boats and marketed its craft to the "individual and great American, who values his own initiative, rather than mass-oriented and ecology-disturbing pastimes." Today there are many manufacturers: Folbot, Feathercraft, Nautiraid, Pakboat and Fujita, to name just a few. And although the coated canvas cover has been superseded by synthetic cloth coated with synthetic rubber – PVC, Hypalon or polyurethane – and the wooden frame components have been replaced with aluminum or polycarbonates, these folding boats remain true to Klepper's vision of a boat-in-a-bag, ready for travel.

If one was handy with tools, though, prefab folding boats were not the only option. The 1911 book *Boat-Building and Boating*, by D.C. Beard, provided plans for Ozias Dodge's Umbrella canoe, which seemed a very close cousin of the Klepper. Beard assures the reader that Mr. Dodge is a Yale man, an artist and an enthusiastic canoeist whose little craft has navigated many picturesque rivers in the United States and Europe.

Dodge's Umbrella canoe was actually an early folding kayak that could be easily manufactured at home by the intrepid reader. The boat frame consisted of four notched formers, eight stringers and two sheet-metal thimbles. To assemble the boat, you laid out the stringers, inserted them into the notched formers, and gathered the ends of the stringers and inserted them into the thimbles. A painted canvas skin was drawn over the hull. The author concedes that the resulting boat does "look like a starved dog, with all of its ribs showing through the skin but does not in any way impede the progress of the boat through the water." To disassemble, you simply popped the stringers from the notches in the formers, rolled up the canvas around the stringers, slid the formers over the bundled poles, put the whole thing on your shoulder and carried it home.

For the impecunious basement boatbuilder, kits for rigid boats began to emerge. A 1938 *Popular Mechanics* magazine carried an ad for the Mead's Glider Company of Chicago touting a 30-pound CK-2 Sportsman's KiYak "at amazing factory-to-you prices – home-assembly in 9 hours at nearly HALF factory-built cost." Some of the folding-kayak companies also began offering economical rigid versions of their craft. With simple woodworking skills and a modest investment, almost anyone could afford to get out on the water.

Plywood and Strip-Planking

New technologies and glues changed the way builders looked at working with wood. By the Second World War, truly waterproof and durable glues had been developed – no more messing around with adhesives made from horses' feet. These new glues made waterproof plywood possible.

Plywood is a manufactured wooden panel or sheet composed of many thin wooden layers, which are called veneers or plies. The veneers are sandwiched at right angles to one another and glued together under great pressure. Initially, primitive adhesives relegated these manufactured panels to furniture and other protected applications. Then, in the 1930s, truly strong and waterproof glues were developed that allowed the laminated sheets to come out from under cover into the great outdoors. A world of potential applications opened up – including building boats.

Boatbuilders, no longer having to rely totally on solid wood and mechanical fastenings, began looking at new designs and for ways to modify their time-tested methods so that they could be used with the new materials. The technique of strip-planking, for example, has been used for many years in Atlantic Canada and New England. One story says the style was developed by a thrifty fisherman (is there any other kind?) who found he could save money when building his boat by using discarded edgings left over from "four-siding" boards at the sawmill.

Apocryphal tale or not, the idea of replacing stiff full-size planks with flexible strips of wood, which could be bent into place around a pre-made form, had great appeal. It meant the builder did not have to master the art of spiling (patternmaking) required for shaping each full-size plank. Nor did he have to caulk the boat afterward. To hold the narrow planking strips to one another, the builder would edge-nail each strip into the previous one. The result was a very rugged interconnected hull that required less internal framing. For the edge-nail system to work, though, the planking had to be heavy enough to handle the fastenings without splitting. This meant that the strip boats were, by definition, heavy. The introduction of new glues changed that definition.

When strip-planking was combined with polyester resin (then, later on, epoxy resin) and reinforced with fiberglass cloth inside and out, the strips became a high-tech core material. Because the strips no longer needed to be held together by fastenings driven through them, their thickness and weight could be reduced. The epoxy and cloth embalmed the wood, protecting it from the elements; made the boat leakproof; and produced a monocoque hull. The strength and lightness of this composite hull makes it ideal for canoes and kayaks.

Nonetheless, for the conservative home builder, the idea of a bundle of strips held together with glued cloth and with limited or no internal framing took a bit of getting used to. Ted remembers, "When I started experimenting with strip-planking in 1972, it was a vague idea at best, with most of the development coming from the marathon racers in Wisconsin and area. Ross Ellery, a racer in Trout Creek, Ontario, was the first builder in eastern Canada I know of. I rented one of his canoes for a week and

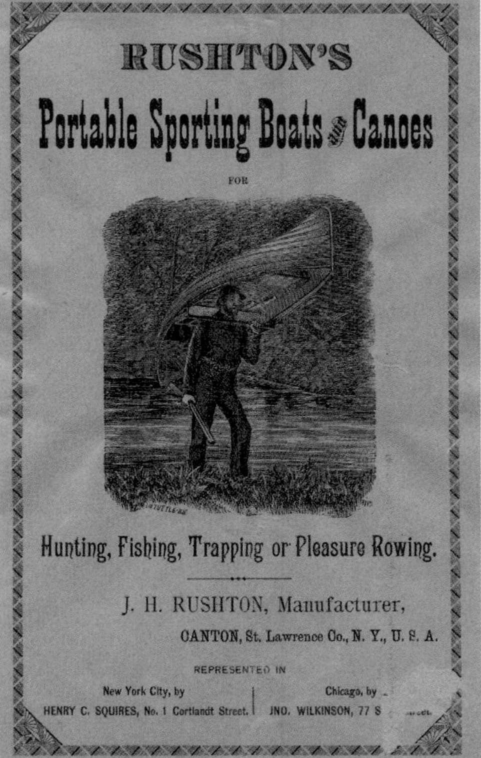

The cover of the 1891 catalog of boatbuilder J.H. Rushton, Canton, New York.

decided they might be fun to build. When my book *Canoecraft* came out in the early eighties, it was still not something that people were doing yet." It didn't take long, though, for acceptance of the technique to take off. Homebuilt strip watercraft – from moose-toting Grand Lake canoes to high-performance kayaks – were becoming a common sight wherever there was a shade tree or a basement boatshop.

Concurrent with the introduction of modern strip-building was the development of sewn-seam plywood construction. Some say Ken Littledyke of England was the first to wire plywood panels together at the chine, much as a tailor would pin or baste together fabric before sewing. The panels would then be bonded together with polyester resin and fiberglass tape. The first commercial use of the procedure is believed to have been in the early 1960s when another Englishman, TV handyman Barry Bucknell, began experimenting with sewn-seam construction methods to build a boat for his son. The project caught the eye of the London *Daily Mirror* and the newspaper recruited designer Jack Holt to refine Bucknell's efforts and design a sailing pram suitable for amateur builders. The result was the hugely popular 10-foot one-design called "the Mirror."

After the introduction of the Mirror boats, relatively few new designs were introduced until the seventies, when inveterate American sea kayaker John Lockwood built his first stitch-and-glue boat, a kayak based on a west Greenland design. In Olympia, Washington, Sam Devlin and his father, Ed, were experimenting with plywood designs that had no interior forms or molds – the shape of the panels dictated the hull's shape. Great idea, but how do you hold it together? Again the stitched-seam method made sense. Sam recounts, "I grabbed a drill and my father grabbed some baling wire and we started sewing the boat together." The initial designs evolved from there. Polyester resin was replaced by epoxy. Glued fiberglass tape over epoxy fillets replaced the venerated longitudinal chine in standard construction.

Sam Devlin describes the concept of stitch-and-glue construction this way: "Picture peeling a banana, eating the fruit, then reassembling the peel to create the banana shape again. That's stitch and glue."

For centuries, kayak builders have been sewing their boats together in one fashion or another. This kayak frame dating from the early to mid-twentieth century represents the Eastern Canadian Arctic kayak type noted for its deep bow, flat deck and low stern. It is easy to imagine this shape clad in plywood.

Since the late seventies Devlin's boatworks has produced a plethora of designs in many sizes that amply illustrate the elegance, flexibility and durability that result from sewing up a plywood boat.

The availability of industrial-strength adhesives and high-quality plywood has inspired a school of boat designers and builders to use the materials to design and custom build graceful yet rugged small craft. Properly built, a monocoque stressed-skin plywood hull is both strong and light. Because plywood is stiffer than fiberglass, the energy expended by the paddler is used to move the boat, not to flex the hull. Plywood also retains its strength despite repeated cycles of tension and compression from rough seas. And as it doesn't shrink or swell, plywood planking stands up well to just about any climate – a boon for the peripatetic kayaker, the badlands-based boatman or anyone whose harbor happens to be a trailer.

A Bit on Bytes

In the decade after he built his Greenland-style kayak, John Lockwood put a lot of miles under his keel. He was not only a long-distance kayaker, but also a software engineer working for Boeing in Seattle. In 1982 Lockwood attempted to modify his original kayak design to make it easier to build. It didn't work particularly well and he decided he needed to go back to the drawing board – this time an electronic one.

Investigation led Lockwood to a mathematical approach to plating that was introduced by Tim Nolan in a 1971 issue of *Marine Technology*. In many ways, the results of a computer plate program is akin to the work of the loftsman who produces templates for the flat iron plates used in a battleship's hull. Both produce pieces that can be wrapped around a hull without buckling and, when fastened into place, look like a boat. The computer, however, is able to design and generate these pieces in moments.

The bad news was that the only existing software was prohibitively expensive and designed to run on mainframe computers. In 1985 Lockwood quit his job to create what would become the first commercially available hull-plate-expansion program designed to run on personal computers. Before long, his new company, Pygmy Boats, introduced a computer-designed precut production kayak kit. Other manufacturers were soon to follow. In 1991 Chesapeake Light Craft (CLC) started up in Chris Kulczycki's Arlington, Virginia, basement.

Computer design was a boon for the stitch-and-glue kayak business. It promotes efficient use of materials, allows for development of very complex hull shapes – either hard-chined or multi-chined – and still lets the panels fit easily and accurately together. Says Lockwood, "You don't have to fight with the pieces, as they are all mathematically predicted." CNC (computer numerical control) machines produce highly accurate kayak pieces while at the same time reducing costs.

For the home builder, the kit-produced kayak is an efficient and relatively economical way to get out on the water. Although not quite the boat-in-a-bag instant craft promised by the folding kayaks, the boat-kit-in-a-box offers much to like. Generally plywood kayaks are either hard-chined versions of the skin-on-frame Greenland style or multi-chined versions of Pacific Northwest ancestry. The kits feature precision-cut components, epoxy and cloth. The straightforward building system requires little in the way of construction forms or tools, and the end product is a lightweight yet rugged and seaworthy kayak.

It seems that with all the various methods of home construction – strip, plywood, folding or traditional – there is a common thread. That is, for a kayak to be successful, not only must the design be safe and efficient and the construction method reliable, but the finished product should feel right to the owner and look elegant on the water. Messrs. Rushton and MacGregor, and perhaps even the ancient builders of the far North, would likely agree.

CHAPTER TWO

Choosing the Right Kayak

BUILDERS OF PLYWOOD KAYAKS are often paddlers first and builders by necessity or choice. They have an advantage when it comes to choosing the right model to build because they most likely have firm opinions about what kayak works best for them. On the other end of the scale is the builder who will learn to paddle after building the boat. Regardless of what you know about kayaks at the moment, the kayak you build should be the right one for you. It will be your mental image of pointing that beautiful varnished deck out into the waters of your favorite place that will keep the project going.

Before buying or building a kayak, it is wise to paddle all the kayaks you can before making a decision. Dealers of mass-produced kayaks often allow potential customers to try out boats before buying. Paddling a specific kit boat is a little more difficult. Unless you know someone who has built the kit you are interested in, all you have to work with are the specifications. The best you can do is collect all the specifications and features from the boats you like and look for a kit that is similar. To begin the search, we suggest making a list to help define and sort out your needs.

Deciding on what to build can be done in two stages. The first is to consider how you will use the boat and what you expect it to do for you. A good exercise is to settle yourself in the virtual cockpit and see where it takes you. The second is to match your wish list to the various kit manufacturers' model specifications. This is not always easy, because there is no standard way of expressing how a kayak will perform, and the hydrostatic data given by suppliers is sometimes incomplete.

Where Will You Paddle?

The contemporary kayak has evolved in a number of directions. New sports have been created, often driven by the evolution in materials and manufacturing. A good example is extreme whitewater kayaking, which would not exist without forgiving polyethylene and roto molding. As a rule, wooden kayaks are built for traditional paddling styles. Kayaks built with plywood are usually traditional sea kayaks or Rob Roy-style double-paddle solo canoes.

If you are heading offshore, speed and seaworthiness are more important than initial stability. For the birdwatcher exploring the marsh, a short boat with initial stability is ideal, and if the boat happens to be easy to enter and exit gracefully, so much the better. In spite of what some ads claim, one kayak will not do everything well. Kayak design is a fine balancing act; having more of one good feature means less of something else. As kayakers, we would like to have both initial stability and seaworthiness, but the broad, flat bottom that is comfortable and safe in the wetland is a hazard in open water because it follows the profile of every wave. A good designer will design a kayak for a specific purpose, but will keep the shape in balance so that it won't be cranky.

Consider Your Skill Level

Are you happy with your skill level or will you continue to improve and push your limits? It is wise to build a kayak that you can grow into. On the other hand, if you are still learning how to get into one, a long, skinny kayak may fit the fantasy but leave you cold and wet.

Design Considerations

Stability

Stability is the design characteristic that keeps a kayak deck side up. The entry-level paddler will be looking for a kayak that isn't twitchy, but for the experienced paddler, too much stability will make it difficult to roll and recover.

Expressing stability in an understandable language is complicated, and most suppliers don't even try. Steve Killing has developed a mathematical formula for his kayak and canoe designs that makes it easy to evaluate stability in understandable terms. *Sea Kayaker* magazine uses a similar formula to plot stability curves for the kayaks it reviews. These reviews are an excellent place to match the kayak that interests you with the technical data on its or a similar kayak's performance. Suppliers frequently do provide testimonials. This can be useful information if it is understood that a testimonial is one person's reaction based on his or her experience and preferences. Web site chat rooms are a good source of personal reactions to the various designs offered and are worth checking out.

Kayak Size

Most serious sea kayaks range in size from 16 to 22 feet long and 20 to 24 inches wide. Fun boats for day trips and exercise measure from 13 to 16 feet long and 22 to 30 inches wide. Rob Roy double-paddle canoes are generally 12 to 15 feet long. Your choice of size should be based on where you will paddle, expected stability, your size and weight, and how much gear you will carry.

Cockpit Size

Another design characteristic to consider is cockpit size and shape. A small cockpit opening is good because the skirt deck will hold less water and is less likely to cave in during an emergency. On the other hand, you need to get in gracefully and you don't want to worry about getting stuck doing a wet exit. Trying out a few kayaks with cockpits of different sizes will give you a feel for your comfort level. If you are having a problem bending your legs enough to slide into a small cockpit, consider a keyhole shape that extends the length while keeping the area of the opening to a minimum.

For the builder, it is easy to reduce the width of the cockpit by trimming the parts on the centerline, but if a wider cockpit is desired, new components will have to be made. Keep in mind when redesigning the cockpit that spray skirts come in standard sizes and it is easier to buy a skirt off the shelf than have one custom made. Some skirts are designed so that you can get at the bungee to make some adjustment.

Rob Roy-style canoes are generally paddled without a cover, so there is no limit on the size of the opening. A typical cockpit would be 4 to 5 feet long, making it easy to enter and exit but unsuitable for rough conditions.

Comfort

If you intend to spend long periods of time in your kayak, comfort is going to be important. The standard seat included in most kits is usually good but basic. Some suppliers will upgrade components for an additional charge. Check out the seat ads in the kayak magazines if you are looking for the ultimate in comfort.

As a rule, for maximum stability the seat bottom should be as close to the bottom of the kayak as possible. Backrests should be low enough that they do not interfere with the movements of paddling, as well as allowing you to lie back over the aft deck when rolling.

If you have big feet or if you paddle with boots on, the height of the foredeck will be of interest to you. While the height on the centerline will vary from 11 to 16 inches, it is the space where your feet will be that is important. Also consider the deck height at the back of the cockpit. A low aft deck will allow for a good layback when rolling.

Displacement

Displacement is the total weight of the boat, the paddler and the cargo. Professional plans will give the displacement at the design waterline as well as the weight to immerse. A good designer will calculate the optimum capacity range, or the safe and efficient upper and lower load limits. You can get an idea of what happens when the load changes by looking at the design waterline on the plans. Use the weight-to-immerse number to see how the waterline shape changes as weight is added or removed.

You will often see a specification called "capacity" that is intended to suggest something about displacement. Unless you know how the calculation was arrived at and how it relates to the design waterline, all it really tells you is that the kayak will hold *x* amount of weight without sinking. Don't be misled by this number; it has nothing to do with how safely the kayak will function with you and your gear aboard. If that is all the plans have to say about displacement, you have to wonder how serious the supplier is about design and customer safety.

Cargo Space

The gear you carry with you will go inside the kayak or ride on deck. One of the advantages of building your own boat is that the choice of how much of what goes where is up to you. Try to be realistic about the number of hatches and the sizes of the openings. Visually, it bothers us to cut a hole in a beautiful foredeck if we can get away with a dry bag or air bags to fill up the space. Keep the hole to the minimum size possible. In theory, a small hatch opening will have a better chance of being watertight, partially because the cover will hold its shape better and the deck will remain rigid.

The hatch components included in most kits may be reduced in width quite easily, but changing the shape or reducing the length will require new parts. On the Coho and the Enterprise, Ted used the components intended for the foredeck in the stern deck. Although the hatch appears small, it is large enough for a comfortable week of self-sufficient cruising.

Deck hatches and bulkheads are simple to add later, so if you are not sure what you will need, consider cutting the hole only when you know what will be going into it. The same holds true for deck rigging; decide what you will use before installing it. There is no point in cluttering up the deck with lines that will never be used, especially when it is easy to add more later.

Finally, building a plywood kayak from a kit is a big commitment in time and money. While the function of the boat is important, it must also look right to your eye to make the exercise worth the effort.

Bear Mountain

CHAPTER THREE

Setting Up the Workshop

The perfect workshop has a level floor, good light and ventilation, a workbench with tools in place, and a nice view. But not having the perfect shop is no excuse for not building a small boat.

Plywood is quite forgiving and a good epoxy system will handle any weather you can. We have built in the steamy rain forest of Belize on a dirt floor under a tarp. Building on the Hyde Street pier in San Francisco is cold and damp, with the wind driving the rain halfway across the open-sided shop. At the Mariners' Museum in Newport News, Virginia, the temperature in the shop hits 110°F by noon. It is nice to be comfortable, but a workspace does not have to be ideal.

As the popularity of kayaks grows, impromptu boatshops are showing up in the most unlikely locations: subdivision garages, in-town garden sheds and even apartment spare bedrooms. By and large, this is a good thing. A lot more people are seeing that they too can build a boat. A boat being built attracts neighbors like a lamp attracts moths, offering plenty of opportunities to visit and extra hands right when you need them. Generally a boatshop next door will be welcomed (or at least tolerated) – except when it comes to noise.

A full-service boatshop can crack out plenty of decibels. To the commercial boatyard owner, saws, planers, routers and sanders are the sounds of progress and money. The neighbors (if there are any) aren't troubled because these shops are usually in industrial areas and are running only during business hours. The home workshop turns that friendly separation from the neighbors on its head. Now the manufacturing is right next door (or maybe right upstairs) and "business hours" are likely to be at night or on the weekends, when everyone else is trying to relax. You may be thinking, "But I'll only be using my sander." To put your sander in perspective, let's substitute the guy with the leaf blower at six on Sunday morning, the teenager with the maxed-out boombox, the executive at the next table bellowing into a cell phone, and you get the general idea. A sander can make a lot of unwanted din.

So, what to do? Fortunately, building from a kit makes relatively little mess compared to other methods of wooden boat building. Making a worktable will require some cutting, but it should not take a great deal of time. Sanding will be the biggest noisemaker, and the amount can be controlled by working neatly. The less excess epoxy you put on, the less you have to sand off. If the epoxy is kept under control when wet, expect about one day of sanding, preferably outside. Tidy glue application brings the additional benefits of less unhealthy dust produced and more efficient – and less costly – use of the epoxy.

Speaking of sanders, diplomacy suggests avoiding using the droning device late at night or on Sunday morning. There are always plenty of more tranquil construction tasks that can be done at these times. Consider hand sanding, and try out that extra-sharp paint scraper on those high glue spots. You'll use less sandpaper and enjoy it more. While you're at it, talk to your neighbors about the project and ask when the best "noise time" is for them. Your boatshop will likely become a hit, and you might even inspire a fleet of new kayak builders.

Working like a Professional

When working with wood and epoxy, there are plenty of good reasons for keeping a clean and organized shop. One is efficiency. Having all your tools, glues, solvents, cloth, clamps and what-have-you in predictable locations can save untold hours wasted thrashing about looking for that one item you didn't know you had run out of.

Another motive is aesthetics. The conditions in your shop can in many ways affect pride taken in workmanship and can set a style of building. It's a little bit like "you are what you eat." We're not looking for the shop of the immaculate construction, but it really is much easier to do a professional job in a tidy shop than in one that is a cross between the La Brea tar pits and a collapsed mine shaft.

Take the time to hang up your tools where you can see them; it will save rooting through the bench clutter when you are in a hurry. One of the most pleasant parts of building anything – and a sign of a professional – is getting into the rhythm of working efficiently. Knowing how to do the next step and being able to reach for the next tool without thinking about it feels good. It is hard for the tool to become an extension of your thoughts if you have to find it first and then sharpen it.

Keep a couple of garbage cans where they will be convenient to use. Get in the habit of dropping trash in the can instead of on the bench; it is the same motion but it goes a long way toward keeping clutter off the bench and cleanup time to a minimum. All rags that have been exposed to solvents, oils and chemicals should be taken outside, aired out and disposed of safely. Dirty piled-up rags are potential shop-burners.

A clean shop and safety are synonymous. Working cleanly in an orderly workshop can reduce your exposure to harmful dust, noise, fumes and toxins. It also helps promote safe use of cutting tools and reduces the chance of fire.

Think Lazy

In order to achieve professional results, each stage of your work should be completed with the least number of steps as well as prepare you for the next stage. For example, if you apply the filler casually with a stick, before the next step can happen the excess will have to be sanded off. Professionals eliminate the cleanup step by placing just enough filler in the right place to do the job. When the masking tape is peeled off, the step is complete and ready for the next one.

Keeping the filler under control saves time and minimizes exposure to the bad stuff. That's a pretty fair payoff, but there's also a bonus that comes with thinking lazy. That bonus is professional results. You cannot build a professional-quality boat when you are doing damage control between each step.

Think ahead and get it right the first time. Trust your instincts. If you feel something you are doing is heading down a blind alley, find out why before going on. Understanding the why of what you are doing is the foundation for making the right decision. We are all good at something; by combining an understanding of what needs to be done with what is already familiar, we find that practical solutions present themselves. It is this process that will make the project your kayak and a graphic representation of who you are. The quality of your boat will be the sum of the integrity going into each piece.

Ruminations on a Good Worktable

Over the millennia countless boats have been built using the eyeball method. The old-time builder of a flatiron skiff would saw out the boat's two sides from heavy lumber, then spike them to the stem. Next he'd whip up a transom and some sort of center form. The center form would be placed between the sides, roughly in the middle, then a Spanish windlass would be used to pull the side planks into the transom. After he spiked the sides to the transom, the bottom could be cross-planked. And there he had his boat. It might not have been symmetrical or shaped exactly as he had intended, but it worked.

Unlike the old-timer, we know exactly what our boat is supposed to look like and we have a limited supply of materials to work with. So, how to begin? One option, of course, is the free-form approach, in which the kayak is built right on the floor or, as one manufacturer suggests, on something flat like three cardboard boxes. Although this lets you get right to work, there are a number of drawbacks. One is the possibility of introducing funky eccentricities and variables to a process that requires precise control. The other is the questionable practicality of spending hours bent over, toiling on the floor. This is a pretty good sized "some assembly required" project, and at some point in the process either your knees or your back will start protesting.

Another way to go is to build a worktable that will raise your assembly surface to a more civilized altitude. With some forethought the worktable also becomes a modification of the traditional boatbuilder's strongback. A big advantage to the worktable is that you are, in effect, working from the same baseline that the designer used to draw the boat. With the addition of a centerline and station lines, the table becomes an accurate reference and a jig for many of the building steps. The effort to construct a reliably straight and level work surface at a comfortable workbench height is time well spent.

Some operations, such as aligning, joining and gluing the components that make up the planks, require a flat surface the length of the kayak you are building. Being able to reach in and clamp along the edge of the worktable is convenient, and a step toward making tidy joints that require very little cleanup. This not only saves time but also reduces your exposure to the epoxy.

Then there is the matter of quality control. As with the old-timer's flatiron skiff, the kayak's shape is developed by drawing the edges of the floppy pre-shaped panels together with some guidance from two or three forms. Much of the shape of the vessel is controlled visually. Keeping on top of the details while working on the floor is a tall order. Assembling the boat on top of a table is another matter altogether; you can see the work better and use the table to measure to when checking the shape.

A table is not only a great place to rest your coffee cup, but also a big step toward working safely. With your body in a balanced position, tools can be used more effectively and are less likely to get out of control. And the more comfortable you are, the longer you can work without fatigue and the inevitable accidents that occur when you are beat.

As an added bonus, a well-built table will make a handy workbench when the kayak project is finished. But don't let us influence your decision!

Building a Worktable

Building the box beam and fitting and leveling the top of the worktable took the best part of one day and consumed two sheets of plywood. If building this beam sounds like too much work, there are other possibilities for getting a stable base under the top. Consider a straight ladder set up on sawhorses, laminated floor joists or anything else that will support the plywood top at a convenient working height. Be sure to tailor the height and length of the table to accommodate your height and the kayak you are building.

Making the long straight cuts necessary for building a straight table could be a challenge for the casual builder. The easiest solution, and one that also simplifies transportation, is to have the plywood sheet ripped into the desired widths when you purchase the board. Some big-box home improvement stores offer this service at little or no extra cost, using extremely accurate dedicated panel saws. If you decide to do it yourself and are using a table saw, keep in mind that the panel must be supported at both the in-feed and out-feed ends for safety reasons and to ensure that the cuts are straight. If you are using a portable circular saw, consider clamping a straightedge to the board to guide the saw.

The simple-to-build box beam consists of two 8-foot open-ended boxes held together with a 4-foot section that fits in the open ends of the boxes to tie them together. The important point to keep in mind is that once joined, the top side of the box must be straight.

Here are the steps to follow in building a worktable.

1. Prepare cutting list and cut pieces to size.

2. Construct three sections of box beam.

Clamp the two sides together to lay out the position of the gables on 16-inch centers. Marking both sides at the same time will ensure that the boxes come out square, even if the numbers are off a bit. Assemble the components with 1⅝-inch drywall screws.

3. Join sections of box beam.

To set the components up straight, clamp them together and confirm, before fastening them together with 1¼-inch screws. Lay the unit on its side, resting on blocks high enough to clear the clamps. Stretch a string line along the edge that will eventually support the top. Pull very tight and clamp the string to anchor it. Take three spacers (small pieces of wood of the same thickness) and place one under each end of the string. Use the third as a thickness gauge to check the space between string and box (3-1). If the string is straight, the spacer should just slide under the string without moving it or having space to spare. Adjust if necessary, then screw the components together.

4. Assemble legs and fasten to box beam.

Clamp the legs into position, using a square to confirm that they will be straight, and screw into place.

5. Turn table over and level.

This is where we begin to make full use of our table as a building reference; take the time to make it as accurate as possible. The table should be level across its width and reasonably level from end to end. Your floor won't be level, so place the level across the box over the legs and wedge the low leg up until the box is level (3-2). Repeat on the other end and then confirm both ends. Clamp a short block to the side of the low leg to extend it; fasten the block with screws after the top has been installed and checked.

In case you are wondering why we are not suggesting checking the level along the length of the beam, there is a good reason.

3-1

In spite of all the care taken to cut the parts as straight as possible, the beam is not going to be perfect. Too much information is confusing – the top will average out the little waves along the length that could be throwing the level off.

6. Fasten top to beam.

Our top is made of two 8-foot pieces with a 2-foot section in the middle to extend it to 18 feet. If the kayak to be built is over 16 feet long, this is the time to add length to the workbench; the ends of the top will cantilever off the ends of the box. You say your boat is under 16 feet long? Building a 16-foot table is still easier than making the extra cuts to shorten the 8-foot sections, and more bench space is always useful.

Center the top over the box, clamp, then confirm with a string line that the edge of the table is going to be straight. Fasten through the top into the box with 1⅝-inch drywall screws. Drilling a pilot hole with a bit of countersink will put the head of the

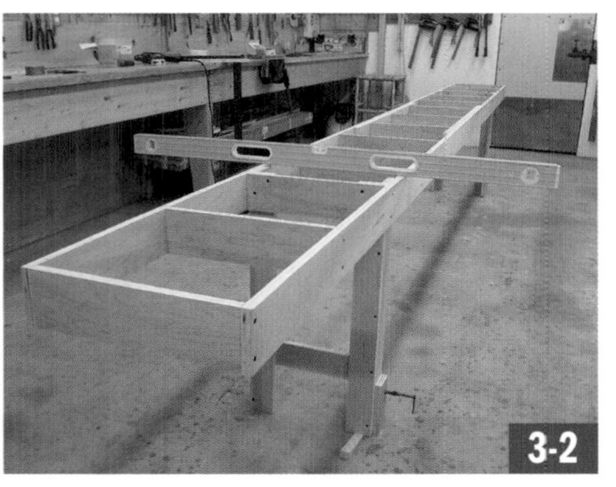

3-2

screw below the surface of the table, where it will not get in the way.

Regardless of what the top will be fastened to, it should be level across its width and reasonably level but very straight from end to end. To check for straightness, stretch a string from end to end, using the same method as in Step 3. Check in a number of places over the length of the table.

This table was built to be as light as we could get away with and it did have a sag in the middle. The string line pointed this out, however, and we fastened temporary legs to the middle of the span to straighten it out.

To confirm that the table is level from side to side, place blocks of equal thickness at the edges to support the level (3-3). Check the ends, the middle and several places in-between.

Keeping the table in this position is very important. If you are working on a wood floor that can be abused, the legs may be stabilized with cleats screwed to the floor. If screwing into the floor is out of the question, mark the position with a felt-tipped pen or masking tape. Should the table get shifted, home base will be easy to find.

3-3

7. Draw reference lines.

To draw a truly accurate centerline down the middle of the table, pull the string tight; then, using a combination square, mark a series of points directly under the string along its length. Connect these points using your longest straightedge. Use a ballpoint pen for a crisp line that will be easy to see. After drawing the line, check it from both ends to be sure it is straight.

Station lines on 12-inch centers are helpful additions to a centerline. These will be handy references when duplicating work from one side to the other. Use a tape measure to mark these points (3-4), because the cumulative error from marking with a short ruler will be significant over the length of the table.

Use a carpenter's square to draw the perpendicular lines (3-5). If you anticipate using the table as a workbench for future projects, a quick coat of sealer will help keep it clean. A good coat of floor or furniture wax will keep epoxy from sticking to it.

3-4

Cradle Forms

Cradle forms are the secret to controlling the shape of a plywood kayak. They can make the difference between a twisted hull with a hogged bottom and the beautiful kayak in your mind. Besides, now that you have a worktable, you might as well add several cradle forms and enjoy the peaceful rhythm of building when the pieces fall into

3-5

place and stay where you put them.

With cradles attached to the predictable base formed by the worktable, the hull will come together at a controlled distance above the baseline and will be centered over the table centerline (3-6); our horizontal reference will be the level, anytime we need it. As flimsy plank is added to flimsy plank, the cradle forms will hold all the pieces where they should be. The pieces will come together without being stressed or having to be bullied into position.

Plans for making cradles are not included in the Coho and Mill Creek kits, but the information needed to build them is there if we look for it. Although these two kit boats use different building methods, the Mill Creek has bulkheads and the Coho has temporary forms that give us some cross-section shapes. Forms are included in the Enterprise kit.

3-6

3-7

Constructing Cradle Forms with a Baseline Reference

The three forms included in the Coho kit are all the reference necessary for picking up an accurate hull and deck cradle shape. Each form is in two parts. The main component defines the hull and deck shape. The "spacer," or extension, is added to each form to bring them all up to the same level for lining up the hull. The combined result is a baseline that is common to all the forms. Make one set of cradles to support the hull in the upright position as well as one to fit the deck, for working on the kayak upside down.

Draw a distinct, crisp centerline on both sides of each form and extension (3-7) to help in making the cradles and also for lining up the hull during construction.

Make the cradles from $1/2$-inch to $3/4$-inch plywood, particle board or solid wood. At 8 inches wide, our cradle form was ideal for supporting the planks – high enough to support the top side plank, yet allowing room to work on the deck-hull joint.

Prepare the cradle form by cutting the construction stock to length (about $1\frac{1}{2}$ inches wider than the form) and drawing a crisp centerline on both sides.

Lay out the mid form first; it will be closest to the table because of the rocker in the bottom of the hull. To find the shape, put the form and extension together and position them over the construction stock by lining up the centerlines. What we are looking for here is a distance from the bottom edge of the extension to a place below the bottom of the hull that will be high enough to clear a wooden cleat across the bottom of the cradle. We have used 14 inches from the edge of the extension to the edge of the stock, which puts the bottom of the hull at the mid form about $1\frac{1}{2}$ inches from the worktable. Confirm that the two horizontal edges are parallel and (in our case) 14 inches apart, and that the centerlines are right on.

If the hull is expected to be straight, keep in mind that the bottom edge of the cradle form must be parallel to the bottom of the extension. The bottom edge of the cradle becomes a new baseline.

When laying out the other forms, it is important to keep the distance from the bottom edge of the extension to the bottom of the cradle form the same as with the mid form, in our case, 14 inches. While the mid form is $1\frac{1}{2}$ inches above the table, the other forms will be at a distance that reflects the rocker in the hull.

Secure the bulkhead to the cradle material with several 1-inch finishing nails. Trace

3-8

onto the cradle stock the outline of the bulkhead plus the thickness of the hull planking. As a guide, choose something slightly thicker than the planking; our planks were 4 mm (5/32-inch), and our guide was a piece of 6 mm (1/4-inch) plywood, to give some room to play (3-8).

Cut the cradle form to shape, then clean up and soften sharp edges that could damage the planking or epoxy and glass covering. A layer of duct tape over the edge wouldn't hurt either. Its rubbery surface will take the bite out of the raw wood and help keep the hull from sliding.

To secure the cradle forms to the table, first fasten the forms to 1 1/2-inch square blocks cut to the width of the table. Secure the cradles to the table at the positions given in the kayak construction manual. Line up the centerline on the cradle with the centerline on the table and secure.

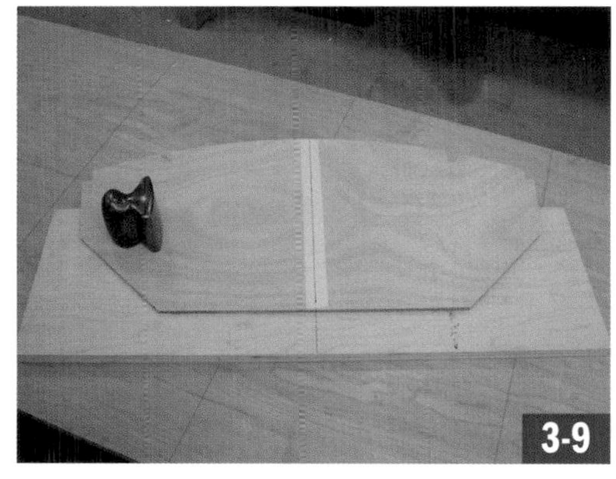

3-9

Constructing Cradle Forms Without a Baseline Reference

Constructing cradle forms for the Mill Creek is very easy. The two bulkheads included in the kit are used as references for the shape, and the fore and aft positions are taken from the plans.

Although we do not have a baseline reference for the bulkheads, it will not matter, because we have only two cradles and the kayak's bottom is flat. All this means for us is that the kayak's design waterline (DWL) may not be parallel to the table. Three cradle forms would give better control over the length of the kayak, but we can add more support to the ends later, when we find out where the ends will be positioned.

Draw a centerline on both sides of each bulkhead. If you intend to use a clear (bright) finish such as varnish, put masking tape down first to draw on. This will avoid damaging the face of the bulkhead. Also draw centerlines on both sides of the cradle stock.

We want the bottom of the hull to be 2 inches above the table, and have positioned the bulkhead on the cradle stock accordingly. Use a block slightly thicker than the planking to scribe a line parallel to the bulkhead (3-9).

Setting Up on Sawhorses

If the best you have to work on is sawhorses, it is possible, but fussy, to fasten the cradles to the horses. Position the horses at the same spacing as the forms and set them up level in both directions. Fasten the cradles to the tops of the horses as we did on the table. It is a good idea to mark the position of the horses on the floor. Use cement blocks or screw them to the floor to keep them from sliding around.

With the workshop space up and ready, let's take a look at the tools, materials and supplies you'll need to build your kayak.

THINK LAZY

Moving the cradles

The cradles will be taken off the table and then replaced several times during the building process. To make this easier, drill pilot holes for the screws and mark the position of the cleats on the table. The screws will be easy to get in and out, and with the position marked, the screws will go back into their old holes when the cradle is replaced.

CHAPTER FOUR

Tools, Materials and Supplies

As Ted often says – usually when lusting over a new tool catalog – "tools make us look good." He is the first to admit, though, that this is only true if the tool is properly maintained and the operator can make it do what it is intended to do. Fortunately for the builder assembling a kit, not many tools are needed that would not be used in regular home maintenance. If a block plane and a couple of chisels are not in your toolbox, they are a good investment and will become indispensable for future projects.

Consider this the list to end all lists. You won't need all the tools, materials and supplies on it, but it will help you choose what to buy and what to borrow.

Plywood: Join the Marines

For plywood to be labeled marine it has to be certified (and perhaps sanctified) by an accreditation agency. APA, the Engineered Wood Association, sets the standards for U.S. marine-grade plywood. Marine plywood certified by the British Standards Institution falls under the rubric of BS 1088. There are U.S. military standards as well. Other, non-marine types may work well in certain situations if you know the stock and the manufacturer. For better or for worse, there are quite a few alternatives in the manufactured panel world – all with their vigorous adherents and detractors.

In all likelihood, your kit manufacturer has supplied you with certified marine plywood. That said, you should know what sort of stuff you will be building with. This is especially important if you are using this book to assist you in building a "from scratch" kayak, from plans only.

Let's take a look at the plywood used in boatbuilding in general. For all-round working craft where durability and cost are a concern and paint is the finish of choice, APA-rated plywood is a good option. For kayaks where the job calls for defect-free stock, when high strength-to-weight ratio is important and a varnish finish is desired, the BS 1088 certified panel is probably the way to go. Whatever your decision, rather than just going to Don's Discount Home Wood-Mart, it is best to buy from a knowledgeable and reliable supplier. Generally, when buying plywood, you get what you pay for.

So what are you getting with marine-grade plywood? For starters, you receive a guarantee that the stock is made with WBP (weather- and boil-proof) glue, which means it is bonded with phenol formaldehyde (or in some American plywoods, resorcinol).

PLYWOOD CONVERSION

Imperial	Metric
5/32 inch	4 mm
1/4 inch	6 mm
3/8 inch	9 mm
1/2 inch	12 mm
5/8 inch	15 mm
3/4 inch	19 mm

Although you are probably not planning to boil your boat, this means you have a glue that has stood up to some rigorous testing.

Beyond similarities in glue, the American and British standards are quite different. For example, British Standard applies to plywood made with untreated tropical hardwood veneers having a prescribed level of resistance to fungal attack. APA standards call for Douglas fir or western larch. The British standard for veneers requires that they be free from knots, other than sound pin knots.

The APA requires that the grade of all plies be B or better (B veneers may have knots but no knotholes; an A grade allows no knots or knotholes). Wood or synthetic patches are allowed. In any edge of a BS 1088 board, not more than one gap is allowed, and it cannot be wider than 0.5 mm (just over 1/64 inch). The maximum APA core gap is 1/8 inch.

Plan Sheets

To be a useful reference, construction sheets need to be visible. Tack them up on the wall or on a sheet of plywood that can be stood up. If possible, consider getting them laminated. This will help them survive rain, coffee spills and wind damage. You can still make marks on them with a grease pencil.

TYPICAL WOODS USED IN MARINE PLYWOOD

- **Douglas fir** Generally used in American marine plywood. Strong, splintery and moderately durable.
- **Lauan, or Philippine mahogany** Also known as seraya (North Borneo) and meranti (Malaya). Most comes from southeast Asia. Moderately durable, though variable.
- **Okume, or gaboon** A hardwood from Africa that is classified BS 1088. Okume is one of the most common woods used in marine plywood. Light to medium mahogany in color, it is stable and glues well. Although generally considered nondurable when unsealed, when it is used as a core material (coated with epoxy and glass cloth), okume is rugged and long-lasting.
- **Sapele** A hardwood from Africa. Stronger than lauan, Honduras mahogany or African mahogany. Moderately durable.
- **Utile and Sipo** Both African hardwoods. Harder than okume or lauan.
- **African mahogany** An African hardwood. Moderate decay resistance and moderately strong.

Measuring and Setup Tools

Batten

A wooden batten is used to create a smooth, fair line. It's nice to have one that is longer than the boat you are building. A batten should be rectangular in cross-section, for example, 3/8 x 1 inch or 1/4 x 1 1/4 inches. The wood should be as straight-grained as possible, without knots, sapwood, rot or other imperfections. Look for resilient woods that resist taking a permanent bend: spruce, fir, basswood or Philippine mahogany. Even pine will work sometimes. Hardwoods such as oak, ash and Honduras mahogany are either too prone to taking a set or have too convoluted a grain to bend into a fair curve.

Level

Used to level the worktable, to confirm that the hull is not twisted, or just as a short straightedge. A 4-foot carpenter's spirit level will give you the bigger picture, but a 2-foot level is adequate for a plywood kayak-building project.

Ruler

A 16-inch to 24-inch steel ruler is handy for accurate measurement and as a short straightedge.

Sliding Bevel Gauge

A tool with two legs that can be adjusted to make various angles. It is used to measure or mark an angle on something.

4-1

Squares

Carpenter's framing square

The ubiquitous 2-foot framing square is just the ticket for plumbing forms, squaring stations, and all sorts of general layout work (4-1). A caveat here – just because something is called a square doesn't guarantee that it actually is square. Even new tools straight from the hardware store are suspect. And the one you found under Uncle Wally's cellar stairs – who knows what it has been used for?

Here is how to check the squareness of your square. First strike a straight baseline on a table or the floor. Lay the long leg of the square on the line and draw a line up the perpendicular (short) leg of the square. Then flip the square over so that the long leg of the square is still on the same side of the baseline, but pointed in the opposite direction. Slide the square over to where the short leg touches the drawn perpendicular line. If the square is indeed square, the short leg should line up exactly with the perpendicular line. If it doesn't, find yourself another square.

Combination square

The combination square, a small square with an adjustable arm 12 to 18 inches long, is a must-have; very useful for bench work, measuring depth and scribing parallel lines.

Straightedge

The straightedge is great for striking long straight lines and setting up a worktable. Although they can be obtained commercially, the easiest way to get one is to take a 4- to 5-inch slice off the factory-cut side of a piece of plywood. (Don't forget to label which edge is the factory-cut one.) An 8-foot straightedge is indispensable for the plans-builder; for the kit-builder, a 4-foot one is fine.

String Line

Fishing line or a similar strong, thin string works best for a string line. It needs to be strong enough so that it can be stretched tight to create a centerline, to confirm the straightness of the hull or to check for true straightness when setting up the worktable.

Tape Measure

The ideal size is 25 feet x 3/4 inches, but a 12-foot tape is adequate for a kayak-building project.

Cutting and Shaping Tools

A new edge tool is rarely ready to be used right out of the box (or, increasingly, out of the plastic). Rough edges may need to be smoothed with a file and emery cloth or with wet/dry sandpaper, using WD-40 (a light oil) as the lubricant. Surfaces may need to be waxed and turn-screws lubricated and, most importantly, the cutting edge will need to be sharpened.

THINK LAZY

Make it a habit to put tools away clean and sharp. It has to be done anyway and a routine of cleaning up and putting tools away at the end of the day creates a good time for reflection on the day's progress and for planning tomorrow's work.

4-2

Block Plane

The diminutive block plane is standard in the boatbuilder's tool kit (4-2). It is the sports car of the plane family, nimble and easy to maneuver. The tool is available in high (20 degrees) and low (12 to 13 degrees) angled versions. Many prefer the paring quality of the low-angle model for shaping plywood edges.

It is possible to build a kit kayak using sanding blocks instead of a block plane. However, for the builder working with sheet plywood these tools are indispensable.

A block plane is the kind of tool you want to be ready when you are. Nothing ruins the rhythm of working more than grabbing the block plane (or any other tool) and finding that the only parts that aren't rusty are covered with paint. Keep this precision tool in a safe place where it won't rust. Remove rust before it has a chance to pit the metal. Wet/dry sandpaper (600 grit) with WD-40 will cut through light rust fast and leave a film that will inhibit further rust. You can also rub a little wax on the sole (working surface) to reduce friction and inhibit rust. For long-term storage, wrap the plane in an oil-dampened cloth and store in a plastic resealable bag.

SAFETY TIP

Keep in mind that most small hand tools are cast iron and will shatter if dropped on a concrete floor. Put them down on a solid surface where they won't be in the way, or keep them available in your apron.

Chisel

You will need a long-handled chisel, 3/4 to 1 1/2 inches wide, to trim planks and epoxy-saturated fiberglass cloth. No need to be fancy here, but it needs to be sharp.

File

A flat steel tool with a rough, ridged surface for smoothing, grinding down or cutting through wood, steel or plastic. Necessary for maintaining scrapers. Look for a 10-inch mill bastard file.

As with all hand-cutting tools, lift the file off the work on the return stroke. Riding back on the cutting edge will roll the edges of the teeth over and change their angle. The tool will have lost its usefulness long before it becomes dull.

File Card

A brush with short wire bristles for cleaning and unplugging a file. A must if you have a file or a rasp.

Knives

Putty knife

This knife is used for applying and cleaning up filler and for adjusting planks.

If there is a choice, choose one with a flexible blade. Keep it clean. Scrape the epoxy grunge into a can, then wipe the knife clean on a rag dampened with lacquer thinner. If there is epoxy on the handle, clean that as well. Using a putty knife with stuff building up on the handle feels disgusting.

An old flexible putty knife ground down to about 1/4 inch wide will place a little bit of filler without spreading it around. An artist's palette knife is a classy alternative if you happen to have one.

Utility knife

Utility knives are cheap and come with replaceable blades. Surprisingly, this tool probably causes more accidents than any other. Incautious whittling and attempting to catch the knife when it falls off the bench are common causes of mishaps. Be careful cutting hard material – the blade can break and the knife can fly out of control, and the part of the blade that is left is very sharp. Keep both hands behind the blade and always slide it back into the housing when it is not being used.

4-3

Laminate Trimmer

This small router has a straight bit with a pilot bearing on the bottom that is the same diameter as the cutter (4-3). As the bearing rides along a surface or pattern under the material being cut, the material is trimmed flush to the pattern. Useful for trimming the oversized deck on the Mill Creek kayak or for cutting plywood planks to a pattern.

Linesman Pliers

Used for cutting and twisting wire, linesman pliers are cheap and readily available.

Rasp

A rasp is really just a coarse-toothed file. It's great for shaping filler and trimming cured fiberglass cloth. In contrast, a file – a mill bastard, for example – that is ideal for hard material would plug up in three passes and simply ride over the surface.

Always use a rasp by cutting on the push stroke and lifting off as you return. When you're finished using it, clean the teeth with a file card because the filler will harden and be very hard to remove later.

Router

See laminate trimmer.

Saws

Japanese pull saw

A boatbuilder friend once said, "I resisted it for years, but after trying it, there is no turning back." The Japanese saw (4-4) has a very thin blade with fine teeth and it cuts on the backstroke, as opposed to the forward cutting action of the Western-style saw. It is very sharp and very fast to use. There are a number of different styles and models, including a series of novel double-edged saws that have a rip set on one side and a crosscut on the other. For cutting and trimming on the kayak, a small saw with a reinforced back or spine and a fine single cutting edge is a good choice.

4-4

Until recently, Japanese saws were available only in specialty tool stores or through mail order catalogs. Now decent little pull saws at reasonable prices are beginning to turn up in big-box home improvement stores and even at Greg's local general store (right next to the chainsaws and stump pullers). But if you are looking for top quality and variety, shop the specialty tool sources.

Jigsaw

A jigsaw is a handy addition to your tool kit. Fast and agile, it is a top choice for cutting openings in the deck for cockpit or hatches. If you don't own a jigsaw, consider borrowing or renting one for this step.

Scissors

Elegance isn't necessary, sharpness is. Use them for cutting fiberglass cloth and plastic film.

Scrapers

Cabinet scraper

The cabinet scraper works well for removing epoxy runs and for working filler down to size. Despite its fancy name, this tool is really just a thin, flat piece of spring steel that can be bent by hand. Although the most common version – and the one most useful for our purposes – is rectangular, it also comes in curved shapes. Like all edge tools, it needs to be kept sharp.

Sharpen this scraper by filing the edge flat and square to the side of the blade, then rolling the edge with a burnisher or a hard piece of smooth steel (such as a nail set) to produce a hook or burr. This hook is what makes the cut.

Paint scraper

The underrated $1\frac{1}{2}$-inch paint scraper is the poor builder's profile sander. It is great for knocking glue down to size and shaping filler or sneaking into hard-to-reach corners. The edge is easy to file into an appropriate profile to produce consistent shapes.

Keep it sharp – being easy to file also means that the edge will not last long. Sharpen it with a mill file on about a 45-degree angle. File the edge until a burr begins to develop on the back, then make a couple of passes to remove the burr.

Sharpening Stone

In recent years the hand-powered edge tool has earned an ill-deserved reputation for being slow, working poorly and being hard to use. Most of this bad press can be traced to dull or maladjusted tools. A good sharpening stone will alleviate the problem of dullness. Either a traditional oil (or water) stone or a low-maintenance diamond-coated stone will do the job. A pair of good whetstones large enough to be convenient is a substantial investment; they will require maintenance to keep them flat. For a

CHEAP TRICK

Sandpaper-on-flat-surface honing system

The perfect edge that this trick produces might seem impossible with such a low-cost system. But the only skill needed for predictable sharpening results is being able to hold the iron at the correct angle every time it is passed over the stone or abrasive surface. Maintaining this precise angle consistently by hand is difficult, even with years of practice. Although sharpening jigs that hold the iron at the precise angle are common, their usefulness is limited by the size of affordable stones. These jigs become practical, however, when used with a sheet of wet/dry sandpaper on a flat, smooth surface.

Note: Major stock removal, such as removing nicks in the blade or changing the angle of the bevel, should be done on a grindstone before honing.

Setup

The base can be any flat, smooth surface – plastic laminate, Plexiglas, metal or glass. A piece of 10-inch x 14-inch window glass is cheap and easy to find in any hardware, home improvement or building supply store. Tape a piece of 400 grit wet/dry sandpaper to one side and 600 grit to the other side. (The tape will be broken down by the lubricant in time, so you might want to consider using a spray adhesive.) Cover the edges of the glass with tape, for obvious reasons. To protect the grit on the bottom, set the base on a clean piece of cardboard.

Upgrade this setup by using two pieces of glass secured to a portable plywood base or ¼-inch plate glass with the edges finished for safety. You can also upgrade the wet/dry sandpaper to a micro-abrasive sheet with a pressure-sensitive adhesive backing. The PSA backing will not be broken down by the lubricant. We use 15 micron (abrasive grit 1000) to bring the surface up to a certain level of smoothness, then switch to 5 micron (abrasive grit 2500) to polish it to a mirror finish. This is a very sharp edge, but if you want to go all the way, finish up with 0.5 micron (abrasive grit 9000).

Lubricant

The purpose of the lubricant is to keep the fine grit from getting plugged up before it wears out, by

floating away the particles of metal as they are removed. Add a few generous drops of lubricant to the paper, or enough to spread over the surface being worked on. Choose a light oil such as sharpening oil, a mixture of kerosene and motor oil, WD-40 or water. WD-40 is a good choice; it is readily available, comes in a handy package and leaves a protective coating on the tool. As with natural stones, if you start with oil, stick to oil – water and oil don't mix.

How to use the sharpening jig

Set up the blade in the guide and adjust the angle. Most jigs have a holder for the blade with an adjustable guide wheel on the back. The angle is set by adjusting the blade back and forth in the holder or by moving the wheel up or down. If the blade is new or when the angle is correct, position the blade so that the entire bevel is riding square on the sandpaper. For a good look at the angle, place the jig and tool on a straightedge and hold it up to the light.

A good way to get a handle on sharpening is to use a magnifying glass to keep track of what is happening between the abrasive and the blade. To confirm that the setup is correct, check the blade after the first few passes. Look for a change in color or degree of gloss made by the new scratches. When this new surface extends out to the pointed edge, the beveled side is finished.

Keep in mind that if you start sharpening at the back of the bevel, it will take a long time to work out to the edge. However, avoid beginning to sharpen at the edge of the blade and working back; this will give you a fast edge, but you will begin to change the cutting angle of the blade, and it will eventually need to be reground to correct the angle.

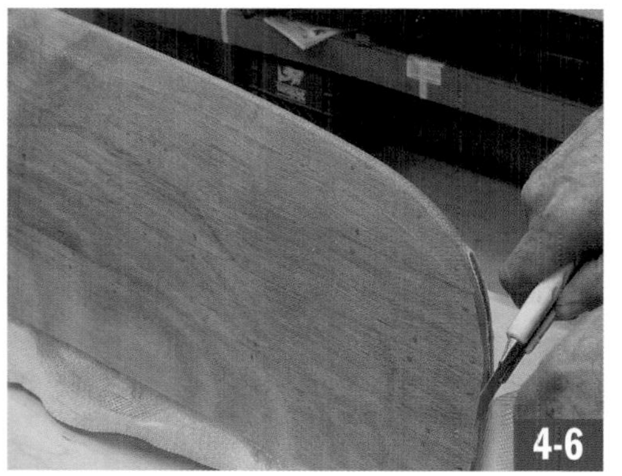
4-6

low-cost alternative that is easy to use and effective, consider the sandpaper-on-flat-surface honing system (→ page 34).

Spokeshave

Think of the spokeshave as a two-handed shaving plane or a short-bodied sport block plane. A spokeshave (4-6) will plane, smooth and sculpt wood with ease and, in many cases, faster than a power tool. The trick is to have the blade sharp and set correctly. The blade needs to be set to just pare the wood (you need a road grader, not a bull-dozer). It will often cut more easily if used at a skewed or oblique angle rather than at 90 degrees to the work. If the tool is not performing up to expectations, check that the iron has been installed correctly. The manufacturer's name must always be on the visible side of the iron.

The spokeshave may be hard to find at your local chain hardware store. Try a store that sells nails from a bin and locate a clerk with gray hair. If this doesn't work, the tool can be ordered from most woodworking catalogs. Choose a flat-bottom model if you are buying just one – it is much easier to use than the curved-bottom type and can shape most inside curves encountered in small boat construction.

4-7

Fastenings and Fastening Tools

Clamps

Building a plywood kayak kit is mostly an exercise in clamping and gluing. Before the components become a kayak, they will be held in place by several different kinds of clamps (4-7).

C-clamps

When you need a lot of gripping oomph, C-clamps are the way to go. Application is two-handed, but the direct and powerful clamping action they provide and the great variety of sizes and depths of throat available make them a must for the boatshop. They are generally sold by the inch – a 3-inch clamp will clamp stock that is 3-inches thick. If the throat size is given, the number indicates how far in the clamp will reach. For this scale of boatbuilding, the 3-inch clamp is a versatile size to start collecting. C-clamps are called G-clamps in Britain.

4-8

"Schedule 40" clamps

If you are faced with a paucity of spring clamps and the local tool emporium is closed, consider the sewer-pipe spring clamp (4-8). Manufacturing these little wonders is cheap and easy. The raw material is common 3-inch or 4-inch Schedule 40 plastic sewer pipe, available at most hardware stores and lumberyards.

Simply slice the pipe crosswise into roughly 1-inch sections to produce a plethora of plastic doughnuts. Then lay each ring on its side and make a single cut through the ring with a bandsaw or hacksaw. That's it – they are ready to go. The newly minted clamps have naturally deep throats and enough bite to handle many light-duty clamping tasks. Adjust the clamping pressure by varying the width of the slice and diameter of the pipe.

4-9

STRETCHING YOUR CLAMP SUPPLY

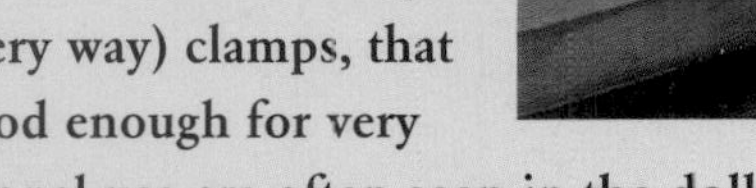

4-10

Several times in the building process you will need a large number of clamps, but only for a few days.

- Consider borrowing rather than investing in a mess of clamps that may not get used again or that you can't afford.
- Check tool sales. Cheap (in every way) clamps, that are good enough for very occasional use are often seen in the dollar bin.
- Yard sales are always worth checking for cheap tools.
- C-clamps are preferred for their controlled clamping pressure and should be used in critical positions. At other times consider using less-controllable clamps, such as spring clamps, and weights.
- See the Cheap Trick for "Schedule 40" clamps on page 35.
- Make homemade clamps using threaded rods or bolts (4-10).

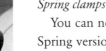

Spring clamps

You can never have too many clamps. Spring versions (4-9) that you can use with one hand are great for temporarily holding planks, rails and panels in place. Plastic clamps are inexpensive yet have plenty of gripping power, with little chance of damage to the surface. You might want to consider the new generation of spring clamps, which have a ratchet action that combines the one-handed adjustment of the spring clamp with the controlled pressure of a screw-type clamp. Simple spring clamps range in size up to about a 3-inch capacity. Start your collection with a few medium-sized ones.

Clamp Blocks

Also called clamp pads or stop blocks, these wooden blocks or pads are put between the clamp and your stock to protect the surface and spread out the clamping pressure.

Drill

Either a 1/4-inch or 3/8-inch electric drill will do. Cordless versions are especially handy. A basic set of high-speed bits from 1/16 inch to 1/4 inch is adequate for assembling a plywood kayak.

A great many holes need to be drilled if the kayak panels are wired together, but the thin plywood is easy to drill. Drilling these holes by hand is not impossible, or extremely tedious.

Hot-Melt Glue

Hot glue is used for provisional fastening.

4-11

It's a handy material for small plywood boat construction.

Mallet

A wooden mallet will save your chisel handles, plus give you greater control than a framing hammer (not to mention a quieter shop). Which shape to buy is a matter of personal preference, but many builders opt for flat-sided models – they allow a good swing in tight quarters. An important shop tool but not necessary for the one-time kit-builder.

Nails

Brads

These small wire nails are used as temporary fasteners and to anchor string lines.

Brass escutcheon pins

Used anywhere a light fastener is needed (4-11).

4-12

4-13

CHEAP TRICK

4-14

Don't want to feel like a klutz trying to dig up the end of the tape when you want to use it? Try folding the end of the tape back on itself before sticking it down (4-14).

Bronze ring nails

Non-ferrous bronze boat nails with a box-nail head and rings formed around the wire provide a tenacious hold.

Pushpins

Pushpins are used for anchoring errant cloth, hanging up construction plans and anywhere else a small, temporary fastener is required. Look for the ones with long, thin pins.

Keep in mind that the plastic ends can break when the pins are pushed into something hard. If you are pushing with your thumb and the top breaks, the pin will hurt you. Consider tapping them in with a small hammer or putting something hard over the top to protect your thumb.

Screws

Use stainless steel, brass or bronze screws wherever they will become a permanent part of the kayak. Drywall screws are ideal for assembling jigs and as temporary fasteners.

Tape

Clear plastic tape

Packaging tape makes an excellent non-destructive clamping device for pulling awkward shapes together. Use the stretching action of the tape to develop clamping pressure.

Fiber tape

Useful for heavy-duty clamping where stretch is not desirable (4-12).

Fiberglass tape

Woven fiberglass tape in weights from 4 to 9 ounces is common in plywood kayak construction. It is used to strengthen and reinforce chines, corners and stress points. The bow stem, for example, should be reinforced – this exposed area is usually the first point of contact when you run out of water. For most joining applications on a light-weight kayak, 4-ounce tape is fine, especially if used under the fiberglass cloth.

Masking tape

Two or three rolls of 1-inch masking tape are necessary when applying a clear coating. Other widths are nice to have in some situations but not necessary. Use for general masking duties (4-12). Keep a roll of low-tack tape handy for delicate surfaces.

Tie-down Straps

Nylon straps (4-13) are handy for clamping deck panels into position as well as for tying the kayak to a car rack.

Vise

Boatbuilding can be habit-forming, but we are talking here about the tool with two jaws that is used to hold an object immobile. For this scale of work it does not have to be massive or expensive. A light 6-inch vise that will clamp onto the bench is a good choice.

Wedges

Used for shimming and aligning. Cedar shingles work well.

4-15

Weights

Used to provide clamping pressure where conventional clamps won't reach. Also great as an extra set of hands to hold components in place. Look for compact, heavy items (4-15), such as chunks of iron or lead, old flatirons, railroad track or coffee cans filled with sand.

Wire for Sutures

Copper or mild steel wire for "sewing up" the hull and deck panels. Eighteen to 20 gauge wire works well (18 gauge diameter = 1.024 mm, or just a bit less than 1/16 inch).

Epoxy and Fiberglassing Materials

Epoxy Resin and Hardener

Well-mixed epoxy will glue, embalm and encapsulate your boat (4-16). The resin as it comes from the can is formulated to be thin enough to allow it to saturate the fiberglass cloth and bond with the wood. Add hardener and a little reinforcement to the resin and you have an adhesive. Add a bit of sanding dust and you have a color-matched structural filler. If used properly, the resulting stuff is tougher than a boiled owl. But if the builder takes short cuts or is cavalier with the manufacturer's instructions, the results can be disappointing and frustrating.

There are many epoxy formulations tailored for specific functions. For kayak building, the resin must be compatible with wood in a marine environment. The epoxy used to build the kayaks featured in this book came from well-known suppliers; other brands may or may not work successfully. Outside North America we have heard of regionally available epoxy being used successfully, so there are alternatives to the brands we are using here. The main problems with lesser-known epoxy brands seem to result from poor or no directions on how to use the product safely and no technical backup support for problems that arise.

Some epoxy manufacturers have done

AMINE BLUSH

Amine blush is a waxy byproduct of the epoxy hardener that appears as a hazy area on an otherwise shiny surface coat. Wipe it with your finger and it will feel greasy. This unused portion of the hardener is water soluble and must be removed before the next application of epoxy. It is not a problem as such, but it is another step to take care of before getting back to work.

How to Avoid Blush

Blush has not been a problem when using the slow hardener available with the three brands tested. Two of the suppliers offer a fast hardener (accelerator) that can be blended with their blush-free slow hardener to accelerate the cure time. However, fast hardeners do blush; the more you add, the greater the chance of blushing.

Curing slowly in a cold, damp environment will encourage blush. The snag here is that if the shop is cold, adding a fast hardener will promote more blush. The choice is to let the slow mix cure at its own speed or add some fast hardener and take a chance on having to clean up the blush. If you anticipate being cool to the point of discomfort, or your time is limited, choose a brand with the fastest slow hardener.

Dealing with Blush

Amine blush may look innocent, but it is a chemical byproduct. Handle with the same care as uncured epoxy dust.

Remove the blush with clean, warm water and a Scotchbrite-type abrasive pad. Fortify the water with a mild abrasive containing ammonia, such as Ajax, to give it more of a bite. Rinse well with plenty of clean water and towel dry; then go back and scrub any remaining greasy areas. Amine blush must also be removed before applying paint or varnish.

If the surface is smooth, it is possible to sand off the greasy residue, but washing it off is the better option.

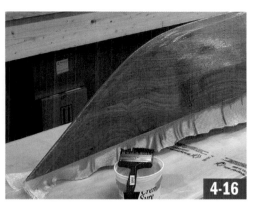

4-16

such a good job of packaging and promoting their products you might get the idea that mixing and applying the stuff is foolproof and that success is guaranteed. Well, almost. Things can go wrong and do, and most of the problems can be traced to operator error. The builder must be scrupulous in following the manufacturer's recommendations for mixing and preparation. If there is too much or too little hardener, the epoxy won't set. Adding more hardener will not speed up the cure time. We are talking chemical reaction here, and the system has much in common with making bread. Mess around with the recipe, leave out the yeast, get impatient with the kneading, and the whole process will likely leave you flat.

Choosing a Brand

Boatbuilders ask a lot of their epoxy. They want it to cure quickly (sometimes in just minutes) to do a quick repair job. They want it to cure slowly so that they can fabricate a large keel assembly or cover a hull in one shot. And while most marine epoxy is formulated for use at room temperature, 70°F–72°F (21°C–22°C), builders use the stuff in shops without climate control from the Arctic to the rainforest.

In an attempt to accommodate these many conditions, epoxy manufacturers have developed hardeners with different curing times: fast, medium, slow, extra slow. Keep in mind that these are relative times, sort of like geologic terms. Fast epoxy is not as fast as five-minute epoxy, but it is faster than medium or slow epoxy. One supplier's conception of slow will be different from a competitor's slow.

The temperature in which you work also affects cure time. Fast epoxy will set up a lot faster at low temperatures than the slow will, but it will still take a long time to cure. On the other hand, mix up a batch of fast epoxy at your tropical island hideaway boatshop and you will barely be able to get it out of the pot before it goes off. In such conditions, a very slow hardener (and some cold lime juice and bubbles) would be called for.

Resin-to-hardener ratios will range from 1:1 to 5:1 depending on the brand. Mixing in equal proportions (1:1) can improve the success of the "marks-on-a-stick" metering system. A mix of equal proportions of resin and hardener is more forgiving of a slight imbalance than using a small (5:1) quantity of hardener. With care the stick will work, but it is messy, time-consuming and wasteful. Pumps that dispense resin and hardener in the correct ratio are cheap and available from the epoxy supplier.

Some epoxy systems encourage combining fast and slow hardeners to get a curing speed in between. This is most often done when the amine blush-free characteristic of the slow hardener is desirable but the temperature calls for a little more oomph. The important thing to remember when combining hardeners is that the ratio of hardener to resin doesn't change. The hardener quantity comprises a combination of the two hardeners.

It could be a coincidence, but the most successful epoxy systems seem to have been developed by boatbuilders for their own use. And, like boatbuilders in general, they all have strong ideas about what makes a good epoxy. The brands we tested (→ page 40) all gave good results using the slow hardener. They differ in the ratio of resin to hardener, cure time, sanding ability, odor and color; all, however, had good clarity using our application method.

When choosing an epoxy, do some homework and look for features that fit your building environment and work style. Talk to people who have used the brand you are considering (for example, in Web chat groups). Ask about workability, cure time, smell, safety, technical support, how well it sands, color and how it ages. Price should not be a deciding factor; it is not worth taking a chance on your health and your kayak to save money.

Before starting a project, we suggest that you do a test in your environment of the brand you have chosen. If working with

EPOXY TEST

The objective of this test is to compare the basic working characteristics of three popular epoxy systems. While in no way scientific, it is an honest assessment of how they worked in our workshop environment.

What we are looking for in our test

- The time it takes for the mixed epoxy to kick. The green stage is often the stage where work may progress to the next step.
- Time to sand without plugging the sandpaper, useful information for feathering edges between buildup coats.
- How long it takes the mixed epoxy to wet out the cloth and how transparent it is. If the cloth does not wet out clear, it may not be compatible with the epoxy.
- The number of coats it takes to fill and bury the weave of the cloth so that it can be sanded flat.

Blush-free (low-blush) resin and hardeners tested

- MAS low-viscosity resin with slow hardener
- WEST 105 resin with 207 hardener (slow)
- System Three resin with slow hardener

Control

- All resins and hardeners were warmed together; containers were slightly warm to the touch.
- Temperature was typical of Ted's shop in the winter – 65°F to 75°F (18°C to 24°C) for the first 24 hours; beginning the next day, the heat was turned down to 60°F (10°C) overnight (7 hours).
- Mixed epoxy was applied to dry cloth over raw plywood.
- Plywood was 4 mm stock, 8 x 31 inches, cut side by side from the same piece of material.

Observations

- It was interesting to apply all three brands side by side and note the speed at which the mixed epoxy saturated the cloth. I would have guessed that the low-viscosity MAS would be much faster than the others, but it was no faster than the WEST, with the System Three only slightly behind.
- The odors from the WEST and System Three were not strong or unpleasant, just enough to remind us to work safely. MAS had a pungent chemical smell that suggests good ventilation is necessary. Odors trigger different reactions in all of us, so this is not a comparison but rather what our noses were telling us.

Time	WEST	System Three	MAS
3 hrs.	rubbery	sticky	sticky
6 hrs.	ready to cut	sticky	sticky
8 hrs.	ready to sand	rubbery	sticky
11 hrs.		ready to cut	rubbery/ sticky
14 hrs.		ready to sand	rubbery/ sticky
18 hrs.			rubbery/ sticky
21 hrs.			ready to cut
24 hrs.			rubbery
29 hrs.			able to sand, still rubbery

- The first coat of mixed epoxy appeared to have saturated the wood and cloth equally well with all the brands tested.
- An interesting phenomenon was that the mas and System Three panels warped as the epoxy cured, while the WEST panel stayed flat. The panels curled away from the coated side, suggesting that that side had expanded. The lengthy cure time seems to have allowed the wood fibers to absorb the epoxy and swell, much as a dry board on wet grass will curl away from the wet side. This might explain why the one with the longest cure time, MAS, had the most warping.

epoxy is new to you, this will be a simple introduction to take some of the mystery out of it. Get a feel for its viscosity, pot life (the amount of workable time the mixed epoxy has in the pot before it begins to thicken and the material is no longer useful) and working time; the time to kick (become rubbery) and sand will help you calculate a realistic time line for your project.

Mix up a one-shot batch and apply a scrap of fiberglass cloth to a piece of scrap wood. If you are unfamiliar with the brand of epoxy or the pumps are new, this will give you a feel for the material as well as confirm the reliability of the pumps. Here are some points to consider: smell (can you live with it?); viscosity (how well and fast does it spread and saturate the glass cloth?) and cure time (how long does it take to kick or reach the green stage – when the mixed epoxy is firm enough to cut without sticking to the knife – and how long does it take to sand?).

Because specifications given by the manufacturers are expressed in different ways, we ran a few simple tests using three brands – MAS, WEST and System Three – to see how they compared in our shop environment.

Five-Minute Epoxy

A fast-setting two-part epoxy glue suitable for quick repairs, five-minute epoxy is not the first choice for general construction. It is quite thick, which limits how far it will penetrate to make a mechanical bond.

Epoxy Glue

Although other marine adhesives could be used to construct a plywood kayak, it is hard to beat waterproof epoxy glue for versatility, flexibility, resilience, gap filling, forgiveness (sometimes) and (relative) ease of use.

Catalyzed epoxy resin (mixed epoxy) is an ideal base for a waterproof marine glue. Adding a fiber reinforcement such as cotton fiber or wood dust to the epoxy makes it into a structural adhesive. Epoxy by itself is excellent in compression, but it is not very strong in tension. Compensating for this by adding a reinforcement could be compared to adding straw to adobe, horsehair to plaster or rebar to concrete. The mixture will fill cracks but will be tough to sand because the fiber absorbs the epoxy.

A number of reinforcements are available in several colors. Some materials designed for high strength (Cabosil, for example) have silica as a component. Silica is stone, and when mixed with epoxy is tougher to work than a piece of sidewalk. Cotton fibers are much easier on edge tools and are plenty strong enough for kayak and small boatbuilding. Wood flour is a reasonable substitute for cotton fibers. However, although the price is right, the glue will be dark and harder to brush out and sand.

Reinforcements

Collodial Silica

A thickening additive used to control the viscosity of mixed epoxy. It is often used in combination with other fillers to control and improve the working characteristics of an epoxy mixture as well as to thicken the bonding adhesive when filleting. It also improves abrasion resistance, making it difficult to sand, so not recommended if it must be worked in the future.

Microfibers

A cotton fiber used as a thickening and reinforcing additive. Added to mixed epoxy, it creates a strong multi-purpose adhesive.

Wood Flour

Wood flour is finely ground wood fiber. We call it sanding dust, and it's available from the bag of your sander. Use 120 grit or finer and save jars of it in a variety of colors for color-matching filler. For the professional boatbuilder, sanding dust is the profit; until we get around to bagging and selling it, we must again be content with breaking even.

Wood flour is not the greatest fillet material because of its high resin content and coarse texture. When thick enough not to slump, it drags behind the scraper and leaves a very rough surface. As a filler, the saturated wood fibers make the filler heavy, tough and hard to sand, and much darker than the original dust.

Epoxy-Based Fillers

Non-structural epoxy-based fillers are used to tack the planks together, mold fillets and fill suture holes. Synthetic fillers such as Microlite or microballoons are soft, sometimes hollow and do not absorb the epoxy. This limits the amount of epoxy in the filler, making it lightweight and easy to sand but a very poor glue.

Choosing a filler has everything to do with your expectations. If you are aiming for a high-quality bright finish, controlling the details must happen at each stage of the process. You can't expect to end up with a masterpiece by doing damage control. Understanding how filler works with plywood will help you make an intelligent decision when choosing the appropriate additive. Look for a consistency that is smooth for workability and full-bodied enough to hold a shape that can be sanded at the same speed as the plywood.

The color of epoxy-based filler is controlled by using a colored filler or by adding sanding dust as the coloring agent. For a suture-hole filler to match the okume plywood, Ted used a base of off-white #410 Microlite and added brown WEST #407 low-density filler/fairing additive as a coloring agent. Keep in mind when blending color-matched filler or glue that you are matching the color of the wood after you have varnished or stained it. Dampen a little patch of wood with water or lacquer thinner for an approximation of the final color.

The way the plywood surface has been prepared has a lot to do with how much epoxy from the filler will be absorbed by the wood, and the amount of epoxy absorbed will affect the color density. If the filler is applied over unsanded plywood, it will absorb more epoxy and look darker than it would if the surface had been sanded.

The difference in the viscosity of the epoxy in the filler compared to the epoxy that will eventually bond the glass cloth to the plywood also has an effect. A thin material will always soak in deeper than a thick material. Viscosity is affected by both temperature and pot life. Picture an area around a suture hole where some old filler has been wiped over and around the hole. Being old, thick and cool, it will soak in – not far, but far enough to seal the wood. Later, when the

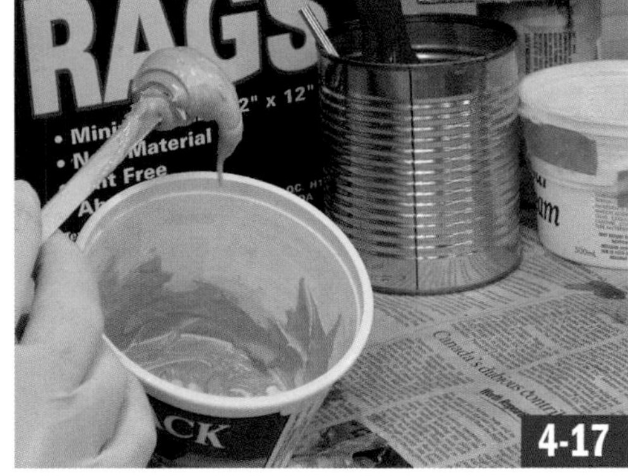

glass is being wet out with lots of fresh, warm epoxy, the epoxy will penetrate most of the way in to the first glue line of the plywood. This saturation will deepen the color of the plywood. The contrast between the sealed area around the suture hole and the glassed area will be very obvious. Match the method to your expectations.

When you are using a filler to tack the planks, a filler mixture with a very low epoxy content will limit the amount of staining and cleanup on the inside. For our purposes, a full-bodied mixture of #410 Microlite and WEST #407 mixed to a smooth peanut-butter consistency was ideal (4-17).

Microlite

An easily mixed low-density filler for making a light, easily worked filling compound. Add it to mixed epoxy – the light tan shade is a good base color. Add sanding dust to create a color match. If more red is desired, add some microballoons to the mix.

Microballoons

Microballoons are microscopic hollow spheres that resemble reddish brown flour. Blend them into mixed epoxy. Use the dark mahogany shade to color-match glues and fillers.

Other Fillers

Plastic Wood

A point to consider before using plastic wood or similar fillers on okume plywood – or any type of open-grained wood – is that the pores in the wood will trap the material deeper than you want to sand. The contrast between the filler in the open grain and the unfilled area around it will be obvious. This problem can be compounded if you leave a thin film of plastic wood over the surface that may be invisible after sanding. When the epoxy is applied, it will not penetrate as deeply in the sealed area, which will look lighter than the clean wood around it.

Plastic wood is available in a variety of colors. We used a teak color in a few places and on okume plywood it was the least conspicuous of all the filler colors tried. Although the consistency of the plastic wood did not appear to be stiff, it could not be worked all the way through a suture hole in 4 mm plywood. For this reason, it would not be our first choice for filling wire holes. Plastic wood is not appropriate for tacking the planks together either, because it is brittle and does not penetrate deeply enough to make a structural bond with the wood.

If you choose to use this type of filler,

taping off the space to be filled will confine the staining to the smallest area possible. As long as the filler is in the pores of the wood, it will be visible to some extent. Sanding deeply enough to remove it is not recommended because the damage caused by the sanding will look worse than leaving the filler where it is.

Water-based wood filler, a type of plastic wood, is a good alternative to solvent-based fillers. It is quick-drying and premixed in a variety of colors.

Polyester Body Filler

Body filler is another good possibility for bonding the planks. We were skeptical that this filler would have enough bite to hold on to the planks; in practice, this was not a problem. The big advantage of using body filler is that it is a fast way to tack the planks together. In about 15 minutes it is hard enough to remove the wires, compared to 12 to 24 hours with epoxy-based filler. Body filler can cut days off assembling the hull and deck components. It could be very useful for a complicated assembly job requiring a number of steps.

Because polyester body filler does not saturate the fibers of the wood, the bond is not as strong as that produced by an epoxy-based filler. It worked for us because we used cradles and forms to support our kayak components; consequently, they were under very little stress. If you are building "free-form" (on the floor), an epoxy-based filler would be a better choice.

Good or bad, polyester body filler comes (to our knowledge) in light blue-green, denture pink and white. The white may be tinted. Check automotive supply stores for available colors.

Epoxy Thinners and Solvents

Solvents are a necessary evil when using epoxy, paint or varnish. There are a number of them, all with their own good and bad features. If they are aggressive enough to work fast, they are hazardous; if less harmful, they have less bite. Denatured alcohol deserves some consideration because it is in the middle of the spectrum.

Remember that solvents work by evaporating, so everything that comes out of the can goes into your air. Wear gloves when practical (some solvents will eat disposable gloves) and be sure there's good ventilation in the shop.

Acetone

Acetone, while serviceable and efficacious for cleaning epoxy from your work and tools, is also flammable, volatile, explosive and foul-smelling – all qualities generally considered less than desirable in the shop setting. Also, it is bad for the skin. As an alternative, consider lacquer thinner or denatured alcohol.

Denatured Alcohol

Denatured alcohol is easy to find at your local hardware emporium. Inexpensive and effective, it does a good job of cleaning up

CHEAP TRICK

Grunge can

Cut a ¾-inch-wide slot down the side of a cardboard frozen juice can, heavy paper hot beverage cup or inverted plastic milk jug with the bottom cut off (4-18). To use, slide your epoxy-loaded squeegee into the slot and pull it back out, scraping the offending epoxy into the can.

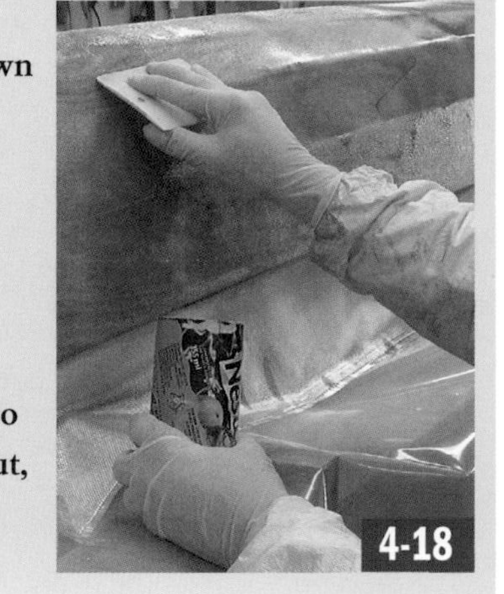

4-18

epoxy. It should not be used directly on any joints on the kayak that have been made with a polyurethane flexible adhesive (for example, 3M's 5200 and Sikaflex). Instead, try mineral spirits or a citrus-based cleaner. However, denatured alcohol is great for removing stray smudges of intractable polyurethane flexible adhesive from surface areas that are not near the joint; it doesn't leave a residue or drive the product into the grain.

Lacquer Thinner

As a thinner for uncured epoxy, lacquer thinner is a good choice. It is foul-smelling enough that you don't forget it is a nasty chemical, and it is a good cleaner that evaporates moderately fast without leaving a residue. Use it for cleaning brushes and tools and cleaning up spills.

Lacquer thinner does its job by evaporating. This puts it high on the list of shop hazards. Always use it with a good cross-draft of fresh air. However, because it evaporates fast, the fumes are not going to last long – a consideration when working in the basement or when it is –40°F outside.

Vinegar

In a pinch, vinegar (dilute acetic acid) is another alternative for tool cleanup. Using balsamic is unnecessary; el cheapo white vinegar will do a reasonable job of removing uncured epoxy. However, keep in mind that vinegar removes oil from the skin as effectively as lacquer thinner, so don't forget the gloves.

Fiberglass Cloth

All fiberglass cloth (4-19) and tape are made by twisting filaments of glass into thread, then weaving the thread into a variety of weights and widths of cloth and tape. The weight of the glass is governed by the number of filaments in the thread and how tightly it is woven. After weaving, the cloth is fired to remove residual wax and oil and then finished with a coupling agent. The coupling agent is the interface between the glass fibers and the epoxy. Many different finishes are available, but few are suitable for our purpose. Buy your cloth from an epoxy dealer and ask if the finish is compatible with the epoxy.

THINK LAZY

Cloth care

Unfold the glass as far as you can onto the clean hull, tape the end of the cloth to a piece of 4-inch plastic pipe, then roll it carefully onto the pipe. Care must be taken to keep the cloth rolling smoothly onto the pipe without folding or kinking. Once it is on the pipe, it is easy to position the cloth when needed and to cut it accurately to length. As well, by the time the inside is ready to glass, most of the folds will have settled out.

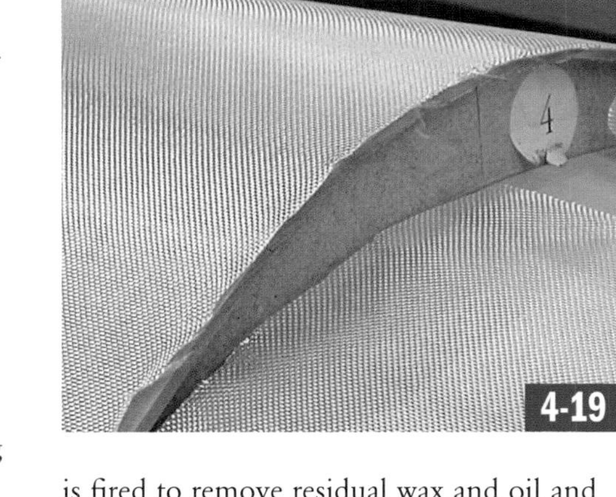

4-19

When you buy glass cloth, insist that it be carefully rolled. If it is folded, the hard creases may not come out. On the outside of the kayak you might be able to sand them flat, but there is always a possibility of hitting the glass and then having to patch it. On the inside, if only two coats of epoxy are used, the wrinkles could remain visible.

If you have purchased a kit, you may not have this option. The glass cloth in most kits is in one piece, folded into a bundle that is clean, dry and easy to pack. Unless you have a large, clean table, the folded cloth is awkward to handle without damaging it.

For the plans-builder, you have a choice of cloth weights. Using 6-ounce cloth will result in a strong boat, but if you can give the kayak reasonable care, consider using 4-ounce cloth to save some weight. Using the lighter cloth will make a difference of about 4 pounds on a 17-foot kayak. If you anticipate surprise forces from the outside, consider 6-ounce cloth or a second layer of 4-ounce in strategic places on the inside – for instance, the center of the bottom.

Glass cloth comes in a variety of widths; choose a width that will result in the least amount of cutting or waste. Try to avoid doing a lot of cutting and piecing. Joints in cloth are time-consuming, plus they must be feathered before subsequent coats of epoxy, which means significant waiting, sanding and cleanup time.

To determine the width of cloth needed, measure around the widest section on the plans and note the width of cloth needed for the hull and deck. To calculate the length of cloth needed for the outside, add 12 inches to the overall length of the kayak. For the inside, use the actual length of the kayak.

Epoxy Tools

Brushes

Acid brush

An acid brush is a 1/2- to 3/4-inch-wide bristle brush with a metal handle that comes from the plumbing department. Use it for applying glue and small amounts of mixed epoxy and for working out bubbles in the epoxy. They are cheap, but they don't have to be disposable; soak them in lacquer thinner when not in use.

Chip brush

This el cheapo brush with blond bristles is sometimes used for applying epoxy. Cheap in every way, it sheds excessively, and the bristles are hard to find and pick up on the light-colored plywood. Also available is a slightly higher-priced "disposable" brush with black bristles. It is just as bad – the dye on the bristles dissolves and leaves black streaks in the epoxy.

Epoxy brush

The ideal epoxy brush is a moderately priced 2-inch-wide natural bristle brush. Look for a brush with short bristles that are not too thick. If you can only find one with long, flexible bristles, trim them back with sharp scissors. A brush with a mixture of light and dark hairs is most likely natural bristle. If the bristles are all black, the color may have been altered. In case the bristles have been dyed, rinse the brush in lacquer thinner before using it.

An expensive varnish brush is not a good choice because it holds more epoxy than is useful and is hard to clean. Because of its greater viscosity, mixed epoxy does not flow out of a brush as freely as paint or varnish. Old epoxy collects up inside the brush and hardens before the project can be completed.

All brushes are going to shed when they are new, but dark bristles will be easier to see. Shake out as many bristles as you can before using the brush for the first time.

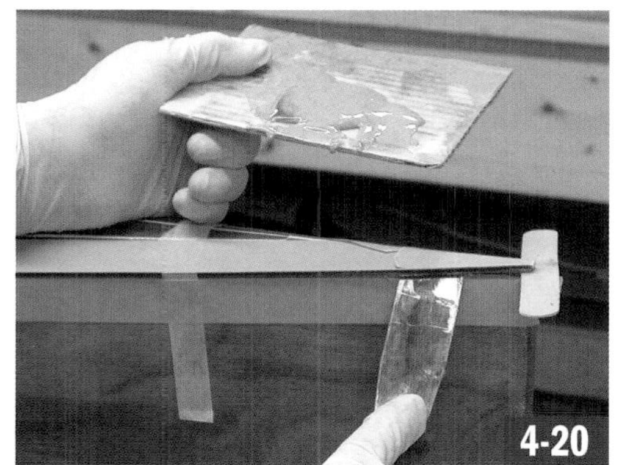
4-20

Take care of your epoxy brush. The more it is used, the better it will become. When you are finished using the brush or you feel it beginning to get stiff, scrape as much of the excess epoxy as possible out of the brush into a grunge can, then rinse the brush in lacquer thinner. Shake it completely dry before using. Store the brush in clean lacquer thinner between coats, then wash with soap and water or a water-soluble brush cleaner. When the brush is soaking in the thinner, cover the brush and can with a plastic bag or glove to slow down evaporation and contain the fumes.

Hawk

This homemade tool for holding filler (4-20) was inspired by the bricklayer's hawk, used to hold mortar, or maybe an artist's palette. The advantage of using a hawk is that the edge can be used to keep the putty knife clean, allowing you to pick up the precise amount of filler needed for the space you are working on. Spreading the filler out will keep it fresh, extending the working time.

A square of cardboard makes a fine hawk. The first time you use it, it will absorb some of the resin out of the filler. Take the time to scrape the hawk clean when you're finished; it won't absorb resin the next time you use it and the edge will remain firm. Keep the edge crisp with 180 grit sandpaper.

Hot Air Gun

A hot air gun – or the home version, a hair dryer – can come in handy around epoxy-built boats. Used with care, it will speed up the curing. However, we have seen people smear on a sloppy fillet, then later use the hot air gun to soften it so they could scrape it clean. This is not recommended, for obvious health reasons, but also consider the filler that was softened and not removed, the glue melting in the plywood, and the pointless waste of time to clean these up. Work neat and clean; it is the lazy way.

CHEAP TRICK

Forgot to clean the putty knife? With a hot air gun or a hair dryer, heat the filler on the knife enough to soften it, then scrape it clean. Do this outside – the fumes are lethal.

CHEAP TRICK

Solvent bottles

The plastic squeeze bottles used for maple syrup, ketchup and shampoo are invaluable for dispensing solvent in a controlled quantity – much better than holding a rag over the hole of a large can and sloshing out the contents. If the cap is misplaced, the hole is small enough that very little solvent is lost through evaporation. This cheap trick will cut the amount of thinner you use in half.

Mixing Pots

These are available commercially, but plastic yogurt or margarine tubs work fine. Gourmet cat food tins and other small cans are great for mixing small amounts of epoxy glue.

Polyethylene Film

Used as a barrier between a part being glued and the clamp block. The best weight is 6 mm because it will hold its shape and is reusable. Waxed paper will do the job but is flimsy.

Rollers

If you use rollers, use the real deal 7-inch yellow ones marketed by marine hardware and epoxy companies. Bargain-basement gray ones will unwind on your work like a long gray slug or dissolve into a resinous gray glob.

Rollers work fine for applying mixed epoxy on large, reasonably flat surfaces. On a little boat like a kayak, which is all chines and tight inside curves, the roller is awkward and has a tendency to pick up the cloth and move it. Because the roller has no control over the position of the cloth, a brush must be used in conjunction with it.

On the buildup coats, if the roller hangs over an edge as it is being rolled along a chine, a large ridge of foamy epoxy will be deposited along the edge. The only possible solution to this problem is to roll directly across the chine at a right angle. A roller cut in half will fit the scale of the kayak a little better and reduce the amount of epoxy wasted.

There is a much greater chance that a first-time builder will overwork the epoxy with a roller than with a brush. Overworking introduces air into the epoxy that may or may not come out with careful squeegeeing. Overworked epoxy has a milky look.

Then there is the cost of the roller and the wasted epoxy. Rollers retain a substantial amount of epoxy after use. (Avoid rolling the last bit of epoxy onto the boat; it is foamy and should be discarded.) For this reason, they do not tend to be reusable – lacquer thinner destroys them – plus getting the roller off the frame always gets epoxy on your gloves or pliers or whatever it takes to remove the roller.

In general, a roller is a costly nuisance if the area is small and there is an easier-to-clean, reusable way of applying the epoxy or finish.

Roller Tray

Used to hold a supply of material and as a ramp for rolling drips off the roller. To save on cleanup time, liners are available to fit the tray. We use several plastic bags pulled over the tray and taped around the edges.

Spatula

Any small, flexible spreader. It can be cobbled together easily from a piece of a thick plastic bottle or a section cut from a standard squeegee. Or simply use an artist's palette knife.

Squeegee (Plastic Spreader)

This ubiquitous yellow flat, flexible tool is popular for spreading polyester body filler and can usually be found in auto and marine supply stores or where you purchase your epoxy. It is a precision tool that will give you an epoxy-and-fiberglass surface that, with very little sanding, will look like 12 coats of varnish.

Keep the edge trimmed straight. A couple of passes with a sharp block plane will get the big nicks; use 400 grit wet/dry sandpaper to soften the edge and remove any small nicks.

Stir Sticks

Homemade stir sticks work just fine for combining epoxy resin and hardener. For the builder with no scrap wood pile, consider tongue depressors.

Syringe

A disposable plastic syringe is used for injecting filler and glue; it's similar to a medical syringe but without the needle. Available from epoxy dealers and woodworkers' supply stores, or talk to your dentist.

Tongue Depressors

Used for fillet sculpture or as stir sticks. Cut them into short pieces for use as clamp pads.

Sanding Tools and Materials

If you are building on the beach and don't have power, a plywood kayak can be sanded by hand. It need not be an endless job if reasonable care is taken during construction.

File Board

If you must sand your kayak by hand or if you want an incredibly fair surface, consider using a file board such as the Speed File, a commercially available tool that uses 2¾- x 14½-inch strips of sandpaper (4-21). Purchase one at an auto body supply store; it is used extensively in auto bodywork as a fairing tool.

Sanders

Round-bottomed orbital sanders are the handiest, but the half- or quarter-sheet flat models are fine for flat and outside curves.

Random orbital sander

If you are in the market for a new sander to use on a variety of projects, the round 5-inch random orbital sander will do everything from 80 grit rough shaping to 220 grit scuffing between varnish coats. Most brands are available with either a PSA (pressure-sensitive adhesive) or hook-and-loop pad system. Hook-and-loop is handy if you don't anticipate wearing out the disc before having to change to the next grit, but if you anticipate wearing each disc out, it is not cost-effective.

The advantage of the PSA system is that you can make a disc from any sheet of sandpaper. Cut the disc out of a sheet and coat the back with a spray adhesive such as 3M Super 77. If removed while still hot from being used, the coated disc will peel cleanly off the pad.

Flat half- or quarter-sheet sander

Flat-pad sanders operate by moving the pad in a fixed orbit to make overlapping random scratches in the surface. Useful for sanding epoxy on the outside of the hull and deck.

4-22

Sanding Blocks

For this project you will need three types of sanding blocks: a hard block to create and maintain flat surfaces (cleaning up plank joints), a firm block to follow long curves (hull and deck) and a soft block to shape and soften curved edges (joint between hull and deck).

While sanding blocks are commercially available in a variety of sizes, densities and clamping systems, they are also easy to make from common materials. For a hard block, a piece of wood with ¼-inch cork glued to the surface works well. A firm block can be made out of surplus high-density foam packaging material. Insulation foam or softer packaging foam make a good soft block (4-22).

Foam insulation can easily be shaped into the shape you are going to sand. Put sandpaper with the grit up over the piece you will be sanding. Run the foam block back and forth long enough to sand the profile into the foam. Turn the sandpaper over and start sanding.

Sandpaper

The following grits are needed for a professional finish:

- 80 for rough shaping and rough sanding of epoxy
- 120 to 180 for finish sanding of planking and epoxy and for shaping hardwood trim
- 220 to 280 for finish sanding of hardwood trim and sanding between varnish coats
- 400 wet paper for optional sanding before the last coat of paint or varnish

"Open coat" refers to paper that has grains covering 50 to 70 percent of the backing. This sort of sandpaper is used in applications where the surface being sanded tends to plug up or load the abrasive surface, reducing both the cutting ability and the useful life of the paper. "Closed coat" refers to paper that has grains all over the backing. Faster-cutting, it is used in situations where loading up is not a problem. Paper weights range from A to F. A is the most flexible, but is so light that it really is suitable only for hand sanding. C or D is a good compromise – less flexible but much stronger and works well in power sanders. F is belt sander grade. Silicon carbide and aluminum carbide grits are much sharper and tougher than either garnet or flint.

CAUTION

Never use lacquer thinner or acetone with oil-based finishes. They work as a mild paint stripper and will dissolve the finish. Conversely, never use paint thinner with epoxy.

Scotchbrite

A plastic abrasive pad used in place of steel wool. Use it for softening and sanding edges and for aggressive scrubbing to remove epoxy blush.

Steel or Bronze Wool

Steel wool is most useful for cutting the gloss on tight corners where taking a minimum of material is important. The resulting steel particles are hard to clean up. To keep them from becoming embedded in the epoxy, vacuum the debris as soon as possible.

Bronze wool is a somewhat more expensive alternative. Unlike steel wool, though, any stray particles that become embedded will not rust. Available at specialty paint and marine supply stores.

Finishing Materials and Tools

You will no doubt have decided on paint or varnish by now, so it is just a matter of getting on with the job. Oil-based paints and varnishes are similar to work with and require the same prepared surface. Keep in mind that an unfair surface will be the least conspicuous under varnish or a light-colored paint. Dark colors like black or dark blue will show all your sins.

4-23

Marine Spar Varnish

Choose a premium modified oil-based varnish with at least 3 percent ultraviolet (UV) inhibitor (4-23). Also confirm that it is compatible with your epoxy. One of the few things that will break epoxy down is ultraviolet light. When you apply four coats of varnish, the surface of your kayak will be protected with the recommended 12 percent UV inhibitor.

Some two-part polyurethanes are compatible with epoxy and make a hard, durable surface. The downside is that they are more toxic than a spar varnish and more difficult to apply with a brush.

Adding color to varnish

An interesting way to add color is to combine a pigment with the varnish. This method will give a different effect than changing the color of the surface. Picture the difference between what you see through colored glasses and the effect of a colored reflective surface on the back of a mirror. The color is more in the depth of the finish than a reflection of what is underneath it. Because the varnish is transparent, defects and stains will not be hidden as they would be under paint.

The pigment we use is an artist's oil color available at any art store. We used Winsor & Newton #23 Indian red on the outside of the Coho to reduce the strong contrast between the forest green deck and the pale okume plywood.

There are no secrets to mixing. Choose a color, add some to the quantity of varnish necessary for the project and stir well. Put a dab on your finger and rub it out thinly on a piece of white paper. Keep in mind that each coat will build the intensity of the color. When you reach a color intensity that looks right, varnish as usual. Watch how the color develops as the coats build and adjust the color if necessary.

It is a very good idea to finish up with at least one coat of straight varnish. This will simplify touching up the varnish in the future by avoiding having to repair and match the color.

Paint

Paints sold for marine applications are a safe choice. Exterior-grade enamels from the home supply store are also worth considering. We have had good success with porch and floor paint. Since it is intended for a similar environment, the finish ages well on a boat and the scuff resistance it provides is a great asset for a kayak that will be dragged up on the beach. Porch paint is available in a full range of colors and priced for the home improvement market.

Our experience with coating WEST epoxy with a wide variety of oil-based finishes has always been successful if the epoxy is completely cured and well sanded. Always follow the epoxy manufacturer's recommendations for compatible finishes and/or do a test before putting the finish where it matters.

Graphite

This black coating is most appropriate below the waterline, where the color looks logical and where it will do the most good. No finish is bulletproof, but a mixture of graphite powder and collodial silica in mixed epoxy is one of the toughest we know of. The graphite is a lubricant and makes the surface slippery while the silica makes it very hard. Up to 25 percent (by volume) of graphite powder and 10 percent of collodial silica are added to mixed epoxy to make the coating.

Graphite coating should be applied over sanded epoxy after the other finishes have been applied. Application is tricky because the lubricating properties of the graphite make it prone to flow over the tape masking off the waterline. If the tape is removed too soon, the finish will continue to run across the line. But if the tape is left until the coating is hard, you will have to use a file to remove the mixture in order to get at the tape. Remove it when the epoxy is still uncured but solid to the touch.

For an attractive matte finish, buff the surface when the coating is good and hard with 0000 steel wool to cut the gloss. A glossy surface shows scuffs. When you remove all the gloss beforehand, scuffs will blend right in. When the surface begins to look scruffy, rubbing it down with steel wool will restore an even matte finish.

Solvents

When the instructions on the can specify the company's own thinner, take those instructions seriously. When they specify mineral spirits, they mean paint thinner, which is sold under a number of brand names such as Varsol. As a rule, paint thinner is compatible with spar varnish and enamel paints, but if there is any doubt, go by the instructions.

The curing speed of the finish may be controlled by adding a thinner. Brushing thinner is a retardant and will help keep a wet edge on a hot day. Spraying thinner is an accelerator and is useful on a cold, damp day.

Brushes

Foam brush

Foam brushes are cheap, available and disposable and don't shed bristles. They're not appropriate for epoxy. For applying paint or varnish, use a 1-inch brush for the trim and a 2- to 3-inch brush for hull and deck. Since the varnish does not build up as fast with a foam brush as it does with a bristle brush, consider an extra coat if a foam brush is being used.

CHEAP TRICK

Instead of scrunching up a rag, fold it neatly like a dinner napkin so that you can expose a fresh face when one side becomes charged with dust.

Don't choose a foam brush for economy. When the cost of all the foam brushes it takes to finish a kayak are added up, a good badger-hair brush will look like a bargain and a good nylon brush, a steal.

Paint or varnish brush

A badger-hair brush is a joy to use, but good results are also possible with a first-rate natural bristle or flagged nylon brush. Even the best brush will lose a few bristles when it is new. Before using, loosen the bristles that would fall out anyway by rinsing the brush in paint thinner, then spinning the handle between your hands to dry it. Most likely there are more bristles to come, so keep an eye on it. If you take care of a good varnish brush, it will last forever and keep getting better with use.

Brush Cleaner

If a brush is to get better with use, it must be well cleaned and maintained. Brush cleaner makes the oil-based residue in a brush water-soluble, allowing you to wash it well in lots of warm water.

After using a brush, wipe the handle clean, then scrape all the grunge into a can. Rinse the brush well in paint thinner, shake it out, then rotate the handle rapidly between your hands to remove the remaining solvent. Soak the brush in the brush cleaner, then rinse with water. Spin dry, smooth out the bristles and hang to dry in a dust-free area. When the brush is dry, store it in a plastic bag.

Paint Filter

Use a paint filter to strain the finishing material to be sure there are no uninvited particles floating about. Although this is a greater problem with cans that have previously been opened and used, there is sometimes contamination in a new can.

Tack Cloth

Tack cloth is a piece of cheesecloth that has been impregnated with a sticky substance that will pick up and hold difficult-to-see dust particles. Traditional boat finishers made theirs by working a mixture of varnish, raw linseed oil and solvent into the cheesecloth. Today they are available at most paint and auto supply stores.

When using a tack cloth, wipe gently; if the cloth is pressed down too firmly, the sticky residue will be transferred to the surface. If the residue is not removed, the varnish will not stick to the surface. Count on dust settling out of the air continually, so wait until you are ready to apply the finish before the final wipe-down.

Safety and Cleaning Supplies and Other Necessities

These items relate to health, safety and boatbuilder comfort. The coffee pot you most likely have; the rest will not be hard to round up.

Coffee Pot

Used to produce the universal sacramental mood enhancer and clarifier.

Dust Mask

There are dust masks and then there are real dusk masks. Those thin economy models with the single elastic strap are about as effective as wearing a doily (and nowhere near as stylish). Get the industrial NIOSH/MSHA-approved paper mask.

Ear Plugs or Earphones

Remember that hearing loss is cumulative. Your ear plugs need to be comfortable. They are especially helpful for machine sanding.

Gloves

Gloves are handy when applying dye with a sponge (4-24) and, needless to say, should always be worn when working with epoxy. The effects of epoxy exposure are cumulative and can lead to serious health problems. Keep a box of latex, vinyl or, better yet, the more durable and less allergenic nitrile gloves handy – and wear them. Keep two pairs on the go; when one gets damp inside, remove them by turning them inside out and put on a dry pair.

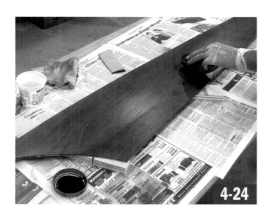

4-24

Make a habit of wiping the drips off your brush handle with a dry rag. This will keep the handle clean and keep you conscious of working clean. Once epoxy gets on your gloves, it is guaranteed to get deposited where it will not be noticed until somebody sits in it.

There will be times when, despite your best efforts, you will end up with epoxy on your skin. Steer clear of aggressive solvents when cleaning your skin. While they will do the job, they will also drive the chemicals into your body and remove the protective oil from your skin, leaving it exposed to the next careless contamination. Neither situation is desirable. Instead, consider pumice soap and water or a waterless hand cleaner containing lanolin. To get a bit more scrubbing action, add a dash of sawdust to the hand cleaner.

Rags

Use white cotton rags for epoxy cleanup. Epoxy solvents will dissolve the dye in colored fabrics and transfer it to the surface being cleaned. Well-washed white sheets are lint-free and make premium rags.

Fabric softener residue in rags has been known to cause epoxy bonding problems. Rinse your rags well with clean water to remove the silicone and soap residue.

Respirator

If you have allergies or are sensitive to chemicals or dust, look for a full-fledged (and properly rated) charcoal filter canister respirator. Be sure it is well fitted and has a fresh, properly rated canister. Storing it in a sealed plastic bag will extend the life of the active charcoal filter.

Safety Glasses, Shield or Goggles

Select eye protection that doesn't fog up and is comfortable enough that you will use it. We suggest wearing eye protection for handling and using epoxy, paints, varnishes and thinners and for machine sanding or cutting.

Vacuum Cleaner

A heavy-duty shop vacuum with a good filter is nice to have, but most home versions will handle the volume of dust generated by a plywood kayak building project. Reduce cleanup time by sanding epoxy outside when possible.

Waterless Hand Cleaner and Paper Towels

A waterless hand cleaner and paper towels are handy to have if running water is not available in your shop. Even if it is, we recommend this kind of cleaner for removing uncured epoxy from your skin. It usually contains lanolin, which replaces the natural protective oil in the skin that washing removes.

TWELVE STEPS TO A KAYAK

Building a plywood kayak involves a series of simple steps. Here is a quick look at the major steps and the order in which the Mill Creek kayak pieces go together.

Join the components into planks.

Assemble the hull.

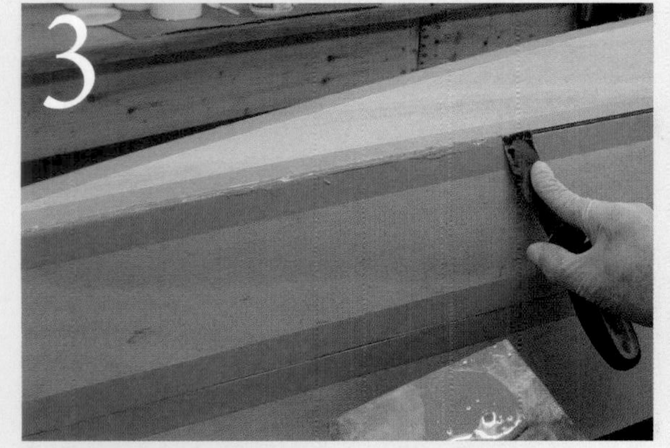

Tack the plank seams.

Apply the fillets.

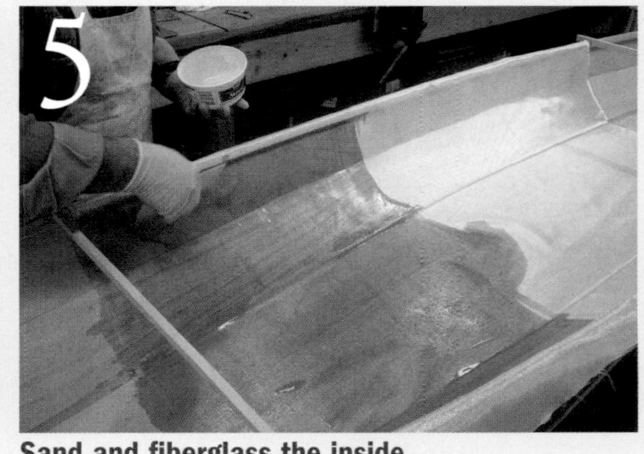

Sand and fiberglass the inside.

Do the end pour to cast a stem and breast-hook.

Install foot braces.

Sand and fiberglass the outside.

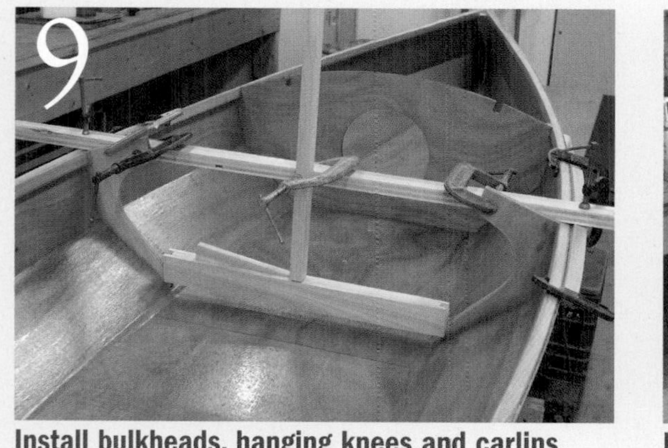

Install bulkheads, hanging knees and carlins.

Install and fiberglass the deck.

Install the trim.

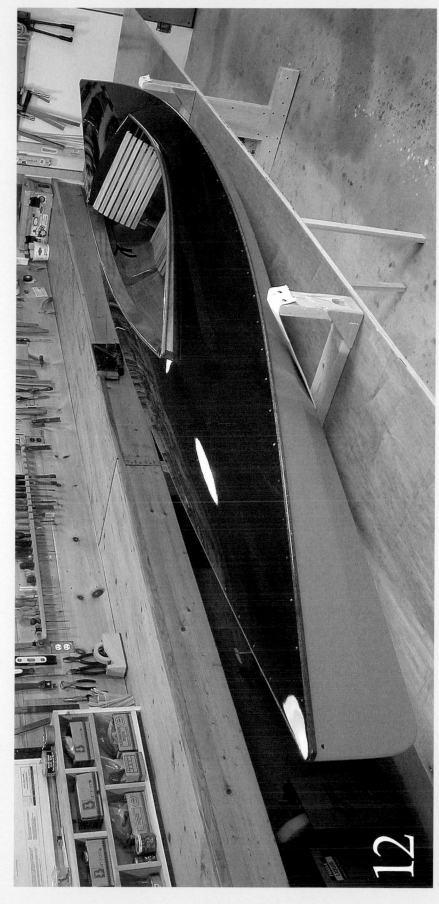

12

Sand and varnish or paint.

CHAPTER FIVE

Plywood Boat-Building Techniques

TED STARTED BUILDING BOATS with the assumption that a person can achieve professional results if good materials are used and simple steps are performed with care in the proper order. Over time his techniques have evolved, as have the materials, but that basic assumption has always served him well. As you begin to build your kayak, it will serve you well, too.

The techniques for building with plywood and working with fiberglass cloth and epoxy are common to all plywood kayaks. They can be grouped together into seven major areas: joining the plank components, assembling the hull and deck panels, fiberglassing the outside and inside, sanding, installing trim, fitting out, and finishing.

Joining the Plank Components

Assembling the Hull and Deck

PLYWOOD BOAT-BUILDING TECHNIQUES

Joining the Plank Components

If you're building from a kit, the planks are precut for you. But because each plank is longer than a regular 4x8 sheet of plywood, it comes in two or more pieces that must be glued together.

A number of ways of lining up and joining the planking components are used by the various kit suppliers. Regardless of the method used, accuracy is very important. Take your time joining the pieces together. The old saying, "Be sure you are right, then go ahead," works here. If the plank components are not assembled into the smooth shape the designer had in mind, the planks will not fit together as intended and it will require a great deal of work to achieve a compromise fit. If you try to force into place plywood planks that are incorrectly shaped, chances are they will bulge in or out at all the wrong places. Keep in mind that wherever we have to do damage control, it will never look as good as it would have if

5-1

we had got it right the first time.

Follow the system in your instruction manual for identifying the components and organize them into sets for each plank. Look for the good side of the plywood, as this is the side you will want on the outside of the kayak. The manufacturer's identifying marks are often a good clue; they're usually on the inside surface. Although there is a difference in quality between the two sides, if the grain pattern of the inner surface intrigues you, don't hesitate to flip the components over. Compare the quality of the sanding on both sides; the back or inside face may need a little more attention to get it to match the adjoining plank.

Lining Up the Components

As an aid to lining up the components, some suppliers will provide distances from a baseline to the joint or to specified points along the length of the plank. For assembly, draw a centerline or use the edge of the table if it is straight. If you don't have the benefit of these aids, a tightly stretched string line is a reliable reference. Shim the ends of the string up enough to clear the table to guarantee that it is straight. Because accuracy is so important, a chalk line is of little use. When it's snapped, the chalk can spread out up to ⅛ inch, making it difficult to decide where the middle is.

Lining up plank components without a baseline reference is more difficult and requires extra attention to the shape before committing to the glue. The following tricks will give you a good look at the curve; when it feels right, it most likely is.

Standing at the end of the plank, squint as you sight down the edge, looking for a fair curve on both edges. For a good view, look from just above the surface of the table. Check from both ends until you are satisfied with the shape. Your eye is a powerful tool; trust it. Although you may not have the experience to recognize the right shape, most builders are able to see or sense that something is out of place and can adjust the position until it feels right.

You can also check for a fair line by springing a batten around the edge. If the batten lies comfortably along both edges of both components, and if your eye is happy, there is a good chance you have the intended shape.

To keep both sides of the kayak the same shape, join all the planks for one side first, then use them as a pattern for assembling their mates. For this operation the two outside plank faces will be together. The shape of the hull and deck may not be what the designer drew, but this trick will help keep the hull and deck symmetrical.

Working with Epoxy

Once the plank components are lined up, you're ready to join them together with epoxy glue (5-1). This is the first, but certainly not the last time you will be working with epoxy during this project. The secret to a healthy relationship with epoxy is keeping a clean and organized shop and being constantly aware of the potential hazards. Take the time to understand the dangers and to implement the following simple steps to keep safe and healthy:

- Plan ahead to keep epoxy exposure time to a minimum. Choose methods that will give the best results with the least amount of exposure to resins and solvents.
- Be sure you have good cross-ventilation inside, or work outside.
- Wear a dust mask when sanding epoxy. If you are sensitive to dust, use a properly rated charcoal filter canister respirator.
- Wear gloves when handling wet or uncured epoxy. These can be the ubiquitous latex or the less allergenic nitrile or vinyl gloves. Try cornstarch, talcum powder or baby powder in the gloves to absorb the sweat; a rash similar to diaper rash is commonly caused by wearing sweaty gloves for long periods of time and is sometimes mistaken for a reaction to the epoxy. Wear an old shirt with long sleeves that can be

tucked inside the gloves. Disposable overalls or sleeves are great for protecting your arms and clothing, especially when working on the inside of the hull.

• Dispose of unused epoxy (grunge) in a container with a couple of inches of water in the bottom to dissipate the heat. Left to its own devices, a can filled with grunge will soon start to smoke, boil and froth over the top, Vesuvius-like, producing extremely toxic fumes in the process – interesting, but not productive or healthy. An overheated shop or a hot summer's day only makes the problem worse.

Get rid of the grunge by carefully moving the container outside as soon as possible. If the stuff has heated up, wear gloves or handle the container with a rag to protect yourself from burns. Avoid breathing any fumes.

• Avoid using epoxy as a condiment with lunch. The glue bench is not a dinner table. Smoking cigarettes (resin-dipped or not) is also verboten.

• Before discarding thinner-soaked rags, drape them over something (preferably out of doors) to allow the thinner to evaporate. Fires often start in a garbage can from balled-up rags containing thinner.

• To catch the inevitable drips, lay cardboard or heavy kraft paper on the floor. (Plastic film is slippery and newspapers can stick to the floor.) Working on a 24-inch table does not expose much of the floor, but take the time to cover the exposed portion of the table.

• Contain the drips. A few conveniently located cardboard "coasters" will protect the bench from a trail of wet epoxy. A rag around the container just below the rim will catch the epoxy before it gets to your gloves.

• Take the time to read and understand the safety information provided for the epoxy system that you are using. In the U.S. and Canada, manufacturers of chemical products are required to publish product safety data sheets that give you the lowdown on what the product contains and the associated hazards. These are available for the asking from the manufacturer, and retailers are required by law to provide them to customers buying these products.

• Reduce your exposure to toxic uncured epoxy. Allow the epoxy to reach a full cure (one to two weeks, depending on the brand and temperature) before sanding.

Mixing the Resin and Hardener

Epoxy manufacturers sell inexpensive calibrated metering pumps in ratios tailored to their particular product. The most popular type resembles the ketchup dispensers popular in fast food restaurants. If your resin and hardener are to be mixed in a 5:1 ratio, pumps are set up so that one squirt of the resin pump will give you five times the amount from one squirt of the hardener pump. There are, alas, documented cases of folks who reversed the pumps or, insisting that the instructions said 5 to 1, by golly, they just had to give that resin pump five squirts for every one of the hardener. Don't do it.

Check new pumps

Don't take anything for granted when it comes to epoxy pumps. We have received pumps that were packaged with the wrong ratio of hardener pump and with barrels that were cracked. If there is ever any doubt about whether a pump has the correct ratio of resin and/or hardener, dispose of it or, better yet, return it to the manufacturer.

These pumps work by drawing the liquid up into the barrel with pull created by a spring. When the spring stops pulling the liquid into the barrel, a ball valve closes on the bottom and the liquid is held in place until it is dispensed by pressing the plunger down. If the resin or hardener is cold, it will be stiff, like maple syrup in the refrigerator, and the spring will have a hard time pulling it up into the pump. Before using a new pump, prime it by pumping until the resin begins to come out; if you don't know whether you have dispensed a full shot, give it a couple of trial squirts into the grunge can.

With cold resin, the pump will often dispense air (of varying quantities) along with the resin. Sometimes, at the beginning of the stroke, the plunger will suddenly drop a short distance before getting firm again. To maintain the correct ratio, let the plunger come back up the distance it dropped, then continue to the bottom. Little belches shouldn't be a problem.

CHEAP TRICK

Ill-fitting joints

It is hard to imagine, but if for some reason a joint does not fit perfectly, use the gap-filling ability of thick, color-matched epoxy glue to hide your sins. Use plastic-covered smooth-faced clamping blocks on both sides to hold the components in line and mold a smooth joint (5-2). Clamp just enough to draw the joint into the shape you want; any more and your sins will be revealed.

5-2

Maintain the correct ratio

Pump out the resin and hardener in alternate strokes, beginning with the resin: one of resin, then one of hardener, then one of resin and so on. Not only will the liquids be layered in the mixing pot, already beginning the mixing process, but you also won't lose track of the number of squirts you have put into the mix. For example, if you have just taken your hand off the hardener pump, you can be sure that the ratio is correct; if your hand just came off the resin pump, a shot of hardener will complete the ratio.

Combine completely

After you have dispensed an appropriate amount of the ingredients, it's time to mix. In order to get all those molecules properly socialized with one another, plan on at least 60 seconds of mixing per batch. Be sure to scrape along the sides and bottom as you mix, and reverse rotation from time to time. Sixty seconds can seem like forever when you're mixing; to check that you are mixing long enough, try using an egg timer.

How much to mix at a time?

Mixed epoxy generates exothermic heat, which in turn promotes the cure. The more epoxy you have and the smaller the container, the faster the cure and the more heat it will generate.

For even saturation of wood and fiberglass cloth, the mixed epoxy must be of a consistent viscosity. Epoxy that has begun to cure will be thicker than when it was mixed. To extend the pot life,

• Keep the batch size small. Choose a quantity that you can comfortably use up in 10 minutes or less. This is a conservative length of time that should be safe in most instances. To check for the end of the pot life, see if you can feel any heat through the container (a metal container will give you this information faster than a plastic one). If you feel any heat, discard what is left of the batch.

• Use a shallow, wide-bottomed container (an aluminum pie plate or paint roller pan, for example) that allows the epoxy to spread out without having too much depth.

Epoxy Glue

Mixed epoxy (the catalyzed or combined resin and hardener) becomes a glue when a reinforcement is added. It will take some experimenting to get a feel for the ratio of additive to mixed epoxy. The amount of fiber added is adjusted to suit the surfaces being glued together. A glue with a high fiber content is appropriate between two hard surfaces that will not absorb much epoxy (for example, between sanded epoxy and the hardwood trim). Between two raw wood surfaces, some of the epoxy in the glue will be absorbed into the pores, so a thinner mix is desirable.

A fiber additive mixed into epoxy can be deceiving. A mix that looks right initially can go dry in a minute or two when the fibers have had a chance to absorb the epoxy. To avoid this, make your glue a bit thinner than you want it to be. Remember that fiber should be added only to premixed epoxy.

Sanding dust or a variety of fillers can be used as color additives to hide or accent the joint.

Pre-coat the end grain

Epoxy is thin, which is usually a good thing because it is able to penetrate the wood to give you a strong, well-anchored joint. But if the wood is really absorbent, most of the glue will migrate into it before the epoxy has a chance to cure. This will leave you with a weak, "glue-starved" joint. To prevent this, simply apply the glue to both surfaces (if they are both absorbent).

This is particularly important for any exposed end grain and open-grain woods. When gluing exposed end grain – in a scarf joint, for example – it is necessary to pre-coat the surfaces with mixed but unthickened epoxy. This will give the wood a good drink and limit the amount of epoxy that will be absorbed out of the glue. When gluing raw wood to a sanded epoxy surface, there is no need to coat the epoxy side.

Work clean

Try to keep the glue off your gloves. From your gloves it will get on anything you touch and make a terrible mess on your clamps. Dirty clamps are a nuisance to use and they make you feel like a klutz when they won't clamp. Keep a clean, dry rag handy to catch the drips when they happen.

Clamping

The number of clamps you use will have a lot to do with how many you have in the first place – you will use them all. Building methods that require gluing the sheer clamp to the sheer plank will require a minimum of three clamps per foot; cockpit coamings will require a dozen plus. In general, the thinner the material, the closer together the clamps should be. Thin material is not stiff enough to stay straight and tight between clamps spaced widely apart. For a consistent joint between layers of thin plywood, use clamps on 3- to 4-inch centers.

Once again, the key to success is planning ahead. Do a dry run and see how things fit together. Do you have enough clamps set to the right opening? Do you have clamp blocks? If you are gluing up on a table, is the throat of the clamp deep enough for it to reach your work?

How Much Pressure?

Pressure is an important consideration when clamping. We want to have epoxy glue in the joint; indeed, it is the joint. But epoxy is a different critter from the old standard glues such as urea-formaldehyde and resorcinol glues, which required high-accuracy joinery and heavy-duty pressure from industrial-strength clamps. That sort of clamping pressure isn't necessary or desirable with epoxy. In fact, heavy clamping can force too much glue out the sides and leave the joint with a glue deficit. All you really need is enough uniform pressure to bring your mating pieces together without distorting them and to hold them in place until the glue cures.

Clamp-Control Theory

Will your work move when you put pressure on it? This is especially likely to happen when gluing panel components together with scarf joints, which are essentially two inclined planes put together with a lubricant (fresh epoxy glue). Putting pressure on the joint is a little like squeezing a watermelon seed between your fingers – something is likely to move. To stabilize the joint, clamp around the edges of the panel to immobilize the patient.

Unless the clamp is applying pressure straight down, the clamp block will want to shift when the clamp is tightened. If the joint is not pulling up tight where you want it, there are a few things you can try. Check that the pad portion of the clamp under the table is flat to the table surface. Assuming that the clamp is not bent, this should put the screw in the right position, perpendicular to the clamp block. If there is an excessive amount of glue on the part being glued, one technique is to twist it back and forth a few times to work some of the glue out of the joint and create a vacuum.

THINK LAZY

Cleaning up squeezed-out glue

It is much easier and healthier to clean up squeezed-out glue before it has a chance to kick than to sand and file it off later. Pick up large quantities of glue with the putty knife, then wipe the area clean with a rag dampened with lacquer thinner. Trying to wipe up a lot of glue with a rag will smear it around enough to make it a messy job to clean up.

Butt Joints

A butt joint is sometimes used to fasten the ends of two components squarely together without overlapping. A butt block backs up the joint. Traditionally this would be a short piece of hardwood bedded and fastened to the back of the plank between the ribs or frames. For our plywood kayak, the function of the butt block is the same, but the considerations are different.

In traditional wooden boat construction, the integrity of the hull structure relies on the strength of the adjoining planks and ribs and the tension that results from bending them in different directions. But when plywood is sandwiched between layers of fiberglass cloth, the wood becomes a core material. The integrity of this monocoque, or self-supporting, structure relies on the strength of the glass skins and maintaining the distance between them. As long as the core does not cave in or the skin break, the structure will remain strong. How the pieces are held together does not matter. Our only concern is to have a joint strong enough to hold until all the planks are tacked together and the glass is put on.

Glass Butt Blocks

Glass butt blocks are pieces of fiberglass cloth glued to one or both sides of the butted pieces of wood. After experimenting with various combinations of fiberglass weights and amounts of epoxy, we have come to the conclusion that this joint can be inconspicuous and strong, as well as quick and easy to clean up. The ideal combination for both hull and deck is 4-ounce bias-cut cloth or 4-ounce fiberglass tape applied with minimal epoxy on the inside of the plank only. Unlike glassing both sides, this method will keep the color density on the outside consistent and eliminate half of the epoxy application and sanding exposure time needed to assemble the joints.

Always begin by assembling the planks on a flat surface and securing the components in position with clamps, weights or brads. Before committing to the glue, take all the time you need to confirm that you are happy with the shape. One set of clamps should be located 8 to 10 inches from either side of the joint. This will give you lots of space to position the clamp blocks, yet hold the plywood flat to the bench. Slide a piece of plastic film under the joint (or cover the surface with plastic packaging tape) to mold the epoxy that will be squeezed through the joint into a smooth surface and to keep the plywood from becoming bonded to the table (5-3).

5-3

The number of joints you do at one time is limited only by the space you have to work in and the number of clamps available. Set up as many planks as possible, because it does not take long to apply the glass butt blocks with epoxy glue and position the clamps. Cure time before the next setup will be from 6 to 24 hours, depending on the temperature and the brand of epoxy resin and hardener used.

5-4

For each joint, prepare a smooth-faced clamp block beforehand. Cut them slightly wider than the joint and about 6 or 8 inches long. Cover one side with plastic packaging tape as a second line of defense.

Prepare the bias-cut cloth or tape by cutting it slightly longer than the width of the plank.

Do a dry run to confirm that everything is in order and to set up the clamps. Use weights (10 to 20 pounds) over the joints only if clamps are unavailable or you are working on the floor. Too much pressure is undesirable when working with epoxy glue, and weights can't provide the precise adjustments possible with a clamp. Another problem is that the size of a weight that is heavy enough to do the job may also obscure the clamp block. Then if there is a problem with the joint, it will not be discovered until the weight is removed after curing.

Mix up a one-shot batch of epoxy resin and hardener. The objective of this step is to apply just enough mixed epoxy to the glass patch to saturate the fibers without buildup

5-5

and without floating the glass on excess epoxy (5-4). The weave of the cloth should be distinct, with no shiny puddles. When pressure is put on the clamp block, the fibers will be flattened to a smooth surface and some mixed epoxy will be forced through the joint. There should be enough epoxy to have a bit squeeze out and feather into the plank. With the right amount of mixed epoxy, a quick sanding will be all that is needed to prepare the joint for the next step. Any more epoxy will result in a bump in the plank or need aggressive sanding and scraping to get the joint close to what it should have been.

With an acid brush, apply the mixed epoxy to the area covered by the glass patch. Press the glass into the wet epoxy. Give the epoxy a minute to soak into the glass before deciding how much additional mixed epoxy to add. If the glass looks shiny, there is too much epoxy. Pick up the excess with a dry acid brush (that is, with the wet epoxy scraped out).

Cover the wetted-out glass tape with a layer of plastic film. While holding the edge of the film in place, smooth out any remaining air with a squeegee. If needed, use firm pressure to work any excess epoxy out to the edge, where it can be cleaned off later (5-5).

Position the clamp block over the joint and secure it (5-6). The clamping pressure should be firm enough to exclude any air and press the glass tight to the plank, but not so much that epoxy is squeezed out to the point of starving the joint.

Before removing the clamp block, be sure the mixed epoxy has kicked. Uncured epoxy will stick to the plastic, and removing the plastic prematurely will pull the glass off with it.

Cleaning Up the Joint

If you have followed the above steps, a quick scuff with 180 grit sandpaper on a hard block will finish the joint. On the other hand, if glass tape and a generous amount of mixed epoxy have been used, the following is for you.

The cabinet scraper is a good tool for working down excess epoxy to the desired shape. The straight edge of the scraper will ride on the high points first and bring them down to meet the low areas. At this stage anything flexible, such as a power sander or soft sanding block, will have a tendency to follow the profile of the surface, taking equal amounts off both high and low areas. The low spots (the wood) will be damaged before the high points (the epoxy and glass) have been leveled off. This is compounded

5-6

by the fact that the wood, which is the softest of the materials being shaped, is removed the fastest. Not only will this get us away from the fair surface we are trying to achieve, but it also risks cutting through the first plywood lamination and hitting the glue line. The glue line appears in high contrast to the plywood, and if you are at all concerned about how your kayak will look, you won't like it.

It is important to keep the scraper sharp enough to make a decent shaving. A dull scraper will slide over the hard parts and dig a hole where it hits the softer wood. A sharp paint scraper with a straight blade will work fine here, perhaps better, because it is easier to see what you are doing than with a cabinet scraper.

As you work the epoxy down with the scraper, at some point you will run into the glass tape. Stop scraping here, as two things could happen: cutting the glass will defeat the whole purpose of the exercise and the

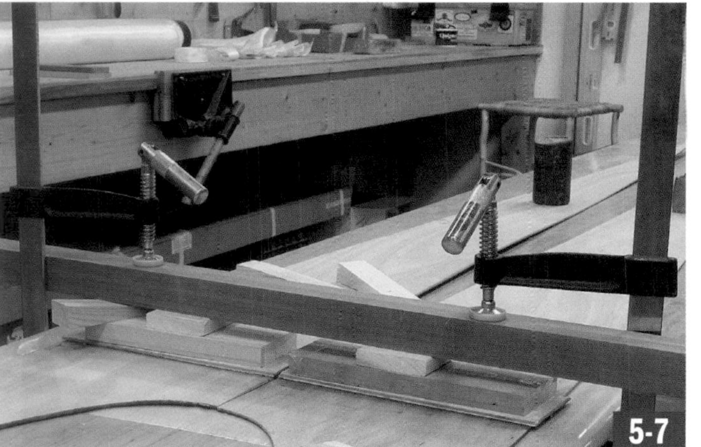
5-7

glass will take the edge off the scraper.

Complete the shaping with a firm sanding block loaded with 120 grit paper. The epoxy should be feathered into the plank surface and all the gloss should be removed. This is not quite as easy as it sounds if you are cutting through the thick selvage edge of the glass tape to feather it into the plank. The edge of the glass is hard and the wood beside it is soft. Make every effort not to remove any of the plank's surface. If you try not to remove any wood, you will get away with removing an acceptable amount.

If you don't have a scraper or haven't mastered sharpening one, a hard sanding block will clean the joint up just fine, but it will take a little longer. Wondering why we are not suggesting using a power sander to clean up the joint? The problem with the machine is visibility. Without being able to see what is happening – and it happens fast – you could end up with more problems than solutions. Ted recalls, "After becoming impatient with cleaning up one of those thick joints, I have to admit that I did fire up the random-orbit sander to get it over with. It only took one joint to remind me what I knew already. That was the only joint that broke in handling. Having to redo it was a just reward for my impatience and took a whole lot longer than doing it right the first time."

Plywood Butt Blocks

The plywood butt block is a conventional alternative to a scarf joint. Both are heavy-duty techniques for making structural joints in plywood panels that will be as strong as the surrounding plywood. A structural joint is most appropriate when both surfaces are not being reinforced with fiberglass cloth. The deck panels on the Coho call for a plywood butt block backing up the joint just forward of the cockpit (5-7). In this application, it is being used to stiffen the deck structure as well as to join the components.

Plywood butt blocks in a kit are generally made from the same material as the planking. Cut the block about 3½ inches wide by slightly longer than the width of the panel. The block will likely slide around a bit when the clamps are tightened, so the extra length is insurance.

Prepare the block by beveling the edges for a graceful transition into the panel. This will make it look like the block is intentional and the epoxy will coat the edges more effectively. If the inside or interior is glassed, the block should have a shape the cloth will follow. If you want to get technical, a long bevel on the edges will reduce the hard spot created by suddenly doubling the plank's thickness. Of course this could be done after the block is glued in place, but it is awkward to do and could damage the panel surface.

For glue, use a structural mix of epoxy resin and hardener reinforced with cotton fibers or wood flour. Judge the amount of glue to be applied by guessing how much will be absorbed by the plywood and how much will be left in the joint after it is clamped up. Applying an excessive amount of glue, then having to clean it up later, just makes extra work that you don't need.

Clean up the glue that has squeezed out with a putty knife, then wipe the joint clean with a rag dampened with lacquer thinner. There should be nothing left to sand later.

Scarf Joints

The scarf joint is another traditional boat-building method of joining the ends of two plank or panel components. This process involves cutting complementary bevels, or scarfs, into the joining ends of the two pieces. Epoxy glue is applied to the bevels, the pieces are put together and clamped, and when the glue has cured we have one continuous plank. Are there drawbacks? Certainly – this is boatbuilding after all.

Cutting the bevels requires hand-tool skills and attention to craftsmanship. (The kit-builder can skip down to Gluing the Scarfs, if the bevels have been precut for you.) The bevels have to be truly complementary – matching exactly and cut to the same angle. Any crown left in the bevel will keep the joint from closing (and gluing) properly. And you will be gluing what is essentially end grain, so care must be taken to ensure that the joint is thoroughly saturated in order to avoid glue starvation.

Another thing to keep in mind is that scarfing the planks will make them shorter. If you have two 8-foot pieces of plywood cut exactly to shape for your plank, when you scarf and glue them, because of the overlapping scarfs the plank will no longer be 16 feet long. If you need that 16 feet, unless you want to add a second scarf, consider either glass or plywood butt blocks. That warning aside, scarfing does produce a remarkably strong joint.

How Long?

The scarf on each of your plywood pieces needs a minimum length of eight times the thickness of the plywood. A ratio of 12:1 rather than 8:1 is preferable, and indeed is the best ratio for sawn wood pieces such as clamps and rails. The reason is that the longer the glue line, the more the two bevels will react as one piece of wood. In addition, the wood will bend more naturally, with less chance of developing a hard spot.

Check to make sure your pieces are long enough. For example, using a 12:1 ratio, 1/4-inch pieces of plywood need 3-inch bevels (12 x 1/4 inches = 3 inches). An 8:1 ratio for 6 mm plywood will give you 48 mm bevels.

Cutting the Bevels

There are many ways to cut the bevels into your plywood. It is easier than it sounds. But, as always, whatever method you use, if this is your first attempt, make up a test piece to work out your technique.

Scarfs can be planed in with a power plane (overkill for this situation), belt-sanded in (kind of sloppy and likely will need to be cleaned up with a hand plane) or simply hand-planed in. For our purposes, hand-planing is the way to go.

For the builder working from plans, some instructions will recommend assembling the stock as an oversized panel that can be cut to shape after the glue has cured in the joint. If the full-length plank is being lofted from offsets, this method involves much less angst than trying to align very narrow pieces that have already been trimmed to size.

To help ensure a properly aligned fit, your two joining ends should butt together tightly. Overlap one piece the required amount over the other. Lay your full-length pattern over top. Still long and wide enough? Brightly mark the sides of the plywood to be beveled (the bottom of one and the top of the other) with an inscription that says something like "bevel me." Mark the end-of-scarf line onto the plywood. Use a non-staining lumber marker or pencil in case it is not all planed away.

Lay the first piece, bevel side up, onto the worktable with the edge to be scarfed flush with the end of the table. Then lay the second piece on top of the first to form a step, lining up the edge of the second piece with the end-of-scarf line marked on the first. Repeat for the third and fourth pieces. Secure the staggered stack of plywood to the table with clamps.

5-8

Next begin to cut your scarfs with a very sharp block plane set for a big bite (5-8). The "steps" will help maintain the angle. Soon the steps will start to turn into a ramp and the laminations will appear as strips or

CHEAP TRICK

Masking with plastic packing tape

Before setting up the components, use plastic packing tape to mask off the inner unplaned edges of the scarfs. The epoxy will migrate under the tape, but this is way ahead of having to sand off the mess later. Masking tape will work but is not as easy to remove.

Remove the tape carefully by pulling slowly at a low angle tangentially to the joint. Plastic tape gets a good bite on the wood after it has been clamped, and the wood is often the weak link rather than the glue. If the tape is pulling wood up with it, consider warming the tape with a heat gun or hair drier to soften the glue.

5-9

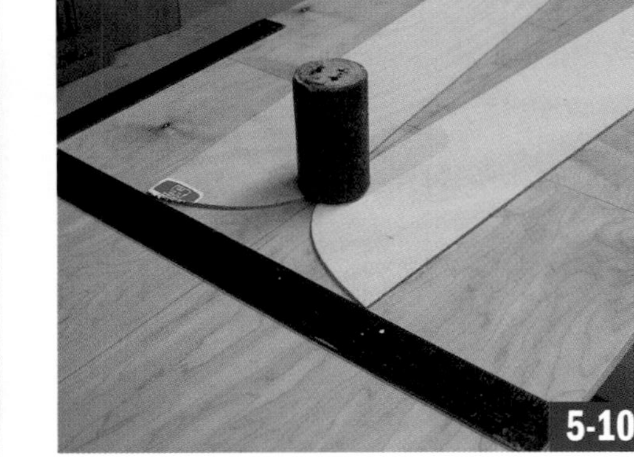

5-10

5-11

bands. The lamination bands act as an indicator; they should all be straight and of equal width. Wobbles in the bands could be registering disquieting hollows or crowns in the tapered cut; these should be planed out. Check the ramp with a straightedge to make sure it is flat in all directions. When the lamination bands are all straight and the bevel is uniformly flat, the scarf is done.

Gluing the Scarfs

Position the first plank component with the edge on the baseline and adjust the joint to the given distance. Hold it in position with weights or clamps. Add the next piece and adjust the overlapping ends of the scarfs.

Check the overlap

To ensure a good-looking plank, check that the overlapping scarfs end up lying flat and level relative to each other. This simple check will help get it right the first time and could avoid a step in the plank or cutting into the plywood glue line to try to correct it.

Clamp the components in position and place a straightedge across the joint. The straightedge should lie tightly on both sides; adjust as necessary. Note that in these pre-fab kit scarfs (5-9) the blunt ends of the scarfs cause a space between the two machined edges. This is intentional on the part of the manufacturer – a feathered edge would be difficult to package and ship successfully. One option is to work the scarf down to a better fit or, as we did, simply use a color-matched glue to fill the void.

When the first plank is settled, lay out its mate using the same routine. Use a square to position this piece parallel to the first plank (5-10). If we use the square to set up the other end, the planks should be the same length.

Plank pairs may also be stacked and glued as a sandwich, but as some planks require two scarfs to give us the proper length, that wouldn't be our first choice (there are simply too many parts to slide around). Although sandwiching will guarantee that the shapes are symmetrical, it is very awkward to apply glue to all four surfaces with a piece of plastic in between the layers. The sandwich idea is more manageable if two steps are used: first gluing the first set of scarfs and then gluing the second.

Apply the glue

Polyethylene film is used under the joint to protect the table and to mold the squeezed-out glue into a smooth, tight joint. Position the clamp on the top layer far enough back from the joint that the plank can be propped up just enough to apply the glue without stressing the plank.

Apply the glue in two steps. The first application is mixed epoxy to saturate the exposed end grain (5-11). The second has fiber reinforcement added to the epoxy to make it into glue.

The saturation application is complete when the surface stays shiny; dull means it is still hungry. If puddles remain after the epoxy has stopped soaking in, pick them up with the brush.

The glue used here is a mixture of cotton microfibers as the structural component,

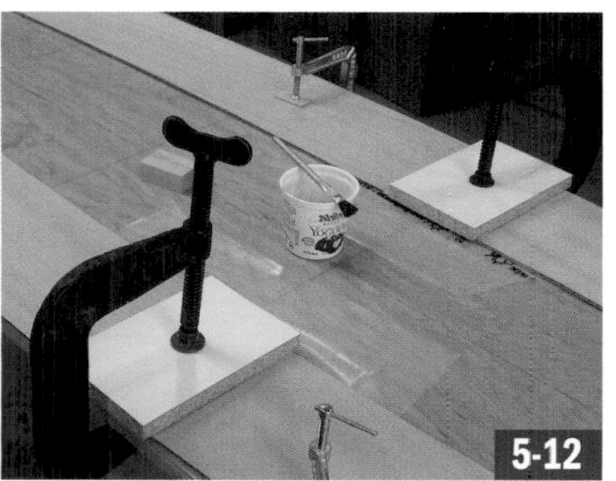

5-12

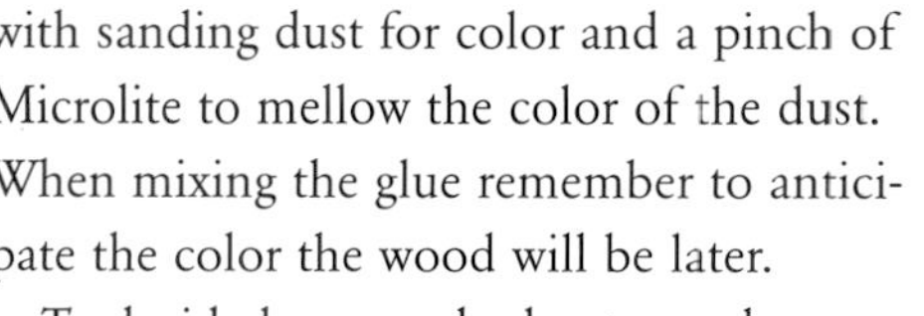

with sanding dust for color and a pinch of Microlite to mellow the color of the dust. When mixing the glue remember to anticipate the color the wood will be later.

To decide how much glue to apply, picture the space between the two surfaces when they come together. Applying more than this volume will cause several problems. If the joint is being clamped with a weight, it may not provide sufficient pressure to squeeze the excess glue out of the joint, which in turn will leave a step between the components. If there is enough pressure to pull the parts together, the squeezed-out excess will have to be dealt with later in some way. Optimistically speaking, a little squeezed-out glue is an indication that the joint is full.

Clamp the joint

Another piece of plastic is used to mold the top of the joint. Over it we are using a piece of melamine-covered particle board as a clamping block (5-12). It's very flat and the epoxy will not stick to the melamine.

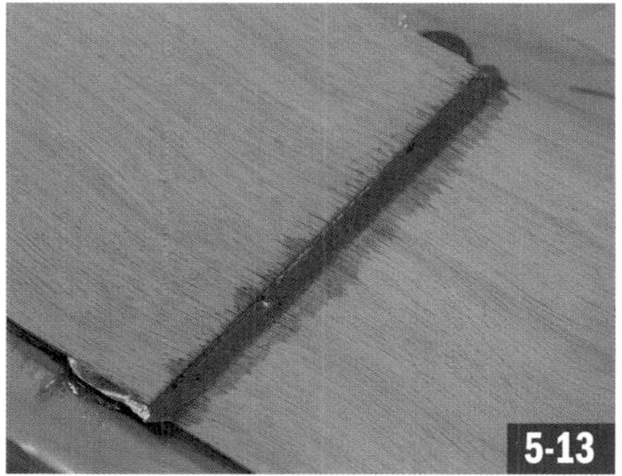

5-13

Clamp with enough pressure to pull the joint together and squeeze out any excess glue. Think firm rather than tight. Check the joint after a few minutes; the clamps will loosen a bit as the glue squeezes out or as more epoxy is absorbed. Retighten the clamps.

If the optimum amounts of glue and pressure have been used, the joint will be filled and all the excess glue will have squeezed onto the tape or out the end. Removing the tape will leave a joint that requires a few passes with a firm sanding block to finish (5-13).

Scarf Joints in Wide Panels

The bottom of the Mill Creek 13 is a flat panel with one joint in the middle. The scarf joint is perfect for this application. Joints in a flat-bottom panel are more structural than in a multi-panel V bottom. The triangulation created by joining two panels at an angle increases the stiffness and integrity of the structure, which in turn puts less stress on the joints.

THINK LAZY

5-14 5-15

Tape the edges of scarf joints

Getting it right the first time will avoid time spent in damage control and a repaired-looking kayak when you are finished. We were curious to see what would happen if we didn't tape the edges of the scarf joints. It didn't look bad, because an optimum amount of glue and moderate clamping pressure were used (5-14).

A sharp cabinet scraper brought the glue down to the level of the wood (5-15). It was then sanded with 120 grit sandpaper on a firm block. Balancing 15 minutes of cleaning up the mess against the seconds it would have taken to tape the edges answered our question.

Lining Up the Components

This step is important because it guarantees that the sides will be the same length and the boat will track straight.

Begin by finding the midpoint of the joint on both components. If you are working on a table with a marked centerline, center both ends of the first panel on the line and secure them. Add the other panel and it should be close. If you don't have a centerline, position the panels by eye.

Take time to confirm that the bottom

5-16

5-17

really is straight. A string line stretched from tip to tip should pass directly over the centerline mark at the joint (5-16). Also make a final check on the overlap with a straightedge.

CHEAP TRICK

Clamp trick

Place a clamp just past each end of the scarf. These will anchor the two pieces and keep them from sliding apart when the third clamp is tightened over the joint.

Gluing and Clamping

The problem with clamping a long scarf in plywood is the difficulty applying even pressure across the full length. A stiff cross-spall with clamps at the ends will bow up in the middle; tightening the clamps only makes the problem worse. This simple method, on the other hand, requires two C- or bar clamps and a few wedges and allows controlled pressure along the full length of the joint.

We are using a plastic-covered clamp block over the joint with a small square block sitting in the middle (a piece of loose plastic would have been easier to remove than the tape-covered block). When a stiff cross-spall is laid across the center block and the ends are clamped down to the table, pressure is applied to the middle of the panel and it begins to squeeze the excess glue out to the ends. Add wedges on both sides to distribute the clamping pressure out to the ends (5-17).

Scarfing Sheer Clamps and Guards

Use two plastic-covered clamp blocks that are longer than the scarf joint to help line up the joint, distribute the clamping pressure and keep the joint from sliding apart when the clamps are tightened (5-18).

Do a dry run before gluing to eliminate surprises and to adjust the clamps to their approximate opening. When you are happy with how it fits dry, draw a reference line across the joint as a guide for gluing.

5-18

Apply the glue using the two-step method used on the plank scarfs (→ page 66). Clean up the squeezed-out glue with a putty knife and wipe clean with a rag dampened with lacquer thinner.

Assembling the Hull and Deck

As already mentioned, preparation is a major part of building a boat, and our approach to assembling the hull and deck will underline this.

Wiring the hull planks together is often the image we have of building a stitch-and-glue kayak. In most cases the hull assembly can be wired together in a day if you are prepared and all the pieces fit. This step is all about control; take time to measure carefully, position the wire holes in a logical pattern and keep the edges of the planks lined up. The shape of the planks will do much of the work of generating the hull's shape. Nonetheless, wiring up a kayak's planks is a balancing act that can be quite frustrating unless the pieces are being assembled in a cradle.

There are a number of different ways to assemble the hull planks and deck panels. Three of these are covered in Chapter Six. What follows are some basic techniques,

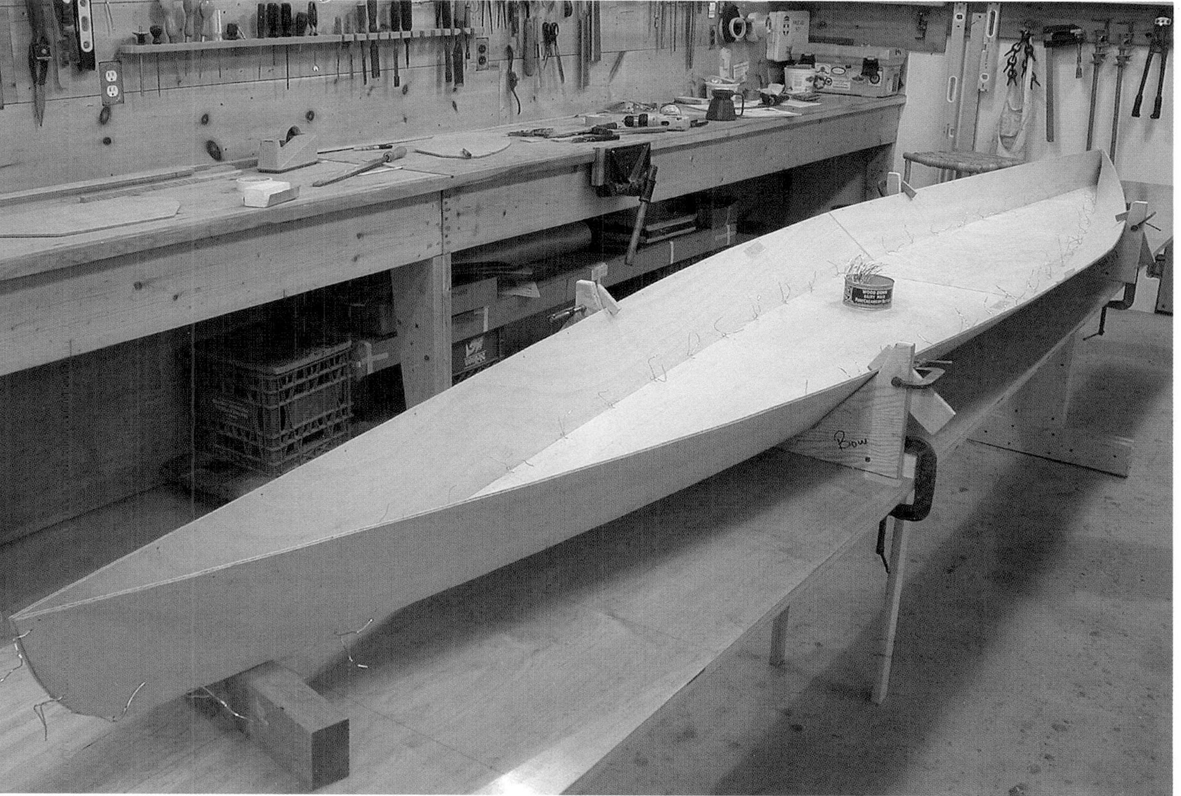

THINK LAZY

Drill spacer jig

5-19

Make a jig from scrap wood to guide the drill. This will eliminate the time it takes to measure and the associated potential for error. Generally we want the holes to be 1/4 inch in from the edge of the panel and 6 inches on center. Our jig is 1/2 inch wide and 6 1/2 inches long, with the holes centered on the width and 1/4 inch from the ends.

To use the jig, locate the position of the first hole, place the hole in the jig at this position and be sure the jig is flush to the edge of the plank. Drill the first hole and, holding the jig firmly in position, drill into the other end (5-19). Now stop the drill with the bit in the hole, swivel the jig around to the next position, fire up the drill to remove the bit and drill the next hole.

Ted had a problem with the guide holes in a 4 mm plywood jig. They became enlarged from repetitive use, with a corresponding lack of accuracy. We suggest using hardwood for the jig or making several jigs from scrap plywood and discarding used ones periodically.

some time-saving tips and tried-and-true error avoidance strategies that will help you build a great-looking kayak.

Drilling Suture Holes

The most important thing to remember when drilling suture (wire) holes is that the pair of holes must be positioned directly opposite each other. If they aren't, when tension is put on the wire, the wire will try to straighten out, shifting the plank.

You have a few options for when and where the holes are drilled. A common practice is to drill the holes on one edge of the plank at the bench, then drill the holes for the mates as the planks are wired together. Although this may look like the safest method, the uncontrolled position of the planks while drilling will introduce an unnecessary variable.

Put the worktable to good use; drilling all the holes before assembling the panels is accurate and fast. To reduce both the number of holes to drill and the variables, drill the planks in pairs. Use a 1/16-inch bit for 20-gauge wire.

5-20

Making Wire Sutures

Prepare the wire sutures or stitches by cutting 20-gauge wire into pieces about 3 1/2 inches long (5-20). To bend the wire into the "staple" shape, try linesman pliers. The jaws are about 1/2 inch wide and will bend five or six wires at a time.

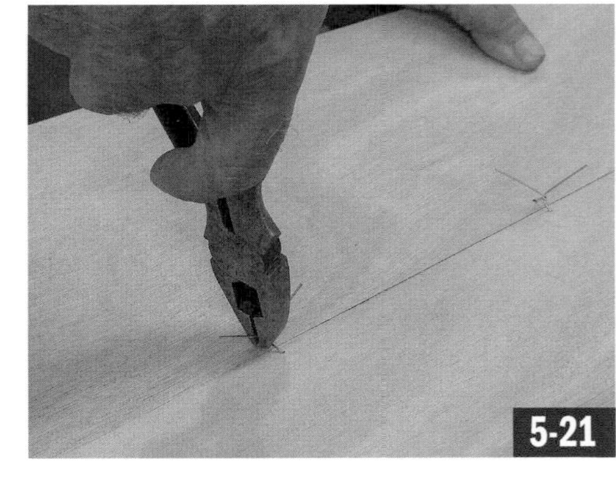
5-21

Wiring Panels

After inserting the wire sutures through the holes, you must tighten the wires just enough to draw the edges of the planks together. They should be just snug enough to hold the edges in line long enough to get the filler into the joints.

To tighten the wire, grab the ends where they cross, squeeze tight and rotate to tighten (5-21). It helps to pull up on the wire while twisting; this takes the slack out of the loop and keeps the twists close together. The direction you rotate in is not important.

Tacking Planks with Filler

Tacking the planks together with filler (5-22) is one of the key steps in building a plywood kayak, but it may be the least understood. In most cases we see joints that are overbuilt. Considering the evolution of the technique, this is not surprising. Before the stitched-seam method was developed, plywood panels were joined together with chines and battens. A large fillet as a substitute for the

5-22

5-23

chine or batten may be appropriate in a heavily built craft, but it results in excess weight and stiffness in a lightweight kayak. In a monocoque structure with plywood as the core, a chine substitute is not necessary.

So if we are simply making a plywood core in the shape of a kayak, how strong does the bond between the planks need to be? The short answer is "strong enough to apply the epoxy and fiberglass to one side," but there is a longer answer worth looking at. Some builders use a process in which unthickened mixed epoxy is injected into the joint, allowed to soak into the plywood, then followed with another shot of epoxy thickened with wood flour. This two-step epoxy application is useful on end grain in a structural joint, but perhaps more than needed for simply tacking the planks together.

The problem with this routine is that the unthickened epoxy runs down the outside and will have to be cleaned up while wet, which means breaking out those unpleasant solvents, sanded off later, and/or left as a stain. Inside drips will be more of a problem because they will be harder to see and clean up. If they are left until the hull is turned over again, there goes another Sunday with sander in hand. Shorter and healthier ways to tack the planks do exist, with the bonus of a clear finish at the end.

Reduce the Stain, Choose a Color

Choose a low-resin-content filler such as Microlite mixed to a workable (thick but not stiff) consistency. It will be easy to sand, and since there is not much resin in it, there will be very little discoloration around the joint (5-23). The beige color of the filler is close to the color of dry okume plywood, but will end up being a lighter shade than the wood after a clear finish has been applied. Changing the color with sanding dust is a possibility, but the trick is in keeping the same shade with both filling steps.

Work Clean

Masking the joints before applying the filler is about looking good, but it is also about staying healthy while thinking lazy.

5-24

Because the wood is protected, the filler can be worked in as aggressively as necessary to fill the crack without worrying about staining the plank surface. Taping off this hull (5-24) used about one roll of 1-inch low-tack masking tape that took less than one hour to apply and remove. Balanced against the sanding time needed to clean up filler that has been casually applied, this is time well invested. If you are thinking of a clear finish, or don't like sanding, let the tape do the work for you.

Before applying the tape, check that the inside plank edges are in line. On this kayak the planks did not move because they were stabilized by the forms, but it might just have been luck. Keep aware of the edges while masking and filling. If you happen to bump a plank out of place, fix it before you forget or can't find it again.

Try to keep the masking tape just slightly ($^1/_{16}$ inch) outside the line. If the tape is over the line, the filler will be pulled out when

5-25

5-26

5-27

the tape is removed, leaving a void and another detail to attend to later.

Use a Palette

A pile of filler on the putty knife has a way of crawling up until your finger is in it. Instead, place the filler on a small board or piece of cardboard to make it easier to pick up a precise amount on the end of the blade. This allows you to place the filler where you want it and to work it in without leaving a big mess to clean up. When you spread the filler out on the palette, heat will not build up in the epoxy as quickly and the filler's working time will be extended.

Fill It the First Time

Use a flexible putty knife to fill the joint completely (5-25). Make a point of forcing the filler down to the bottom of the opening. When it hits bottom you will see the filler rise up around the sides of the knife. Pay special attention to narrow joints or small voids, as these will take more time to work the filler to the bottom.

When the joint is full, scrape the filler flush with the top of the tape. This will leave the filler the thickness of the tape above the surface – an insurance policy in case the wood absorbs more epoxy.

Working Around the Sutures

Build the filler up around the sutures, but try not to bury them; this will save digging the wire out. Around the stem, look for enough buildup to round over without cutting into the plywood glue line (5-26).

Don't worry if you miss a few spots at this filling session; there will be time when the cracks around the wires are filled after the sutures have been removed.

Remove the Tape

Remove the tape as soon as the joint is full and the filler has been cleaned up. Removing it during the early sticky green stage could pull filler out of the joint. But after the epoxy has cured, the edge of the tape will be glued down, making it a nuisance to remove.

If the filler is forced through a crack, it is best not to try to clean it up with a rag at this point. You will succeed only in smearing it around. The contained extrusion can be scraped and sanded clean more easily after it has hardened (5-27).

Fill the Remaining Seams

After the filler has cured, cut the sutures in the middle, bend the wires upright and carefully remove them.

Clean up the filler by hand with a firm sanding block. This will make it easier to do a neat job of filling the seams around the sutures, as well as show up any joints shy on filler. The outside of the hull will be sanded after all the filler is in, so don't take any more wood than necessary at this point. Work the filler down to the flat surface of the plank, but don't round over the edges until the final sanding before the fiberglass is applied. Crisp edges will give your eye something to follow when checking for fair lines and missing filler. Rounding the edges all at the same time will also result in a

CHEAP TRICK

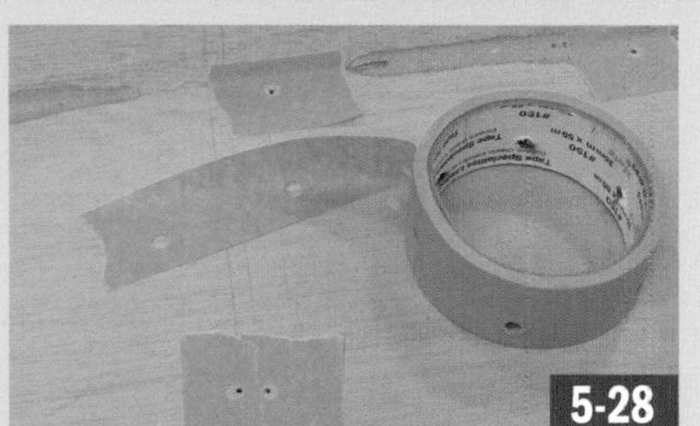

5-28

Drilling holes in tape

You can save a lot of time when masking the holes by drilling small holes in the tape beforehand (5-28). Drill 1/4-inch holes about 2 inches apart into a roll of masking tape. A Forstner-style wood bit will make a very clean cut; a regular high-speed bit will make a usable hole. It helps to use a sharp bit and to keep the speed of the drill slow in order to cut cleanly and avoid melting the glue on the tape.

more consistent shape than one that is developed through various building stages.

Using Polyester Body Filler

Keep in mind that the working time for polyester body filler is limited. Be sure everything is in order and start with a small batch to get an idea of how much you can keep up with. Try to keep it as fresh as possible. Once the filler begins to move into the green rubbery stage (called cheese) – and it happens very fast – it will have no bond at all.

CAUTION

When combining any two materials where the results matter, do a small test beforehand to reduce surprises.

Read the instructions on the can for mixing the filler. Adjust the speed of the mix with the amount of hardener added. Expect this to take a little practice, because the amount of compound is measured by eye and the hardener is added by drops or squirted from a tube, with the resulting amalgam being mixed with the putty knife.

Masking with tape beforehand is recommended. The very unwoodlike colors of these fillers make an interesting accent in the joint, but will be very obvious if worked into the grain of the plywood.

Filling Wire Holes

The decision to fill the wire holes is as much an epoxy-exposure and labor-saving consideration as it is about taking pride in the appearance of your boat. When fiberglass cloth or tape is laminated over the hole, the glass will wick the epoxy through the hole to build up on the inside. Before you can get back to work on the inside, the hard blobs and runs must be removed by sanding or scraping.

Covering the holes on the inside with masking tape would keep the epoxy from running through, but the air trapped in the hole could cause problems. As the epoxy cures, heat is produced and the air expands, resulting in a bubble. Also, most of the holes will still be open and the problem will repeat itself on the other side.

The only reasonable alternative is to fill the holes with a full-bodied filler (→ page 42) that can be forced all the way through the holes without leaving a stain.

Fillets

A fillet is a sculpted cove-shaped bead of epoxy-based filler that bridges and reinforces the joint between two intersecting components. Structurally, a fillet increases the surface area of the bond between two components, thus spreading stress over a larger area and avoiding stress concentrations. When joining pieces that come together at near right angles, a fiberglass and fillet joint is the way to go.

A fillet also eases the transition between the bonded surfaces, allowing the fiberglass cloth to flow smoothly from one to the other. The cloth doesn't like to bend around sharp corners; if forced to, the result will be weak, with air-trapping gaps behind the cloth. Not only does this defeat the purpose of glass over the joint, it is also unsightly, and repairing the problem could turn into a career.

Before stitched-seam construction, plywood panels were joined together with chines and battens. A large fillet in a stitch-and-glue craft is a substitute for the chine log in a more heavily built craft. However, because we are building a monocoque structure and the plywood is a core material, a

FILLETING TOOLS

- Choose a flexible putty knife for application and cleanup.
- There are a number of options for tools to shape your fillets. Some prefer a plastic spatula trimmed and bent to the curve of the fillet. Others use a wooden paddle – either a large tongue depressor or a homemade tongue-depressor-shaped stick – or even the radius end of a PVC sewer pipe. The kind you choose depends on the job, what you have to work with and personal preference.
- Make a palette to hold the filleting compound.
- Other tools include 1-inch-wide masking tape, a glue syringe and a plastic bag for the cake-decorator trick (→ page 75).

fillet as a substitute for the chine is not necessary. In theory, all of the components in a monocoque craft should act as a balanced unit. In a plywood kayak, fillets that are larger than necessary simply add weight and become hard spots that can concentrate stress.

As always, take the time to run a practice fillet on a dummy setup. It will give you a chance to work out any bugs in your technique and your tools before you have to deal with the real thing.

Epoxy-based Filler Used as Filleting Compound

Generally speaking, two types of fillets can be made – high-density or low-density. The high-density fillet features a smaller radius and uses silica and/or microfibers as the filler material. The cured high-density

5-29

mix is strong – indeed, stronger than many woods. It is also heavier and somewhat more difficult to sand than a low-density compound. The low-density version has a larger radius and uses a combination of lightweight components, such as microballoons and Microlite, mixed with the epoxy. It's not as strong, but certainly strong enough for our purposes, and it's lighter and easier to sand than the high-density compound.

The overall goal is to use ingredients that will produce the best joint for the purpose and that will be easy to work and to smooth. All recipes begin with a mixed epoxy base. Combine resin and hardener and stir well before adding the thickener.

Double-check first

Before mixing up the filleting compound, do a last check that all the parts are stabilized in the correct position. Like the filler between the planks, the fillet is another step toward locking the pieces into the final kayak shape. If the shape is not right at this stage, trying to accommodate precut components at a later stage will mean distorting the plywood, leading to even more complications.

The putty knife is a safe tool for making height adjustments between the plank edges (5-29). Press the knife blade in as far as it will go and lever the low side up. Avoid using a knife with a narrow tip to adjust planks; it is a poor lever and will damage the edge of the plank.

Mix the filleting compound

This is one of those "season to taste" recipes that will need a little tinkering to get just right. Microlite is a good additive to begin with. It is very easy to sand and the light beige color is close to that of okume plywood. The texture we are looking for is stiff enough to hold the shape yet wet enough to smooth into a clean fillet (5-30). Blend until the mixture begins to lose its gloss and is stiff enough to support itself with very little slump (like chunky peanut butter or meringue). Keep the batch-size small, as heat will build quickly and cause premature cure.

5-30

5-31

To alter the color, a small amount of wood flour may be added to the lightweight filler. Keep in mind that a large concentration of wood flour will make the compound hard to work with. For a darker color, begin with a darker filler such as microballoons or WEST #407, or use a darker shade of sanding dust.

Shaping a Graceful Fillet

On the inside of a kayak, where most of the surface is hidden by the deck and seat, the stain left behind after the filler has been cleaned up will be visible. If keeping the plywood clean around the fillet is important to you, mask off the area to be covered by the fillet. This would be most appropriate for the portion of the deck used for the hatch cover or around the cockpit opening.

Place the filler

Try to apply the fillet using this three-step method. The first step after masking is to place the filler roughly in the joint. Moving the filler from the cup to the joint is awkward, but using the side of a thin wooden spatula (5-31) worked as well as anything we tried. Where there is working room, another method of placing the filleting compound is to use the putty knife to transfer blobs of it to the joint. Work these piles out with the spatula and smooth the filler to shape. Make it easy for yourself by picking up controlled amounts of filler from a palette.

It is important to push the material into the joint, forcing the air out in the process. If you don't find the air while you're placing the filler, the air will expand later and leave a large hole in the fillet. Work in sections about 12 inches long at a time.

Shape the fillet

Next, begin to draw the filler out and shape the fillet, using a number of passes (5-33). Move slowly and deliberately, using consistent pressure. You will notice that the angle at which the spatula is held affects the radius of the cove. Begin using a low angle and gradually increase it until you reach the edge of the tape. Draw the filler out in stages by building up pressure and increasing the angle with each pass until you reach the optimum shape. Each pass will pick up extra filler; deposit it at the end of the fillet and spread it out with the next section.

To work a new section seamlessly into the previous section, begin a short distance from the end of the finished section. As you move slowly along with the squeegee, gradually increase the pressure until the squeegee

CHEAP TRICK

The amazing plastic-bag cake decorator device

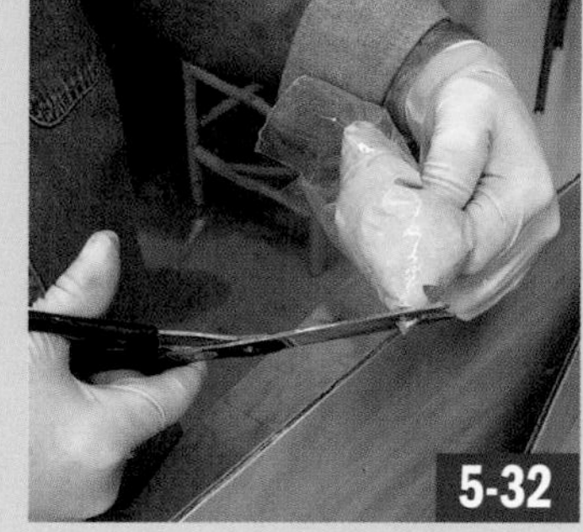

5-32

Take one heavy-duty bag, such as a recycled frozen food bag or a freezer bag. After mixing the filler, turn the plastic bag inside out with one hand inside the bag. Pile the filler into the palm of your bagged hand and, holding the pile of filler in your fist, fold the bag back over it. The filler will be in the bottom of the bag. Twist the top of the bag up tight. When you snip the corner off the bag (5-32), it's ready to deposit a thick bead of filler down the joint.

Some provisos. It does take a few minutes to load the bag, and if the bag is used a second time, it gets messy. This becomes time-consuming when many small batches are needed on a big project. (Small batches are recommended to keep heat from building and the filler fresh.) Also, guessing the correct amount of filler to squeeze out takes a while to get a handle on. This trick is most appropriate in places where it is too awkward to reach into the hull and lay the filler down with a knife.

5-33

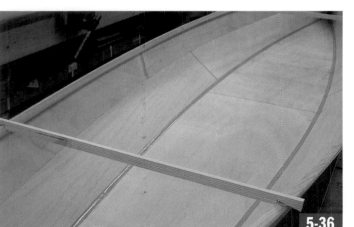

5-34

5-35

5-36

is bent enough to just touch the finished surface. Hold this angle and pressure as you move into the fresh area.

Use a putty knife to pick up the filler on the tape (5-34).

Finish tooling the joint by using a narrow plastic squeegee to shape the cove and feather the edge of the filler out to the tape (5-35). Use a standard squeegee with a slice cut off the end to make it about 1⅝ inches wide. The squeegee is flexible enough to bend into a cove shape and follow the changing angle of the joint. A spatula with a pre-shaped edge is appropriate for consistent angles, but is unable to adjust to the changing angle. A wider squeegee will spread the excess over a large area of the plywood, necessitating a larger cleanup.

Pick up the excess filler and remove the tape when finished (5-36).

When the filler has cured, it will take very little hand sanding to feather the edge of the fillet (basically the thickness of the tape) into the plywood.

Small Fillets

A quick method of applying a small fillet is to apply the filler with a glue syringe, then mold the fillet with masking tape.

Run a bead of filler down the joint between the wires. Don't try to get too close to the wire; shaping the fillet with tape will draw the filler out to the ends.

Place a piece of masking tape over the joint and gently smooth the filler under it into a neat cove. When the tape is removed after the glue has kicked (5-37), there will be little if any cleanup to do before the major fillet is applied.

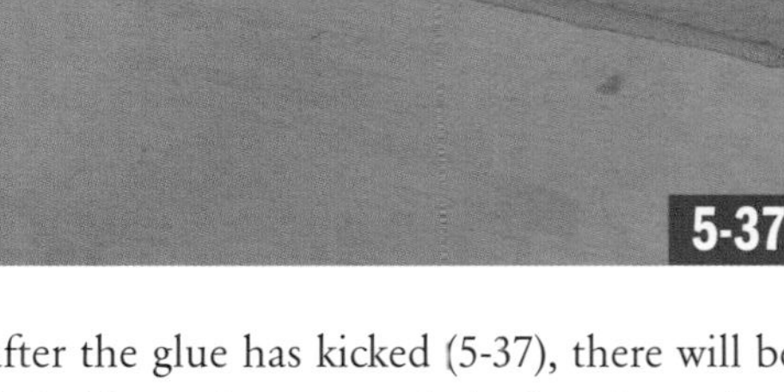
5-37

Bad Fillets

There are good and bad fillets. These are nothing to be proud of (5-39).

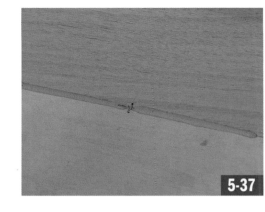

CHEAP TRICK

5-38

Glue syringe

The problem with using a syringe is loading it with filler that is stiff enough not to slump when it is placed. Try a fillet mixture that is just thin enough to pour (with patience) into the syringe (5-38).

5-39

Fillet and Tape

There are a number of methods for using glass tape reinforcement over a fillet. Choose a method that is appropriate for both the application and your expectations.

One-Step Fillet and Tape

When time is tight and you don't plan to do the ultimate job, there is no reason why the tape cannot be applied over a wet fillet. We suggest getting the fillet as close to perfection as possible in the beginning, because we are proud people. But if the fillet is less than perfect, this is a second chance to rescue it after a fashion – by shaping the wet compound under the dry tape with the tip of a gloved finger. This will work on a routine filleting job, but if you have to take care of a lot of tricky details, it might be better to break the process down into steps.

Combine a Saturation Coat with Fillet and Tape

Saturate the plywood first (→ page 89). Apply the fillet and clean up as much as possible on the wet surface. Press the fiberglass tape into the wet filler; get it in the right position the first time, because moving it is out of the question. Apply mixed epoxy to the tape with an acid brush to complete wetting it out. When the tape is saturated, scrape off the excess epoxy with a small squeegee. Draw the excess onto the plywood, pick it up and discard.

Now, if you are really on a roll and the area to be covered is manageable, the fiberglass cloth can be positioned and wetted out at the same time. Care should be taken when positioning the cloth not to get it stuck to the wet tape and pull the tape along with the cloth (→ page 157).

Fillet and Tape in Two Sessions

Complicated applications, such as the underside of the Coho deck, require a lot of filling and shaping before the tape is applied. In this case, or if you just want to be sure that the fillet is tidy and the plywood clean before committing to the tape, apply the tape after the fillet has cured and been cleaned up.

To apply the glass tape over a cured fillet, begin by cutting the tape to length. Being prepared beforehand will save getting your scissors sticky, and it is nice to know that there is enough tape for all the joints.

Use an acid brush to wet out the area to be covered by the tape with mixed epoxy and press the tape into the thin coat of epoxy (5-40). The epoxy will hold the tape in position as well as begin to saturate the

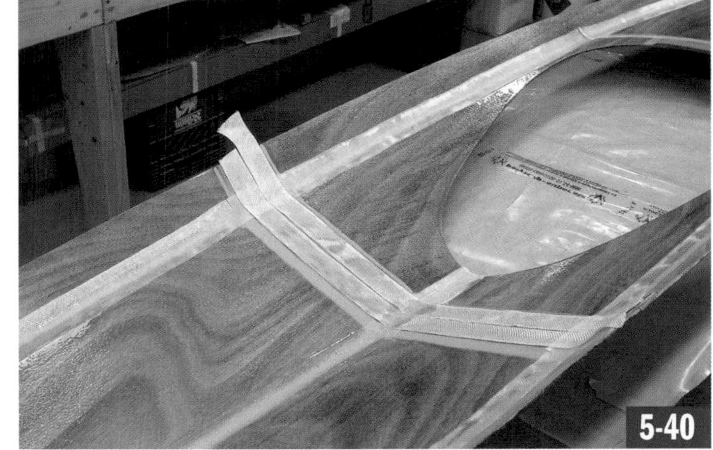

5-40

glass from the bottom. When all the tape has been positioned, use an acid brush to carefully apply just enough epoxy to finish wetting out the tape and to press it into the cove.

To clean up, go over the surface with a small squeegee (→ page 84) to scrape off and pick up all the excess epoxy. Work the grunge out onto the deck, then pick it up off the plywood with the squeegee. The tape will want to pull out of the cove at times; keep an eye on it and work it back in when necessary. The glass tape should be saturated but not floating – no shiny puddles. Any more epoxy than this will be sanding dust later.

It is very important to check the tape for air trapped in the cove. Press down gently with the end of a clean acid brush; keep checking until the epoxy has firmed up.

For this application, we are using two continuous pieces of tape running the full width of the deck, positioned over the butt

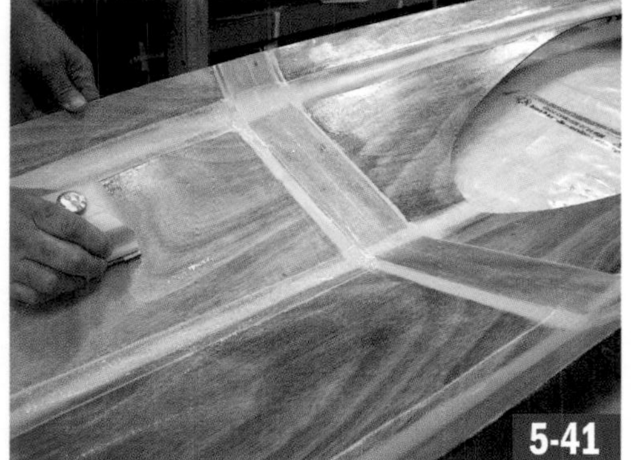

5-41

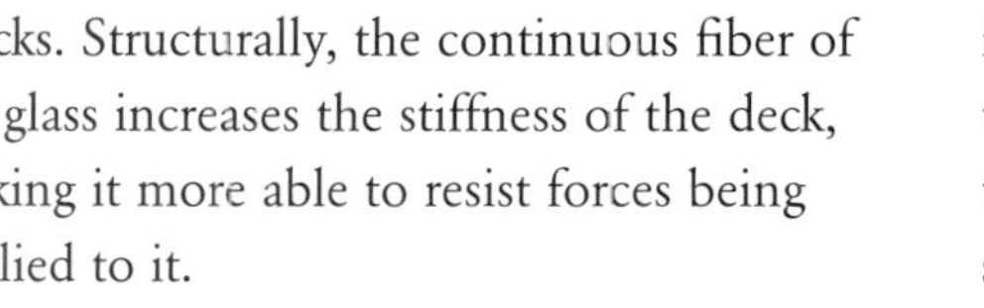

5-42

5-43

blocks. Structurally, the continuous fiber of the glass increases the stiffness of the deck, making it more able to resist forces being applied to it.

When the epoxy has cured, soften the edges of the tape with a firm sanding block and 120 grit sandpaper (5-41). Since this particular deck will not be glassed on the inside, consider whether you need to feather the tape to a perfect transition into the coated plywood surface. Balancing the amount of work needed to do this and the danger of damaging the coating on the plywood against a persnickity finish that will not be seen, it's an easy choice for us. We aim for a soft edge that will be safe to the touch, feel as if it were planned, and be easy for the next coat of epoxy to cover.

Vacuum up the dust and wipe the surface clean with a rag dampened with lacquer thinner or water.

Reinforced Fillets in Hard-to-Reach Places

A need for a discreet glass-reinforced fillet is often needed in a corner that is awkward to work in. If it is going to be difficult to get the filler in, it will be even more difficult to sand it clean later. This little trick will do it all in one step, with no sanding.

Wet out the fiberglass cloth or tape on a piece of plastic that is slightly larger than the tape. To do this, apply the mixed epoxy to the plastic, then place the glass reinforcement into the wet epoxy. Add enough additional epoxy to saturate the glass.

Apply a consistent bead of filler to the joint, using a syringe (5-42). We could shape the wet filler with a spatula, but given the awkward position, we would probably make a mess.

Position the wet glass and plastic over the wet filler (5-43), shape the fillet with your finger, and work the air out to the edge of the plastic (5-44). Remove the plastic after the epoxy has kicked – no sticky fingers, a perfectly smooth cove and very little cleanup.

There will be situations where it is impossible to get the filler in, even with the syringe; behind the hip brace is a good example. Using this trick, you will be able to make a reinforced fillet in the dark – well, almost. Prepare the wetted-out glass as above, then place a bead of filler across the middle of the glass. To keep the end of the fillet crisp, mask off where it should end beforehand (5-45). Place the plastic, glass and filler on the joint and smooth the filler and glass through the plastic. When the epoxy has cured, remove the plastic.

The End Pour

Plywood kayak building incorporates techniques from a number of trades, including the concrete business. We use fibers to reinforce epoxy that are similar to the rebar in concrete, and the breast-hook is made by setting up a form similar to the forms used in concrete work.

The purpose of the breast-hook in a traditional boat is to tie the sides of the hull together at the sheer line. Called the deck in open canoes and small craft, the breast-hook is often expanded to make a visual state-

5-44

5-45

5-46

ment. Builders of kayaks that don't have a sheer clamp are faced with an awkward problem when tying the ends of the hull and deck together. Much of the inside joint between the hull and deck can be filleted and taped by working through the cockpit and hatch openings, but a ferret couldn't get all the way up to the end. There are several ways of casting something that will hold the pieces together in the end and make an anchor for securing a rope or grab handle.

End Pour After Hull and Deck Have Been Attached

Many builders, including fiberglass production builders, rely on the stand-it-in-the-tree, trip-bucket method of doing the end pour. With the kayak set on its end, the trick is to get the container down to the bottom, then dump the thick filler close to where you want it. The major concern is dealing with the heat that can be generated by this mass of epoxy-based filler. Try keeping the shop temperature low, use a slow hardener, keep the resin content of the filler low, and fill in stages, letting the filler cool between steps.

Some builders use a small plastic bucket with a wire bail (or a can and a coat hanger). The bucket is lowered on a rope fastened to the bail. A second string, fastened to the bottom of the bucket, follows the rig down. When it reaches the bottom, the string is pulled and the filler is dumped. Filler will more than likely spill on the sides of the boat, but gravity should take it the rest of the way down.

End Pour Before Deck Is Attached

An alternative end-pour method in the Coho instructions suggests casting this piece in the end before attaching the deck (5-46). This eliminates some of the gymnastics.

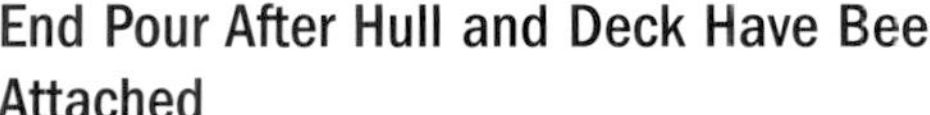
CHEAP TRICK

When doing a vertical end pour, set the end of the kayak in a bucket of cold water to dissipate the heat from the filler.

Although it does not tie the deck to the hull at the end, we have not heard that this is a weak point and did not hesitate to build our Coho using this method. If you are worried about it, consider getting the bulk of the filler in before attaching the deck and then finishing with a small vertical end pour.

Fit the dam or form snugly enough that it does not leak and strongly enough that it can take some expansion pressure if the epoxy begins to cook. Dams may become part of the kayak or be covered in plastic and removed later. To keep the epoxy filler from overheating and boiling over, keep the shop temperature low, use a slow hardener, keep the resin content of the filler low, and pour in small batches, with about six hours between batches.

PLYWOOD BOAT-BUILDING TECHNIQUES

Fiberglassing the Outside and Inside

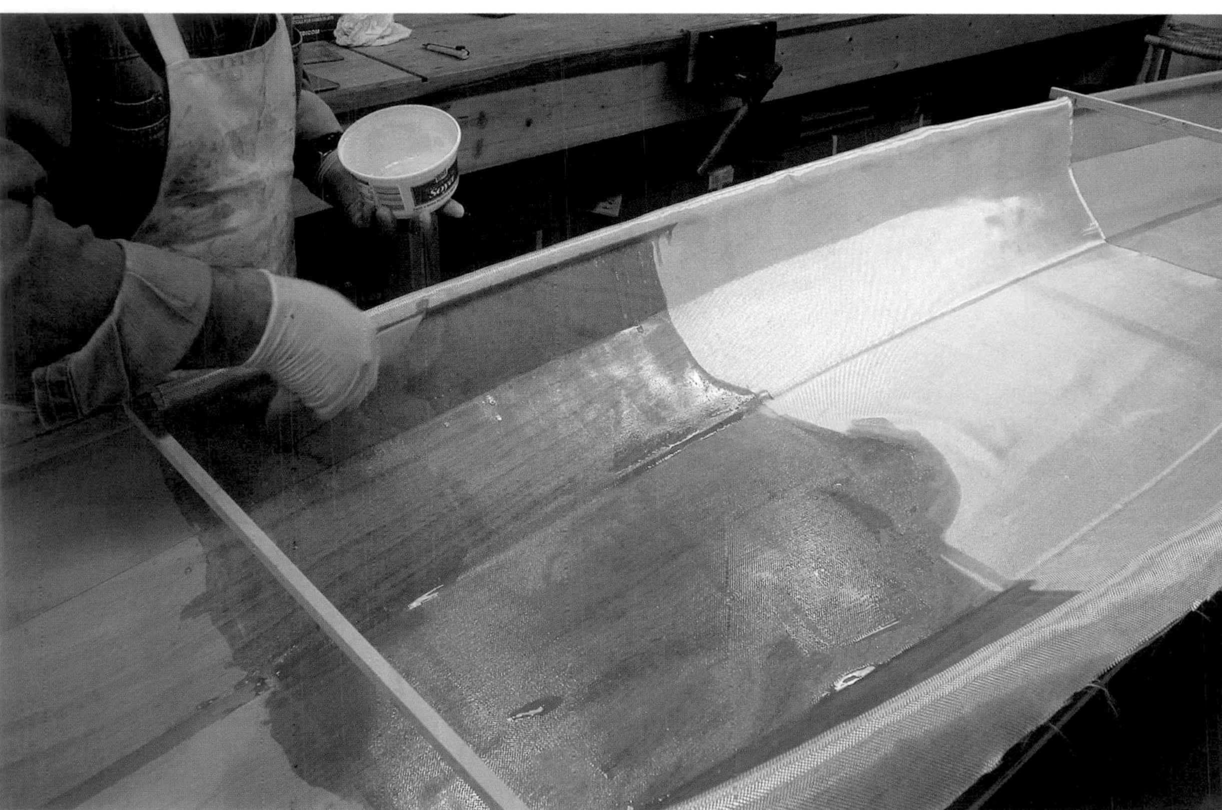

WE USE A CLEAR epoxy-and-glass coating to enhance the surface of the wood beneath. A blemish-free, well-sanded plywood hull will radiate warmth like a well-finished piece of furniture. Conversely, the hull that has scratches, sander swirls, laminates sanded through, and glue stains will have those features highlighted.

The only way to achieve a clear coating is to build up each epoxy layer evenly. The results from doing damage control with the sander between each coat will never look as clean as the results from controlling each layer. Each layer does a specific job and will require different techniques to apply. For the outside of the hull, where durability and clarity of finish are prime considerations, three layers of epoxy and one layer of glass fabric are used. The glass cloth is laid up in the first coat of epoxy, the second coat fills the weave of the fabric and the third buries the cloth, providing a thick enough layer of epoxy to sand smooth without hitting the fiberglass. For the interior, the third coat of epoxy may be omitted if desired. This will leave a non-skid textured surface on the inside while still allowing the beauty of the wood to show through.

The ideal situation is to apply the coats of epoxy as close together in time as possible. The layers will bond together chemically and there will be less chance that the surface will become contaminated. If more than 24 hours have passed since the last coat kicked, promoting a mechanical bond becomes important. Give the surface a quick scuff with 120 grit sandpaper to scratch it up and give the next coat something to hang on to. Another reason to keep the process moving along is to limit the possibility of amine blush contamination (→ page 38).

There will be times when work must be done before the second coat can be applied; for example, reinforcing the stern stem with a glass patch. If this patch is feathered into the glass after the first coat of epoxy, the second and third coats will bury it and it should be easy to sand and virtually invisible. This will require another epoxy cure cycle, so in this case sanding before the second coat is recommended.

Preparing the Surface

While epoxy can create a tenacious bond, it will not stick to certain things – oils, grease, most plastics, silicones and wax. This non-stick quality can work to your advantage in some situations. When gluing up plank scarfs, for example, a sheet of polyethylene between the glued epoxy plank and the worktable can make all the difference between whether the plank will go on the boat or stay permanently affixed to the table.

On the other hand, oil, wax or silicone on the surface of the wood that you want to laminate is bad news; it can result in "fisheyes" (round craters), an imperfect bond or even joint failure. Contamination can come from many different sources – a tack cloth, a rag washed with fabric softener, a misaimed shot of WD-40, contaminated solvent or the wrong type, an out-of-place salami sandwich, sweat from your hands or even residue from a belching oil heater.

Some contaminants can be cleaned away with lacquer thinner or acetone and then sanded, but the best solution is to keep the bonding steps close together, keep your workplace clean and watch out for those rags (you don't know where they've been). Also avoid mixing epoxy in waxed paper cups or cups with solvent-unstable linings. And, if you can, keep fondling to a minimum between the critical layers.

As always, preparation is the key to success. See page 95 for information on sanding.

Positioning the Fiberglass Cloth on the Outside

Roll out the glass cloth over the hull, leaving about 4 to 6 inches extra at each end. With a person at each end holding the cloth in the middle, tug it back and forth in a gentle seesaw motion to center the cloth on the hull and straighten out the fibers. While holding the cloth at the middle with one hand, use the other hand to work down to the edge, tugging against your partner every 4 or 5 inches. This exercise will straighten the threads and shape the cloth perfectly around the hull. You should be able to manipulate the entire piece of cloth from the ends.

Use this technique if wrinkles develop in the cloth during the layup. Trying to brush them out with your hands or an epoxy brush could put a permanent crease in the cloth.

Watch for unidentified foreign objects under the cloth. Fabric- and epoxy-trapped bits of detritus can grow to boulder status, causing unsightly lumps that can't be sanded out without cutting through the fiberglass.

Fit the Bow Stem

If the cloth is centered on the hull, it is possible to work the glass around the bow stem of most kayaks without having to cut

> **SAFETY TIP**
>
> **If your floor matters, cardboard is the best protection; plastic is slippery to the point of being dangerous and newspapers will soak up the epoxy, which could glue the papers to the floor.**

5-47

and overlap the cloth (5-47). Stern stems are more difficult; they have to be wrapped before the second coat of epoxy is applied.

Don't Trim the Cloth

Leave as much cloth around the sheer as possible until all the epoxy work has been completed. The cloth will catch runs and wick the epoxy away from the edge as it begins to settle (5-48). It also makes an easy path for the excess epoxy to run off the boat during the second and third coats.

SAFETY TIP

Positioning and smoothing the cloth while wearing disposable gloves is tricky and only marginally successful. The gloves will periodically grab the cloth when you least expect it and pull everything out of position. Although gloves are usually a good idea, a rash from handling glass cloth with bare hands is rare. If you have tender hands or are at all worried about it, do wear gloves and make the best of it.

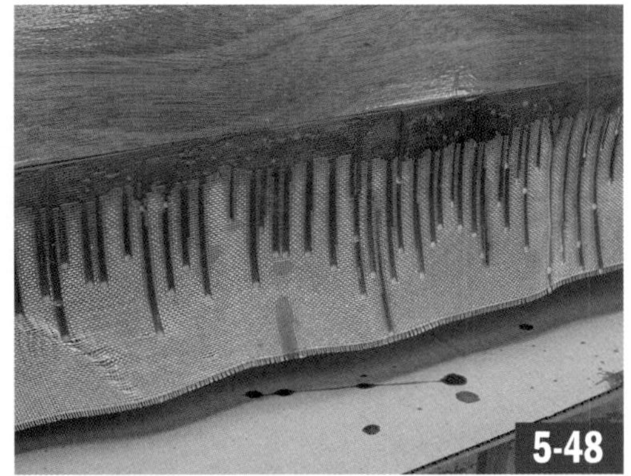
5-48

If the cloth is trimmed closely, three problems can occur. Loose glass hairs can stick to the brush as you work along the edge. As the wet epoxy begins to flow out, it will collect along the edge and build up into a large ridge before it begins to drip. At some point this will become a hard ridge, which will have to be removed. And finally, the cloth will float on the epoxy so that sanding it flat later will cut through the glass.

The First Coat of Epoxy

The first coat of epoxy is one of the key steps in building a plywood kayak, and because of this it is often regarded with fear, or at least tense anticipation. A little concern will keep you focused, but if you understand what is happening and follow the simple steps in order, you have nothing to lose sleep over.

You can apply the mixed epoxy to the cloth in several different ways. Keep in mind that all we are doing is transferring the epoxy from the can to the surface of the cloth in the most graceful manner possible. When the mixed epoxy saturates the glass cloth, it will change from white to clear. No effort should be made to work the epoxy into the cloth; working the epoxy will introduce air and could result in a milky finish. Allow the epoxy to soak in on its own.

How to Apply the Epoxy

Using a roller

As we mentioned in Chapter 4, we don't recommend rollers for applying epoxy to the cloth of a kayak. It is more difficult for the first-time builder to control the position of the cloth with a roller than with a brush. As well, the roller encourages overworking the epoxy.

Pour-and-spread method

There are several ways to transfer epoxy from the can to the cloth. If the surface is horizontal, pour the mixed epoxy into a

CHEAP TRICK

Mixed epoxy check

A simple test of the success of the mix is to set aside the container that had the epoxy mixed in it and check the residue in it to see if it has hardened. It's better to poke at the epoxy left in the container than at the epoxy on the kayak. Knowing that the mix was correct when it left the container will help limit your search for the cause of problems that may occur.

small puddle and move it around with a squeegee. Note, however, that the squeegee has a tendency to spread the epoxy quite thin. Keep an eye out for starved areas (the cloth will have a glassy, whitish, dry look); go back and add a little more fresh epoxy. This method works best on the deck or inside, where the epoxy is contained. On the outside, where the surface is mostly vertical, trying to pour it on will make a dreadful mess.

Using a brush

For the small, mostly vertical surfaces on the outside of a plywood kayak, a brush is the most graceful way of applying the epoxy. It can spread just the right amount of epoxy gently over the surface without disturbing the position of the cloth. Should the cloth need to be repositioned, the brush is the tool to use. Pulling the cloth with the brush is more successful than pushing. Point the handle in the direction that you want the cloth to go, lay the side of the brush on the cloth and draw the cloth along.

Squeeze all the epoxy out of the brush at the end of applying each batch. If the epoxy is clean, deposit it onto the boat; if it is getting foamy, scrape it into a grunge can partially filled with water. If old epoxy is allowed to build up in the brush from batch to batch, it may be deposited after it has begun to thicken, or the brush may stiffen and go hard before the end of a long session.

COLD-WEATHER BLUES

Most warm-weather application problems can be taken care of simply by switching to a slower hardener, mixing smaller batches that can be spread out quickly, and dumping the mixture into a paint roller tray or other large pan. A very effective method is to catch a little hammock time and wait for a cooler time of day.

Cold-weather application of epoxy offers additional challenges. Low temperatures will definitely slow the cure time. CLC uses this rule-of-thumb: starting at room temperature, the cure time of its epoxy doubles with each 10°F drop in temperature. Tests indicate that epoxy cured at very cool temperatures may be weaker. Like honey kept in the refrigerator, epoxy components thicken, causing them to cling to the surfaces of the pumps. This can cause the pumps to belch air and fail to meter out the resin and hardener in the correct proportions. And the thicker stuff is much harder to mix. Both conditions can lead to a questionable bond.

Cool, thick epoxy is also much more difficult to spread and is slow to wet out the cloth. This will waste a lot more epoxy when it is squeegeed and could require more sanding. As well, the epoxy will not penetrate as far into the surface of the wood, resulting in a lighter color and a less secure bond.

Finally, air bubbles may be introduced during mixing or application and held in suspension in the thick epoxy. The bubbles not only show up in a clear coating, but they can also reduce the epoxy's strength and moisture-barrier capabilities.

What to do?

Begin by reading the manufacturer's instructions about the operating temperatures of the various hardeners. Then investigate the possibility of adding additional heat to your shop to at least 55°F (12°C), although 65°F to 70°F is better (5-49).

Tenting off a section of the shop or the boat itself can help confine heat. Some builders use spotlights or heat lamps, but avoid using unvented space heaters; they produce elevated CO_2 levels that are not only bad for you but may also inhibit the epoxy's cure. Unburned hydrocarbons from kerosene and fuel oil burners may contaminate the bonding surface. Whatever heat source you use, be extremely mindful of any fire danger. Remove any liquids that have flammable fumes and keep your heating units well away from combustible surfaces.

Store the resin and hardener in a warm place (room temperature) until you are ready to use it. Warm epoxy is thinner and flows out better. Keep your fiberglass cloth warm and dry as well so that it doesn't draw heat from the mixed epoxy.

Choose a brand that will cure the fastest with slow hardener; if recoating is anticipated, avoid adding fast hardener (→ Amine Blush, page 38).

5-49

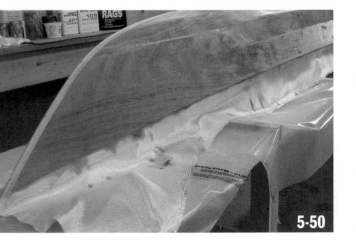

Batch Size

Begin with a one-cup batch for wetting out the cloth. The ideal quantity is what you can apply in 5 to 10 minutes – the fresher the better. If you have a mixer, he or she should time the beginning of the next batch so that it is ready just as you run out. Don't mix batches ahead of time for efficiency. If a container of epoxy has been around for a while and you can feel the heat through the container, discard the epoxy into a grunge can.

Where to Begin?

Give some thought to where you will begin applying the epoxy. The idea is to find a place where it will be easiest to maintain a wet edge. Unless the edge is kept fresh (10 minutes' working time) there could be a visible line where it meets the next batch. When applying the first coat, having a reliable helper to do the mixing will make the job go much faster and allow you to concentrate on applying the epoxy.

5-50

If you are working alone, begin about 4 feet from the end to anchor the cloth, and apply epoxy to a section that is a comfortable brushing length (24 to 36 inches). Work from the keel line down to the sheer, then move along to the end to pull the cloth out tight. Move to the other side and do the same, then come back to the side you began on for the next batch. Work down the hull, alternating sides. If working with a helper, begin on opposite sides and work down the hull in tandem.

Apply a sufficient amount of epoxy to saturate the cloth and the surface of the wood, plus a little more to soak in later. For a clear finish, apply it quickly, with the least amount of agitation. Yes, it does look ugly – if you are a good painter, it will drive you crazy. Don't play with it; it will look better soon. The only reason to go back is to break big bubbles that are lifting the cloth and to add more to starved areas.

If the epoxy has been applied quickly, as it should be, there will be bubbles, puddles, runs of streaky epoxy and a few brush hairs (5-50). Rather than sand this mess off later, we suggest removing it with a squeegee (see below for instructions). Keep in mind, though, that you must begin to squeegee about 30 minutes after the epoxy has been applied. Try to get all of the epoxy on within this time so that you can concentrate on working with the squeegee. If you run out of time with more to apply, squeegee the area where the first batch was applied, then go back and apply the next batch. Continue going back and forth like this until all the epoxy has been applied. If you have a mixer who is also handy with the brush, he or she can maintain the fresh edge by working both sides.

The Squeegee Is Your Friend

A little piece of plastic – the squeegee – is the secret to a beautiful clear coating with very little sanding. If you're looking for something that can reduce all those dismal, tedious hours of sanding, this step is for you.

Elapsed Time

For even saturation, the elapsed time between application of the epoxy and removal of excess epoxy must be consistent. If the cloth is squeegeed before the wood is thoroughly saturated, the wood will continue to act like a sponge, drawing the epoxy from the cloth and leaving it dry. This is more critical on a softwood strip-planked surface, where each plank will absorb a different amount of epoxy, than on a plywood surface, where the depth stops at the first glue line.

Using the Squeegee

Using the squeegee is a skill that requires practice to get a feel for the correct angle and pressure. The idea is to apply enough pressure to leave the wood and glass saturated but with the pattern of the cloth plainly visible. Easy to say, but there is a fine balance between squeezing the cloth

5-51

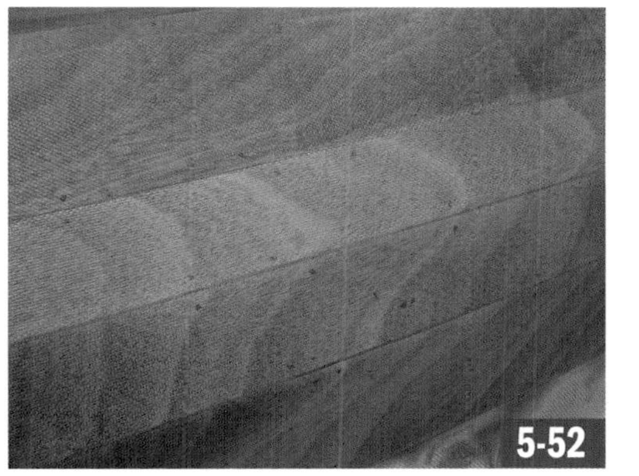
5-52

dry and leaving it floating in excess epoxy; both are to be avoided. Dry cloth will have a slightly white, dry appearance; these unsaturated threads will remain visible in the finish. Excess epoxy will look wet and shiny and will flow over and under the glass.

Take control

To use the squeegee, hold it at a shallow angle to avoid removing too much epoxy. For the best control over its edge, place your thumb and little finger under the squeegee and the three middle fingers on top (5-51). If you keep your thumb almost dragging on the surface, there is little danger of removing too much epoxy. The three fingers on top are spread out to control the pressure along the edge. Remember, you aren't hard-pressed for time here because you want to keep the same elapsed time between the application of each batch and the cleanup.

Begin by making light passes to pick up the bulk of the grunge. If the squeegee is loaded, stop short of the edge of the surface being worked in order to keep from pulling it over the edge. Do a little J-stroke at the end, which flips the squeegee over before the epoxy can drip off. After each pass, clean the squeegee blade by passing it through the slit in the grunge can. This will avoid transferring the waste back to the beginning of the next stroke.

Adjust the angle as conditions change. If the cloth starts to shift, reduce the angle and pressure. As the epoxy begins to thicken (and you're picking up runs after the epoxy has begun to kick), use slightly more pressure and a little steeper angle. Keep in mind that this increases the chance of taking too much off and dragging the cloth out of position.

Aim for an even texture

Look for an even texture (some say leathery); try to work out any tracks left between passes (5-52). Since the inside of the kayak is receiving only two coats of epoxy, the texture of the weave must be consistent in order to look good. The outside is a good place to practice achieving that even texture.

Systematically work the sections of epoxy in the order they were applied. Finish each section before moving on to the next section. Begin at the keel line and try to work across the chines at a right angle. Take as many light passes as necessary to remove just the right amount of epoxy. Check around the edge of the cloth for drips, buildup or other defects.

Dry-brush

A dry brush can be used to work out any tracks that might be left behind by the squeegee. Brush aggressively, working fore and aft by drawing the brush along at a fairly low angle to pull the epoxy into a consistent film (5-53).

Final check

Take time to check over the newly covered hull before cleaning up the squeegee and taking off your gloves. A good view is from the end with your head low, keeping your

5-53

eyes even with the edge of the hull. Move around and look from both ends. Check the places that are hardest to see. The edge of the hull will often have a buildup of epoxy along the edge, or the cloth will sometimes pull away around the stern stem.

If possible, keep an eye on the boat for a while watching for cloth coming away from the edge, bubbles or runs. With the slow, slow hardeners, there is a lot of time to pick up the occasional run or shiny spot that might show up. At some point the epoxy will get so sticky that it will smear rather than pick up cleanly; this is the time to leave it alone. Deal with anything you don't like when it is hard.

Allow the epoxy to kick before prepping for the next coat. It will be ready for the next coat when the cloth hanging over the stern has reached the rubbery green stage and can be cut with a sharp knife without the epoxy sticking to the knife. This will be from 4 to 21 hours, depending on conditions and the brand of resin and hardener you are using.

Reinforcing the Stems

The curve of the bow on most sea kayaks is usually gentle enough that the cloth may be worked around it without cutting the glass.

> **CAUTION**
>
> **Never use paint thinner (mineral spirits, turpentine, etc.) for cleaning up amine blush or anything else between epoxy coats; it will leave an oily film that inhibits the bond between epoxy layers.**

At the stern, or if the curve on the bow is too tight to follow, this isn't possible. You can cut the cloth an inch or two past the end of the hull and wrap the ends around the stem, overlapping the two pieces of wet glass. Or you can cut the cloth flush to the end of the stem after the first coat of epoxy has kicked, then reinforce with a glass patch around the end.

Wrapping the ends of the cloth around the stem and lapping one side over the other is a very direct way of finishing the end. If time is tight and you just want to go paddling, try it. But frankly, our experience with this technique has been more miss than hit. When it doesn't work, it adds several more steps to repair the places where the cloth would not stay down and is trapping air.

If you are not a gambler or have the time to play, try finishing the end using the second option.

The best and most convenient time to reinforce the stem is between the first and second coats of epoxy, anytime after the epoxy has kicked. Make a clean cut with a sharp utility knife to carve the glass smoothly into the stem (5-54). If the epoxy has just reached the firm stage, don't bother trying to feather the edge with sandpaper. Sanding it will plug the paper and smear the epoxy over the surface. Plus it's not healthy.

Why no gloves in this photo? When this was taken, it had been several days since the epoxy was applied, in other words, past the green stage. Until the epoxy reaches a full

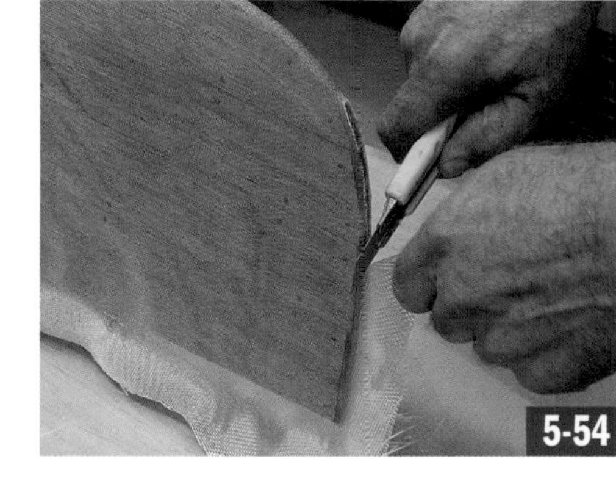
5-54

cure, which can be from 9 to 14 days, the partially cured epoxy is a chemical hazard. Wearing gloves at this stage would be a good idea, but if the epoxy has just reached the green stage, definitely wear the gloves.

If it has been a while since the epoxy was applied, scratch the surface with 120 grit sandpaper to ensure a good mechanical bond (5-55).

Wrapping with Fiberglass Tape

Glass tape will wrap around the vertical portion of the stem reasonably well. Cut enough slits in the edge of the tape to get it

5-55

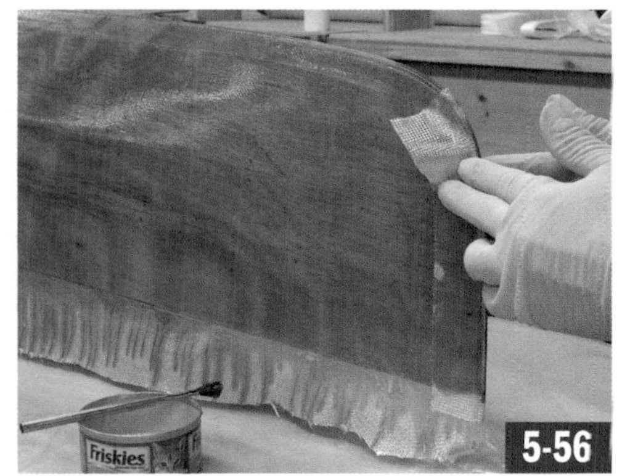

5-56

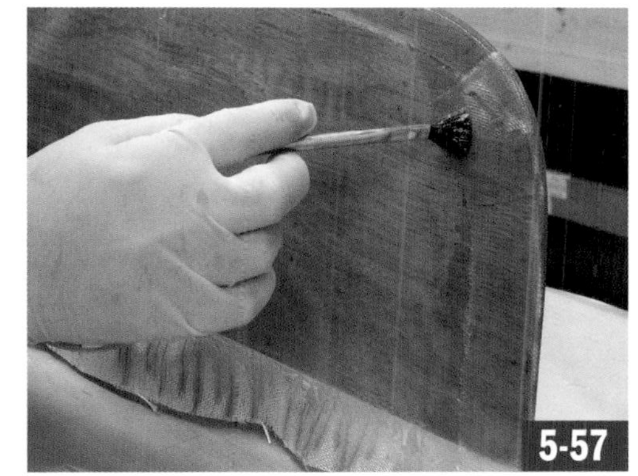
5-57

5-58

to fit around the tight curve without bunching up at the edges. Tape is not our first choice, though, because it is difficult to feather the thick selvage edge into the hull surface.

Wrapping with Bias-cut Cloth

A piece of scrap cloth cut on the bias makes the easiest patch to work with and clean up. The piece we are using is about 3 inches wide and long enough to fit the stem with a bit left over.

Apply epoxy to the area that will be covered by the glass patch in order to hold the glass in position and begin saturating the cloth. Notice in the photo (5-56) that the glass is almost completely saturated where it has been pressed down and will require very little additional epoxy.

Although the cloth is cut on the bias, if the edge is overworked it will begin to fall apart. Use a sponging motion with the brush to transfer the epoxy (5-57). Squeegee off any excess epoxy and dispose of it.

Keep an eye on the patch until the epoxy begins to kick. Use the acid brush to work out any air bubbles and to pull the glass tight around the curve when needed.

When the epoxy is hard enough to sand, use a firm sanding block to feather the edge of the patch into the previously coated surface (5-58).

The Second Coat of Epoxy

The purpose of the second coat is to fill the weave of the cloth and level the surface. After the first coat, the surface is rough, with open spaces between the threads. If the first coat of epoxy is hard, give the hull a quick sand with 120 grit sandpaper before applying the second coat. This should be a quick pass with the paper folded in your hand. The objective is to cut the small points of epoxy-reinforced glass that are sticking up. Any more than a zip-zip sanding will cut into the glass fibers. If the coats are being applied close together, this sanding step is not necessary because the surface will not be as abrasive in the rubbery green stage.

If you do sand, pick up the epoxy dust with a vacuum cleaner, then wipe clean with a rag dampened with lacquer thinner or water before applying the second coat.

How to Apply the Epoxy

Mix the epoxy in half-cup batches. To take the pressure off finishing before the

CHEAP TRICK

Glass patch cut in direction of weave

If you don't have a piece of cloth big enough to cut on the bias, there is a way to use a patch cut in the direction of the weave without the edge of the glass falling apart. Cut the cloth about 8 inches wide and the appropriate length. Apply epoxy to the stem and about 1½ inches back on both sides, then position the glass over this wet area. Press the cloth into the wet epoxy and use masking tape along the dry edge of the patch to hold it tight and secure to the hull. Add more epoxy if necessary to saturate the wet area, and pick up any excess with the squeegee. After the epoxy has cured, slice off the dry part of the cloth with a sharp chisel held almost flat to the hull. The chisel will start feathering the edge and it will take very little work to finish with sandpaper.

epoxy begins to kick, apply and scrape off the excess epoxy one batch at a time. Maintaining a wet edge and overlapping batches is not a concern here because the epoxy is not soaking in on this coat.

When transferring epoxy from the can to the surface, avoid pouring it onto the outside of the hull and pulling it down the vertical sides. It will run all over the place and you will miss places along the sheer.

What works for us is to apply the epoxy along the sheer with a brush (5-59) and draw it up with the squeegee to spread it around the bottom. Moving the epoxy over this rough texture will introduce air, so keep the distance that you will move it to a practical minimum. Try to judge the amount of epoxy you apply so that drawing it up to the centerline uses up the entire amount that you brushed on. Apply it liberally with the brush, about one-third of the distance to be covered.

The object of the next step is to pack the

5-59

5-60

epoxy into the spaces and force the air out. Use firm pressure on the squeegee and a steeper angle than you used on the wet fiberglass (5-60). Don't try to make it look pretty at this stage. If the epoxy you are moving is starting to get foamy, let it sit, add fresh epoxy and move on.

Cleanup

When the whole batch has been applied and packed in, systematically scrape off all the excess epoxy flush to the top of the glass threads. Practice achieving an even texture with no horizontal squeegee tracks. Tracks that you can't get with the squeegee can be worked out with a dry brush using long fore-and-aft strokes.

Final Check

Since this is what the inside of the hull will look like with two coats of epoxy, now is a good time to identify any problems you may be having with getting a continuous texture. Check from a low angle. Look for dry patches; these are easiest to see looking

5-61

from the end in low light. Check along the sheer; to be sure, do a horizontal pass with the squeegee to catch any runs along the edge or identify places that have been missed. Listen to the squeegee; as it passes over dry glass, it will have a higher pitch, almost a whistling sound. Keep an eye on it for a while to be sure there are no surprises.

The Third Coat of Epoxy

The purpose of the third coat (5-61) is to bury the cloth under enough epoxy that it can be sanded smooth without hitting the glass. For some people, this coat is the easiest one to apply because it involves familiar painting techniques.

How to Apply the Epoxy

Apply a heavy coat of epoxy, preferably with a brush (5-62). By heavy we mean as much as possible without its sliding off onto the floor. A thick coat will stay in place without runs if it has an even film thickness. Runs and curtains happen when a thick patch of epoxy flows over a thinner patch.

Apply it in about one-cup size batches; it will brush out better when the epoxy is fresh.

Load up the brush and spread the epoxy over the surface using horizontal strokes. Work on a section about 3 feet long (a comfortable brushing arm's length). When this section has been covered, work on the diagonal in both directions to blend the horizontal application strokes. Use a draw stroke, pointing the handle in the direction of travel, to pull the epoxy along – as opposed to a pushing stroke, with the handle held vertically, which is used to transport the material to the surface and spread it around.

Notice how the resistance you feel through the brush will change as the uneven densities begin to blend. When satisfied with the consistency you can feel when working on the diagonal, finish with long horizontal strokes. At this point, gloss is gloss; you can't expect to control the thickness of this coat by what you see. Concentrate on the feedback from the brush for all the information you need. When the resistance is consistent over the whole surface, move on to the next section.

Blending Sections

Adjoining sections are applied in the same manner but will require attention where the sections join. If the sections are overlapped, the extra thickness of epoxy on the overlapping portion is tricky to sand out; if left in place, the extra thickness is noticeable on a shiny finish.

To avoid lap marks, work from the wet to the dry. Place the epoxy beside rather than on the wet edge and draw it away. After the section has been drawn out using long horizontal strokes, the blending will be completed. It is very important to avoid digging holes in the epoxy with the brush at the beginning or end of the stroke. These holes will end up as low spots in the final finish that will take a lot of work to feather in, with a possibility of hitting the cloth. To avoid this, keep the brush at a low angle to pull the epoxy; lift off gently at the end of the stroke, switch direction on the brush and come in like an airplane touching down gently. Move at a reasonably slow speed so that the epoxy has time to react and adjust to the new position. Think ballet.

To avoid runs, use this method of application with paint or varnish.

Taking Care of Runs

There is a time limit to how long the runs can be worked, but generally speaking, until the epoxy has begun to get sticky they can be brushed out. Most runs come in the form of curtains. Keeping in mind that the thick is running over the thin, first work the run down over the thinner area by brushing on the diagonal, then draw it out on the horizontal to blend it in. Work the smallest possible area. When the epoxy begins to roll up in waves and not flow out, it is time to leave it alone.

Sealing Plywood with Epoxy

There are several situations in which applying mixed epoxy directly to raw wood is appropriate. Some plywood building methods will use thick enough plywood to carry the load without the need for fiberglass cloth reinforcement. Cloth will sometimes be used on one side only for durability. In this case, it is very important to have the unreinforced side well sealed to balance the moisture content on both sides of the panel.

Protecting the surface of the plywood during construction is another good reason for pre-coating the planks and deck panels. If the ultimate clear coating is desirable or if the panels have been dyed, this step is the place to start. Once the plywood is sealed, joints and fillets can be made without staining or scratching the wood during assembly.

The discriminating plans-builder can save time by coating the plywood sheet before marking and cutting out the parts. This will save having to deal with the edges while coating and sanding. If the surface is sanded, it will accept pencil lines – wipe the ones you don't like off with a rag dampened with lacquer thinner. The downside is the safety hazard of cutting epoxy-coated plywood.

It is worth noting that if controlling the surface is not a priority, pre-coating the panels is unnecessary because the glass will bond to raw wood as well as or better than it will to a pre-coated surface. With reasonable care, a kit may be assembled without causing damage that cannot be cleaned up in a reasonable amount of time.

Applying the Epoxy

Over a prepared surface (→ page 81) apply the epoxy with a brush or roller, or simply pour a puddle and move it around with the squeegee. Pouring on a small puddle and spreading it with the squeegee works best on horizontal surfaces; use a brush on vertical surfaces.

The problem

Notice the bubbles in the photo (5-63) caused by epoxy soaking into the wood fibers and displacing the air in the fibers. This happens because wood fibers work as a wick to draw the epoxy in. The epoxy has been sitting on this surface for about 20 minutes and is still bubbling as the air inside expands.

If the bubbles are left unbroken, thick craters will remain around them requiring aggressive sanding to flatten but leaving the open pores still open. Working the surface with a brush after the epoxy has begun to thicken is dicey because it will introduce more air into the epoxy, and bubbles will keep coming anyway until the epoxy is stiff. Either way, the surface will need a lot of sanding to level the surface before it is ready for the second coat. The next application will not fill the openings much better; you can get into a cycle of put-it-on-and-sand-it-off that lasts until you get fed up with the nonsense.

5-63

5-64

The solution

Cut out all the nasty sanding and get on with building a kayak. Let the epoxy soak in for 20 to 30 minutes, then remove all the buildup. Squeegee tangent to the direction of the grain, using a low angle and firm pressure to press the epoxy in and force the air out (5-64). If the squeegee is picking up a substantial amount of epoxy, lift off before reaching the edges to avoid messing them up any more than is necessary. When working around the edge of a panel, try holding the squeegee at an angle that moves the epoxy onto the wood rather than pushing it over the edge. Clean the edge of the blade after each stroke by passing it through the slit in the grunge can. When finished, scrape the edge of the panel with a putty knife.

This is a simple step that will leave the wood fibers completely saturated and the surface stable. But the real bonus is that there is nothing to be sanded off later; the surface is sealed, ready for the next step. Depending on the reason for the sealer, there are several ways to go from here.

Quick Sealer

If the plywood is to be coated but not glassed or varnished (for example, on the underside of a taped-seam deck), the objective is a well-sealed and reasonably smooth surface. Sand the first coat but don't cut down to the wood. Look for a balance of shiny (low spots) and dull (sanded and flat spots). Clean as if it were the last coat of varnish, because specks of dust will cause sharp points in the finish. Brush or roll on another full coat of mixed epoxy and draw it out into an even film (→ page 88).

Added Protection for a Surface to Be Worked on Later

This is a quick step that will provide good protection and a smoother coating on a hidden surface. It can also provide extra protection during construction for a colored panel that will be glassed later. In the latter case, a quick sanding is sufficient to knock the tops off the high points and scuff up the surface. Apply the epoxy coat with a squeegee, then scrape off the excess. The surface should be brighter than it was because it is almost flat, with a thin film of epoxy.

When the epoxy has cured, clean up the edges of the plywood with a rasp or hard sanding block. Try not to alter the shape of the wood – the edge is the guide for assembling the pieces. Check the ends that will be joined together; they should be square, flat and clean. Components that will be glassed after assembly are now ready to go. A quick sanding will smooth the piece to the touch. Leave the rest of the prep work until later when you are doing cleanup before glassing the structure.

Fiberglassing Inside of Hull

Before we get going here, it is worth noting that not all kayak plans and kits require fiberglassing the interior. Some boats rely on filleted and taped joints to hold them together. The exteriors of these kayaks are fiberglassed for abrasion resistance and the interiors are epoxy-coated to seal them.

Fitting and wetting out the cloth inside (5-65) require a few tricks to accommodate the shape. Bending materials into the inside of a curved form is always more difficult then bending around the outside. This is true whether you are steam-bending oak ribs or laying up epoxy-saturated fiberglass. The stock always tries to come away from tight bends in the form to make the easiest natural curve possible, leaving an air-filled gap behind. In the kayak, these bends occur at the plank joints and at the stem. Gracefully sculpted fillets can go a long way toward easing these transitions.

Understanding How the Cloth Works

If the glass pulls away, you won't make it go down by poking at it with the brush or adding more epoxy. The epoxy might fill up the void, but we don't want the glass to be floating. Poking at it will most likely pull it up somewhere else. To get it to stay down, hold the glass off the edge of the hull and feed more cloth down into the joint. The fiber that you feed over the edge should go directly into the void you are trying to fill. Expect the cloth to react at some distance from where you are feeding it.

Before working the cloth with the brush, scrape all the grunge out of the brush. Hold the brush with the handle pointing in the direction you are feeding and pull the cloth rather than pushing with the ends of the bristles.

If you are unlucky enough to have to piece up the interior, take time to dry-run the operation. Trim out your pieces and see how they fit – handle with extreme care so as not to distort the shape of the cloth. Plan for where your overlapping glass joints will be. A bit of preemptive strategy can mean the difference between a pleasant artistic exercise and man-to-man combat with a slithering squid.

5-65

THINK LAZY

Controlling the cloth

The secret to a successful glass layup is to be aware of how what you do with the brush or squeegee affects the cloth. Assume that it will move the cloth; if the cloth pulls out of the joint when you work in one direction, put it back in place by reversing the action. It is quite easy to control the cloth if you note what is going wrong and use this knowledge to your advantage. Keep in mind that the cloth is made up of continuous glass threads running in two directions. This means that what you do in one place will be evident some distance away in the direction that the thread is running.

Some Tricks That Might Help

• Work out the most convenient order for building up the pieces. Lay up awkward shapes first and hide the edges under the adjoining less-worked piece; the edge will be straighter.

• To keep the threads straight along the selvage edge, always brush and squeegee straight out from the edge. The alternative is a ridge of something that looks like glass-fiber felt reinforced with epoxy.

• While it is possible to overlap the edges of two pieces of dry cloth and wet them as one, with larger pieces there can be problems; the bottom layer may have shifted by the time you get there and the ends of the threads may be standing on end. One possibility is to start wetting out at the join and work out from there in both directions.

• If there is a choice, overlap a selvage edge over a cut edge.

• Pull off as many loose strings as possible or they will stick to your brush later.

• Make something like a selvage edge by cutting parallel to the thread and pulling off the first two or three rows.

• Use a sponging motion with the brush to transfer the epoxy straight down in order to avoid disturbing the edge by brushing over it.

Taming the Glass Inside

A simple way of keeping the glass on the inside from getting away from you is to have pieces of cloth running from side to side rather than a single piece running from end to end. Each section will be wetted out and squeegeed before adding the next section with a 1-inch overlap. Breaking the cloth into sections will give you time to get each piece right and a short break before the next one, if you need it. Although dealing with the joins between each section is extra work, having a selvage on both edges is a big help. The joins do not have to be obvious if they are placed outside the cockpit area. Keep this in mind when deciding where to put the first piece of cloth.

We are using 6-ounce fiberglass cloth that is 60 inches wide. Cloth included in your kit may be a different width but it can be applied in the above way with very little waste of cloth. If the instructions direct you to some tight measurements and tricky cutting and piecing back together, it is a good idea to measure the cloth you have to work with before committing to that method. Having a few inches hanging over each side will hold the cloth in position and protect the outside of the hull from drips. Do what you can to avoid making joins on a

5-66

5-67

5-68

cut edge of cloth or ending the cloth short of the edge of the sheer line.

There is no future in trying to overlap the cloth at the stem. It will end up in a mess and take a lot of sanding time to clean up. Stop the cloth about 4 inches short of the stem fillet, but keep in mind that the exposed plywood should be well sealed with epoxy.

Brushing over the cut edge of the cloth will unravel it, so we have stopped the mixed epoxy just short of the edge of the glass. The cloth is then carefully folded back (5-66) so that epoxy can be brushed over the bare area. Carefully unfold the cloth back over the wet epoxy and press straight down with the flat side of the brush; add a little more mixed epoxy if needed and finish with the squeegee.

Begin by wetting out an arm's-length section of the glass, beginning along the centerline and continuing up the hull (5-67). When you reach the sheer, try not to shift the cloth or leave a big glob of epoxy that might run down the outside (if it does, wipe it up with a thinner-dampened rag). Using a sponging motion can help avoid shifting the cloth.

When this section has been completed up to the sheer, repeat to the end of the cloth. Now wet out the opposite side. By the time the second side has been wetted out, the first section will be ready to be squeegeed. Fifteen to 25 minutes will be enough for the cloth and the surface of the plywood to absorb all the epoxy they want.

The direction you work along the edge of the cloth is important. The short fibers sticking out of the selvage edge of the cloth should be kept straight and flat. If they are bunched up the overlapping cloth will not lie flat.

Use the squeegee to pick up excess epoxy (5-68). Remember that the hardest-to-see places are the places that get missed; look there first.

Applying the Second Piece of Cloth

To center the next piece of glass in the hull, fold the cloth in half, then position the fold along the centerline (5-69). After getting one side roughly settled, fold the other side into position and smooth it out.

Start by positioning the cloth to overlap the wet section by about 1 inch. Press the dry cloth into the wet epoxy to anchor it; smooth from this point forward along the centerline, then work it up to the sheer (5-70).

Using a brush to transfer epoxy from the can to the cloth is most effective when working on vertical surfaces, on small areas or in confined spaces. In this section of the hull, where there is lots of room to move, simply pour a small puddle of epoxy in the middle, then use the squeegee to spread the epoxy over the cloth (5-71). Keep the puddles small so that the epoxy does not have to be moved any farther than necessary.

5-69

This is what the glass looks like where the two pieces overlap (5-72). Notice how the ends of both pieces blend together, with all

5-70

5-71

5-72

the end fibers lying flat. The trick here is to squeegee the edge of the cloth with the small squeegee, working in the direction of the loose fibers to remove excess epoxy while keeping the fibers straight.

The Second Coat of Epoxy

On the inside of the hull, two coats of mixed epoxy are recommended rather than the three coats used on the outside. This will result in a pleasing texture that will be easy to keep clean and less slippery than a high-gloss finish.

When the first coat of epoxy has cured, give the surface a quick sanding by hand with 120 grit sandpaper. Feather any rough joints where the glass overlaps. Vacuum-dust and wipe it clean with a rag dampened with lacquer thinner or water.

Apply the second coat of epoxy with the squeegee, then take a break and congratulate yourself on a job well done.

Sanding

We are not suggesting that you learn to love sanding, but when it changes from being a frantic cleanup that goes on forever to being an intelligent, controlled step in putting the kayak together, sanding is neither unpleasant nor time-consuming. Think sanding from the time you open the box – be conscious of ways to avoid it or keep it to a minimum as each step progresses.

Working clean is the secret of building a beautiful boat without wasting pointless hours of exposure to hazardous substances. Control epoxy at the source. If there is epoxy on your glove, wipe it off with a dry rag. That one blob of sticky stuff will end up in more places than you can imagine before you know it. Once it begins to spread, the job gets unhealthy, and more steps – wiping, scraping and sanding – must be worked through before you go paddling. Instead of building a kayak, the project can become an

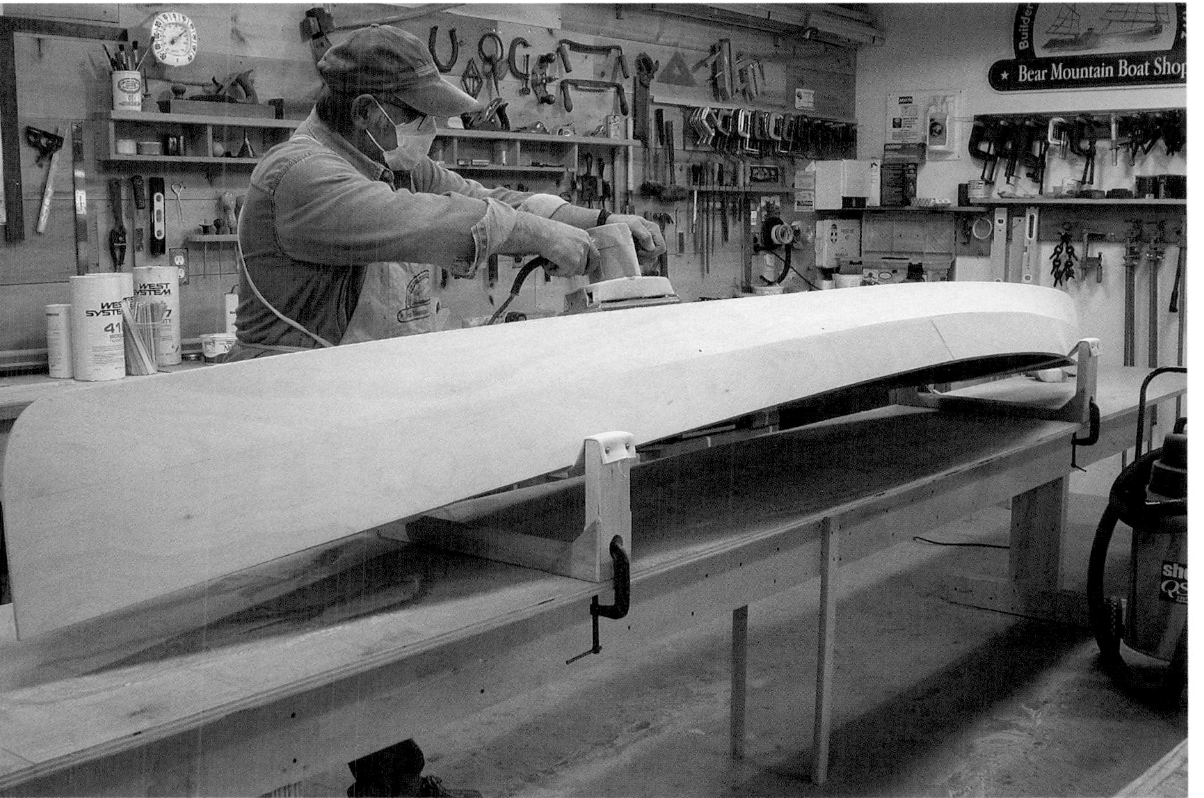

exercise in damage control.

One of the big differences between a plywood kit and a strip-plank or traditional small boat is how little dust is generated by the plywood method. To build a round-bilge boat with flat planks means that the flats must be worked into curves. Planks in a plywood kayak must stay flat, with the shape being developed at the joints. Considering how thin the face veneers are in 4 mm plywood, it is in our best interest not to do any shaping on the plywood. What this means is that if you are producing a lot of wood dust, the boat is in trouble.

Why Are You Sanding?

It is very important to understand exactly why you are sanding in order to know how to proceed and when to stop. The reasons for sanding range from structural considerations to simple pride in workmanship. When you understand the why it is possible to match that up with your expectations for the boat and to tailor a sanding schedule to achieve the desired results. Finishes can range from workboat grade to obsessive Steinway piano. The finer the finish, the more you need to pay attention to detail.

The secret to a clean color with an even density is in how the surface of the wood has been prepared. Think of making a mirror – the wood surface is the reflector; if the back of the mirror is uneven, the reflection will be distorted. The plywood as it comes from the manufacturer has been sanded to size the panel to a specified thickness. While relatively smooth, the surface will be rough for our purposes and bruised from the aggressive sanding. When moisture is applied to this surface, it swells the roughly cut fibers and stands them on end. Before the next step can happen, this very rough reinforced surface must be sanded flat. Sanding varnish is labor-intensive and sanding epoxy is just a lot of unhealthy work. Getting rid of the fuzz before it is coated saves a lot of construction time and hazardous dust exposure time.

Before installing small parts such as hatch trim, take the time to sand and soften the edges. It is much faster and easier to do it on the bench than after the piece has been glued onto the kayak. Breaking the edge is not just for the perfectionist to consider. When any material is applied to a sharp corner or edge, the film breaks and pulls back from the corner, leaving it exposed.

Machine Sanding

Using a machine sander on small surfaces can very quickly take off more material than needs to be removed. Power sanders are invaluable for many projects, but their usefulness is limited on small surfaces where precise control is important. Lack of visibility is the big problem. With the size of the pad, machine vibration, dust, noise and protective gear, keeping track of what is happening is a guess at best.

If you do use a machine, be aware of what the sander is doing at all times. Watch how and what it is cutting and how fast. Watch how the surface is changing as it emerges from under the pad with each pass. There should be a window of clean surface around the pad. Watch that the pad of the sander does not wrap over the hull-deck joint or sand along the joint between planks; the machine will cut the edge a lot faster than you think.

For anything other than large sheets, hand sanding is recommended for preparing plywood for a coating or finish.

Hand Sanding

Hand sanding is healthier than machine sanding and actually quite pleasant; you can see where you are going and hear yourself think. If you are working in a confined space or if noise could be a problem, sanding by hand will easily solve your concerns.

Sanding Plywood

Preparing the plywood surface before applying the epoxy-and-glass covering is another important step in meeting your expectations. Begin by sanding with 120 grit paper on a firm block, working slightly across the grain. When working with precut components that must be fit together in the future, care must be taken not to round the edges. The hard block will help by projecting over rather than following around the edge.

For a paint-grade finish, you could stop here. The epoxy will bring the bruised grain up, but the glass will bury it, and when the surface is squeegeed, the fibers will be pushed back down.

5-73

Raise the grain

For a bright finish, before the final sanding dampen the surface with warm to hot water to raise the grain. Use a clean rag or sponge with most of the water squeezed out. Avoid puddles – they could stain the wood and will take time to dry.

Remove the fuzz

After the surface looks dry, remove the resulting fuzz with 180 to 220 grit sandpaper, working slightly across the grain to cut the fuzz rather than push it back down. Work systematically, because it won't look much different after it has been sanded. To check, vacuum the dust, then run your hand over the surface feeling for anything that is less than smooth.

Clean

Vacuum to remove the dust. Half of what we are doing here is cleaning, so expect the vacuum cleaner or compressed air to do a better job of getting the dust out of the pores than brushing will.

SANDING SAFELY

- Reduce sanding to a professional minimum by controlling the material as it is applied.
- Wear a dust mask. If you are sensitive to dust, use a properly rated charcoal filter canister respirator. Woods that are "naturally rot resistant" are so because they are naturally toxic.
- Allow the mixed epoxy to reach a full cure before any major sanding – the dust is toxic in its uncured state.
- When sanding epoxy, cover up; wear long sleeves or coveralls and a hat (5-74).
- Wear eye protection, especially when machine sanding.
- Whenever possible, control the dust at the source. This is more a consideration for machine sanding than for hand sanding. Hand sanding plywood in the basement is not that disruptive if the dust is vacuumed up before it has a chance to spread. A good shop vacuum or dust collector with the intake hose rigged up close to where you are sanding will do a lot to capture flying dust at the source. Most vacuum cleaners are not made for continuous duty, so watch that the motor doesn't overheat. Cover shelves and other hard-to-clean areas with plastic film to aid in cleanup. Machine sand outside when you can, and make a point of it when sanding large areas of epoxy.
- Set up good cross-ventilation; use a fan in the window or move the kayak outside if the weather is good.
- Take the time to rig up adequate lighting.
- Work in a balanced position; it is safer on your body and the boat.
- Wear ear protection; machine sanding is noisy and will be amplified in an enclosed space.
- If you are not wearing coveralls, a shower and a change of clothes is recommended after a major epoxy sanding session. It might also be wise to wash your work clothes separately from the regular wash to avoid contaminating your other clothes.

5-74

Sanding Epoxy

It is not a ridiculous idea to consider sanding the epoxy on a little sea kayak by hand. If care has been taken to do a good layup, a reasonable day's work will prepare the kayak for varnish or paint. Compared to machine sanding, the surface will be extremely fair and there is very little danger of cutting through the fiberglass. If you sand inside and vacuum as you go, flying dust will be limited. Sanding our Coho deck (5-73), which was mostly hand work, took about 90 minutes, including cleanup.

What grits to use

Use a firm block or sanding board, with nothing coarser than 120 grit paper. We used 180 grit, which, while not as aggressive as

CAUTION

5-75

What to avoid

While you are working your way down through the gloss, watch for glass cloth appearing along the edges (5-75) as well as around any low spots. If it looks like you are getting close to the glass, leave a bit of gloss. Before finishing, dull these areas with a folded piece of sandpaper or fine bronze or steel wool.

120, did not require a second pass to clean up the deeper 120 scratches. It takes about the same amount of time and there is less chance of cutting through the glass fibers along the edge. Use an open-coat paper of the best body-shop quality you can find. Work the plank or panel as a flat surface; avoid rounding the corners until you've finished sanding.

When you are happy with the flat surfaces, finish the edges with a soft block and fine bronze or steel wool. On these exposed corners you should try to leave as much epoxy built up as possible.

5-76

Sanding epoxy is another step that has a lot to do with how the finished kayak will look, but it also has a lot to do with the structural integrity of the boat. The surface must look smooth and fair, but we must be able to get it that way without cutting through the glass along the edges.

Control visually

Keep track of where you are by watching for these four visual stages: (1) gloss; (2) a balance of dull and gloss; (3) dull and flat – stop here; (4) glass threads exposed – you don't want to see this.

The idea is to bring all the high spots down to meet the low spots, then stop sanding. When you begin to sand, the sandpaper will scratch the gloss off the high points first. This tells you where the high points are because the low parts will still be shiny (5-76). In theory, sand until the shiny parts disappear. In practice, there may be some areas where getting rid of all the gloss will cut the glass, so use your discretion. Sand until the majority of the hull surface is dull and flat. Any gloss that remains should be cut with fine bronze or steel wool to remove any chance of amine blush and to give the finish something to hang on to.

Sanding Filler

If the surface has been filled, dampening it will let you know if all the filler has been cleaned up. Look for areas that are a lighter color; this will indicate where the filler is sealing up the grain. If you can live with it, great; if you can't, note the places that bother you and work them a little more after the surface has dried.

Go easy when sanding epoxy stains and out-of-place filler. There is a limit to how far you can go before hitting the glue line. If you are going for perfection, think lazy and tape well before filling.

PLYWOOD BOAT-BUILDING TECHNIQUES

Installing Trim

WITH THE HULL and deck fastened together, we have a shell that looks like a kayak. These next steps will make it function as one. Take the time to be happy with each step, because this is the stage at which the kayak really becomes your boat.

Building a Safe Kayak

To tailor the kayak for its anticipated use, many levels of safety can be added as it is being built. When you consider the harsh environment in which the kayak evolved, it is not surprising that it could be the safest small craft afloat – that is, after you manage to get in and get settled. Once he or she is seated, the paddler's weight is positioned below the waterline and acts as ballast, similar to the keel on a sailboat.

Safety begins with the cockpit. Unlike most small boats, the opening is just big enough to accommodate the paddler, thus

5-77

limiting how fast water can come aboard uninvited. Add a spray skirt and the craft is as buoyant as a duck. Add to this watertight bulkheads, a cockpit coaming to hold the spray skirt, waterproof hatches, seat and foot pegs plus a large number of optional rigging possibilities, and the kayak is ready for a serious expedition.

Ways to Divide Up the Space

The first level of protection deals with the "big wave comes over the deck and caves your skirt in" event or the "it's a hot, calm day and you are wearing a skirt but you pull it off the coaming to get a little air and some fool comes charging past on a jet ski and swamps you" event. There are a lot of ways water can get inside the kayak, turning a pleasant paddle into a not-so-pleasant one. A kayak hull full of water is extremely heavy. On a sand beach it's a chore for two people to empty one, but in open water it could be a disaster.

The least you must do is find a way to fill up most of the space in the kayak that is not being occupied by the paddler. This will limit the amount of water the hull can take on as well as provide buoyancy. The most common way to divide up the space in the hull is with bulkheads.

Air bags are a good alternative to installing bulkheads. Made of tough plastic, the bags are pushed up into the ends of the boat and inflated to fill the space. For the traveler, dual bags or dry bags packed with gear will perform the same function. This is a good route to take if you don't have the heart to cut a hole in your beautiful deck.

A sea sock is the next level of protection. It is a waterproof sock that the paddler's lower body slides into, with the top secured around the coaming beneath the spray skirt. Water coming into the cockpit is limited to the inside of the sock.

Motor Mounts

The seat and foot pegs provide another level of safety. When the occupant is locked between the seat back and the foot braces, the kayak becomes an extension of the body; in a sense, the paddler wears the boat. With practice, the boat will be where you expect it to be. Your positive attachment to the boat also effectively transforms into forward motion the energy produced by the paddle pulling against the water.

Deck Rigging

On deck are more safety features. One that all kayaks should have is something on the slippery bow and stern to grab on to easily. A rope loop or handle on each end will also help two people carry the boat without fear of dropping it. Add deck lines leading from bow and stern to the cockpit and there will be something to hang on to at any point along the length of the kayak. This line will also be available as a towline.

A method of securing gear on deck is the final way the builder can rig a kayak for safety. Elastic deck lines or tie-downs are used to hold extra paddles, maps, bilge pumps, paddle floats – in fact, anything light that might be needed in a hurry. Going offshore? Mount a compass on the foredeck to get you home when the fog rolls in.

Bulkheads

Bulkheads may be made from glass-reinforced plywood or a dense closed-cell foam such as Ethafoam (5-77). Foam set in a flexible bedding compound, such as Sikaflex 241 or 3M Fast Cure 5200, is the best choice because it allows the hull to absorb shock evenly. A rigid bulkhead in a monocoque structure is like an egg meeting the side of the frying pan. Whatever bulkhead material is used, it will have to be trimmed to fit the shape of the hull's interior. If the designer has not thoughtfully provided a template for the finished shape of the bulkhead, you will have to make a pattern.

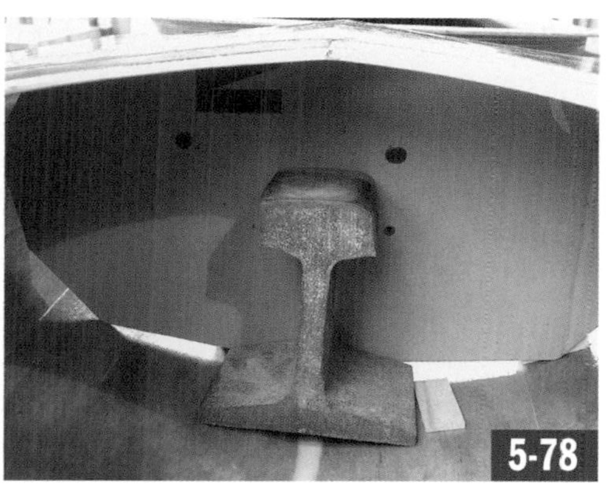
5-78

5-79

Making the Template

The first step in making a template is to set up a reference point for the position fore and aft. Without this reference, you could be fitting to a different place every time. We are using a small length of railroad track as a backstop (5-78), but a small cardboard box full of junk would work just as well.

Begin by making a rough pattern. Trim a piece of cardboard enough to fit it into the space up against the backstop.

Use a small block large enough to bridge the biggest gap in the rough pattern to scribe (trace) the true interior shape onto the cardboard (5-79). The shape drawn will be what you are looking for, minus the thickness of the scribing block.

Before cutting the shape in the bulkhead material, it might be worth the effort to take the template to another level just to be sure. Place the rough pattern over a fresh piece of cardboard and use the same scribe block to project the scribed line out to full size (5-80). Cut the cardboard to shape and check it in position. Adjust the shape by scribing with the spacer block or hot-gluing paper shims (sticky office notes also work if you are pushed for time).

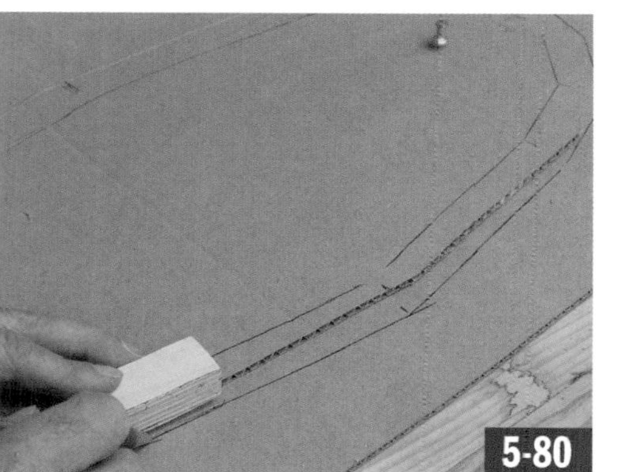
5-80

5-81

Cutting the Bulkhead

Secure the template to the bulkhead material (5-81) and trace the shape.

Cut the foam or plywood bulkhead to shape with a jigsaw or band saw. Since the shape is a series of straight lines, cutting by hand is also feasible.

If the template was accurate, there is no reason why the bulkhead should not slip right into position (5-77).

Installing a Foam Bulkhead

Install the bulkhead after the deck has been attached and the interior has been varnished. Choose a flexible adhesive-sealant, such as Sikaflex 241 or 3M Fast Cure 5200, that matches the foam color.

The bedding compound can be gunned around the edge of the foam bulkhead and spread into a cove shape with your finger, but the edge will not be as crisp as it could be. Consider putting the compound between the foam and the hull and finishing it off flush with the foam. Trim the foam back about 1/8 inch and in about 1/2 inch around the edges to make a space for the bedding compound. Save a little cleanup time by first masking the wood next to the edge of the bulkhead. Scrape the sealant off flush and remove the tape before it begins to cure.

Consider sealing the top edge with the kayak upside down on horses.

5-82

Installing a Rigid Bulkhead

Install this bulkhead before varnishing the interior and before the deck is glued into place (5-82). A plywood bulkhead is secured with a fillet and glass on one or both sides.

Fine-tune the shape of the bulkhead to fit comfortably and stay in position long enough to spot-glue it to the hull. A stick was clamped across our hull as a guide for fitting and gluing. The bulkhead forward of the cockpit was 5/16 inch short, so wedges were used under the sheer clamp to force it down to the bottom board. This kept the visible part looking tidy and we dealt with the missing part on top later.

Fillet both sides?

It is customary practice to fillet and tape both sides of a plywood bulkhead. Considering how this 40-pound craft will be used, we questioned the necessity of filleting both sides. Also, we don't mind eliminating unhealthy steps to get a better-looking job.

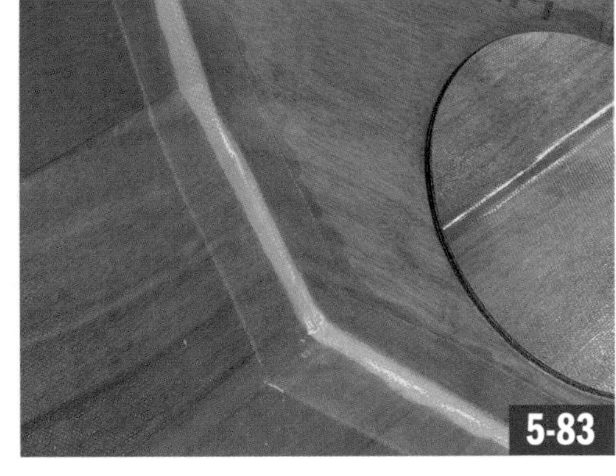

5-83

The most destructive stress on a bulkhead comes when the hull is twisted – something to be expected on a high-performance sailing dinghy but a remote possibility on most kayaks. When the hull and deck are bonded together and working in conjunction with the triangulation at the chines, the glass-reinforced plywood kayak is a very rigid structure.

Tack with a small fillet

Because the bulkheads were being held only by friction, we thought it safer to bond them in two operations rather than risk pushing the bulkhead out of position trying to do everything at once.

A small fillet was applied to each bulkhead on the cavity side of the hull. The objective was to tack the bulkhead to the hull in such a way that it would not have to be cleaned up before applying the primary fillet and tape. Using a syringe to force filler into the crack and to deposit enough for the fillet worked well and was neater than using a putty knife.

Glass the fillet

When the filler has kicked, apply more filler and shape it into a tidy fillet. Wet out the glass tape or bias-cut cloth on a piece of plastic and position the glass over the wet fillet (5-83). Press it down with the acid brush to work the air out. Add more epoxy only where needed. Refine the shape of the cove with a gloved finger.

Cockpit Coaming

The kayak coaming serves several important functions. Like an egg, the combined hull and deck unit is very strong until the continuous shell is broken. When holes are cut for cockpit and hatches, these breaks in the shell must be reinforced. An important feature of the cockpit coaming is the rim extending around the edge to capture the spray skirt. The coaming is made up of a rim and a spacer. The spacer raises the rim enough to capture the elastic cord sewn into the edge of the spray skirt. Structurally, the spacer is just a spacer. Its job is to maintain the space between the upper and lower strength layers, the rim and the deck. It is the neutral piece of the sandwich. The coaming also keeps small amounts of water from entering the kayak. A simple and effective method of constructing the coaming on homebuilt kayaks is to stack precut plywood layers to make up the spacer and the rim.

The rim is a very exposed part of the deck structure and will take the most stress and abuse, yet it needs to look light and remain attractive. It should be engineered to take

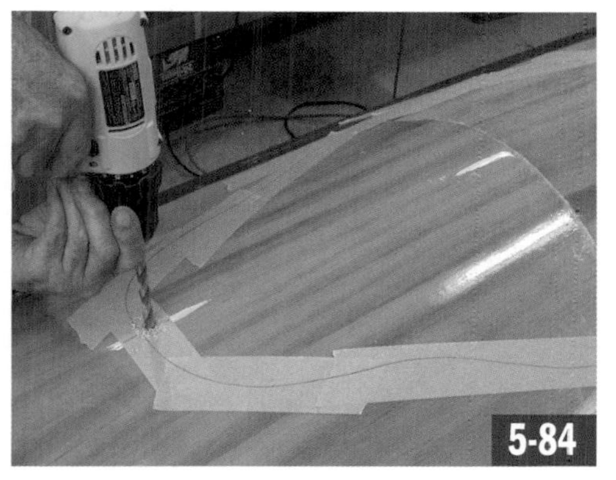

5-84

5-85

5-86

the standard abuse of paddling as well as panic situations when the skirt must be ripped off.

For the kit-builder, the choice of cockpit coamings is limited to the components supplied. The number of components to be assembled will depend on the amount of shape in the deck. The flat sections of a multi-paneled deck will generally accommodate a solid spacer; a tortured plywood deck or the compound curve of a strip-plank deck will require a laminated spacer.

Before you begin to build the coaming, there should be a cockpit-shaped hole in the deck. Kit deck components may be supplied with the exact opening already cut, an approximate opening cut, or no opening at all. There are good reasons for all of these variations; follow your kit instructions to prepare the opening.

Cutting the Opening

If the hole must be cut, information for the shape of the opening will be found on a full-size drawing, a template or a precut coaming spacer. Double-check the specifications for its placement on deck; once that hole is cut, it is cut.

Cover the path of the cut with masking tape to provide something to mark on and to protect the deck and the edge of the cut. Drill a hole inside the line big enough for the jigsaw blade (5-84).

Take your time making the cut. Trust the line and follow it; it is easier to make the first cut to the line than try to clean it up later. As the cut progresses, bridge the joint with tape to keep the cutout from falling into the hull (5-85). Peel off the tape when you have finished making the cut and clean up the shape with a rasp or a hard sanding block if needed. This opening will be the pattern for trimming the parts to come, so getting a smooth shape now will save correcting the same problem on the spacer and rim later.

Building a Solid Spacer

The Coho coaming is made up of one 3/4 x 3/4-inch spacer with a 1/2-inch-wide by 5/32-inch-thick rim per side. Fitting this spacer is a simple matter of lining it up with the opening and trimming it at the centerline (5-86).

Building a Laminated Spacer

The price of the Enterprise's nicely cambered strip-planked deck is having to laminate the components to fit the deck shape.

Our Enterprise kit included five precut pieces of 4 mm (5/32-inch) plywood for each side. They are cut oversized to allow for creep as they bend to the contour of the deck and to leave something for trimming at the centerline. After laminating, they are trimmed to fit the deck opening.

Because the glue may run down, begin by covering the area around the opening, top and side, with plastic packing tape. A piece of cardboard inside will catch any drips as well as provide something safe to pile clamps on.

Consider attaching clamping blocks, one for each clamp, under the deck with

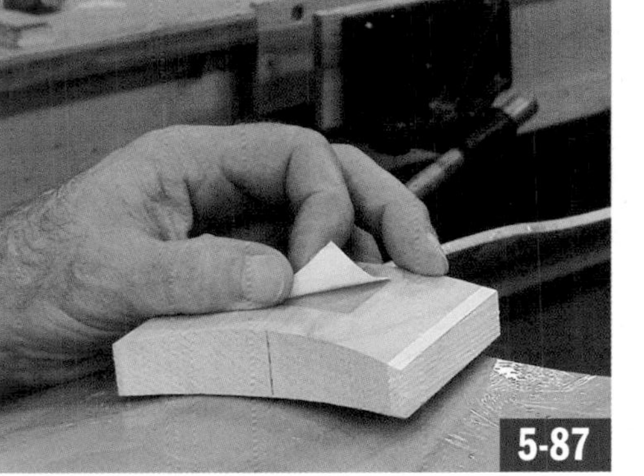

5-87

5-88

5-89

two-sided tape. They will be used a number of times before the coaming is finished, so they are well worth the effort.

Give some thought to the considerable stress that will be put on the deck centerline when the stack of plywood is bent from the centerline outward. To spread the stress over a larger area, shape a special 4 x 4 x 3/4-inch softwood clamp block to fit the deck contour on the centerline at both ends of the kayak (5-87).

Do a dry run to set up the clamps before mixing the glue. Stack the layers and hold them together with spring clamps. Begin clamping at the centerline and add clamps from both ends, working into the middle (5-88). If you have lots of clamps, consider clamping up the other side. Having one side in place is a good reference and guide for clamping up the mate; this is especially useful after the glue has been applied.

Spread the glue (mixed epoxy fortified with cotton fibers) over all the mating surfaces (5-89). Consider the space between the layers when deciding how thick to apply the glue. Stack the layers neatly as the glue is applied, then use two spring clamps to hold them together for positioning on the deck.

Begin with the laminations stacked vertically at the centerline of the deck. If they look like a staircase, you will waste a lot of the spacer width fitting it later.

The number of clamps you use will have a lot to do with how many you have (→ page 35). In general, the thinner the material, the closer together the clamps should be. Four

5-90

inches between clamps is the minimum; closer can only help (5-90).

C-clamps are preferred for their controlled clamping pressure and should be used at least at the centerline joint. Once the spacer is pulled down in a few places by C-clamps, filling in with less controllable clamps such as the spring-loaded variety is fine.

Clean up the squeezed-out glue on the outside and what you can get at on the inside without getting it on the clamps.

Ted was able to continue on the other side (5-91) because he has, as he puts it,

5-91

"a disgusting number of clamps to work with." To keep the sides of the pieces we were gluing from sticking together, a small piece of plastic film was used between the ends. If you have run out of clamps and are planning on putting in hatches, this would be a good time to get them started.

Building a Laminated Rim

The rim we are using on the Enterprise is made of two layers of 4 mm (5/32-inch) plywood laminated by using the same routine as for the spacer.

Building a Glass-Reinforced Rim

The Coho rim is made from one layer of 4 mm (5/32-inch) plywood that must be reinforced on both sides with a layer of glass cloth. The bottom of the rim is glassed before it is glued to the spacer, and the top after the coaming has been shaped.

The bottom of the rim is generally glassed with the same method used to glass the hull. However, the three applications of epoxy may be reduced to one application because the rim does not require a full buildup of epoxy. What we are doing is wetting out the glass just enough to saturate the cloth and wood surface, then molding it under moderate pressure into a thin, smooth surface.

The base can be any flat surface with a protective piece of plastic between it and the wet cloth. This could be plastic on the bench, with the rim and glass clamped upside down to the bench.

We are covering both components at one time and using one rim as the mold for the other side.

5-92

Our base is a piece of scrap plywood cut slightly larger than the rim (to make it easy to position the clamps) and covered with plastic. Position the first piece bottom side up on the base, wet out the wood and position the cloth in the wet epoxy. Apply just enough mixed epoxy to saturate the cloth, then lay a piece of plastic over the wet cloth. Apply the glass cloth to the bottom of the mate, turn it over and place the wet side down on the plastic directly over the first rim.

Be careful repositioning the wet glass after it has been stuck onto the plastic; it may shift and bunch up.

Clamping pressure should be firm enough to force the air out without squeezing out more epoxy than necessary (5-92).

If you can catch the green stage for removing the clamps, the epoxy and glass will cut cleanly with a sharp knife. At this stage of the cure, peel strength is minimal, meaning that it won't take much to peel the cloth off the wood. Cut with a motion that forces the cloth down into the wood.

Fitting Components on the Centerline

If the coaming components are joined in the middle, the next step will be to fit the pieces together on the centerline. This measuring and cutting routine will work for solid or laminated components, as well as the hatch trim.

The pieces for the solid Coho coaming spacers are cut to shape but need to be trimmed to make a clean joint at the centerline.

Begin by clamping the shaped spacer slightly (1/16 inch) inside the edge of the deck, just enough to clear all the way around yet leave a little insurance for adjusting the centerline cut. It is a lot easier to work the

CHEAP TRICK

Saw-blade joinery

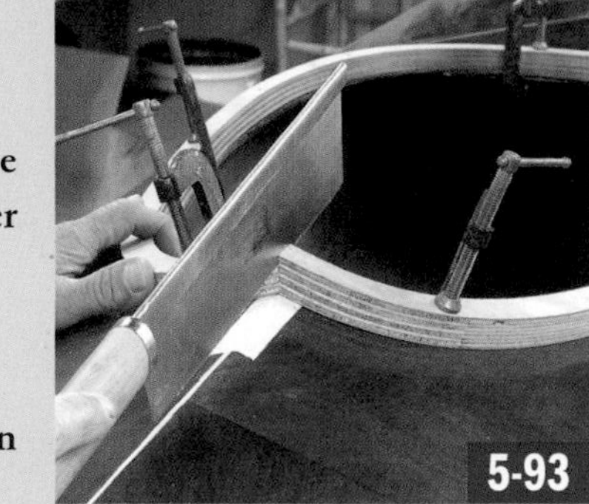
5-93

This trick is so easy, it is not just for the perfectionist. When the ends are fitting together as close as the thickness of a fine saw blade, clamp the ends together tightly and run the saw down between them (5-93). The saw will average out the space so that the ends make parallel lines. If more than one pass is needed, alternate ends so that they both come together at the same time. Do keep an eye on the deck.

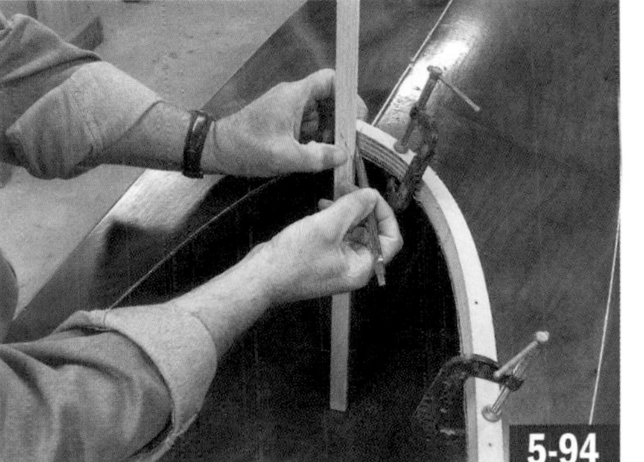

5-94

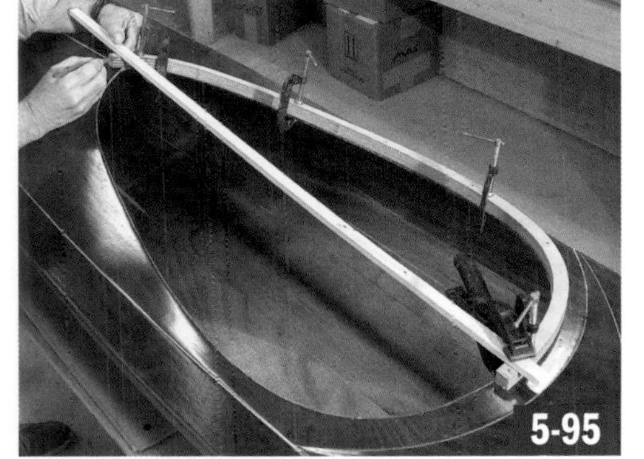

5-95

edge of the deck back to meet the spacer than to reshape the thick spacer to fit the deck. Also, the precut spacer is defining the shape of the opening; reshaping it will make it into a free-form shape that takes a lot of work to look intended and symmetrical.

Pick up the vertical angle with a straightedge projecting from the centerline of the bottom panels past the centerline of the deck. Draw a distinct line with a sharp pencil (5-94). Repeat at the bow.

Join these two points with a straightedge and draw the centerline on the top of the spacer (5-95).

Make the cut on the bench, cutting up to but not removing the line. Mark and cut the other side using the same method and clamp both pieces back into position. From this point on it is a good idea to keep one side clamped in position at all times as a reference. It will indicate the original position and ensure that you are fitting to the same place each time.

Protecting the Deck

Before setting up the next step, lay several layers of masking or duct tape over the centerline to show where the deck is. It won't stop the saw, but you should see the saw bite into the tape in time to stop before the next stroke; that's better than the first bite being the deck. If the ridge down the centerline is not too sharp, a thin piece of plastic will offer even more protection for the deck. Try material from a plastic bottle.

If the pencil was sharp and your saw followed the line, the ends should come together reasonably well. If the joint is open and needs major work, keep an eye on the amount of deck showing on the inside as you touch up this joint.

Taking a little bit off the end for a better fit is not as easy as cutting it right the first time. Try clamping it in the vise and use a rasp or hard sanding block to work the end. Watch for a crown developing in the middle, making the end dome-shaped; think about the middle and the edges should take care of themselves.

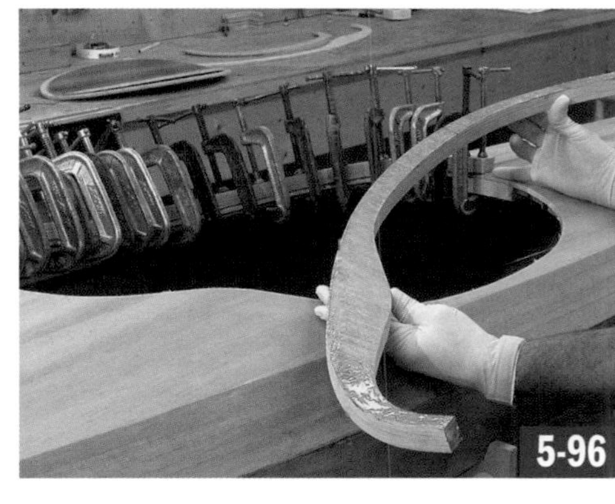

5-96

Trimming the Laminated Spacer and Rim

Fit the two components together at the centerline. Trace the deck opening onto the bottom of the spacers and trim to the line, 90 degrees to the bottom. Trace the outside shape, using the pattern and the trimmed edge as references, and trim to the line. Clean up the outside edge with a rasp or a hard sanding block, then sand.

Attaching the Spacer

This is a good time to sand the epoxy (→ page 97) on the deck. The surface needs to be roughed up before gluing anything on the deck, and the portion of the deck that will become the hatch cover will be awkward to sand after cutting. After sanding these areas there isn't much deck left to sand, but leave the outside edge for now; this area may get beaten up a bit when the guard is being shaped. After sanding, vacuum up the dust before it has a chance to spread.

If possible, leave one side of the spacer clamped in place as a guide for fitting its slippery mate (5-96). Having something to press against and to locate the fore and aft positions is a big help. Glue and, after clamping, pick up the squeezed-out glue around the outside edge with a putty knife and wipe clean with a rag dampened with lacquer thinner.

Reinforcing the Centerline Joint

The joint between the two coaming components should be locked together in some way. Unreinforced, the butt joint will be under more tension than it can handle if the loaded kayak is lifted up by the coaming at the centerline.

There are several ways to do this, some more graceful than others. One common method is to apply a glass patch over the joint on top of the rim. Although functional, it looks like a patch or an afterthought. If it is feathered in enough to look smooth, there will not be enough fiber left to do much good.

We suggest thinking along the lines of hiding some reinforcement between the spacer and the rim. This could be a strip of glass fiber or carbon fiber bridging the joint – strong but a little fussy to get it in and clamped up without the wet fibers sliding out of position.

Another way to reinforce the centerline joint is to build a spline joint. This is a simple method of tying the sides together that avoids messing with the slippery stuff. When the rim is glued over the top, it makes an attractive feature. For the spline, use a piece of easy-to-shape hardwood with the grain running across the joint (5-97).

5-97

5-98

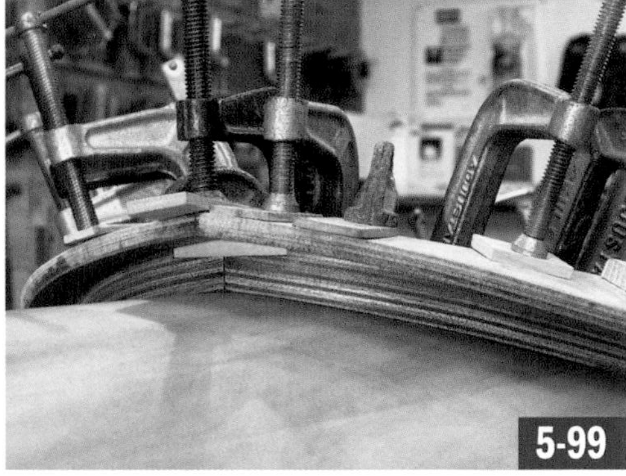
5-99

5-100

Cut the spline to length and use it as a pattern to mark the mortise with a knife. Try for a snug fit in the mortise with some extra wood at the top and ends; trim it to shape after the epoxy glue has cured.

Fitting and Trimming the Rim

Fit the rim at the centerline and clamp. Mark the opening on the bottom of the rim (5-98) and cut it to shape. Use the pattern and the cut edge as a reference to locate and mark the outside shape. Trim to the line and clean up the outside edge.

Do a dry fit and confirm that both sides meet on the same level (5-99); shaping to fit later could expose the glue line. If one side is higher than the other, trim off the top of the spacer to adjust.

Sealing the Spacer, Gluing on the Rim

With the rim in place, the outside edge of the spacer will be hard to get at, so this is a good time to make sure it is sealed. When the rim has been prepared for glue, saturate the edge of the spacer (5-100) with "super sealer" (→ page 135). After it soaks in, rub it

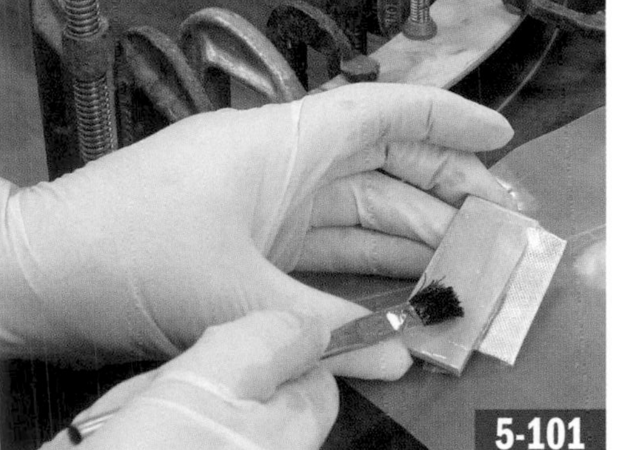

5-101

5-102

in with a Scotchbrite pad, wipe up all the excess, then glue on the rim.

After the clamps are settled, be sure to clean under the rim with a putty knife and a thinner-dampened rag; this is a miserable place to sand later.

Reinforcing the Joint between Rim Components

The joint in the overhanging portion of the rim should fit so that it looks like one piece, and the bottom surface should be tied together. Here is a way to accomplish these objectives in one shot.

5-103

5-104

Cover a thin clamp block with plastic tape and apply mixed epoxy to the block (5-101). Place the glass tape or cloth in the wet epoxy and add just enough epoxy to wet it out. Carefully place it under the joint and, with another plastic-covered block on top, clamp everything up snugly and allow the epoxy to cure (5-102).

Cleaning Up the Opening

Cleaning up the opening will go fast if the shape has been kept under control – the payoff for making each layer fit the previous and for cleaning up the wet glue. To refine

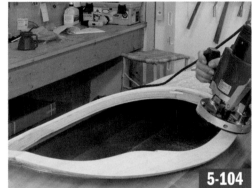

5-105

the shape, Ted used a length of 6-inch cardboard tube (used for casting concrete pillars) with a sheet of 80 grit sandpaper glued to one side (5-103). Its length allows it to be used on the diagonal to average out the high spots. Other useful tools for this job are a rasp, a spokeshave and a firm sanding block.

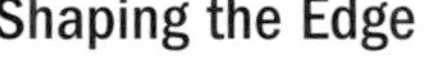

Shaping the Edge

If you are planning on using a router with a pilot bearing to shape the edge, it is important to refine the shape of the opening before rounding over the edge; the machine will simply follow the shape you have made (5-104). A ½-inch-radius round-over bit will remove a lot of weight and leaves a comfortable, safe edge. If you are shaping by hand, this ½-inch-radius round-over is a good shape to aim for. Sand with 120 grit paper on a firm, then a soft block. Dampen the surface. Sand it when dry with 180 or 220 grit and the coaming is ready for sealer.

Sealing the Wood

Super sealer (→ page 135) is the ideal

5-106

5-107

foundation for varnish on awkward shapes such as the coaming and hatch trim. After it soaks in, rub in the thinned-down mixed epoxy with a Scotchbrite pad (5-105), then buff the surface clean with a dry rag. When the epoxy has kicked, rub the surface down with 0000 bronze or steel wool and the surface is ready for varnish.

Reinforcing the Top of a Glass-Reinforced Rim

A rim made from a single layer of 4 mm (5/32-inch) plywood must be reinforced on the top as well as the bottom. This is a three-step application that will give us a thick, smooth coating.

Cut the 4- or 6-ounce glass cloth about 5 inches wide by the circumference of the opening. Since the glass is being cut from waste cloth, several pieces may be necessary; try to keep the joins to a minimum, because each will require careful feathering to blend in.

Protect the inside of the hull from the inevitable drips with polyethylene film or cardboard.

Apply the mixed epoxy to the coaming first; this will tack the cloth in place as it is fitted around this complex shape. Before fitting the cloth, clean off any drips that may be collecting along the bottom edge. Once the glass is on, drips on the wood will not be a problem, as the cloth will wick the epoxy away. Since the fore end is too complicated to follow with one piece, start the cloth here and let the ends overlap about an inch. The epoxy on the wood will begin to soak through, but it will take a little more to saturate all the glass. Use an acid brush to apply the optimum amount of epoxy, as it will be awkward to remove the excess later (5-106).

To keep the joints in the cloth under control, position and wet out one piece at a time (5-107). As it is wet out, there will be too much movement in the cloth to expect the ends not to move. Work the end of the cloth with a sponging motion to keep the cut edge from falling apart. When all the glass has been wet out, check it over with a small squeegee. The cloth should be saturated but not floating (5-108).

5-108

5-109

Trimming the Glass

Try to time trimming the cloth for early in the green stage. It will cut like hard cheese and may be trimmed close enough to eliminate most of the sanding.

When the epoxy is hard enough to sand, clean up the edges with sandpaper and give the glass a quick scuff. Vacuum up the dust and wipe the surface clean with a rag dampened with lacquer thinner or water.

Applying the Second Coat of Epoxy

Use an acid brush to apply a thin, even coat of mixed epoxy over the sanded coaming (5-109). Applying a thin coat to the thin edge will be tricky; use a fairly dry brush to apply just enough to cover it. Once the coaming is covered, the epoxy on the top surface will flow around the curve and drip off the bottom. This is good because we want a smooth film over the edge, and the drips on the bottom can be picked up later.

To pick up the epoxy when it starts to flow out, use a small squeegee and scrape the bottom of both edges. If you really don't like to sand, dampen the corner of a rag with lacquer thinner and carefully wipe the bottom clean. Do not scrape or wipe either of the vertical edges – they need all the epoxy they can get. There is a good chance that you will have to repeat this routine several times before the drips stop.

5-110

Applying the Third Coat of Epoxy

Apply the third coat using the same routine as for applying the second.

Hatches

The size and placement of hatches is a matter of personal preference; consider the smallest opening that will accommodate your needs. If you have not paddled long enough to know what will be most useful for you, consider adding hatches later when you are sure of what you need.

Hatch cover retainer systems range from simple shock-cord systems to blind fastener systems that would be at home on a submarine. Complexity does not seem to guarantee watertightness, so give your hatch cover some time to earn your confidence before you stow your unprotected sleeping bag.

When designing or building a hatch cover, here are a few things to watch for that will increase the odds of a watertight hatch.

Do what you must to keep the cover the same shape as the deck. The plywood deck panels hold a fair curve when all the pieces are fastened together as a unit. When a section of a stressed panel is removed, the piece is no longer restrained by the shape of the unit and will try to flatten out. Glassing both sides of the deck before cutting the hole will go a long way toward maintaining the cutout shape.

On kayaks with stressed plywood decks and no glass on the inside (for example, the Mill Creek), the cover is a separate piece of plywood that is cut larger than the hole so that the top overlaps the deck by the width of a gasket. The cover is shaped by gluing the plywood to cleats that restrain it in a shape close to that of the deck. These covers usually rely on thick gaskets to absorb discrepancy in the fit.

A gasket that is compressed consistently all around will have a better chance of keeping water out than one that is cranked down in some places and floating in others. Another potential problem with a thick gasket is that the unreinforced plywood buckles easily under the straps. The more tension on the strap, the more the cover will leak.

The secret to a hold-down system that works is in devising a way of directing downward pressure to the edge of a rigid cover to compress the gasket evenly. The crown of the foredeck is generally high enough to get enough triangulation out of straps fastened at the sheer to hold the hatch cover tight. The stern deck is usually flatter, making straps fastened at the sheer only marginally effective (5-110).

The Coho, which uses a flush cover, addresses the problem with a piece of half-round molding glued to the top edge of the cover; the strap passes over the molding, which transfers the pressure to the edge of the cover. A great deal of tension can be developed using the kit's cinch cams, which work in a similar way to a trucker's load binder.

The Enterprise uses a technique that takes the strap over the raised trim on the cover and down to deck level close to the cover.

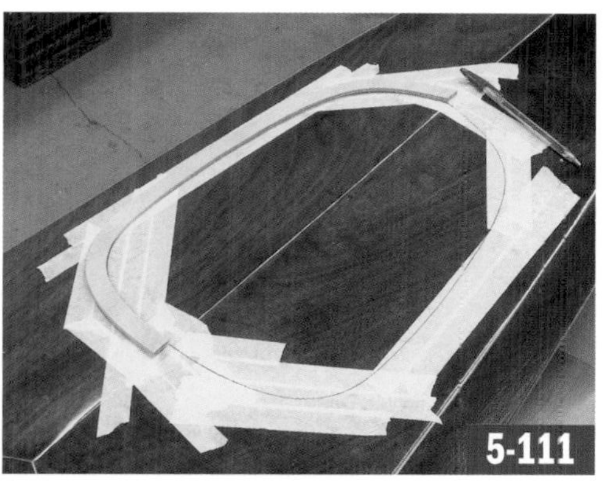

5-111

5-112

5-113

5-114

Snug pressure on the strap is sufficient to pull the edges of the cover down and compress the double gaskets.

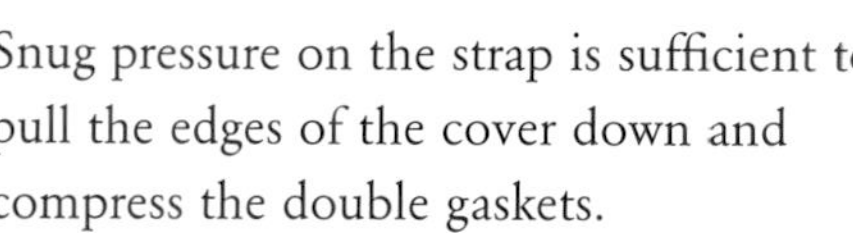

Cutting the Hole

If the hatch cover is to be a cutout piece of the deck, the method for cutting the hole will be the same whether the cover is flush or raised.

Mark the opening with a template taken from the plans or a shape of your own devising. Masking tape is good to draw on with a ballpoint pen and will protect the top edge of the deck when it is cut (5-111). To insure symmetry, use the same pattern for laying out both sides; flop it on the centerline.

To start the cut, drill a series of closely spaced 1/16-inch holes along the line (5-112).

Use a fine saw that has teeth cut to the end of the blade to work the series of holes into a slot big enough to get the jigsaw started (5-113). A hacksaw blade with very fine teeth will work well with masking or duct tape wrapped around the upper part of the blade. To avoid buckling, hold the blade so that it is cutting on the pull stroke.

Take your time making the cut, as you will have to live with it; this cut is one that you will see. Start with a sharp jigsaw blade that will cut the wood fibers cleanly rather than tearing them off (5-114). A blade that has teeth worn more on one side than the other is impossible to steer. Choose a blade that cuts on the upstroke so that any chip-out is on the top, where it will be covered by the coaming. A down-cutting blade could peel the glass from the plywood on the bottom of the deck.

The jigsaw will cut most aggressively when running at slow speed. For a cleaner cut, run it at a fast speed so that the teeth are making many small bites close together. If the machine has a variable speed, choose the fastest speed that does not compromise control.

Jigsaws are prone to steering themselves, particularly with a change in forward pressure on the blade. Keeping the feed rate consistent goes a long way toward keeping the cut smooth. Also, watch out for side pressure on the blade. This will also steer the blade and is tempting for making small corrections. The problem is that the instant the pressure changes, so does the direction, making the saw very unpredictable to control.

As the cut progresses, it is a good idea to add duct tape across the joint to hold the cover in position.

If the cut is less than perfect, you will want to do something about it. Keep in mind that what you do to the shape of the opening will affect the space between the deck and the cover; there is a limit to how much you can do to make the shape look nice without getting a sloppy fit. Clean up the opening in the deck first. After the lip has been installed is a good time to adjust the shape of the cover to follow that of the refined hole.

Use a firm curved sanding block to clean up the curves and a straighter one for the sides. Maintain a right angle between deck and edge so that the spacer and lip will fit cleanly.

Installing a Flush Hatch Cover

A flush hatch cover is the deck cutout supported by a lip. The lip consists of a spacer the thickness of the gasket and a rim glued to the underside of the deck.

Use the inside edge of the spacer as a pattern for the cutout. For a neat job, the tolerances must be quite close and the cut smooth. This isn't hard to do; just draw the outline crisply and accurately, trust the line and follow it with the jigsaw.

The spacer and rim may be glued in one shot if you are pushed for time. Several complications to anticipate include taming two slippery pieces under the deck, getting the clamps on and keeping the centerline joint tight. A bigger consideration is the visible joint between the deck edge and the spacer. It will be difficult to clean up this joint after the lip is glued in place. Being lazy, we have glued ours in two steps.

Fit the spacer and glue it using the same methods as for the cockpit coaming (→ page 106). Protect the top of the deck with clamp blocks (5-115).

5-115

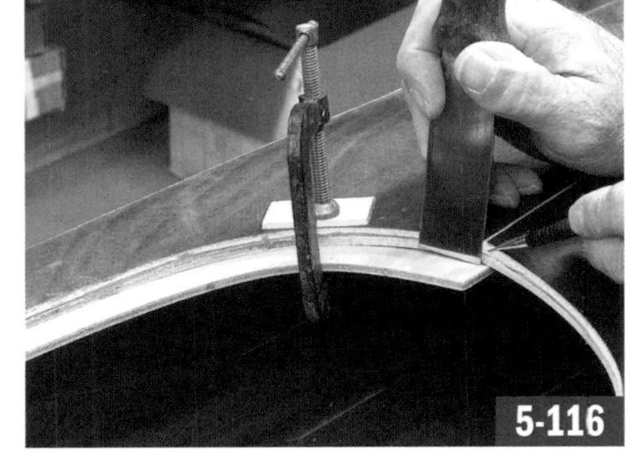
5-116

When the glue has set on the spacer, clean up the joint, maintaining a 90-degree angle to the deck; at this point it should look like one piece of 8 mm (5/16-inch) plywood.

The joint between the rim components is visible and should make a continuous shelf, so try to make it clean. Clamp one side of the rim into position, use a thin straightedge to project the centerline straight down to the rim and mark (5-116).

After marking the other end in the same manner, remove the piece to the bench and join the points with a straightedge; cut to the line. Mark and fit the other side using the same centerline and it should fit perfectly (5-117). There is a bit of latitude here for adjusting the fit; a little more overhang will not be noticeable.

5-117

When you are happy with the dry fit, make small reference marks at each end to help get the wet pieces back in the same position. Keeping one side clamped in position also makes a good reference. However, avoid drawing a strong pencil line around the perimeter, as it will remain visible and be very hard to remove later. Make a very light pencil line as a guide for applying the glue and make a point of washing it off with thinner when the glue is cleaned up.

Try to anticipate the amount of glue necessary, because cleaning up any excess blobs later will be tedious at best. A thinner-dampened rag around the end of a flat screwdriver will get into the corner; reach underneath to get the glue on the inside.

When the clamps (5-118) can be removed,

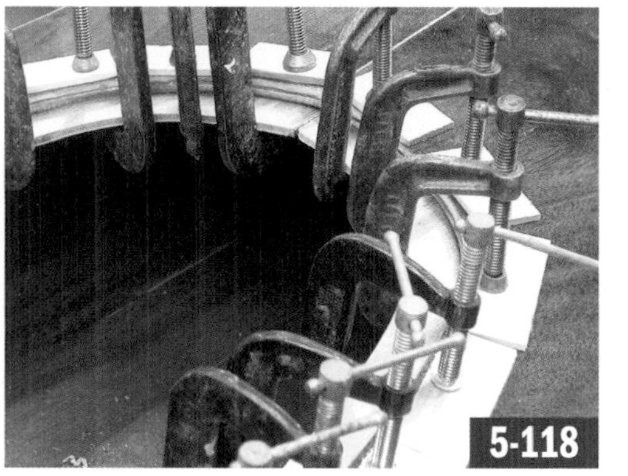
5-118

5-119

reinforce the joint on the bottom with glass tape (→ page 108).

Installing a Raised Hatch Cover

The Bear Mountain style of raised hatch cover was introduced in *KayakCraft* and has proven to be easy to install and very effective. It uses a cutout section of the deck with a rim to make the cover and a lip glued to the underside of the deck to support it. This makes it possible to install a double gasket, one on the cover and one on the lip. To create maximum downward pressure, the cover is held in place with straps anchored

5-120

to the deck close to the cover (5-119).

Use the deck as a mold for shaping the two plywood layers that make up the rim (5-120). By laminating it to shape beforehand, there is little chance that the rim will distort the cover.

When the glue has cured, clean up the edges and soften the top corners. Center the cover on the rim and draw a light pencil line around the edge of the cover. Use this line to show where to apply the glue (5-121) and for positioning the cover on the rim.

Plastic spring clamps are ideal for clamping the rim to the cover (5-122). The plastic jaws save fumbling with clamp blocks and they are fast to position. Clean up both sides of the cover; pick up all the squeezed-out glue with a putty knife and wipe the surfaces clean with a bit of lacquer thinner on a rag.

The lip is one layer of 4 mm (5/32-inch) plywood cut to the same shape as the rim. Do a dry fit and mark the area for glue coverage. Clamp blocks are important on the deck (5-123), but on the bottom of the

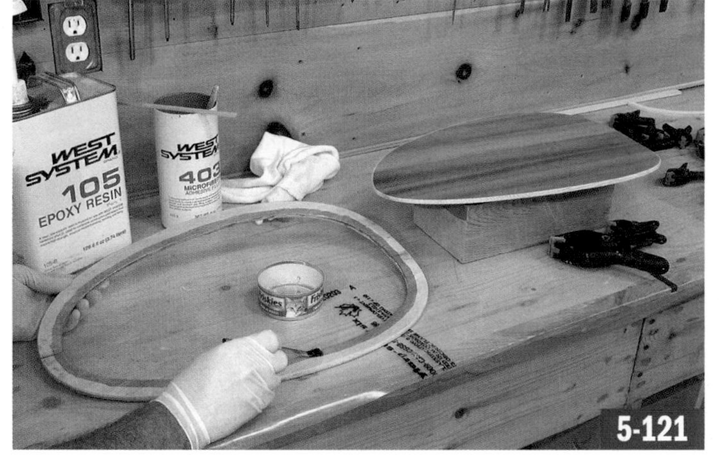

5-121

5-122

SAFETY TIP

A utility knife used with a steel straightedge makes a good job of cutting the rim components. That being said, holding the straightedge while cutting does leave the holding hand very exposed if anything shifts and the knife goes out of control. Clamping the straightedge to the work allows two hands on the knife. Using a fine pull saw to make this cut would be a safer bet.

5-123

5-124

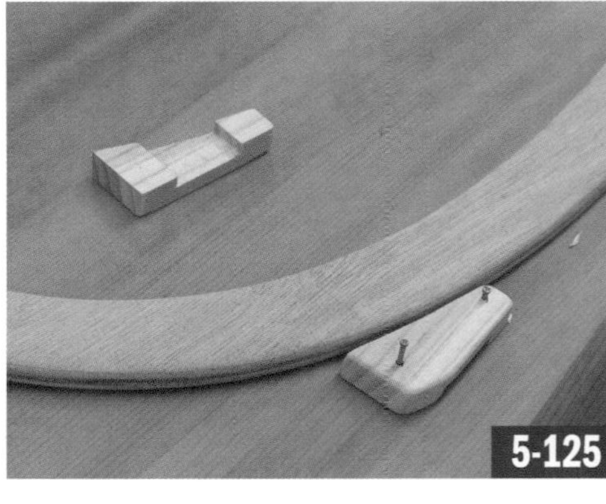

5-125

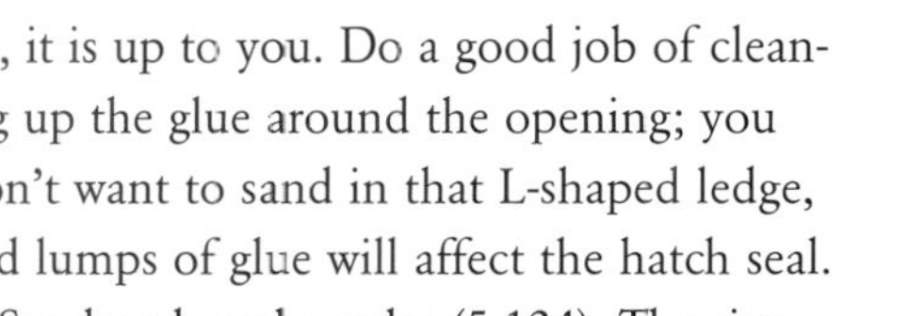

lip, it is up to you. Do a good job of cleaning up the glue around the opening; you won't want to sand in that L-shaped ledge, and lumps of glue will affect the hatch seal.

Sand and apply sealer (5-124). The rim and the lip are awkward shapes to seal using a buildup of mixed epoxy. Consider the super sealer used on the cockpit coaming.

Install the Strap Anchors

The strap anchor system for the Enterprise is one of Ted's better tricks, up there with the slit in the juice can for cleaning the squeegee. It is basically a U-shaped wooden cleat under which a loop in the strap can be slid and then held in place with a small brass pin. For varnishing and maintenance, the pin can be removed and the strap pulled out. The cleat is positioned about $3/16$ inch from the edge of the cover in order to direct the strap straight down (5-125).

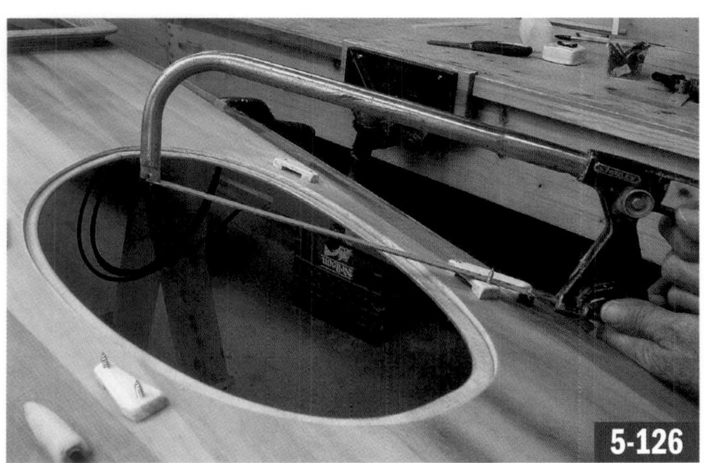

5-126

Put the cover in place and position the cleats, one for each end of each strap. For the strap to pull straight across, the side of the cleat that will capture the pin should be parallel to the centerline. Shape the side facing the cover to follow the contour of the cover. Confirm that both sides are parallel by measuring back from the stem. To relocate this position after the glue has been applied, drill a pilot hole through the cleat and the hull and drop in small finishing nails as a reference.

Apply the epoxy glue, position with the nails, and clamp. It is a good idea to coat the underside of the cleat with mixed epoxy when the glue is being applied as it will be very hard to seal this area later. Keep the nails in place until the clamp has been positioned; the cleat will want to skate when the clamp is tightened. Try spring clamps if you have them. After setting the clamp and removing the nails, clean up all the extra glue and wipe clean.

The cleat is well anchored to the epoxy-and-glass covering on the deck, but it might let go over time from the continuous upward pull of the straps. To tie the cleat to the inside of the deck, drill pilot holes from the outside down the path of the nails. From the inside, drive a #8 brass screw with a finishing washer through the deck and the cleat. Cut the screw off with a hacksaw (5-126) and file it flush. After sanding, the cleat will look like it is held with two polished brass pins. Seal the wooden cleats when convenient.

Steam-Bent Outer Stems

When wood is exposed to heat and moisture, it becomes pliable. Once softened, the fibers may be stretched and/or compressed into a new shape. Steam bending gets more complicated as the thickness of the wood increases. A piece of wood 1½ inches thick that has been bent into the shape of the Enterprise's stern stem will be 2 inches longer on the outside after bending. To keep it simple, cut the wood into thin laminations to minimize distortion. You can then get away with a very low-tech source of steam and a simple steam box and bending form (5-127).

Included in the Enterprise kit are three ⅛ x ⅝-inch hardwood strips for each stem. While the bow is an easy bend, the stern is very sharp, so three thin layers will have a better chance of bending successfully than one thick piece. A multilayered laminated piece is also less likely to straighten out.

In theory, the wood is steamed for one hour per inch of thickness. Since our laminations are ⅛ inch thick, we steamed them for about 10 minutes. The thin strips heat up quickly, but they also cool down quickly. Plan on completing the bend within 45 seconds of removing the strips from the steam.

The Steam Generator

Your steam generator can be anything you cobble together that will safely produce steam and direct it into an enclosure containing the wood. We are using a household kettle because they are readily available, but other possibilities may be kicking around the garage (a camp stove for heat, an old metal gas can for water). Modern kettles are equipped with a safety feature that shuts them off when the water reaches a boil. Your steam generator, though, needs a continuous boil. To fool your kettle's thermostat, remove the bottom and look for a little bimetal switch. The switch should be in the ON position. Use a little wooden wedge to hold it in this position and replace the bottom. Fill the kettle and it is ready to cook. Watch the water level; the heating element will self-destruct if the kettle boils dry.

SAFETY TIP

Steam is hot! Keep in mind that heat rises; don't get exposed body parts over the escaping steam. Wear leather gloves to handle the pipe and the wood.

The Steam Box

Once again look for a simple, cheap solution. All you need is a way of containing the steam around the wood. We are using a piece of 2-inch plastic pipe, but a cardboard mailing tube would hold together long enough to steam two little stems. As we have no desire to create a pressure vessel, a rag wrapped around the kettle spout and another in the top of the pipe is sufficient to contain the steam.

The Mold

The patterns for the bending molds are the stems. This means that the decision to use outside stems should be made before setting up the stems. Trace the outside shape of the stem onto ½-inch or ¾-inch board and cut to shape. Drill holes on about 2½-inch centers around the perimeter to accept the clamps (5-128). While three or four clamps are sufficient to hold the steamed laminations, clamp spacing should be as close as possible for gluing.

5-127

5-128

The Bend

The wood is going to cool fast, so being prepared is very important. Having a routine worked out in your mind beforehand will make it go smoothly. Adjust all the clamps and have them handy to the form. If possible, organize a helper to place the clamps.

Think lazy. Before putting the wood into the pipe, bind the three pieces together at one end with electrical tape. This will identify the end to begin the bend at and save having to fumble with three hot loose pieces. For the bow stem, and as a general rule, begin the bend at the end of the stem that will end up down inside the hull.

Place the taped end of the bundle on this end of the mold and immediately begin to tighten the clamp. Tighten only enough to hold the stem in place; any more than this will mash the softened wood. As soon as the clamp has been snugged up, begin the bend.

THINK LAZY

A square deal for laminations

It is a good idea to have all the layers of the stem in line to make up a clean rectangular section. Having to plane the edges square later will reduce the width and make it tricky to center on the hull. Lining the pieces up with your fingers will get glue on your gloves, which goes directly to the next clamp. Avoid this by using a clamp and a short clamp block on either side of the stem. The clamp will pull the laminations together square and the glue will be on the clamp blocks. After lining up the layers between the first two clamps, keep the blocks advancing ahead of the clamps as you work around the curve.

5-129

Use a strong, steady pressure to draw the wood around the form. It helps to place one hand firmly over the hardest part of the bend as you stretch the wood around the curve. Your speed should be slow enough that the wood fibers have time to adjust, but fast enough that the bend is made before the wood cools.

Because the bend in the stern stem was so tight and Ted was working alone, the wood was bent over the tight curve first, then clamped. This meant that the wood was as hot as possible for the hard bend.

Laminating the Pieces

Before gluing the pieces together, the wood needs time to dry. Twenty-four hours should be enough in a reasonably warm and dry environment. For faster drying, consider removing the pieces after the wood has cooled and started to take a set; tie the ends together to keep them from straightening out.

To prepare the mold for this step, cover its edge with plastic packing tape. Lay the pieces out in order on a piece of plastic film and apply to the mating surfaces a thin coat of mixed epoxy reinforced with cotton fibers. Press the bundle together before moving it to the mold.

Begin clamping at one end, placing the clamps on alternate sides of the mold (5-129). The purpose of this is to balance the pressure and keep the stem flat; the bonus is more room between the clamps for cleaning up the glue.

Pick up the excess glue with a putty knife and wipe it clean with a little lacquer thinner on a rag. If the pieces have been clamped up square and all the excess glue has been cleaned up, the stem is ready to be installed.

Guard

The guard is a thin ($^{1}/_{4}$- to $^{5}/_{16}$-inch) piece of hardwood that covers and protects the joint between hull and deck. The many profiles and widths seen in wooden kayaks are more a matter of taste than function. It doesn't take very much to cover the joint and protect the edge.

The Guard Debate

Whether to use a guard at all is a matter of debate. A valid point for the no-guard camp is the wisdom of keeping the kayak's surface as unobstructed as possible for safety reasons. Another important consideration is the fact that the closer the shape of the kayak is to a cylinder, the better it will roll.

Nevertheless, when you're coming alongside that concrete pier in the future, the edge joint is going to be the first point of contact. You don't have to doubt the integrity of this joint, but visually this situation will break your heart. A smooth impact (the corner of a well-worn wooden dock) on the edge will stretch the fibers; they may not break but the bond with the epoxy will be broken and the glass threads will appear white. Should the surface be coarse (a concrete pier), it will do all of the above as well as cut through the epoxy and glass threads. Not only has the appearance been damaged, but the integrity of the joint is also now in question. A repair will never bring the kayak back to how good it looked the first time around. But all boats are a compromise, so define your objectives and do it your way.

Making the Best of No Guard

Our Coho will probably not be used in harsh situations, so it is a reasonable gamble that it won't have to be repaired. The few dings it gets will be pleasant reminders of where they came from.

Painting a stripe along the sheer can make the kayak look good by drawing attention to the line of the sheer as well as hiding a lot of sins committed in joining the hull and deck. Paint will wear better than varnish and it hides damaged glass fibers. It is simple to mask the stripe and repaint it when necessary. Touching up a varnished edge, however, requires varnishing the whole kayak if a professional-looking repair is desired.

If you are building this kayak for serious use, contact with solid vertical things will happen. The least we suggest is covering the edge with plastic striping tape. Available in a variety of colors at automotive supply stores, it is cheap, reasonably tough and easy to repair or replace. To remove the tape, heat it slowly with a heat gun or hair drier and peel it off slowly enough to remove the glue with the tape. Removing the glue residue is a miserable job, but paint thinner and steel wool will help.

For tougher stick-on abrasion protection, consider automotive trim tape (the kind that goes across the door to protect it from other doors). Tougher but bulkier than striping tape, it comes in standard colors plus black and chrome.

On the high end of the tape scale is UHML low-friction tape. It is so tough and slippery that injurious things slide over it rather than cutting into it. The translucent white color is not offensive and enough of the surface is visible beneath to monitor for damage, something not possible with an opaque covering.

Wooden Guards

Unless an industrial-strength rigid tape such as automotive trim tape is used, adhesive tape edging does not supply much protection from a blow. Protective tape might take the edge off the bite, but you still have to deal with the bruise from the teeth. A good blow will cave in soft plywood or brittle filler and stretch the glass threads. When stretched enough, they will break.

For this level of protection, a longitudinal wooden trim piece may be installed flush to the edge of the deck. If it is made of hardwood of greater density than okume plywood, it will support more of an impact than the plywood will. As long as the edge is reinforced by the guard, the glass under it will not be stretched enough to break. Deciding on a size for the guard is a question of balancing appearance and functionality. Half-oval molding $1/4$ inch thick by $1/2$ inch high is enough protection for the average plywood kayak; any more than this is a personal design choice.

The Guard as Splash Rail

A larger guard extending out from the hull will function as a splash rail and help turn back some of the water before it comes over the deck. Sounds like a good idea, but kayaks were not meant to be dry. Splash rails on a kayak have a lot of strikes against them. Rails wide enough to do any good will add 2 inches to the width, which may or may not be a problem with your style of paddling. More important from a safety standpoint is how it affects the kayak's ability to roll.

Installing the Guard

Our $5/16$ x $3/4$-inch guards were prepared beforehand by gluing precut scarf joints and rounding the bottom outside corner. Shaping the lower corner is much faster and safer on the bench than after it has been installed.

5-130

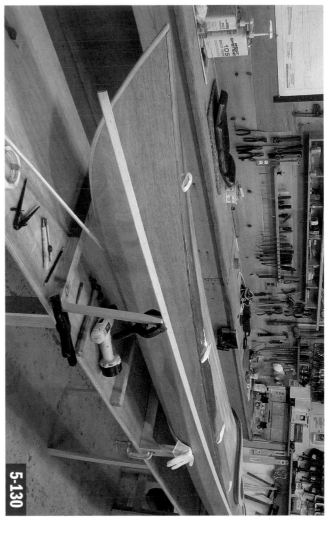

A dry run is a good idea to work out a routine and make sure the guard fits (5-130). If the deck is wider than the hull, it is easy to trim; if there is going to be a space between deck and guard, consider color-matching the glue. Fiber tape works well for the dry run. This is also a good time to mark where the fasteners will go. Keep in mind that there are screws under the guard and that the odds of hitting a few are good; consider marking their positions beforehand.

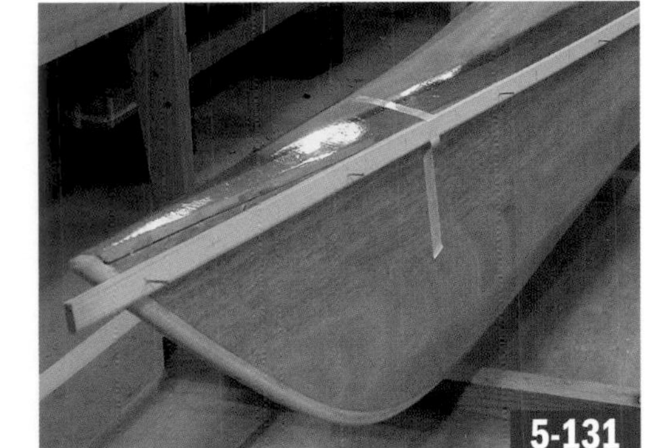

5-131

Although the guard will be attached to the kayak with epoxy glue, mechanical fasteners are useful for the initial clamping pressure. Ted used 3/4-inch 20-gauge brass finishing nails on 4-inch centers; they are much faster to use than screws and plugs yet retain the traditional look. Close spacing between the fasteners is necessary to keep waves from developing in the thin guard.

To begin, drill all the 5/64-inch pilot holes in the guard while it's on the bench. Tape the guard back onto the hull (5-131). Before drilling the pilot holes, line up the top of the guard with the surface of the deck or slightly above. It is easy to shape the guard down to the level of the deck, but there is nothing to work with if the deck is high. Drill 1/16-inch pilot holes into the hull every 12 inches and start installing the nails into the guard. Putting in the initial fasteners some distance apart will insure that the guard finds the fair curve.

5-132

Removing the guard completely will make it difficult to find the pilot holes again, so leave one end taped in place while you apply the glue and fasten the other end. Be generous with the glue; it is easier to scrape it off than pack it into a joint that is not full. After the glue has been applied and the first set of nails driven home on both ends, drill the missing pilot holes and drive in the remaining nails.

Check the joint between the deck and the guard to confirm that it is full of glue or slightly over-full for insurance. Pick up all the squeezed-out glue and wipe the surface clean.

5-133

5-134

Shaping the Guard

When the glue has cured, shape the top of the guard as an extension of the deck line. Remove the bulk of the wood with a block plane and finish with a cabinet scraper (5-132) or hard sanding block. Consider putting masking tape on the deck during the initial shaping and a temporary fence on the plane. The cabinet scraper works well because the wide blade keeps the wood coming down at the correct angle; when it reaches the epoxy, it scrapes it flat. After scraping, very little sanding is required to prepare for the varnish coat.

Complete the shaping step with 120 grit sandpaper on a hard block (5-133). You could do this step with the random orbital sander, but there is always a chance of cutting waves along the edge.

Round over the edge using long strokes with the block plane (5-134); keep an eye on the nails. Finish with a firm sanding block, raise the grain by dampening with water and finish with 180 or 220 grit sandpaper.

Retrofitting a Wooden Guard

A wooden guard could be installed after the kayak has been used long enough to determine the level of protection appropriate for the way you paddle. For the epoxy glue to hold, it is important to remove all of the old finish where the guard will go. To avoid refinishing the whole kayak, tape off the area covered by the guard and work clean. Another approach is to install the guard in a semi-adhesive flexible bedding such as Boatlife Life Caulk or 3M's 4200. It will save removing the old finish as well as making the guard more repairable.

Fitting Out

Seat

The seat is another area where the kayak builder has a number of choices. Seats range from homemade and manufactured versions to hybrids made by combining available components. The Mill Creek seat is similar to a traditional wooden double-paddle canoe seat, while the Enterprise seat components come from the factory (5-135). The Coho combines a deluxe Therm-a-Rest Sport Seat and a homemade plastic back

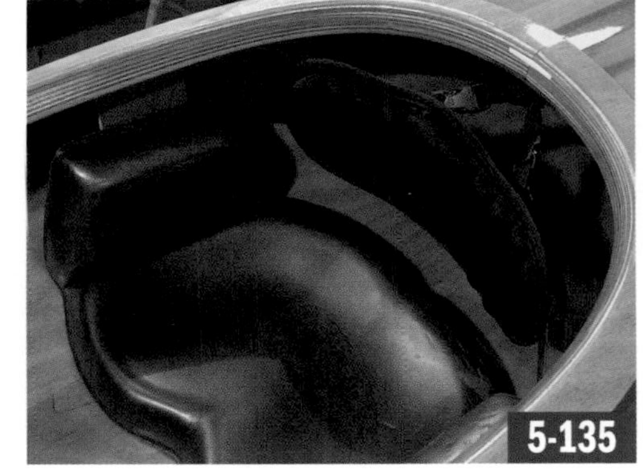

5-135

5-136

5-138

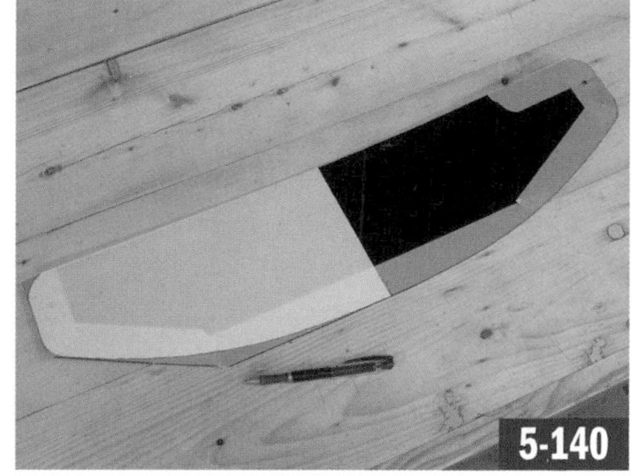

5-140

5-137

5-139

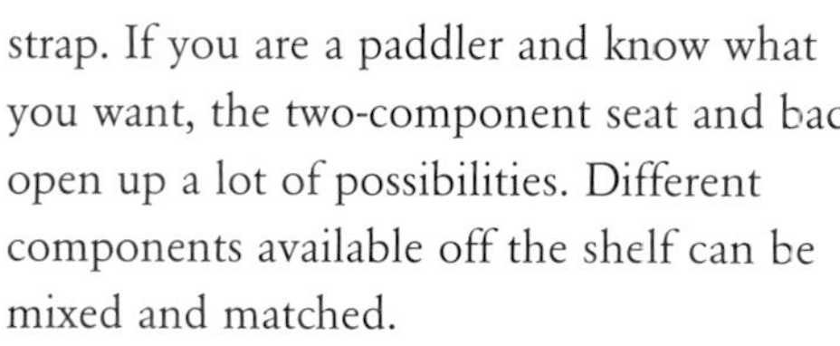

strap. If you are a paddler and know what you want, the two-component seat and back open up a lot of possibilities. Different components available off the shelf can be mixed and matched.

The Coho-style Seat

The seat included in our Coho kit is a simple system consisting of a high-density black plastic back strap and a Therm-a-Rest Sport Seat pad (5-136). The seat is secured to the bottom of the kayak with Velcro – a hook-and-loop fastener – installed after the cockpit has been varnished.

The manual directs us to drill holes for the bolts in the back strap (5-137) and to glue on the foam pad. However, although functional, this rectangular piece of plastic with the corners cut off is not quite ready for the kayak. Here's how to shape the top edge into a gentle arch that will blend into the curve of the deck, and how to transform its scratched-up glossy surface into a more forgiving matte finish.

Cover the surface to be reworked with masking tape and find the centerline. Use a flexible batten to draw a pleasing shape across one half of the top (5-138).

Add a little grace to the bottom by rounding off the corners. But keep an eye on the holes – they should have at least 3/4 inch of solid plastic around them. We have used a small yogurt container as a template for the corner (5-139), but look around the shop for a shape that seems right to you.

Cut the first side to shape using a jigsaw, band saw or pull saw, and refine the shape with a rasp. When you are happy with the outline, make a template from the finished side and flop it on the centerline to draw the other side (5-140). Cut the back strap to shape and file the edge smooth.

To finish, begin by rounding the edges with 180 grit sandpaper and finish with 220 grit. To take care of the scratched surface, rub it with 0000 steel wool to a soft matte finish; polish the edges at the same time.

When we put the back strap in position, there was a lot of tension on the bolts because the plastic wanted to bend into an arch. To relieve this pressure, we gave the strap a sharp bend about 1 1/2 inches in from the end. Clamp up to the bend line with a

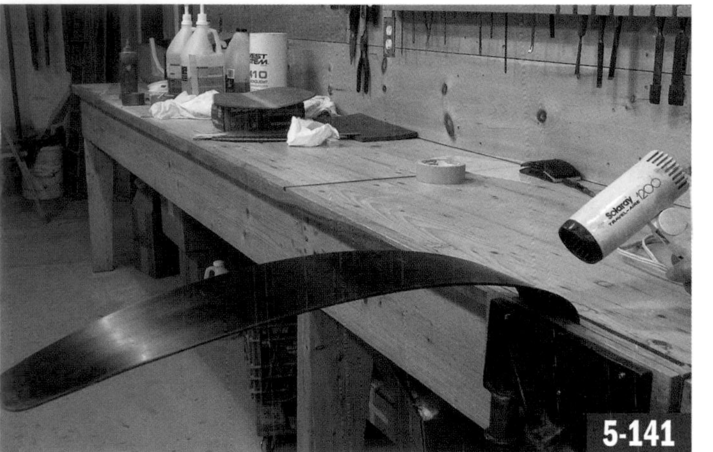
5-141

vise (5-141) or between two pieces of hardwood. Use a heat gun or hair drier to heat both sides of the plastic where the bend will be. When it's uncomfortably hot to the touch, press the strap down firmly, making a slight overbend. Hold on until it cools, and it should hold the crease.

A small eye pad is bolted to the back of the seat for adjusting the angle of the seat back. Countersink the heads on the inside so that they don't dig into your back. Go easy cutting the countersink – the plastic will cut much faster than wood.

5-142

Wait until this piece has been shaped before installing the foam padding; it will save unnecessary handling of the foam. Follow the instructions on the contact cement can for gluing the foam pad to the back.

Bolt the back strap into position after varnishing the kayak. Several washers between the back strap and the hip brace and one behind the nut will keep the back strap moving smoothly without wearing on the finish.

The Wooden Seat

The Mill Creek 13 came with pieces for a slat seat, with some assembly required. While it would save time to install a manufactured plastic seat, we think the wooden seat complements the traditional look of the boat. The trick here is to assemble all the pieces and have the chair come out flat and square. It's also a good idea to work clean, because sanding stray epoxy on all these pieces could go on forever – or at least it will seem like it.

To save time finishing, consider slightly rounding the edges and sanding the parts before assembling. You will do a better job in half the time.

The jig

To keep all the pieces under control and to prevent distortion while nailing on the slats, we cobbled up a simple jig to hold the seat base frame parallel and square (5-142). It will also keep the seat from bouncing around while nailing.

The instructions suggest nailing the ends of the slats to the side rails so that these precut pieces keep the sides in line. This is a good method if the seat is being nailed together free-form. Since the base of our seat is stabilized for assembly, we took the liberty of reducing the span between the side rails to 10 inches, making the jig 10 inches wide as well. The shorter span is more rugged while still complementing the traditional feel of the seat.

The jig begins with a piece of scrap 3/4-inch plywood ripped to the width of the space between the seat base rails. Screw this piece to the bench (or to another piece of scrap working surface) and position the base components on either side. To hold them in place, screw a block to the bench about 1/2 inch from the side of the seat support and fit a wedge into the space. Fasten the block with one screw so that it will pivot to find the angle of the wedge. Repeat on the other side of the seat. Use a square to confirm that the sides are parallel and the base is square.

To find the position of the first slat, we did a dry run back from the front edge to a position around the middle of the seat. A good reason for starting in the middle is to reduce the cumulative error to be expected if the slats are started at one end. Be certain that the first slat is perpendicular to the base, because the other slats will use this piece as a reference. As the slats are being

installed, it is a good idea to check occasionally with the square and adjust if necessary.

Assembling the seat

The seat is fastened with epoxy glue and 3/4-inch brass nails. The 1/4-inch space between the slats is maintained with two 1/4-inch plywood spacers. Pre-drilling the slats (using a 5/64-inch bit) will keep handling to a minimum after the glue is mixed and will be more accurate than drilling as the pieces are assembled. Find the centers on the first slat and use it as a pattern, transferring the line to the other slats. To mark in bunches, use the square to line up the end of the bunch and to project the line across to the other pieces. It is important to drill the pilot holes perpendicular, as the base is not very thick.

Mix up a small batch of epoxy glue reinforced with cotton fibers to a medium consistency. Keep in mind that the plywood base contains end grain and will absorb some of the epoxy as well. Apply the glue to the frame; it is fussy work to clean up the excess, and the cleaner we can keep the pieces, the faster the seat will be finished.

Position the slat in the glue, drill a 1/16-inch pilot hole into the base and nail the slat flush (5-143). It is a good idea to check the first slat with the square, as the slats to come will follow it.

You have a choice here between leaving the head of the nail flush or setting it below the surface and using a wood filler later. The brass nails do look good when shined up and leaving them saves a lot of filling and sanding time.

Our cleanup routine was to pick up most of the squeezed-out glue as the pieces were assembled. Try a slice of plastic squeegee just under 1/4 inch wide to get between the slats. After all the slats were installed, the wedges were released and the seat was turned over for access to the glue on the bottom. Finish cleaning with a bit of lacquer thinner on a rag. It is good idea to wedge the seat back into the jig until the glue cures.

Assembling the backrest

To make sure that the backrest fits exactly, start by bolting the back frame pieces to the seat base frame. Before bolting them together, place a washer between the components at the bored hole. This will help ensure that the moving pieces don't rub together when the back folds down. Consider making it a plastic washer to provide smooth action and really save the finish. A good source of this material is your recycling box.

To save modifying the jig as well as avoid accidental migration of parts, we left the back frame bolted into position for assembly. Set the back in the jig (the seat will be horizontal) and block the ends of the frame so that it is parallel.

Do a dry run of the assembly to find a place to start, then assemble the slats using the same routine as for the seat. After the back is assembled and cleaned up, check that it is not twisted. When the back is folded down to the seat, the back should fit on both ends. If it doesn't, try securing the back with clamps or tape so that it does fit; there is a good chance it will hold this shape after the glue cures.

THINK LAZY

Clamp a guide block to the end of the slat and parallel to the base. When the slats are pressed up to this guide and the 1/4-inch spacers, all that needs to be done is just glue, drill and nail.

Applying the finish

Trying for a neat varnish or paint finish on all these little pieces could be the most frustrating part of the whole project. The number of sides to cover evenly and the corners to work around are endless. It doesn't end there, either; someday it will have to be refinished.

Consider a penetrating oil finish. Look for an oil that will be durable in an outdoor environment and is easy to apply and maintain. Oil finishes sold for wood siding and decks are a good possibility, and they are available in various colors. Marine products

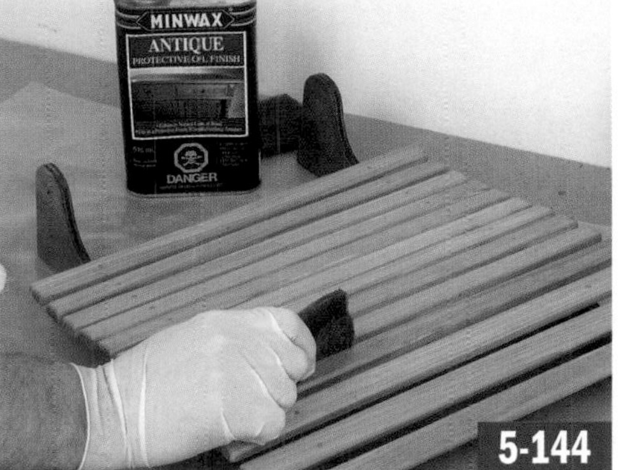

5-144

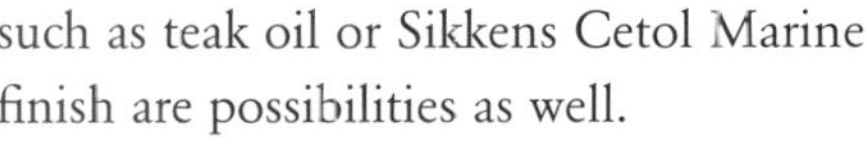

such as teak oil or Sikkens Cetol Marine finish are possibilities as well.

To apply, brush on a generous coat, paying attention to the thirsty end grain. Keep feeding the dry places until they stay shiny. Using an abrasive pad, rub the oil in aggressively to warm the oil and force it in deep (5-144). Wipe off the excess with a clean, dry cloth. If the oil is getting sticky, add a few drops of paint thinner to the rag. Let it dry between coats; two coats are functional, three will make you look good.

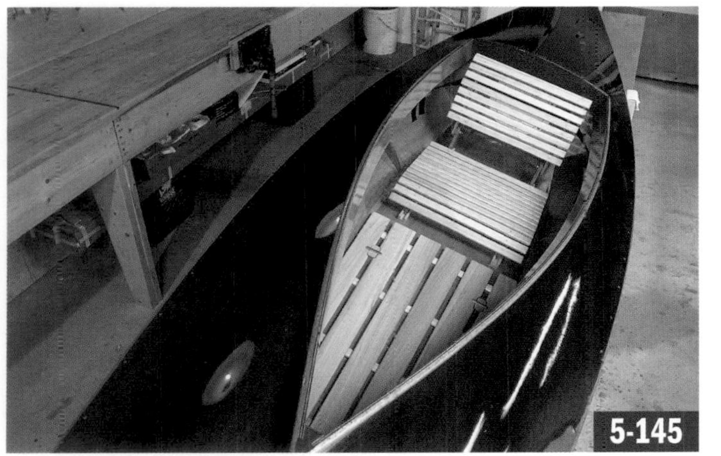

5-145

5-146

Installing the seat

This type of seat could be permanently attached (5-145), but it is convenient to be able to remove it for cleaning the interior and for transport. One way to stabilize the seat is with a pair of tracks that will fit the seat frame (5-146). The tracks are 1½ inches wide by ⅝ inch thick by about 3 inches longer than the seat frame. Cut a slot (dado) the length of the top that will fit around the seat frame. The slot will position the seat on the centerline and allow the seat to be moved fore and aft to adjust the trim.

Positioning the tracks and clamping them is convenient with the seat sitting in the track. Do a dry run to find the track position, then mark the kayak bottom with masking tape. Remove the seat and tracks, apply epoxy glue to the bottom of the track and replace according to the tape marks. Set the seat in the track and add weights for clamping pressure (5-147). Clean up all the excess glue you can get at with the seat in place. If the seat is removed when the epoxy glue has just hit the green stage, the stray glue you couldn't get at will be easy to scrape clean.

5-147

Foot Pegs

Foot pegs, braces or pedals work in conjunction with the seat to anchor your body in the kayak. To be useful, they must be adjustable. Homemade foot braces are a consideration for the plans-builder, but the manufactured foot-brace-and-slider units used in mass-produced kayaks are convenient, available and inexpensive. The foot pad adjusts fore and aft on a track about 16 inches long. The track may also be used with a slider component to control a rudder. Installation is basically the same.

Do a dry fit at the most convenient time during the building process. Although it is possible to do this after the kayak is finished, you will be working in the dark, as well as inviting a possibly damaged finish. A good time to dry-fit the foot braces is after the hull has been glassed inside.

Fore and Aft Position

The position for the foot peg will be given as a distance from the back of the seat. If specifications are not included in the instructions, it is not a hard number to come up with. Sit on the floor with your back against the wall and your knees slightly bent. The distance from the bottom of your foot to the wall will be the distance from the kayak seat back to the middle of the track. This will give you some adjustment both ways as well as accommodate longer or shorter legs.

The distance from the top edge of the hull is not a standard number because it relates to the depth of the hull and the shape of the deck; get this from the plans or instructions. One easy way to ensure that your holes are drilled in the right position is to put some masking tape down and mark the positions on the outside of the hull (5-148). Drill slowly to avoid tear-out on the inside; holding a block of wood against the other side of the hull will help.

Installation

Do the final installation after the kayak has been painted or varnished. To make a watertight fit, the Coho kit includes rubber O-rings for the screws. This is a great idea. It is quick and neat, yet allows the screws to be removed for refinishing. In the absence of O-rings, silicone sealer will make the fasteners watertight.

A Graceful Attachment

Attaching the track to the hull with large screws is quick but it does leave the big screw heads exposed on the outside of the hull. While we might expect to see them on a production boat, for some people the screws will look out of place on their handmade kayak.

If the screw heads are going to bother you, consider gluing wooden cleats to the inside of the hull and screwing the track to them. The most convenient time to install the cleats is when the inside of the hull is complete and before attaching the deck.

A Blind Attachment

Lay out the position of the seat and the track for the foot pegs. The dimensions given on the Enterprise plans are for an average adult; adjust from there for tall and short.

The little L-jigs used to plank the Enterprise will come in handy here. Use them to hold the track while finding the position (5-149), as well as to fit and glue the mounting cleats.

The Enterprise kit includes a pair of cleats $1\frac{1}{4}$ inches wide by $\frac{5}{8}$ inch deep by 16 inches long (the length of the track). If cleats are not included in your kit and you choose to use this method, use a light hardwood (mahogany or cherry) that is easy to shape and will hold the screws. It is important to shape the back of the cleat to fit the side of the hull; when clamped, the hull will bend to take the shape of the cleat, resulting in a flat spot if the cleat is not shaped. In case it is not a perfect fit, use plenty of full-bodied glue and clamp only at the ends. When the clamps are set, remove the L-jigs, clean up the glue and wipe clean (5-150).

5-148

5-149

Before installing the stock track, it will have to be modified for fastening from the inside. Drill and countersink for three #8 x $\frac{3}{4}$-inch flat-head brass screws. If you do a dry run with the screws, the track will be

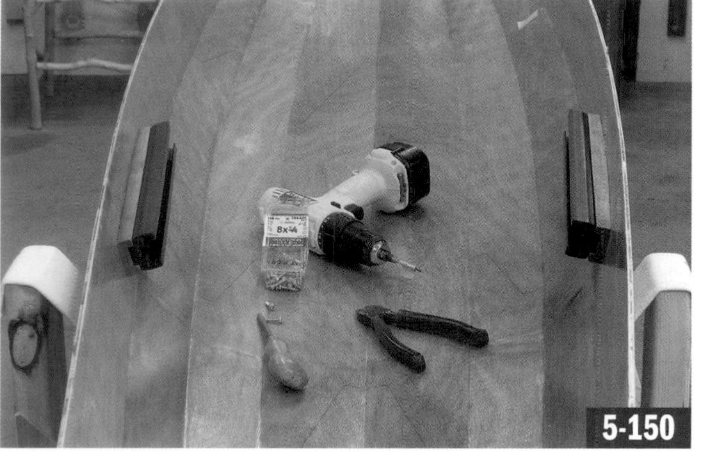
5-150

easy to put back together when the deck is in place. In our case it looked like the screws might be slightly long, so rather than be surprised by seeing it come out the other side, we cut the tip off the screw instead of finding out for sure. Identify the tracks when you take them off; the random pattern of the new holes will mean there is only one way the screws will fit when you put the tracks back on after finishing.

Sliding Foot Pedals

For a sliding foot pedal system used to control a rudder, there is one last detail to prepare. You will need to devise a system to restrain the sliding foot pegs and to keep tension on the rudder linkage. A common way of doing this is to attach a bungee to the slider and anchor it at some point forward. The sheer clamp is convenient if the bungee is anchored far enough forward that it is pulling out more than up. If a ridged bulkhead is used forward, that would be a very good anchor point. The downside of this simple system is that depressing the pedal to turn means stretching the bungee on the other side. Although this may be a comfortable pressure and may help with doing a brace, it is an added strain on the steering linkage and the rudder.

Another method worth exploring is to join the two pedals together with a cable or rope running through turning blocks anchored about 10 inches forward of the end of the track. Splice a length of bungee cord in the middle to keep tension on the linkage and to absorb unplanned shocks. The advantage of this method is that the pedals work together rather than against each other.

Hip Braces

The purpose of hip braces is to position and stabilize the paddler in the center of the kayak. Anything that anchors the body to the kayak contributes to forward motion, balance and control. The hip brace on the Coho is also used to anchor the seat back assembly.

The material supplied for the Coho hip braces was 4 mm ($5/32$-inch) plywood, which needs to be reinforced with glass cloth and epoxy to be strong enough. To save a little time, we used a scrap piece of $1/4$-inch 5-ply that had been sealed with epoxy on both sides.

The trick to fitting and attaching these pieces is to build a series of references. Without these control points, the pieces will be difficult to fit. Our first reference was given in the instructions as 8 inches forward of the aft end of the cockpit coaming. Clamp a straightedge across the cockpit as specified and check that it is perpendicular to the centerline (5-151). We measured from the outside of the rim to the aft edge of the rim centerline joint.

5-151

Locate the Lower Brace Position

The brace should be positioned plumb and parallel to the centerline. Find this position by projecting down from the edge of the coaming (5-152). Adjust the arm of the combination square so it just touches the inside of the hull. We took the liberty of setting the brace just under rather than flush to the edge of the coaming as suggested. This strikes a balance between gracefully hiding the joint and having it out far enough that the seat back does not foul the coaming. A distance of $5/16$ inch looked about right; it was projected out past the end of the square to become our corner mark.

5-152

5-153

Make a Spacer

A spacer is a useful tool for this installation. Cut to a length that is twice the distance from the corner mark to the centerline, it will give the position of the brace on the other side. If the ends are cut square, they will act as guides to keep the braces parallel to the centerline. Clamping pressure for gluing will be created by the spacer and the braces wedged together under the deck.

To find the length, begin by locating the midpoint on the straightedge and position another straightedge from that point to the centerline of the bottom panels. Now measure out horizontally from the corner mark to the centerline; double the distance and you have the length of the spacer.

Cut the spacer to length and mark a centerline across the top and down the sides. Use this line to confirm that it is positioned over the hull centerline. Cover the ends with plastic packaging tape before gluing. Position it on the mark and perpendicular to the centerline, and stabilize (5-153).

Fit the Brace

With a known position for both top and bottom, cutting to length and beveling the ends of the brace to fit the bottom are quite straightforward. Stand the brace in position and scribe a line across the top of the spacer to pick up the bottom angle. After cutting, put it back in position and mark the bevel to the side of the hull. Shape the brace to fit with a block plane or hard sanding block. When you are happy with the fit, use a short straightedge to project the bottom of the deck out to the sides of the brace; mark both sides. Cut and shape the brace to fit. Keeping the fit snug will help hold the pieces tight for gluing.

Glue

In order to survive the anticipated stresses, the ends of each brace will be filleted and reinforced with glass fiber. Since these joints were going to be visible, we broke down the installation into three careful steps. First, apply enough epoxy glue to the ends to tack the brace to the hull and deck. Next, remove the spacer when the glue has cured and fillet and glass the bottom joint (→ page 79). Finally, turn the kayak upside down on horses and apply the fillet and glass to the top. Trying to do this operation without the aid of gravity is bound to end in grief.

Rudder

We are not going to get into the debate of whether or not a kayak needs a rudder. If you are sure you need one, maybe you do. Kayak rudders are a modern invention; the aboriginal kayak was controlled through a combination of hull shape and skill with the paddle. Contemporary kayaks are no different. Nevertheless, rudders will compensate to some degree for undeveloped skill as well as a poor hull shape. (Notice how many bottom-of-the-line plastic kayaks come with rudders as standard equipment.) Be sure you need one before deciding to put up with mushy foot pegs and more rigging to install and maintain. The home builder also has the option of building in a retractable skeg that will either pivot like a centerboard or slide up and down like a dagger board.

Most builders will choose to install a manufactured rudder system, but designing and building your own is not out of the question. The major components are the rudder assembly, a foot-control system and linkage in between.

A rudder consists of a blade, a mechanism for raising and lowering the blade and a yoke for turning it. The rudder is generally

5-154

5-155

5-156

controlled through an adjustable foot-peg assembly sliding on a track. Because this assembly is a source of mushy foot support and undesirable stress on the steering system, kayak designers divide this setup into two separate components: a toe-operated tiller and a push/pull mechanism much like the gas pedal in a car. The linkage is most often light stainless steel aircraft cable.

Rudders can be hung on an external mount (gudgeon) or in the end-pour style, a hole for the pin (pintle) is drilled in the end of the kayak. The pintle we used on the Enterprise has a base that fastens to the deck and a sleeve to capture the pintle. However, the type that fits around the end of a plumb stem is worth considering because it is simpler to install. Mounting systems require some modification to the stern, so the time to begin installation is before the hull and deck have been glued together. If you will possibly be installing a rudder in the future, consider making the modifications under the deck during construction. Except for the stern mount, the components can be put together from the outside through the stern hatch.

Positioning the Pintle

Position the pintle so that the rudder blade will be plumb to the centerline of the hull. In the raised position, the blade should stop just above the deck (5-154). If it stops too high, the catch block must be raised up high to meet it. If it is too low, the blade will chop into the deck if it misses the catch block. To find the correct height, fit the catch block (5-155) to the deck first, then fit the rudder to the block and the pintle to the rudder.

The Cable Path

Put the rudder components together and install the cable guides while you have access to both sides of the deck. The cables go through the top of the deck at some point and travel under the deck to the sliding foot pegs. Under the deck, each cable will travel through a plastic tube that acts as a guide, keeps water from entering the sealed compartment and protects the cable from snagging on gear.

When deciding on where the cable will enter the deck and the path it will take under the deck, try for the straightest line possible between the rudder and the foot pegs. Changing direction will increase friction and contribute to mushy foot pegs.

Begin by hanging the rudder and securing it on the centerline. Tie some light line to the cable holes in the rudder yoke and lead the lines forward toward the foot pegs; knowing where the cables would like to go is a good place to start. In this case, a hole beside the hatch strap anchor would have the cable coming out beside the sheer clamp, which is ideal (5-156).

The next challenge is how to get the cable tube through the deck and anchor it. The tube can be brought through the sheer clamps or a block on the underside of the deck, with the tube cut flush to the deck surface. This looks neat in the beginning, but at some point the cable will wear through the edge of the plastic tube and start cutting into the deck. A fairlead will leave some hardwood under the tube to keep the cable off the deck plus it solves the big problem of drilling a low-angle hole safely through your beautiful deck.

Making and Installing Fairleads

Each fairlead begins as a piece of 3/4-inch hardwood dowel about 4 inches long. Drill a 1/4-inch hole (sized to fit the tube) down the middle. If you are doing this with a hand drill, clamp the dowel in a vise and mark the center with a punch, have a helper stand back to line up the drill perpendicular to the end of the dowel, then drill halfway through; turn the dowel and finish from the other end. Cut the dowel diagonally from end to end, leaving about 1/8 inch solid wood under the hole at one end, tapering down to a point at the other (5-157). For a clean fit, tape some 120 grit sandpaper to the deck and work the fairlead over it until

5-157

5-158

it fits the camber of the deck.

Do a dry run to set up some clamping guides and to work out a clamping routine. The fairlead is an awkward shape to clamp, but it needs only enough pressure to stabilize it until the glue kicks. A bridge arrangement (5-158) worked just fine for us and it also provided good access for cleaning up the glue.

Drilling Holes for the Cable Guides

This is where our fairlead trick really shines. We now have two bushings to guide the bit as we drill holes through the deck. It will take a 6-inch-long bit to make it all the way through (5-159). For a clean exit, keep the bit spinning fast and feed it slowly. Try to anticipate when the bit will break through; really lighten up on the pressure at that point to keep the hole coming out straight. Clamping a block over where the drill will exit will also help prevent tear-out.

5-159

5-160

Installing the Cable Guides

We set our cable guides in epoxy mostly because it was available and fast; however, a flexible bedding compound might be more compatible with the plastic tube (5-160).

Begin by saturating the inside of the hole with unthickened mixed epoxy, then add some filler to the epoxy and work it into the hole. It is a good idea to plug up the end of the tube before inserting it, for obvious reasons. Insert the tube into the hole and far enough through to leave about 1 inch sticking out the other side. Clamp the tube to the sheer clamp, then build up around the

5-161

opening with filler. Clean up the glue that has been pushed outside through the hole and wipe clean. When the filler is hard, trim the end of the tube with a sharp knife.

Hanging the Cable Tube

The sheer clamp is a convenient place to hang the tube. Molded plastic clips are available for this size of tube, but we made ours from ½-inch copper pipe strapping (5-161). Use wire cutters to cut it to length and trim the corners. Fasten with a #6 x ½-inch roundhead brass screw.

For a kayak without a sheer clamp, attaching the cable guide can be as simple as molding a blob of thick filleting material over the guide to stabilize it.

Completing the Installation

Rudder kits usually come with all the bits and pieces needed to complete the installation.

Consider making the connection between the rudder and the cable with a small stainless steel shackle. This will allow the rudder

5-162

5-163

to be removed easily.

Begin by making the cable connection with two swage fittings (5-162).

Trim the cable with sharp wire cutters (5-163) and slide a heat-shrinkable plastic sleeve (5-164) over the swages. (Look for heat-shrinkable tubing where electrical supplies are sold.) Shrink the tube with a heat gun or hair drier.

Rudder Retainer

There are a number of ways to hold the rudder in place, depending upon the style of pin and the way it is hung. Three styles are

5-164

5-165

available: with a threaded end to take a nut; with a cotter pin; or with a straight end for an end-pour mounting system.

The end-pour type is held down by a screw or bolt with a large plastic washer that fits over a part of the rudder (5-165). When it's fastened to the deck, consider using a brass-threaded insert to keep the threads from wearing out and for a more finished look when the rudder is off.

Haul Cord

The purpose of the haul cord is to raise and lower the rudder. It runs forward to the

5-166

5-167

cockpit from the pulley on the rudder and then back again. The forward end of the line is attached to an elastic cord. Anchor it in a convenient position. The plastic eye pad that we used is functional but lacks imagination (5-166); call it an out-of-time solution. A low-profile wooden eye pad would look more graceful; a small plastic jam cleat would be functional and look very acceptable as well.

Deck Rigging

Safety features – grab handles, perimeter deck lines, an anchor for self-rescue systems, and bungee cords to hold bilge pumps, charts, compass, extra paddle and spare life-jacket – depend on anchoring a rope, strap or bungee cord to the deck. A simple yet functional anchor for ropes and bungee cords can be made with a 4-inch length of 1-inch webbing (5-167). Fold the ends back under to double up the strap under the fastener; fasten with a #6 oval-head screw in a cup washer. You may have to melt a hole for the screw if the weave of the strap is tight. If there is no sheer clamp to screw into, use a similar size of machine screw with a nut and washer inside. This method for anchoring the end of a strap is used on some styles of hatch cover restraining straps.

5-168

Anchor Hole

Having a way of hanging on to the end of a slippery kayak is an important safety feature. There are many ways of accomplishing this, from a simple rope loop to a T-shaped handle (toggle) for carrying the kayak and for grabbing on to in a hurry. Handles may be attached directly to the deck or through a hole in the end pour.

5-169

One secure anchor point is a hole through the end pour in the stem that has been lined with a brass tube or plastic sleeve. We used 1/4-inch ID brass tubing.

Lay out the position of the hole on masking tape on both sides of the hull and double-check the measurements. Drill the hole from both sides rather than from one side hoping that you will come out on the other mark (5-168). Make the hole slightly oversized to allow for some glue around the tube.

Prepare the brass tube by cutting it generously long; scratch up the outside with 120 grit sandpaper to clean it and give the epoxy something to hang on to. Plug up the end of the tube so that it doesn't get filled with epoxy. Saturate the inside of the hole with mixed epoxy, then thicken the mix and work some into the hole. Insert the tube (5-169) and clean up the excess filler. Make sure that any space between the hull and the tube is filled.

When the filler has cured, cut the tube off

5-170

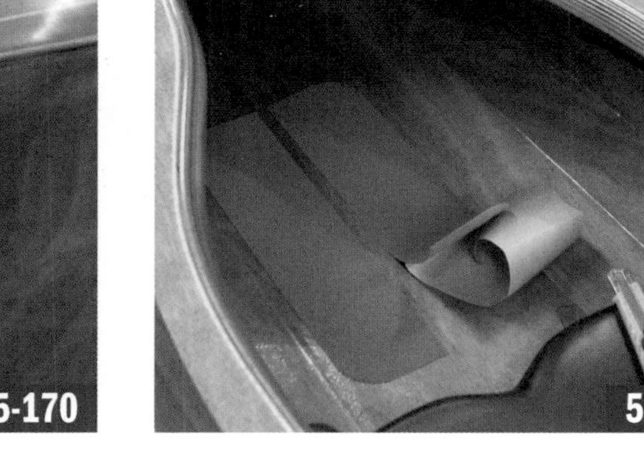

5-171

with a hacksaw (5-170) and file it flush. Flare the ends by rotating a screwdriver or nail set in the hole to roll over the edge.

Nonskid Area

A useful finishing touch for your kayak is a nonskid area in front of the seat. Having your feet slide out from under you while boarding the kayak is painful, embarrassing and potentially dangerous. We used a PSA-backed textured rubber material made for stair treads in industrial applications (5-171). Apply it after the finish has dried. If it's not included in your kit, look for this type of material at safety, auto and bathroom supply stores. It is also useful on deck to protect key areas where hard gear (bilge pump, extra paddles) is carried.

Another way of creating a nonskid surface is to add grit such as crushed walnut shells or very fine sand to the finish to give it texture. The grit is mixed into the varnish and applied evenly with a brush. Mask off the area to be covered and apply after the last coat of finish.

PLYWOOD BOAT-BUILDING TECHNIQUES

Finishing

As it sits, our kayak is a series of components that have been carefully fitted together to create a kayak shape. When the last coat of finish has been applied, all the pieces will become one. But what if the finished surface looks like a nonskid deck decorated with petrified flying creatures? If this worries you, you should do just fine, because you won't leave anything to chance. Understand the importance of preparation, do your best and you will have nothing to worry about. There is always an element of luck in a perfect finish, so if you have lucky charms, use them.

Remember that even though the last coat of varnish is the one that counts, it will only be as good as the building coats under it. If you treat each coat as if it were the last, there will be time to work the bugs out of your system so that the last coat will be your best.

To keep you humble, expect to find at least a little dust in the last coat; the closer

you get to perfection, the more elusive it will be. Don't take it personally. If you have done your best, be proud of it – and go paddling.

Getting Organized

Finishing in the less than perfect environment in which most home builders must work would challenge a professional painter. For most of us the best we can do is cobble together some of the features that make a good paint shop. Achieving that perfect finish can be summed up in three words – preparation, preparation and preparation. Here are some things you can do to prepare your workshop for this final task:

- Having the kayak lit well is important for achieving a good finish. (However, there is a limit to how much you can control the film thickness visually, so expect most of the control to come from what you can feel through the brush.) Fluorescent lights are great because the tube gives a nice long hot spot that will highlight runs or holidays (pinholes, skips, voids or uncoated areas). A portable light is handy for checking vertical surfaces.
- Give the shop a good cleaning, using a sweeping compound to keep the dust down and to pick up fine particles. Allow some time between sweeping and varnishing to give the dust time to settle.
- Vacuum the kayak and all exposed surfaces.
- If your workspace has a lot of hard-to-clean junk overhead or piled around the walls, consider using plastic film suspended or draped where it will do the most good.
- As a rule, the dog and the cat are good company in the shop, but they are slow to learn the difference between wet and dry.
- Many places in the world have a flying bug problem, especially around dawn and dusk. Pick a time of day when they are off somewhere else. To be sure, light one of those bug-killing coils in a ceramic holder when you finish varnishing and lock up.
- If your shop is very dry, there could be a problem with static electricity attracting dust particles out of the air. Try wetting the floor down to settle the dust and raise the humidity in the room.
- Seal the bare wood trim parts first so that the finish will build at the same speed on the wood as it will on the epoxy surface. Use a sealer that is compatible with the varnish you are using, varnish thinned about 50/50 or penetrating epoxy sealer (→ page 135).
- Rinse the brush well after using and store it suspended in clean solvent between varnishing sessions.

Preparing the Kayak

The surface must be free of contaminants for any finish to bond with the epoxy. A freshly sanded surface will be ready to go, but if it has been a while since the epoxy surface was sanded, give it a quick scuff with 220 grit sandpaper to be sure it is clean. After cleaning, avoid handling the surface with sweaty hands, as oil from your skin will contaminate the surface. If you think there is a possibility of oil-based contamination, clean the surface with lacquer thinner or paint thinner.

Vacuum the dust after sanding and pick up the remainder with a water-dampened rag. The moisture will hold the fine dust on the rag and help to discharge the static charge in the boat. Some solvents, such as turpentine, will increase the static charge. Do what you can to keep static electricity from increasing.

Mask off screw holes and any small, hard-to-clean openings; they could hide dust that will be pulled out by the varnish brush. If you have compressed air, blow the tight corners out before the final cleanup with the tack cloth.

Safety First

When working with chemicals that smell bad, it is easy to keep safety in mind. The problem with fresh spar varnish is that it smells so darn good we forget that a significant percentage of what comes out of the can evaporates into the air and is not particularly good for you. A good cross-draft and a supply of fresh, clean air are important. It is not necessary or desirable to have rapid replacement of air. The flow should be gentle enough not to stir up dust but strong enough to sustain a steady supply of fresh air.

Fumes should be treated as a solvent problem and respected as such. Most people will be comfortable with a good supply of fresh air, but if you are sensitive to solvents, wear a charcoal filter respirator.

Super Sealer

Sealers function as an interface between the wood and the coating material. The sealer must saturate the wood fibers for a mechanical bond as well as form a compatible bond with the next coat to be applied. It is also used to control how much the next coat will soak in and to begin the process of flattening the surface. An epoxy-type sealer can increase the density of softwood for greater durability.

Mixed epoxy can be thinned down to make super sealer. Keep in mind this important principle when thinning epoxy – epoxy is all the great things it is because it is 100 percent solids; everything that comes out of the can stays on the boat. This is also what makes it moisture-vapor-proof (or very highly resistant). When you add a solvent that escapes during the curing process, moisture will be able to enter by the same path used by the solvent. Our mixture and some commercial penetrating epoxies will do as advertised, but will not provide the moisture barrier of a 100 percent solid coating.

That said, use a super sealer for soft and absorbent surfaces that are to be covered with varnish or paint. It will perform all the basic functions of a good sanding sealer plus greatly increase the density of the substrata. This technique is perfect for the cockpit coaming, where low maintenance, durability and good looks are important.

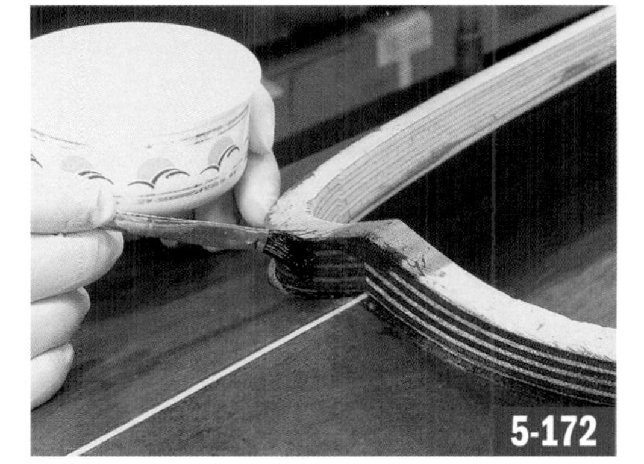
5-172

Mix up resin and hardener, add about 25 percent lacquer thinner and mix well. The mixture will be quite watery, so mask off any areas that need to be covered. Use a bristle brush to apply or, in small areas, an acid brush (5-172). The object here is to give the wood as much to drink as it can absorb. This may require a number of generous applications, especially on end grain. Keep it looking shiny. Watch for dry spots and bubbles indicating that the surface would like a little more, please. When dry patches stop appearing and the surface stays shiny, wipe all the excess epoxy off with a dry rag.

5-173

CAUTION

Our experience with thinning epoxy has been with WEST SYSTEM epoxy; we suggest a test of your epoxy system before committing it to your boat.

Give the surface a good rub with a Scotchbrite pad to pack the pores with natural filler and help drive out any remaining air (5-173). Finish with a quick rub using a clean, lint-free rag; if the rag is sticking, add a few drops of lacquer thinner. For greater penetration, warm the wood with a heat gun before applying the epoxy. As the surface cools, the epoxy will be drawn deeper into the wood.

For a piano finish, it is desirable to fill the pores and level the surface with the least possible number of steps. When working an open-grain wood such as mahogany, try pushing the rubbing step a little further as well as applying a second coat after the first has cured. A harder wood could benefit from an abrasive with more bite than the Scotchbrite. Try 0000 bronze or steel wool, but keep an eye out for loose steel particles getting embedded in the wood. Good marine suppliers carry bronze wool, which avoids the dreaded iron rust curls.

To prepare the surface for finishing, knock down any rough spots with 220 grit sandpaper and finish with a good rub using Scotchbrite or 0000 bronze or steel wool. The result should feel like a baby's bum. Any finish will build fast and smoothly on this surface.

5-174

Varnishing and Painting

Varnish and enamel paint have very short working times, so it is important to lay it on consistently the first time. Finish brushing an arm's-length section to your satisfaction, then leave it alone and move on. Once the surface has begun to skin over, anything you do to it will make it look worse. How long the edge will remain wet enough to work will depend on the speed of the varnish, which is influenced by temperature, humidity and how much and what kind of thinner has been added. A working window of five minutes is safe and not hard to keep up to on a craft this size.

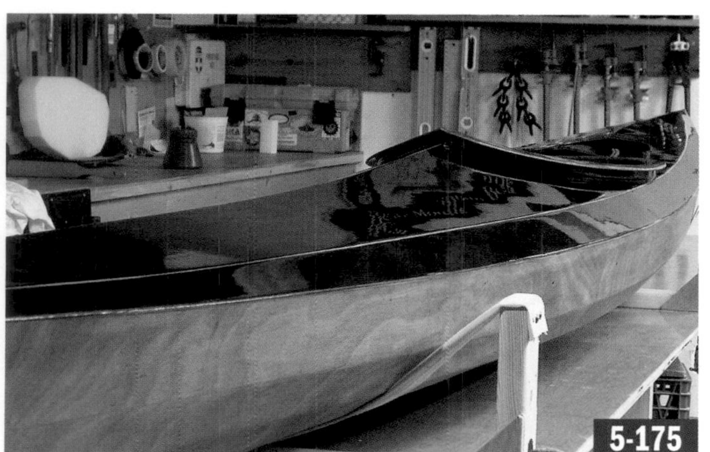

5-175

Have a strategy for applying the varnish that will keep a wet edge and hide the lap marks that cannot be avoided. Break the area to be varnished into the largest segments that you can work on without making lap marks. To blend the sections as inconspicuously as possible, join the sections along corners or in other hard shadow lines. For example, protect the hull by masking to the bottom of the curve around the edge of the deck. When it is time to varnish the hull, overlap the edges by masking to the top of the curve. The tape line will be hidden in the shadow line along the edge and the finish will be a double thickness where it will do the most good.

A Strategy for Finishing the Deck

The first component to be varnished should be the cockpit coaming, a fussy shape to varnish. If we work the varnish down the deck and stop to do the coaming, working under the lip will mess up the deck varnish. When we get back to it, the edge of the deck varnish will have begun to skin over, leaving an ugly lap mark.

A 1-inch foam brush will work better than a thick varnish brush for getting under the rim and cutting in around the deck (5-174). The peak at the forward end of the coaming is a good place to begin, as a lap mark will be the least conspicuous there. Foam brushes have a tendency to promote bubbles if used aggressively; try to use the varnish that is picked up on the outside of the foam and draw it along gently rather than brushing back and forth to squeeze the material out of the brush.

Varnishing the underside of the rim is bound to get some on the deck. Remove it immediately with paint thinner on a clean, lint-free rag after completing the coaming. Carefully pick up any dust or detritus with a tack rag before varnishing the deck.

If your kayak has hatch openings, finish the lips of these at the same time as the cockpit coaming, again using the foam brush.

We used a 2-inch badger-hair brush on the deck, beginning at the bow and working aft. The beauty of this brush is that it holds a large quantity of varnish – an asset on large open surfaces – but it is a little bulky for working around the cockpit coaming. A flagged nylon-and-polyester brush is a good choice for the deck because it is flatter than the badger-hair and the edge is crisper for cutting in around the coaming spacer.

Maintaining the wet edge on both sides of the cockpit gets a bit dicey, but keep moving and try to bring both sides along together (5-175). If you are worried about keeping up with it and your kayak deck has a joint down the centerline, consider varnishing one side of the deck at a time, overlapping along the centerline. The lap mark will be there, but because it follows

CHEAP TRICK

When combining paint and varnish finishes, always apply the varnish first so that the distinctive color of the paint will overlap the varnish and define the edge.

the shadow line along the ridge, it will not be the first thing you see. The line could be masked to keep it tidy if you can live with the extra drying time. Consider doing the buildup coats freehand; before the last coat, sand the lap marks smooth, then mask and apply the final coat in two steps.

Don't overload the brush when cutting in around the coaming spacer. Place the brush at the coaming and draw the varnish out to where you can blend it in.

Hatch openings can also be tricky. If the brush is drawn over the edge, varnish will be squeezed out and run over the edge. Try brushing toward the opening and taking the pressure off the brush as you clear the edge.

Varnish the hatch cover and other loose pieces at the same time as the deck. Balance the cover on a varnish can or something similar for easy access to the edge (5-176).

Preparing the Varnish

The purpose of the thinner in the varnish is to act as a vehicle for the solids that will be deposited on the surface. Shortly after the varnish has been spread, enough of the solvent will have evaporated for the surface to begin to skin over. When all the thinner

5-176

has evaporated, the finish will be hard.

The amount of solvent in a can of varnish varies from brand to brand. A clue here is the price; premium varnish with a high solids content will cost the most and must be thinned before using. A cheaper varnish will contain fewer solids and more low-cost solvent and may be brushed right out of the can. A varnish with a high solids content gives us the option of adjusting its viscosity and drying time to suit the environment and application.

Thin varnish to a consistency that is as full-bodied as possible yet thin enough that it will flow out of the brush without dragging. Brush marks should have time to level out before the varnish skins over. However, avoid adding more thinner than necessary; when it is brushed, a thin varnish will produce more bubbles than you should have to deal with. If you are unfamiliar with the brand of varnish you are using, brush it out on a test panel before deciding whether to add thinner. Add thinner to the mixture a little at a time, then stir well before deciding whether you have the desired viscosity.

Thinners are also used to control the length of time it takes for the surface to skin over. Since the rate of evaporation is influenced by temperature, use a retarder in hot weather to slow things down. In cool temperatures an accelerator can be used to speed up the drying time. We want the brush marks to flow out, enough working time to maintain the wet edge, and the surface to skin over as soon as possible. The sooner it skins over, the less dust will get stuck in the varnish.

Applying the Varnish

Compared to preparation time, it takes very little time to apply the varnish. The application technique is similar to the one used to apply the last coat of epoxy, although the thinner varnish is easier to brush than epoxy.

The first step is to transfer the varnish from the can to the surface and quickly spread it over a section an arm's length long. The larger the section that you can handle, the fewer the lap marks to work out. Be firm with the brush; hold it at an angle that draws varnish evenly over the section.

CAUTION

Check and double-check the lower edge of all vertical surfaces by drawing the brush carefully along the underside of the corner. Drips that are not picked up can take weeks to get hard enough to sand. If you scrape and wash the drips off, the surface is back to where you started.

CAUTION

Always remove masking tape as soon as the finishing material has been applied. This will allow the edge to flow out, leaving a defined but soft edge along the masked line. Once the material has hardened, the edge will be sharp. If you wait to remove the tape, you run the danger of peeling off some of the finish or having to pick at bits of tape to break them free of the surface.

A firm yet aggressive stroke will introduce less air than cautiously applying a little bit at a time.

After spreading the finish in a fore and aft direction, work the surface on both diagonals to be sure that the horizontal strokes have been blended together. Work until resistance to the brush is consistent.

This next step is the one that will make you look good. Blend the diagonal brush strokes by working fore and aft. At this point, the only control you have over film thickness is what you can feel through the brush. Hold the brush at a low angle to draw the material along. Pay attention to what the brush is telling you. Trying to control the film thickness according to gloss will not get you much useful information. Controlling it by what you feel is the only way to avoid runs and holidays.

A thick layer will always run over a thinner layer. A thick coat of varnish that has been worked to an even film thickness will have less chance of running than a conservative amount that has an uneven thickness.

Make a full stroke with the brush as you draw it back and forth. The brush should land gently as it reaches the surface and lift off with the same grace at the end of the stroke. Work the varnish until you feel a consistent fluid drag through the brush, indicating that the material on the surface has been spread evenly over the area being worked.

If the varnish is harder to work than you think it should be, try adding a few drops of thinner before applying the next section.

When you do move on to the adjoining section, be careful not to build up a double thickness of material where the sections meet. Apply the varnish beside the wet area and work it away from the wet. Blend the two sections together beginning with the diagonal and finishing with fore and aft strokes.

While you are varnishing, if the brush begins to fill up with bubbles, scrape the grunge out of the brush into a clean can; the bubbles will eventually disappear and the varnish may be reused after straining.

CAUTION

Never add thinner to a whole can of varnish. Should you happen to add too much thinner or you need a different mix tomorrow, a new can of varnish will have to be opened. Mixing in small batches allows you to adjust the mixture quickly to suit the environment and the size of your work area. Also, once thinner has been added, the varnish will skin over faster in the can.

CHEAP TRICK

That last bit of thinned-down varnish should not go back into the original varnish. To keep the varnish from skinning over, use a glove stretched over the top to seal the container (5-177).

Sanding Between Varnish Coats

Sanding between coats as we build up the finish is a necessary evil that cannot be avoided. The problem is not so much the sanding but that having to clean up after each varnishing session takes time. Sanding between coats gives us a chance to flatten lap marks and runs. More importantly, it scratches up the surface to give the next coat something to lock on to. Choose 220 or 240 grit (used dry) for the optimum balance between efficient preparation and scratches that are small enough for the varnish to flow into and level out.

Try not to contaminate the work area more than necessary when sanding between coats. Use a vacuum cleaner, fan and sweeping compound to help control flying dust. Pick up the remaining dust with a water-dampened rag. If the surface has been contaminated with fingerprints, degrease it with paint thinner.

It is possible that the varnish may not completely level the 220 grit scratches. This could bother some builders. Wet sanding with a finer grit will eliminate them, but the bond between coats could be compromised. If you want to take it further, there is no reason why you cannot sand up to 400 grit wet before the last coat is applied. The reward for your effort will be a slightly higher gloss.

Good luck with the last coat!

Varnishing Inside

We thought it curious that neither the Coho nor the Mill Creek instruction manuals mentioned finishing inside the kayak. Given that much of the inside of a kayak is in the dark or in shadow, UV degradation is not a major consideration in the short term. Abrasion, on the other hand, is going to happen, especially in the cockpit area. It's to our advantage to protect the epoxy, which is a major structural component. We suggest three coats in the cockpit and at least one on what you can reach through the hatch openings. If the deck of your kayak is fastened to a sheer clamp, varnishing before the deck is installed is a very convenient and neat solution.

Surface preparation

The textured surface inside, which is the result of two rather than three coats of epoxy, will require a different approach than the smooth surface outside. Although sanding must be minimal to preserve the texture, it is still important to make sure that the surface is not contaminated with unused hardener (blush), wax, oil or sweat.

When the manufacturer suggests wet sanding or washing the surface with water, it is probably a good idea. We were reminded of this after varnishing the Coho deck. Up to this point, our first experience with System Three epoxy was going well, so we were very surprised when a curing problem developed with some of the varnish. The uncured varnish stood over areas that had originally been low spots but were sanded enough to remove the gloss. The only difference was that the low spots had not been sanded as aggressively as the majority of the deck. Since most of the varnish hardened as usual, incompatibility of the epoxy and varnish could not have been the source of the problem. After two months the varnish in these places was still sticky, which suggests chemical contamination.

Our bad luck was that the varnish had to be wet-sanded completely off to get back to a smooth, clean surface. The good luck was that there could have been several other real disasters. For example, had the textured interior been varnished first, none of the varnish would have cured and the resulting mess would have been one miserable job to remove. This could have happened quite easily. The Bear Mountain Boat Shop ordinarily uses WEST #105/207 epoxy resin and hardener, and we've been spraying varnish over this texture for many years without washing the surface first. Spraying three coats of varnish inside the kayak was next on the to-do list.

The outside could have been equally disastrous. To add a transparent color to the plywood, the varnish was tinted with an oil-based pigment. Since color intensity builds with each layer, repairing uncured patches in one coat never works well. We were about to spray four coats, wet on wet, and would have had a terrible mess on our hands.

The lesson? Read and follow the directions when using unfamiliar products. When working with a new product (in this case, epoxy), it is good practice to lay up a test panel, which can be the proving ground for your experimental finish. Above all, don't assume that experience with one brand applies to a similar product. A test first can save a lot of grief.

How to clean

The contaminants we want to remove are broken down by either water or epoxy solvents (for example, lacquer thinner). Remove any chance of blush (→ page 38) with water that has been fortified with a bit of ammonia. Epoxy solvents will not cut the blush but they will cut sweaty fingerprints and other oil-based contaminants.

Wash with water

Because the interior's coarse texture cannot be wiped effectively, it is better

CAUTION

Most oil-based stains are not compatible with an epoxy coating. The oil, or anything else that stops epoxy from saturating and bonding to raw wood, will compromise the bond and it will delaminate sooner or later. Choose a water- or alcohol-soluble dye.

suited to scrubbing with a brush and water than wiping with solvents. If a household cleanser containing ammonia is added to the water, it should take care of the oil-based contaminants as well. Rinse well with fresh water after scrubbing.

Adding Color with Aniline Dyes

While varnished okume can look pleasant if the workmanship is neat, aniline dyes can take the kayak to another level. According to the package, "Aniline dyes are mixed with water to form a brilliant, fade-resistant stain characterized by deep, even penetration and excellent clarity." Using these dyes is not a complicated process, but it will require careful preparation to be successful. Any of the building and preparation steps that enhance a clear coating are important for a colored finish.

Keep in mind that the color of the wood will combine with the color of the dye to make a new color. Experiment first; it is possible to combine pigments to make the best of the wood's natural tone. A bright yellow deck is a possibility, but requires bleaching the wood first. As a rule, dark colors are best because suture holes and joints in the plank will be less noticeable. On a light-colored deck, glue lines will show.

Dyeing adjacent panels different colors is another possibility as is a combination of bright-finished and dyed panels. These panels can be colored and sealed before assembly with no more effort than for dyeing the whole kayak one color. If the hull and deck have been assembled cleanly, they can be dyed after being assembled and before the glass goes on.

On assembled panels, mask off the area to be dyed and dye it in sections, letting each section dry before taping over it. Use a low-tack tape over a dyed surface and peel it off carefully. The water-based dye will migrate under the tape on bare wood, so try to make the color change at a glue line. The epoxy glue line will stop the dye from moving under the tape.

However, for the most control over the color, individual components should be dyed before assembling into planks and panels. In order to have a consistent color, the dye must be absorbed evenly. Gluing the joints will seal the surface to some extent, no matter how careful you are. Once the wood is saturated with epoxy, it will no longer accept the dye. By dyeing and sealing all the surfaces before joining the components, you will have more consistent color at the joints.

Prepare the Surface

The secret to clean color with an even density is in preparing the surface of the wood well. Keep in mind that the purpose of the dye is to accent the surface; small scratches will become features. Consider an extra grain-raising step to be sure the surface is stabilized (→ page 97).

Prepare the Dye Solution

Our instructions called for dissolving the dye power in hot water in a ratio of one ounce of powder to one quart of water.

Stabilize the Surface

In plywood the grain direction is all over the place. In the dyeing process, the exposed end-grain areas will absorb more dye and looker darker than the straight-grain areas. The following step will help avoid some of these potential blotches and begin stabilizing the surface.

Using a small sponge, apply a weak solution (diluted 50/50) to the surface, working evenly in the direction of the grain. This will put down some base color and raise any fuzz that is left after sanding. Work systematically to move the wet edge forward while applying a consistent amount to keep lap marks to a minimum. Try to get it right the first time, because touching it up later will be dicey. Look for a wet surface with no puddles; puddles contain more dye and will result in darker patches. Let dry.

Remove the fuzz with 280 grit or finer sandpaper, working slightly tangent to the grain. Working at this angle will cut the fuzz rather than pushing it back into the pores. Go lightly – it doesn't take much to cut through the color, resulting in a different color density. If you see that the color is getting scratched, back off. To reduce the chance of cutting through the color, use a quarter-sheet of sandpaper folded in three in your hand rather than a block. The block will cut through any high spots that were missed earlier, while the paper will have a better chance of lightly following the existing shape.

Vacuum carefully to remove dust from the pores. Use a brush attachment and make sure that just the bristles of the vacuum brush touch the surface. The hard rubber hose will burnish the surface and result in a darker color density.

Wipe lightly with a rag dampened very, very slightly with water.

Apply the Full-Strength Dye

Apply the dye full strength using a small sponge (4-24). Then squeeze the sponge dry and use it to even out the dye, picking up any surplus and filling in light areas. It is important to do this while the surface is still wet; working it after it has begun to dry may be counterproductive. Look for an even density – a wet, saturated surface with no light spots or puddles. If an area is too dark, gingerly rub off some of the color with the sponge, or if it's too light, add more dye as needed.

Let the Wood Dry

Allow the wood to dry completely before sealing it with epoxy. This will take at least 24 hours, or more depending on the temperature and humidity. We do not recommend fast drying during the wet stage, as it could warp the plywood. Past that point, putting the wood in the sun should be fine, but keep an eye on it.

After drying, if there is more fuzz standing proud of the surface, it should be removed. At this point sanding is too aggressive and will scratch the dye, so we recommend lightly rubbing down the surface with a fine Scotchbrite pad. Vacuum and wipe clean.

Apply Sealer

Unprotected, the dyed surface (5-178) is very fragile and would not survive being joined together and wired into a kayak. Sanding sealer should be avoided because it inhibits the bond between the wood and the epoxy-and-glass covering that will go on later. Epoxy, on the other hand, is an ideal sealer because it becomes part of the structural covering.

If the surface has been dyed after the kayak has been assembled, lay up the glass cloth over the dyed surface. The cloth will take the place of sealer. But when individual components have been dyed, they require the extra step of sealing the surface with epoxy before assembly (→ page 91).

When you apply the sealer coat of epoxy, use consistent brush strokes, drawing the

5-178

epoxy along in the direction of the grain so that the color is disturbed as little as possible. Warming the epoxy beforehand will make it easier to spread. The object is to cover the surface and let the epoxy soak in on its own. Brushing it into the surface will disturb the color.

Apply a Second Coat of Sealer

A second coat of sealer is recommended over a dyed surface that requires a lot of handling and fitting. Our Coho deck was assembled with only one sealer coat. It was adequate, but there was no room for error when fitting and cleaning up the joints.

When the epoxy has cured, clean up the edges of shaped parts with a rasp or hard sanding block. Try not to alter the shape of the wood – the edges of the wood are your guide for assembling the pieces.

CHAPTER SIX

A Kayak Builder's Journal

ALTHOUGH WE HAVE BUILT many boats using traditional and contemporary building methods, this is the first time we have been able to explore the many variations of sewn-seam construction. Ted was the lucky builder and was able to try out a number of different techniques, some more successful than others.

While Chapter Five describes the techniques we recommend for each of the major procedures (cross-referenced in this chapter with an → and page number), Chapter Six will give you a look at how we have combined what we know of boatbuilding with the kit directions. Use the journals to see how the pieces fit together, how long each step should be expected to take and what you need to get organized. Understanding why some things worked and some didn't will help you adapt Ted's methods to your situation.

Our objectives in building these kayaks were to

• reduce epoxy exposure time to a minimum by finding the shortest route to the best results;

• introduce simple boatbuilding controls that will make the kayak's shape predictable;

• demonstrate that professional quality is a state of mind and applying a few simple shortcuts in the right places;

• demonstrate that building fast does not mean leaving out steps or stopping before the step is finished, but rather making each stage a positive step forward and preparation for the next step;

• explore enough of the why behind what we learned to make our experience valuable to anyone building a plywood boat, regardless of the method.

We invite you to join the crew and become part of building these beautiful kayaks.

A Note on the Time Required for Each Step

The number of days required for each step is most often governed by the time it takes for the epoxy to cure rather than the number of hours required to complete the step. The steps marked with an asterisk (*) require a cure cycle before the work can proceed; two asterisks (**) indicate two cure cycles will be needed to complete the step. Times given are based on an epoxy that is ready to work in 12 hours. The actual time can be anywhere from 6 to 21 hours, depending on the epoxy brand and temperature; adjust your projected time accordingly.

The Coho

THE 17-FOOT PYGMY BOATS' COHO was chosen as a good example of a multi-chined hull and deck kayak kit. The construction method is to wire the hull planks together in the upright position, wire in temporary forms, then turn the hull over to tack it together and fiberglass the outside. After the hull is turned upright again, the deck panels are assembled. The deck is then removed for taping the seams and glassing the inside of the hull. Hull and deck are joined by tacking the deck to the hull, then glassing the outside of the deck and bringing the glass down the sides of the hull.

The Coho has a number of nice details that make this boat strong and functional. These translate into more construction steps, but that doesn't mean this is a difficult kayak to build. You just need to keep all the simple steps in order.

DAY 1
Get Organized

To Do
- O Construct worktable or horses.
- O Unpack shipping cartons and do inventory.
- O Organize tools and materials.
- O Read instructions.

Tools & Materials
- O clamps
- O drill/driver
- O drywall screws
- O level
- O material for worktable
- O material for legs or horses
- O saw
- O square
- O straightedge
- O string line
- O tape measure
- O utility knife

Safety
- O eye protection
- O good ventilation
- O caution with cutting tools

Day one will not necessarily take one day. Many of these details will no doubt be taken care of as you rearrange your schedule and get around to cleaning the junk out of the garage.

1. Construct worktable or horses (→ page 23).

2. Unpack shipping cartons & do inventory.

The Pygmy kayak kit arrived in good condition, with no damage to packages or contents (6-1). One box contained wooden components and the other the System Three epoxy, fiberglass cloth, supplies and deck hardware.

Breaking the Pygmy license-agreement seal fastened to the larger box acknowledges agreement to their terms. When I broke the seal, I agreed to build one boat only and not to make a pattern of the parts. Why so official? It takes a lot of time, effort, patience and experience to develop and produce quality plans or kits. Without fair compensation for the effort, further development by the people who are really good at it won't happen. When someone copies a plan, we all lose.

6-1

3. Organize tools & materials.

After opening the boxes, check that all of the parts for the kit are accounted for and in good condition (6-2). The kit included a handy checklist with drawings, which made this very straightforward.

6-2

4. Read instructions.

All kit suppliers have a recommended method for assembling their kit. Since this project is a little more involved than getting the new barbecue from box to burger, understanding the building method and the order in which the pieces will be assembled is extremely important. Try to visualize the pieces coming together and what your kayak will look like when it is launched. You won't remember everything you read in the manual, but try to remember where to find it.

DAYS 2–4

Join Plank Components

To Do
- O Sort components into sets.
- O Join components into planks.*
- O Reinforce butt joints.*
- O Use assembled plank from one side to assemble its mate.*
- O Clean up joints.
- O Assemble deck panels.

Tools & Materials
- O clamp blocks
- O clamps or weights
- O epoxy resin and hardener
- O fiberglass tape or cloth
- O glue brush or acid brush
- O heavy plastic film
- O lacquer thinner
- O mixing pots
- O putty knife
- O rags
- O firm sanding block
- O 120 grit sandpaper
- O scissors
- O stir sticks
- O straightedge

Safety
- O dust mask
- O gloves
- O eye protection
- O good ventilation
- O caution with cutting tools

Expect Day 2 to be a full one. It takes a while to get everything organized and the first set of planks glued. After this, joining the balance of the planks will happen in small blocks of time regulated by how long it takes the epoxy to kick. An epoxy with an average curing time will allow you to do a set early in the morning and another in the evening.

1. Sort components into sets.

After getting organized, sort the plank components by the numbers on the inside of the panels and stack them up in sets. The planks will be joined on the inside first, in this case the side with the number sticker. This is a good place to practice making a tidy joint because the inside joints will not be as visible as the outside ones.

2. Join components into planks.

This is one of those "hard to recover from gracefully" steps.

6-3

Take all the time you need to be sure the components are positioned to your satisfaction before committing to the glass and epoxy.

Begin by assembling all the planks for one side of the kayak. This set of planks will become patterns for assembling the other side.

The first two planks to assemble are the garboards, the pair that join down the centerline (6-3). As they are the largest and the only pair with a reference for controlling the shape, they will be the least challenging and give us some practice for the ones requiring more judgment. There's no point in working through all the surprises at once.

The construction manual suggests using a straightedge to line up the pieces. To confirm the reliability of the straightedge reference system, I carefully positioned the pieces and checked with the straightedge before gluing (6-4). In addition, a flexible batten was used to check the curved edge for a fair curve. Starboard and port planks were set up the same way and glued up separately.

When the shape was compared after gluing, the forward ends

6-4

were about 3/8 inch out, the aft, a little less. Being out this much did not end up being a problem. The planks are quite flexible and it did not take much to spring them to match up. However, I had expected my 30-plus years of building boats with sweet lines to get me a little closer. The manual is on track when it suggests gluing the planks in pairs. This will at least keep the pairs the same shape and help to keep the hull and deck shapes symmetrical, although they may not be what the designer drew.

3. Reinforce butt joints.

The purpose of the fiberglass tape over the butt joints (glass butt blocks) is to join the components together in the shape of a plank and hold them together until the planks are assembled and reinforced with fiberglass cloth. This much is not hard to do, but I wanted the joint to be easy to clean up and the tape to appear as though it weren't there. It took several tries to find the right balance of fiberglass weight and epoxy quantity to meet both these objectives. I think the various combinations are worth looking at, not because they are right or wrong, but rather as a way of matching up the technique with your expectations.

The first joints were glued up as per the instruction manual. Mix up the resin and hardener (→ page 59) and begin by saturating the end grain. When the components were clamped together, much of this glue ended up on the bottom of the panel, to be scraped off later. Saturating the end grain is important in a structural joint. Pre-coating is unnecessary here because the epoxy will be forced through the joint when it is clamped.

The routine is to place the glass tape over the joint and brush mixed epoxy over the tape (6-5). In practice, the epoxy did not saturate the 4-ounce tape very quickly when applied from the top, partly because the tape was not flat.

6-5

6-6

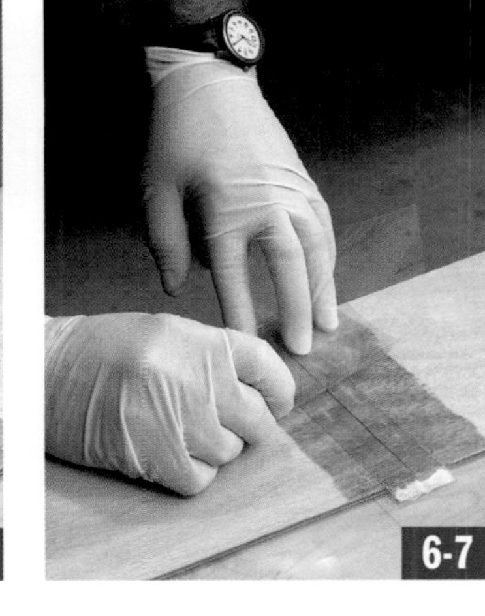
6-7

The instructions direct the builder to "Paint some extra epoxy on the wood for 1½ inches on either side of the tape. Tamp any air bubbles out of the glass tape with the end of a disposable bristle brush. Leave the glass tape and epoxy for several minutes to allow the epoxy to soak into the wood and the fiberglass. The fiberglass should turn completely glass clear. Apply a little more epoxy if you need to, and get the tape completely 'wetted' out. Paint a little more extra epoxy on the tape and enough on each side of the tape to 'float' the tape (so the epoxy on either side of the tape is the same height as the tape). Do not proceed until the tape is glass clear."

This step was a bit of a problem, not with the directions but with the glass tape that would not lie down. After a lot of poking, the tape did wet out clear but only when held down to the surface of the wood with the brush (6-6). Because the tape was puckered, it lifted in places when released, which allowed the air back under the tape (recognizable as a white haze in the photo), even though the tape was well saturated.

Cover the wetted-out glass tape with a layer of plastic film (6-7). To keep from trapping air under the film, begin by positioning it across one edge, press it onto the surface while holding the free end up, then lay it down with a rolling motion. While holding the edge of the film in place, smooth out any remaining air with a squeegee. Using firm pressure will also work some of the excess epoxy out to the edge, where it can be cleaned off later.

In order to apply even pressure over the entire joint, tape and epoxy, I used a 3½ x 6-inch clamp block. One side is smooth and covered with plastic packaging tape. The tape is insurance should epoxy squeeze out from under the plastic film between the plank and the clamp block. The instructions suggest placing the clamp block over the joint and weighting it down with "several bricks (2 lbs. or more is good)." For good measure, I used a 10-pound piece of railway track.

As you can see, the butt block is quite thick, with a step along the edge of the epoxy (6-8). Of

6-8

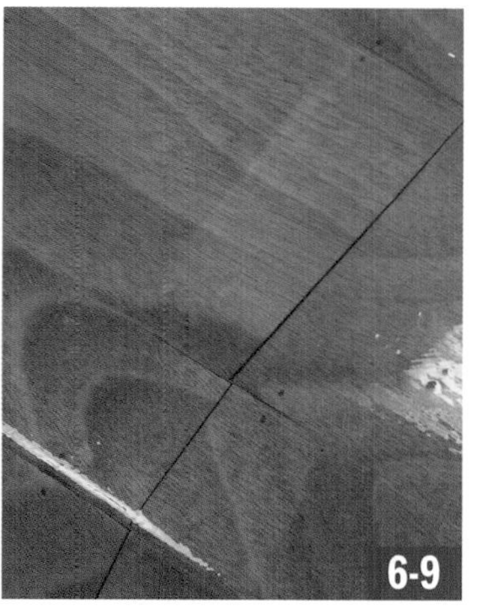
6-9

greater concern is that there was not enough pressure to exclude the air from under the tape and squeeze the excess epoxy out. The problem was a combination of too little pressure and too much epoxy. Also, if my clamp block had been wider the epoxy might have moved out farther, for a smoother transition to the plywood.

If a strong joint were our only objective, this one would do the job with cleanup of a quick scuff and a bit of feathering along the edge. On the other hand, if we are trying to achieve both an attractive appearance and a fair surface, cleaning up this joint is limited by the epoxy between the glass and the plywood; getting any closer to fair will cut into the glass tape. As for the air under the tape, we called that a learning experience and learned to love it.

This joint was made using the above method after three coats of epoxy had been applied (6-9). It is tidy and nothing to be ashamed of, but there is no doubt that the tape is there.

So what did we learn?

1. The first problem was far too much epoxy to clean up on both sides of the plank.

Recommendation: We need to think about what the epoxy is expected to do and the space it will occupy. If we apply the optimum quantity of epoxy, the glass reinforcing will be saturated, the weave filled and the epoxy molded to a feather edge. Cleaning up this joint will then require only a quick scuff with 120 grit sandpaper to cut the gloss and it will be ready for the next step.

2. Glass tape is convenient to apply, but it's tricky and time-consuming to feather the thick selvage edge of the tape into the plywood surface. Leaving enough epoxy in the joint to feather from the thick edge out to the plank leaves a noticeable lump.

Recommendation: Eliminate the thick selvage edge by making the tape from glass cloth cut on the bias. Look for the minimum amount of glass necessary to do the job.

3. Coating the ends of the plank components before clamping deposited far too much unnecessary epoxy on the other side of the plank, which had to be removed before the other side could be worked on.

Recommendation: Pre-coating the ends of the plywood before clamping is unnecessary. Photo 6-10 shows the amount of epoxy that has been forced through a dry joint.

The butt block on the other side of this plank was made with 6-ounce bias-cut cloth and a minimum amount of epoxy. Clamping pressure was from a C-clamp, which probably accounts for why this much

6-10

epoxy came through. Nothing needed to be done to prepare this surface. Because the epoxy was still green, there was no reason to sand.

4. Air was trapped under the tape.

Recommendation: The problem is caused by tape that won't lie flat, too much epoxy and not enough pressure. While the problem is serious, the solution is simple: use bias-cut cloth for tape, less epoxy and a C-clamp for controllable pressure.

A joint made with 6-ounce bias-cut cloth on both sides far exceeds the strength of the plywood around it. To find out the minimum amount of reinforcement, I tried various combinations down to $3/4$-ounce cloth on one side of the plank, with no

6-11

problem assembling the finished plank. My conclusion from trying several different glass weights is that the ideal for both hull and deck is tape cut from 4-ounce bias-cut cloth applied on the inside only. This will keep the color density on the outside consistent and eliminate half of the epoxy application and sanding exposure time required to make the joints.

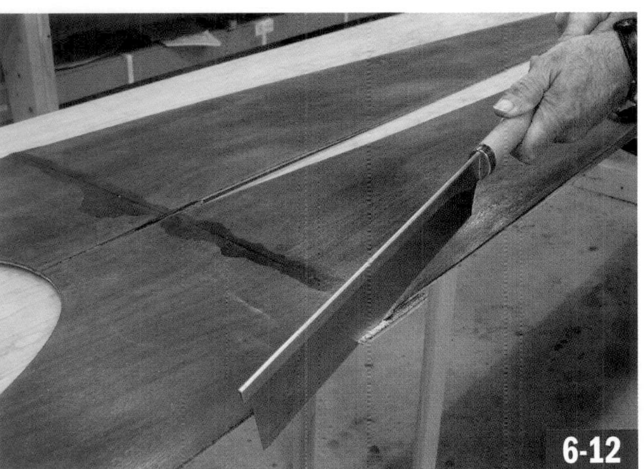
6-12

4. Use assembled plank from one side to assemble its mate.

After all the planks for one side have been assembled and cleaned up, use these as a pattern to position their mates for the other side of the kayak (6-11).

5. Clean up joints.

Do this when the epoxy has cured (→ page 63).

6. Assemble deck panels.

The next components to be assembled are the deck panels. Because our deck panels were dyed and sealed before assembling them, I didn't get to this step until later in the process.

Joining the deck panels gives us a chance to use a more traditional joint – a plywood butt block. To increase the stiffness of the deck forward of the cockpit, plywood is being used to back up the joint.

I started with the two outside panels, lining them up and securing them to the table as we did with the hull planks (→ page 147).

Since the deck on our Coho is green, I used cotton fibers dyed the same green, thinking that a small amount of the glue squeezed through the joint would be visible. Did the dye really matter? In this case, no. All we could see from the outside was a dark line. A similar dark shade could have been achieved with epoxy only slightly thickened with cotton fibers and dark brown wood dust. If the deck is to be finished in a light color, I don't think that using a light-colored glue is of much use. As long as the epoxy in the glue is absorbed into the end grain of the panel, there will be a dark line.

After the glue has set, trim the butt plate flush to the edge of the panel (6-12). Finish with 120 grit sandpaper on a firm sanding block. Bevel the edge of the plate enough to allow the bottom edges of the deck panels to fit together when they are assembled into the deck shape.

For a good fit between hull and deck, the instructions suggest a 45-degree bevel along the inside edge of the sheer plank (6-13). This angle only approximates how the edges will fit together, because the angle changes over the full length of the kayak.

6-13

I would be tempted to skip this step next time, as fitting the deck to the hull would have been a little more precise and there would have been more space for filler if the inside corners had been simply drawn together.

If you do bevel this edge, cut through the first two laminations only, using the glue line as a guide. Cutting into the third layer of veneer will result in a fragile edge and could make fitting the hull and deck a trial.

DAY 5
Assemble Hull

To Do
- O Drill suture holes.
- O Make cradle forms.
- O Make wire sutures.
- O Loosely assemble hull panels.
- O Tune up sutures.
- O Carefully turn hull and check for alignment.

Tools & Materials
- O clamps
- O drill/driver and $1/16$-inch drill bit
- O jigsaw
- O level
- O linesman pliers
- O square
- O tape measure
- O wood for cradle forms

Safety
- O dust mask
- O gloves
- O eye protection
- O good ventilation
- O caution with cutting tools

Day 5 will be intense but rewarding as we get our first look at the kayak in three dimensions. It is a very full day that will go quickly as the planks are wired together into the hull shape.

Hull panels are assembled with wire ties that go through pre-drilled holes. Since the holes will remain visible, positioning them in a logical, repetitive pattern will make them look intentional and help to harmonize with the planking. More importantly, if the pair of holes are not positioned directly opposite each other, tension on the wire will try to shift the panel as the wire tries to straighten out.

1. Drill suture holes.

Various suppliers use different routines for drilling the planks. In the interests of accuracy and reducing the variables, I started by stacking and taping the port and starboard planks together and drilling through both planks (6-14) using the drill spacer jig (→ page 70). I suggest taping the plank pairs together with stretchable tape such as electrical tape or plastic packaging tape. Look for a tape that stretches enough to pull the planks together without leaving a residue; masking tape would be my last choice.

Keep in mind that the edges of the adjoining planks will not fit together until they are drawn up into the designed shape. This means that holes in adjoining

6-14

planks cannot be drilled by simply stacking the planks and drilling one hole. Well, it could be done, but it would be awkward and possibly less than successful.

To take some confusion out of which side to drill the holes in, stack and drill along the lower edge of each pair of planks. This will take care of the sheer plank, which is not drilled along the top edge where it joins the second plank, and will get the holes in the first bottom planks along the keel line – a bonus of using this order of assembly.

There were a few glitches that could have complicated wiring the panels together later on. The manual suggested starting the holes 1 inch from the bow, which I did by measuring and marking one plank, then positioning the next plank beside it with the ends lined up, and projecting the mark across. Using the jig, I drilled the edge of both planks back to the first butt joint (about $2\frac{1}{2}$ feet). When the planks were placed together and lined up at the butt joint, the cumulative error between holes had grown to about $1/8$ inch. To continue like this for the full 17 feet would have been out of the ball park and would have meant drilling new holes.

We can do several things to get this under control. If we start the holes closer to the center of the kayak, the cumulative error is half what it would be if we had started at one end and worked to the other. The first butt joint will be used as a reference for positioning the planks, so it makes sense to start the holes there as well.

Accepting the fact that the jig is handy but not 100 percent accurate, one more confirmation is in order. While it is awkward to bring the plank edges together on the flat, it is possible to position them on the reference mark and draw the edges of the crescent-shaped planks together to add

CHEAP TRICK

To keep from breaking small drill bits, keep them spinning fast when going either in or out; the speed will reduce the friction. Also, avoid changing direction once the bit has entered the hole.

more reference marks. I marked every third hole and found I needed only a slight adjustment of the jig at each of these marks.

2. Make cradle forms (→ page 25).

Taking the time to make cradles that will support the hull is well worth doing before you begin to assemble the planks. I had planned on using cradles but wanted to see how far I could get without them. By the time the first two planks were wired together and the forms wired in, I had run out of patience. If this is your first kayak, you may start to wonder at this point if this rickety assemblage of plywood will ever be a kayak, and if it does become one, whether you will have to paddle it in small round lakes in one direction only.

Cradle forms are simple devices that go a long way toward keeping this a fun project and building a straight boat.

6-16

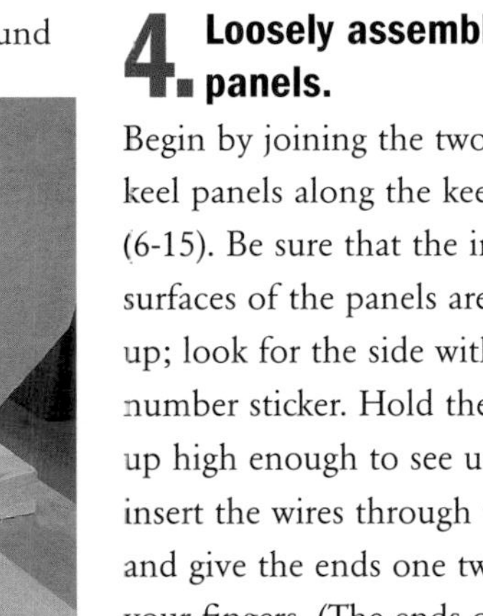

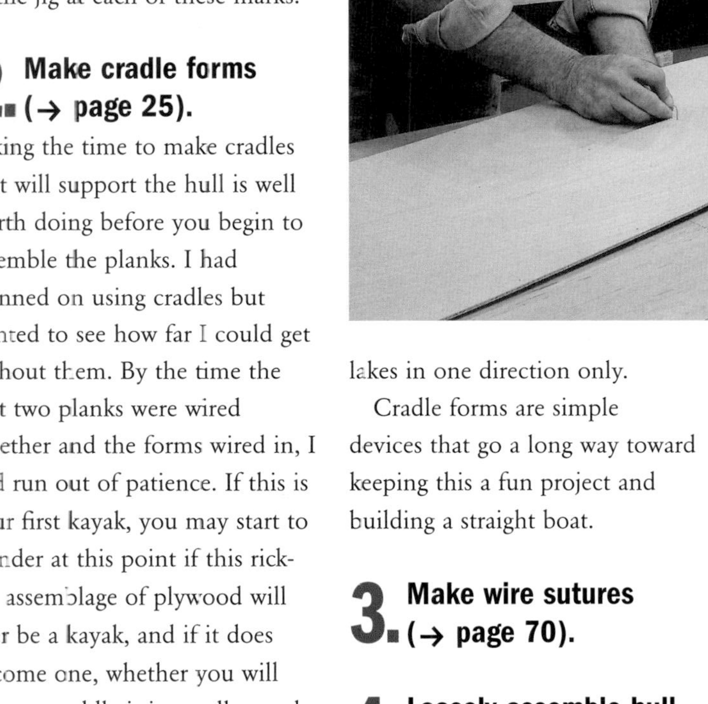
6-15

3. Make wire sutures (→ page 70).

4. Loosely assemble hull panels.

Begin by joining the two bottom keel panels along the keel line (6-15). Be sure that the inside surfaces of the panels are facing up; look for the side with the number sticker. Hold the panels up high enough to see under, insert the wires through the holes and give the ends one twist with your fingers. (The ends of the wires are sharp. My first bandage!) It is a good idea to put the first wires in every 16 inches or so to keep the pieces from sliding around while you are inserting the remainder of the wires. Use the forward plank joint (called the forward butt seam in the manual) as a reference for keeping the panels parallel. Wire as far as you can with the panels lying flat; leave the ends open for now.

Note that the wires for most of the length of the plank will be twisted on the inside of the hull. Beginning about 18 inches from both bow and stern, reverse the direction and place the wires so that they can be twisted on the outside. The reason for twisting the wire on the inside is to keep the outside uncluttered for filling the joint. As we get up into the ends, space inside the hull narrows and we run out of space to twist the wire.

Included in the kit are five temporary forms to bend the planks around and help define the shape of the hull. It is important to position these forms (called frames in the manual) according to the specifications given in the instructions; they don't have to move much before fitting the planks becomes a problem. Find these positions and draw a light pencil line across the panel, perpendicular to the centerline (6-16).

Prepare the forms by drawing a centerline on both sides. Use a ballpoint pen to make a fine line that is easy to see. The centerline will be useful for confirming that the kayak is straight.

Locate the position of the mid form and wire it into place. Drill a $1/16$-inch hole on the centerline of the form about $1\frac{1}{2}$ inches from the bottom corner. The wire will go through this hole, pass through a hole in the left plank, come back up on the other side of the form through a hole in the right plank, and be tightened.

Fastened only at the centerline, the mid form is less than secure, but pulling the ends of the planks together will exert a bit of

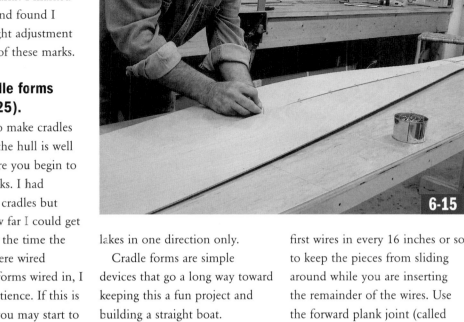

6-17

6-18

6-19

upward pressure on the form and help to hold it in position. If the planks are being assembled in a cradle, this will not be a problem.

Wire in the next two forms in the same manner (6-17).

The ends of the kayak are supported to a specified height to help establish the rocker.

Wire the ends of the planks together by running a suture through each of the paired holes and twisting the wires together. A wire every 2 inches was adequate, but note that the top edges of the planks are pulling apart at the tip (6-18). We will get another chance to pull them together when the stems are clamped and glued.

The second round of planks was then installed and wired to the forms (6-19). This was when I started getting frustrated and made a set of cradle forms.

Installing the final round of planks was a breeze (6-20). As the planks were added, the ends were clipped together with spring clamps. Spring clamps are marginally effective for controlling the pressure when gluing but are convenient for this purpose. C-clamps with clamp blocks have the added advantage of being able to bridge the joint between the rows of planks, keeping them in line.

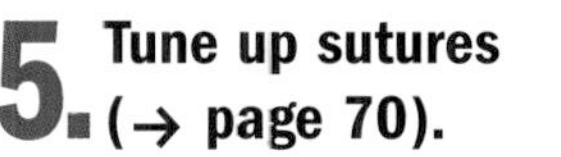

5. Tune up sutures (→ page 70).

Watch that you don't overtighten the wires; the edges of the planks between the wires are not stiff enough to maintain the pressure and will bow out, causing waves to develop. These waves may not be obvious at this stage, but when the covering goes on, they will be. As you tighten the wires, watch the plank edges come together, and stop when they touch with enough friction to hold the inside corners together.

6-20

6-21

Installing the end forms in the specified locations (6-21) will push out the plank ends slightly near the bottom. The wires at the sheer line go through a hole in the frame and are twisted on the outside. Lower down, use a long wire that will pass completely through the hull and come back on the other side of the form; tightening the wire will effectively sandwich the form between the planks.

6-22

6-23

6-24

The instructions suggest hot gluing the forms in place. Since the shape is checked again after the hull is turned over, I thought it would be safer to leave everything flexible at this point.

Before turning the hull over, attach the extensions (spacer pieces) to the forms (6-22). They will rest on the table and hold the hull in the desired position. Make the cleats that attach the extensions to the forms long enough to reach the edge of the table to simplify fastening to the table. It is important to have the cleat flush to the edge of the extension; check that all of the centerlines line up.

6. Carefully turn hull & check for alignment.

To turn it over, carefully lift the hull and remove the cradles. Roll the hull over and position the forms over the centerline; clamp or screw them to secure.

What a sweet hull! This is starting to get exciting. John Lockwood, the designer for Pygmy, certainly knows what a kayak should look like (6-23). I have to admit that I am more of a builder than a paddler, but I am looking forward to paddling this one.

With all of the forms centered and the stems on the line, the hull will be straight. Because the forms are supported on the flat, level table, we can be confident that the hull is not twisted nor the bottom hogged. If the stems are not over the centerline, first check that the forms are on the centerline. If they are, adjust the stems by loosening the wires and repositioning them.

Check the fit of the planks along the centerline and in the area where the bottom becomes the stem; add more sutures as needed (6-24).

Give the hull a final systematic check. Carefully check the fit between the planks on the outside. If we have missed something on the inside, we want to take care of it now. A poor fit at this stage will set us up for problems down the road. There will be waves in the plank line and it will bother you so much that you will try to straighten it up with the sander and cut through the outer ply into the glue line. A poor fit will also leave steps between the planks on the inside that will trap air unless they are filled.

If while applying the filler you see something that doesn't look right, the same applies. Take time to figure out the problem and fix it before locking the planks together.

DAYS 6–7

Glue Plank Seams

To Do
- ○ Tack planks with filler.*
- ○ Cut and remove wires.
- ○ Fill remaining seams.*
- ○ Fill wire holes.

Tools & Materials
- ○ epoxy dispensing pumps
- ○ epoxy resin and hardener
- ○ filler
- ○ grunge can
- ○ lacquer thinner
- ○ linesman pliers
- ○ 1-inch masking tape
- ○ mixing pots
- ○ putty knife
- ○ rags
- ○ firm sanding block
- ○ 120 or 180 grit sandpaper
- ○ stir sticks

Safety
- ○ dust mask
- ○ gloves
- ○ eye protection
- ○ good ventilation
- ○ caution with cutting tools

Expect to work about four to five hours on Day 6 to mask the joints and fill the cracks between the planks. Removing the wire sutures the following day and completing the filler should take about two hours.

1. Tack planks with filler (→ page 70).

To tack the planks together, we used a filler that would be slightly darker than the finished plywood for a subtle accent to the line of the plank. The mixture began with a base of mixed epoxy thickened with beige Microlite. Brown filleting blend was added as a coloring agent. Look for a smooth consistency, stiff enough to hold some shape without looking dry.

Keep in mind that when mixing color-matched filler, you are matching it to the shade that the wood will be after you have stained, varnished or painted it.

The wires on their own were not enough to hold the planks together consistently at the stems. Since I had been using spring clamps in the assembly, these were placed across the joint between the planks and appeared to get everything under control. After removing the clamps, I did have a couple of joints that would have benefited from slightly more pressure. For controlled pressure, I suggest using clamping blocks to bridge the joint between the planks and C-clamps.

2. Cut & remove wires.

Since our forms are held by a wire at the keel line and at the sheer, these wires will be left in until the hull is turned over.

To remove the wire sutures, snip them in the middle and bend the wires upright (6-25). You could simply cut the wire and pull hard enough from the inside to straighten the wire and pull it through, but this would enlarge the holes, a concern if a clear coating is the objective. With the hull sitting on the forms, it is easy to reach under and pull the wire through with your fingers if the ends are straightened first.

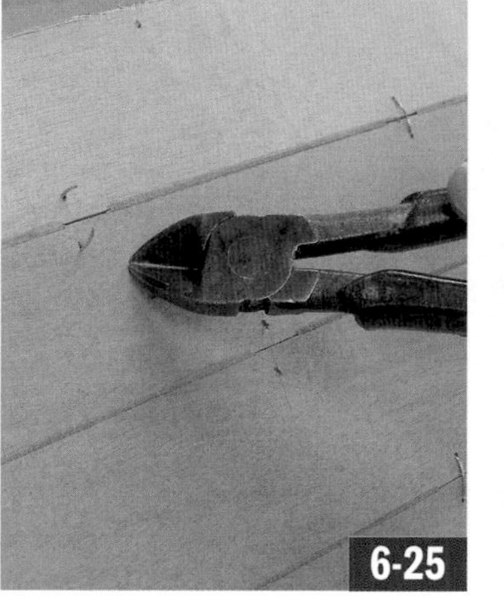
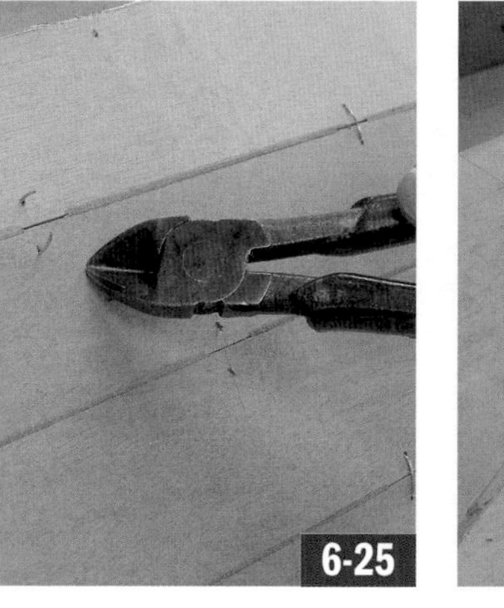

6-25

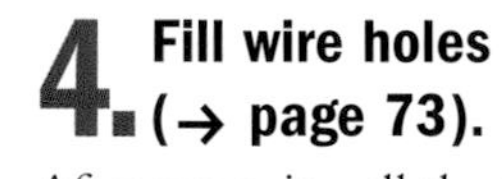

6-26

3. Fill remaining seams (→ page 72).

Do a rough shaping of the filler on the stems (6-26). This will start developing the shape and show you which areas have enough filler and which need more added.

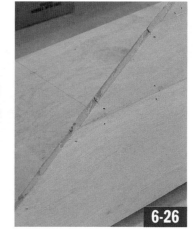

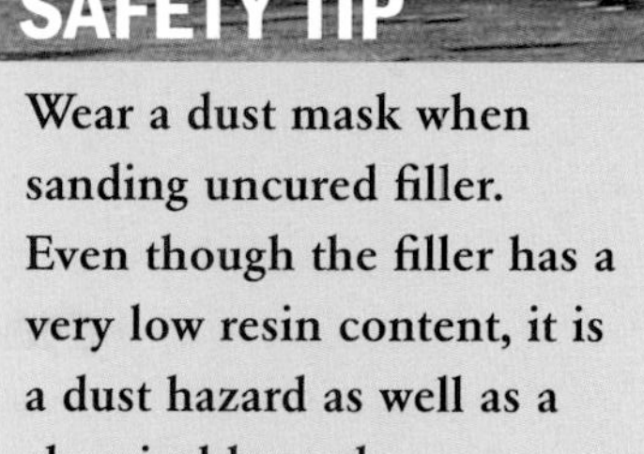

SAFETY TIP

Wear a dust mask when sanding uncured filler. Even though the filler has a very low resin content, it is a dust hazard as well as a chemical hazard.

4. Fill wire holes (→ page 73).

After removing all the sutures and cleaning up the filler, I taped the holes and the joints remaining to be filled and then filled them. If you are using a color-matched filler, try to use the same color today as you used yesterday.

DAYS 8-11

Glass Outside of Hull

This next step will see the outside of the hull reinforced with fiberglass cloth and epoxy. It will take a full day to sand and prep the hull and wet out the glass. If possible, recruit some reliable help for the first day; the following days should not take one person more than a few hours each.

To Do

- ○ Clean up joints and sand hull.
- ○ Stabilize forms from the inside.
- ○ Clean up and assemble epoxy application materials and equipment.
- ○ Position glass cloth.
- ○ Apply first coat of epoxy.*
- ○ Reinforce stern stem.*
- ○ Apply second coat of epoxy.*
- ○ Apply third coat of epoxy.*
- ○ Trim glass around sheer.

Tools & Materials

- ○ acid brush
- ○ 2-inch bristle brush
- ○ epoxy resin and hardener
- ○ fiberglass cloth
- ○ fiberglass tape
- ○ firm sanding block
- ○ grunge can
- ○ hot-glue gun
- ○ lacquer thinner
- ○ 1-inch masking tape
- ○ mixing pots
- ○ plastic spring clamps
- ○ rasp
- ○ 120 grit sandpaper
- ○ scissors
- ○ squeegee
- ○ stir sticks
- ○ string line
- ○ utility knife

Safety

- ○ dust mask
- ○ eye protection
- ○ gloves
- ○ good ventilation

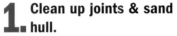

1. Clean up joints & sand hull.

The rasp is a good tool for shaping filler that has been built up on the stem (6-27). Being rigid, the rasp cuts the high points first; this will tell you where to work first and will bridge the shiny low spots until a fair curve is developed.

I suggest shaping the profile first; the crisp edge will give your eye something to follow. When you are happy with the shape, round over the edges into a half-round where the stem comes into the bottom, then let it flatten out slightly as it comes up to the deck.

Use a firm but flexible sanding block to round over the edges. Work with long strokes to keep the curve developing consistently from top to bottom. Finish with a piece of sandpaper wrapped around the stem (6-28).

After the joints have been cleaned up, do a final sanding of the plywood by hand (→ page 96).

6-27

6-28

6-29

6-30

2. Stabilize forms from the inside.

We have a few details to take care of and one last check to be sure the hull is straight; then we can clean up and get organized for the glass-and-epoxy covering.

The hull is still secured to the forms with a couple of wires. Before the outside is glassed, the remaining wires need to be removed and the forms refastened to the inside of the hull.

Turn the hull over and set it up in the cradles. This is a good time to double-check that the hull is straight. Level the forms (6-29), then stand at the end and sight from bow to stern. If the hull is straight, the centerlines on the forms will be in a direct line between bow and stern. If you question your eye, stretch a string from end to end to confirm.

Two small softwood corner blocks, one on each side, are used to hold each form in place (6-30). Keep the amount of hot glue on the planking to a minimum. It is miserable stuff to scrape off, a lot like picking gum off the bottom of your shoe.

Gently turn the hull back over and secure the forms to the table (6-31). Position the forms over the centerline and confirm that

6-31

the bow and stern are centered.

While the forms are just deep enough for the bow and stern to clear the table, the limited clearance at the ends will make applying the glass cloth awkward. I placed a 1½-inch block under each form to get some working room.

Protect the table with plastic or cardboard. Plastic is a good choice on the ends because the wet cloth will touch in places. Cardboard is a good choice for catching drips.

3. Clean up & assemble epoxy application materials & equipment.

This is a good time to clean up the work area, as the next few days will benefit from a clean environment. After vacuuming the dust on the hull that you can get at, carefully pick up the remainder with a rag soaked in lacquer thinner.

Assemble everything needed for applying the epoxy and fiberglass cloth. Because the speed of working with epoxy is driven by its pot life, there will be no time to look for things after the resin and hardener have been combined.

4. Position glass cloth.

The instructions recommend applying a strip of 8.5-ounce glass tape over the cloth to protect the stem and keel line from abrasion. It is a good idea to reinforce this exposed area, as it is usually the first point of contact when you run out of water. To save the step of wetting out the glass tape and to avoid having to feather the edges later, I put the tape under the cloth, where it could be wet out at the same time as the cloth.

Spread the cloth over the hull and cut it slightly longer than the hull. With your helper stationed at the other end, tug the cloth gently back and forth to straighten it out down the centerline. Remember that trying to brush out wrinkles with your hand could put a permanent crease in the fabric.

You might wonder why I went to the effort of getting the glass all settled and then I decided to fold one end back over the other. It's fussy keeping the glass tape centered while positioning the cloth, so we need to increase the odds in our favor. Pulling the cloth out straightens the threads and lets us know where the middle of the cloth is. If we pull the cloth halfway back and keep it centered, we have a reasonable chance of putting it back without disturbing the glass tape.

After drawing the cloth back to the centerline, roll the tape up the stem and down the centerline (6-32), then tuck the roll of tape under the glass. Work the glass tape over the stem and smoothly down the centerline. If necessary, secure it around the stem with several pieces of green masking tape. Don't press the masking tape down too firmly. If you do,

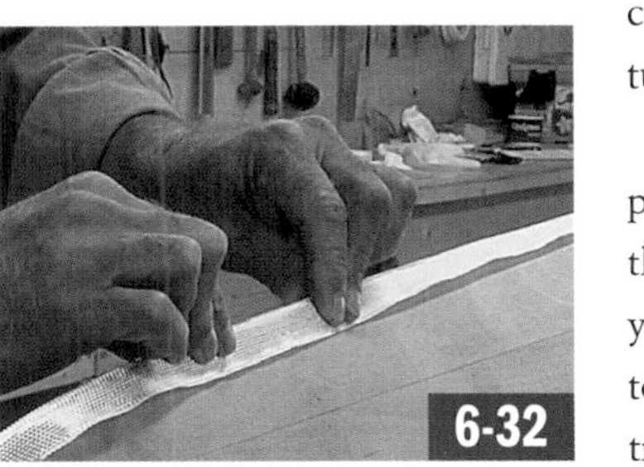
6-32

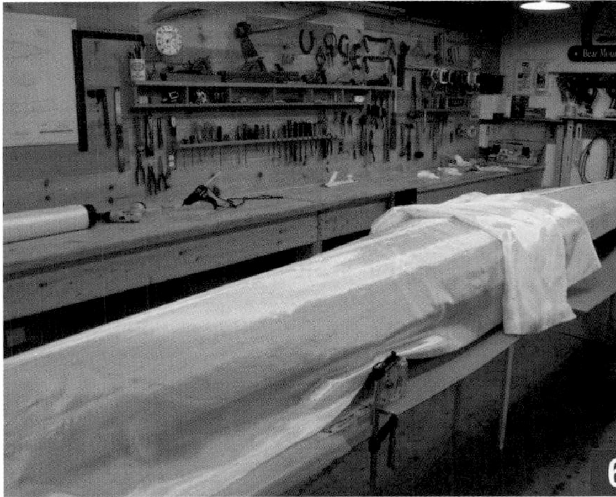
6-33

you may shift the glass tape when removing the masking tape or possibly transfer glue from the tape to the glass.

Hold the glass in the middle and very carefully pull it straight back along the centerline. Keep an eye on the edges; if they get hung up on something, it will mess up the cloth.

Now carefully pull back the glass cloth on the other end (6-33) and continue positioning the tape. Replace the glass by pulling it directly down the centerline and tighten it by tugging gently from the end.

The instructions suggest using pushpins to anchor the tape at the stern – not a bad solution if you are working alone. Hesitating to make more holes in the hull, I tried plastic spring clamps and

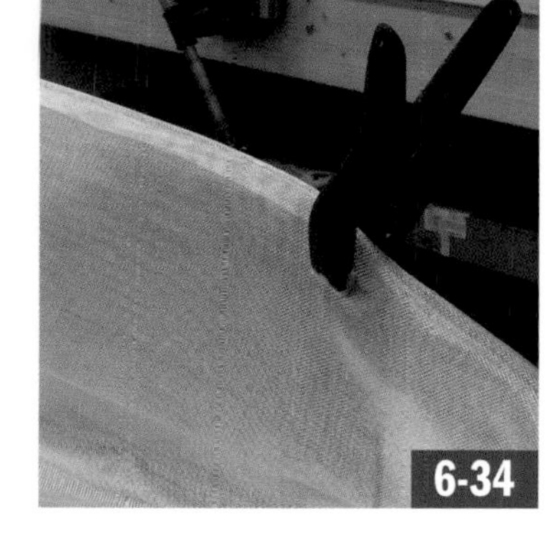
6-34

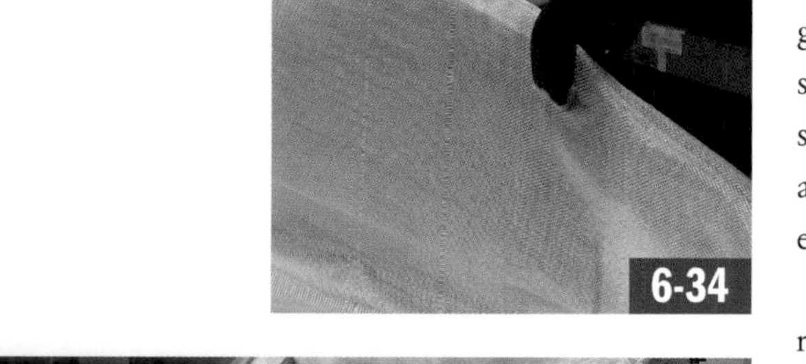
6-35

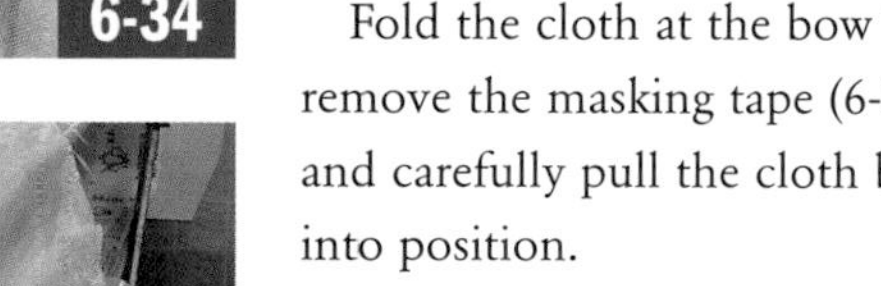
6-36

they worked fine (6-34). Don't try this with unprotected metal spring clamps; they will bruise the wood and snag the cloth. The glass tape will extend around the stern stem about 1 inch past the spring clamp. This is about as far around the stern stem as we can expect the cloth to go.

Fold the cloth at the bow back, remove the masking tape (6-35) and carefully pull the cloth back into position.

It is possible to shape the glass all the way around the bow stem if the glass cloth is centered along the centerline. Begin at the top and work both sides evenly with a down and forward motion. We are not stretching the glass fibers but rather repositioning the threads to cross at an angle other than 90 degrees.

When the cloth is settled, trim the edge of the glass (6-36). Leave as much cloth as possible to catch the runs and wick away the epoxy along the sheer. Save the offcuts, as some scrap will be needed later to reinforce the underside of the deck behind the cockpit.

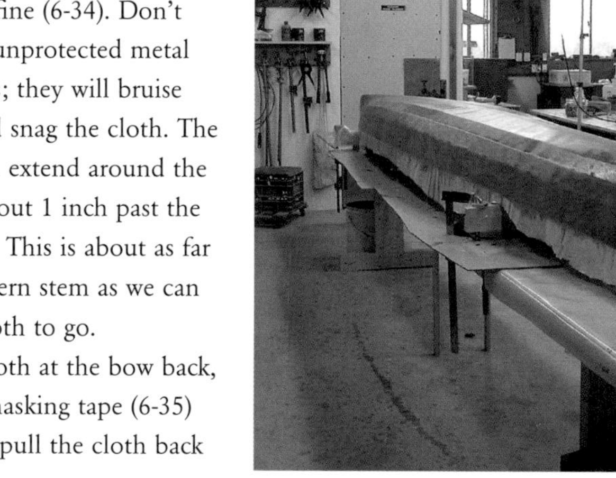
6-37

6-38

5. Apply first coat of epoxy (→ page 82).

We can congratulate ourselves on a job well done (6-37) and take a break until the epoxy has firmed up enough to trim the glass at the stern.

6. Reinforce stern stem (→ page 86).

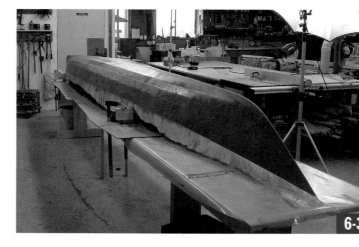

7. Apply second coat of epoxy (→ page 87).

8. Apply third coat of epoxy (→ page 88).

9. Trim glass around sheer.

When the last coat of epoxy has cured, trim the glass around the sheer with a sharp utility knife (6-38). I strongly suggest keeping both hands on the knife for safety. If for any reason the knife goes out of control, at least your hands will be safe behind the blade. Be very careful that the blade does not jump out of the cut and damage the glass covering.

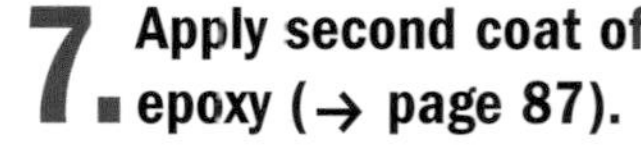

DAYS 12-13

Assemble Deck Panels

To Do
- O Turn hull over and set in cradle.
- O Loosely assemble deck panels.
- O Secure edge of deck to hull.
- O Line up panels and tighten wires.
- O Fill seams between wire sutures.*
- O Cut and remove wires.
- O Fill remaining seams.*

Tools & Materials
- O clamps
- O drill/driver and 1⁄16-inch drill bit
- O epoxy resin and hardener
- O fiber tape
- O filler and coloring agents
- O hot glue
- O linesman pliers
- O masking tape
- O plastic packaging tape
- O putty knife
- O rags
- O rasp
- O firm sanding block
- O scrap wood
- O stir sticks
- O utility knife
- O wire

Safety
- O dust mask
- O eye protection
- O gloves
- O good ventilation
- O caution with cutting tools

Expect the first day of this step to be busy but exciting as you see the deck of your kayak come together. Removing the wires and finishing up the filler should take about three to four hours. Take your time putting the panels together and be sure you are happy with how things fit before committing to the filler. The deck is the part of the kayak that you the paddler will see the most – make it look good.

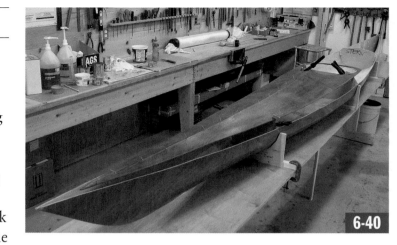

1. Turn hull over & set in cradle.

Turn the hull over and set it up in the cradles.

The first thing to do is clean up the edge of the hull. Glass that was not cut off is glass, and it will cut you. If your hands are soft, it might be a good idea to wear work gloves when turning the hull over. Use a rasp or firm sanding block to remove this sharp edge (6-39); stop when you get to the edge of the hull.

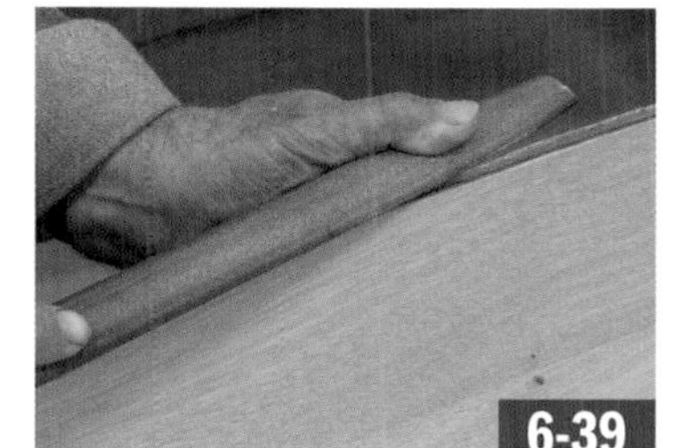
6-39

2. Loosely assemble deck panels.

First we are assembling the two center panels that make up the foredeck (6-40). After finding the holes, insert the wires from the inside and twist them on the outside.

The routine here is the same as on the hull. Assemble the panels with the wires twisted finger-tight. When the pieces are together, go over all the joints, tightening only enough to bring the edges together with sufficient friction to hold the position until the filler cures. Do whatever you can to keep the inside edges of the planks flush. If there is a step

6-40

CHEAP TRICK

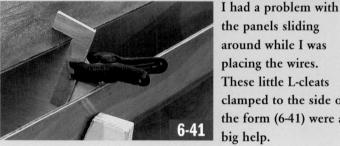

6-41

I had a problem with the panels sliding around while I was placing the wires. These little L-cleats clamped to the side of the form (6-41) were a big help.

6-42

6-43

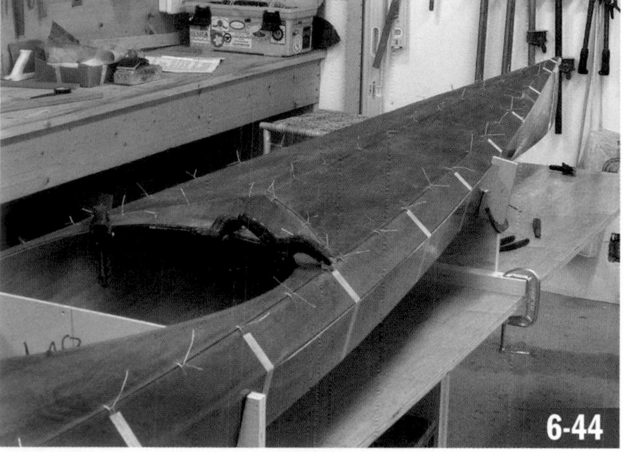
6-44

6-45

between the planks, you may have to cut through the veneer into the glue line while trying to correct it, or air may become trapped under the glass if the step is not removed.

Join the stern deck panels on the centerline. Note the stick across the hull supporting the forward edge of the aft deck (6-42).

A deck recess plate is used in the Coho to make the transition between the aft deck and the cockpit (6-43). This thoughtful detail is another reflection of the pride that Pygmy Boats takes in exploring the limits of plywood for small boat construction. It is not only visually attractive, but is also engineered to stiffen and strengthen the deck behind the cockpit.

Because this piece is bent and sprung into place, it took a bit of fiddling to get all the edges to stay in position. Adding more wires would have helped a lot, but I hesitated to drill more holes in our green deck. If the deck was to be painted, this step would have gone much faster because the additional holes could have been filled and sanded later. I used an off-white filler to accent the joints between the green deck panels, so there was no room for error if I expected an even filler line. I ended up filling the seam in two steps, as getting one part of the plate into position messed up other places. Once part of it had been bonded, the rest was easy to wedge into position and fill.

CHEAPER TRICK

Another problem was getting the wire started up through the hole when working by feel. I found it helped to insert the end of a wire from the top as a guide for finding the hole from the bottom; once the hole was located, it was easy to chase the locating wire up from the bottom with the wire suture.

3. Secure edge of deck to hull.

Tape the deck to the hull with fiber tape (6-44). The edge of the deck must be flush with the outside of the hull. If not, the result will be waves in the sheer line. Compensating for a poor fit makes it fussy to work the filler in, and the results could look less than professional.

4. Line up panels & tighten wires.

Go over the wires and tighten them just enough to draw the inside edges together, no more. If tightened more, the edges of the panels between the wires will bulge out. Work both sides out from the centerline halfway between the bow and the stern in a logical pattern to keep the tension building inward, as well as to keep the parts balanced as they are drawn into shape.

I had a few warps in the plywood that took a lot of attention. In these areas, the edges of the hull and deck would not stay in alignment everywhere at once with just the tape. In retrospect, the trick with the little sticks hot-glued around the edge would have greatly simplified this step and saved time later. Rather than damage the deck with more holes, I tacked the joint where it was fitting and finished it in a second step.

Before committing to the filler, give the joints one last systematic check and adjust the wires as necessary.

If a clear coat is the objective, it is a good idea to protect the plank surface by masking the joints. Nipping the tails off the wires (6-45) will allow the masking tape to go over the wire.

5. Fill seams between wire sutures.

The joints are now taped off ready for filler. You will notice a

6-46

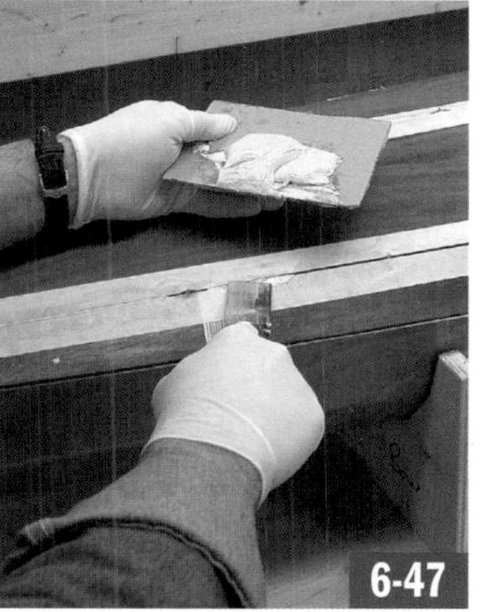
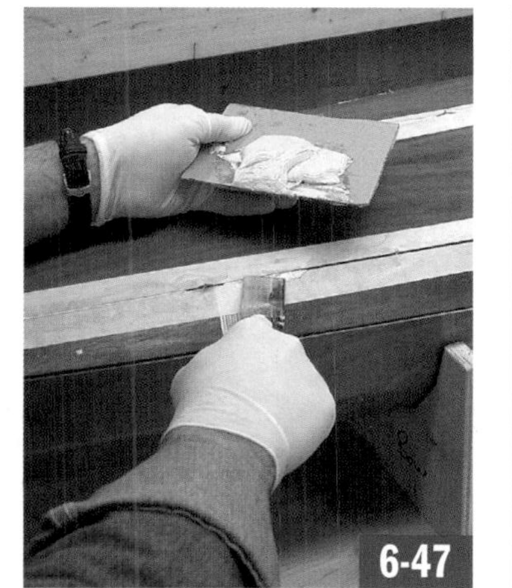

6-47

section in the foreground of the photo that does not have tape on the joint (6-46). These pieces were not fitting, so this section was left until the area around it had been stabilized with filler. Again, this area would have been easy to control with the sticks-and-hot-glue trick. Too soon old, too late smart.

Give some thought to any place where the filler might come through the joint and bond the deck to the hull; protect these places with plastic.

Rather than come up with a green filler to match the deck, I used the off-white color of Microlite combined with mixed epoxy to accent the joints (6-47). Apply it with a downward pressure to force the filler as far as possible into the joint. Work

6-48

aggressively at the ends; as the panels flatten out, the joint gets quite narrow.

Scrape the filler flush with the tape. Anything left behind now will have to be sanded later.

6. Cut & remove wires.

After the joints have been filled between the wires and have had time to cure, cut and remove the wires. Then complete filling the joints.

Because it was resting on the cross-spalls, the weight of the deck was causing it to flatten slightly, so short blocks were clamped to the spacers to maintain the correct width (6-48).

BEST CHEAP TRICK YET

Easy deck-alignment device

This simple little trick is up there with my slit-in-the-juice-can trick for cleaning the squeegee. While attaching the two outside deck panels (called sheer panels in the manual), I felt like a one-armed paper-hanger. Until the panels were secured with a few sutures and taped to the hull, there weren't enough hands to go around.

This idea came later on in the building process, when I was trying to fit the deck precisely to the hull for bonding. But I suggest installing these guides at this point; it will simplify putting the deck panels together and control the shape for a perfect fit to the hull.

Fasten the sticks (tongue depressors can be used) to the hull with hot glue (6-49) in enough places to support the outer deck panel edges and align the panel edges with the edge of the hull (6-50). After the deck is bonded to the hull, the sticks can be popped off the hull without leaving any residue to clean up.

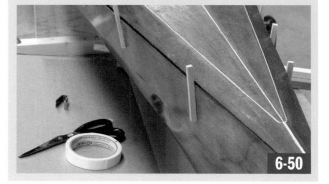

6-49

6-50

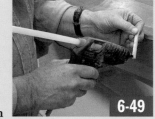

CHEAP TRICK

Clamp block protection

To prevent the heartbreak of gluing the clamp blocks to the hull (something that is surprisingly easy to do), wrap them with clear plastic packaging tape. It saves fumbling with a piece of plastic or waxed paper, plus it allows better visibility and access for cleaning up – you don't need to peek under anything to see what's going on.

6-51

6-52

I had a problem keeping the ends of the panels lined up at the correct angle without adding more wires, so I cut softwood clamping blocks to fit the shape of the deck on both top and bottom.

The stick clamped to the C-clamp was to carry the weight of the clamp and try to correct the twist that was developing in the bow deck (6-51). I am not sure how it got there, but some asymmetrical tension must have developed as the panels were being wired together. I am sure the stick-and-hot-glue trick would have made these gymnastics unnecessary.

7. Fill remaining seams.

Fill the remainder of the joints and peel off the tape (6-52).

Wow! It's a kayak. Since we have been working clean, it is easy to imagine sitting in the cockpit with that long varnished green deck pointing down the river.

We can take a break now until the filler sets, then get organized to finish the inside of the deck.

DAYS 14-16

Seal Underside of Deck

To Do
- ○ Set up cradle to support deck bottom side up.
- ○ Consider filling wire holes.
- ○ Modify any joints difficult for fiberglass to follow.*
- ○ Seal underside of deck and reinforce joints.*
- ○ Feather edges of glass tape.
- ○ Apply second coat of epoxy.*

Tools & Materials
- ○ acid brush
- ○ 2-inch bristle brush
- ○ drill/driver
- ○ epoxy resin and hardener
- ○ fiber tape
- ○ fiberglass cloth
- ○ fiberglass tape
- ○ file
- ○ filler and coloring agents
- ○ lacquer thinner
- ○ masking tape
- ○ putty knife
- ○ rags
- ○ sanding blocks
- ○ 120 grit sandpaper
- ○ scissors
- ○ scraper
- ○ spokeshave
- ○ stir sticks
- ○ utility knife
- ○ vacuum cleaner

Safety
- ○ dust mask
- ○ eye protection
- ○ gloves
- ○ good ventilation
- ○ caution with cutting tools

These will be easy days, broken by the time it takes for the epoxy to kick. The time can be compressed somewhat by using a fast hardener or by adding heat. But unless you are going to be doing more boat work in the future, buying another hardener is hardly justified by saving a day or two.

1. Set up cradle to support deck bottom side up.

Remove the hull, deck and cradles from the table and set up the cradles to support the deck. I used the extensions (spacer pieces) that were part of the frames used to support the hull and added a cleat across the bottom to clamp them to the table. It would have been better if the extensions had been wide enough to extend up the side panel of the deck to keep it from sliding around. I used the ones supplied with no great hardship, but there were times when the extra control would have been helpful.

2. Consider filling wire holes.

There are a number of ways of dealing with the remaining suture holes in the deck. The minimal solution is not to do anything and let the holes be filled with epoxy when the inside of the deck is glassed. The drawback is that the epoxy will ooze through the holes, which means more work on the outside surface.

Since our Coho deck is dark green, I wanted the holes to disappear as much as possible, but making up a green filler to match seemed a bit extreme. However, if your deck is to be bright-finished over raw plywood or dyed another color, you might want to consider mixing up a color-matched filler. The straight mixed epoxy I used as filler was the same brown tone as the dark lines in the grain of the green-dyed plywood. Mixed epoxy was chosen because it wicks into a hole more quickly than thickened filler.

Tape off the holes on the outside and apply the filler from the inside. Taping off the holes not only saves on cleanup time, but also molds the epoxy flush to the deck surface. I used an acid brush to drop a puddle of epoxy over the hole (6-53); unaided, the epoxy soaked partway in. A flexible putty knife was used to force it to the bottom of the hole.

6-54

CHEAP TRICK

If you keep your finger on the tape covering the hole while working the epoxy down with the knife, you will feel the epoxy hit the tape, confirming that the joint hole is full.

3. Modify any joints difficult for fiberglass to follow.

Bevel the aft edge of the butt plate that backs up the joint in the aft deck panels (6-54). The butt plate material is 4 mm (5/32-inch) thick and would require a substantial amount of filler to fair it gracefully into the deck recess plate. Don't bevel the butt plate all the way to the bottom edge, because there is not much

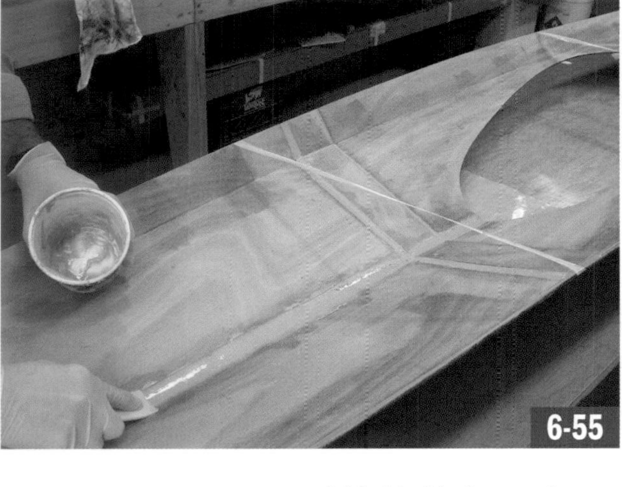
6-55

6-56

6-57

material behind it. I went about two-thirds of the way down (two laminations) and it wasn't hard to fill and feather it into the recess plate. This is an area that will be felt, which is as important as being seen, perhaps more so. People might not see the dust in the varnish, but they will feel an unfinished surface.

I used a spokeshave, but a block plane or firm sanding block would work just as well.

A filler (→ page 75) will be used to ease any abrupt change of direction in the panels so that the fiberglass cloth or tape will be able to follow the shape. The joints that need some help are down the centerline and along the outer deck panel joint. Also needing attention will be the butt block joints.

Notice the piece of fiber tape holding the sides together (6-55). It is important to have the deck sitting in an unstressed position, because once the filler kicks, the shape is locked together for good.

Note the filler along the edge of the plywood butt blocks (6-56). Although the edges were beveled before assembly, a little more filler was needed to blend the block into the deck.

When the filler has cured enough to sand, clean up the fillets in preparation for sealing the plywood and glassing the joints. If you have taken the time to do a neat job on the fillets, the sanding step will go quickly. This is an area that will be felt more than seen, so make it feel good rather than spending a lot of effort to make it look good too.

6-58

When finished, vacuum the dust and wipe clean with a rag dampened with lacquer thinner to pick up the remainder of the dust. Using water at this stage would raise the grain and require another sanding.

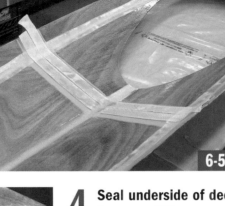

4. Seal underside of deck (→ page 82) & reinforce joints (→ page 77).

I combined the first coat of epoxy with reinforcing the joints with glass tape. Two continuous pieces of tape were used, running the full width of the deck, positioned over the butt blocks (6-57). Structurally, the continuous fiber of the glass increases the stiffness of the deck.

As suggested in the manual, scrap pieces of cloth were used to reinforce the deck aft of the cockpit opening (6-58).

5. Feather edges of glass tape.

When the epoxy has cured, feather the edges of the glass tape and give the coated plywood a

6-59

6-60

quick scuff with 120 grit sandpaper in preparation for a final coat of epoxy. This should have been a quick step, completed and cleaned up inside an hour. Instead, there was something I had to learn first.

I had a problem with the 9.5-ounce tape: one edge kept sticking up a good 1/16 inch, while the other edge lay down just fine. During the cure stage I tried pressing the edge down with the squeegee, but this had no useful effect. Forget feathering this edge with the orbital sander. It would have been hard enough not to damage the sealed plywood with sandpaper on a hard block. I tried several methods to feather the edge. The epoxy cut cleanly with a sharp chisel at the green, rubbery stage (about 24 hours with System Three). This was working well and the first half of the deck was done in less than an hour. It would have been smart to keep going, but I got distracted. When I got back to it the next day, the epoxy was too hard to cut safely with the chisel.

The solution was to use a very sharp scraper to slice off the standing edge of the tape (6-59). I had filed the scraper blade into a crescent shape to keep the corners from digging in and damaging the plywood. It went reasonably fast, but the edge on the scraper dulled quickly when cutting the glass and had to be sharpened often.

6. Apply second coat of epoxy (→ page 87).

Brush the epoxy on and draw it out into a thin, consistent film.

Since I planned to cut a hatch in the deck, I thought it would be a good idea to glass both sides of the deck around the hatch to keep the cover from warping (6-60). It's a good idea to treat plywood in the same way on both sides if holding its shape is important.

The ideal time to apply this reinforcement is when the tape is applied. Because I anticipated a problem with the bulky-edged tape, mine went on with the second coat of mixed epoxy.

When the epoxy had cured, the deck was set in a safe place and the hull was set upright in the cradles.

DAYS 17-19

Glass Inside of Hull

To Do
- O Remove forms and clean up hot-glue damage.
- O Clean up inside and sand plywood.
- O Fillet stems and along centerline.*
- O Clean up fillet and stems after curing.
- O Fiberglass inside of hull.**

Tools & Materials
- O acid brush
- O 2-inch bristle brush
- O cake decorator bag
- O chisel
- O coat hanger
- O drill/driver
- O epoxy glue
- O fiberglass cloth
- O fiberglass tape
- O fiber tape
- O filler and coloring agents
- O file
- O lacquer thinner
- O masking tape
- O putty knife
- O rags
- O sanding blocks
- O 120 grit sandpaper
- O scissors
- O scraper
- O spokeshave
- O stir sticks
- O utility knife
- O vacuum cleaner

Safety
- O dust mask
- O gloves
- O good ventilation
- O caution with cutting tools

Set aside two full days to prepare the hull and apply the fillets and glass and epoxy to the inside of the hull. Applying the second coat of epoxy on the third day should take about two hours to complete.

6-61

6-62

1. Remove forms & clean up hot-glue damage.

Some of our forms were held in place with two small softwood blocks and hot-melt glue. To simply pry the blocks off would have been a gamble. To avoid a potential problem, I split the block above the plywood, then removed the balance by shaving the block down with a sharp chisel (6-61).

2. Clean up inside & sand plywood.

Filling the wire holes from the outside is not all about vanity. To get a feel for cleaning up damage from epoxy running through the wire holes, I left a few of the holes open. Notice how much epoxy has wicked through these holes and piled up (6-62). These bumps must be sanded flat before the fiberglass can be applied. Otherwise, the glass will not follow the shape and air could be trapped around the mound of epoxy.

It is difficult to work the hard bumps down level to the wood. Epoxy is so much harder than wood that it is easy to cause as much damage as is being repaired. A safe method is to use a hard sanding block that will follow the inside curve yet concentrate its pressure on the high glob of cured epoxy.

Because the filler I used had an easy-to-sand Microlite base, this part of the sanding and cleanup was a piece of cake – under one hour (6-63). Another case of pay me now or pay me later. If I had not made an effort to keep the interior clean, sanding would have seemed like endless tedium in tight quarters, and still it would likely never be as clean as an undamaged surface.

Vacuum out the interior and pick up the remainder of the dust with a thinner-dampened rag.

3. Fillet stems & along centerline.

The manual suggests using the supplied tongue depressor to make a dam or form at the stern stem. As an alternative that will ensure an epoxy-tight fit, I suggest shaping a longer dam from a thin, easily carved wood such as pine, basswood, cedar or 4 mm (5/32-inch) plywood. Because the stern stem fillet is the backer for a rudder fitting, the instructions suggest forming a fillet about 2½ inches deep. The form, which

6-63

is about 7/8 inch wide at the top, will be left in and epoxy-coated when the interior is glassed.

The form is braced in place with a stick cut to fit tightly to the outside and clamped to the side of the hull to secure it (6-64). Be sure the backup stick provides support across the full width to keep the dam from twisting as

6-64

the pressure of the filler builds. The backup stick also needs to be positioned high enough that we can go ahead with the centerline fillet.

Before making the end pour (→ page 78), it's wise to mask off the outside of the hull below the top of the stem, just in case the epoxy expands and flows over the top.

After dry-fitting the dam, remove it to place the first batch of filler. The cake decorator bag (→ page 75) did a good job of getting the filler up into the narrow end of the hull, then the dam was wedged back into place and more filler added from the top. Use a piece of coat hanger to work out any bubbles trapped within the filler. Note that the dam was filled to about 1 inch below the top because some expansion was anticipated.

Well, it did expand (6-65), and I had to rush to protect the side of the hull with tape before the filler began to overflow. Even after I scraped off the froth twice (sort of like knocking the head off a pint of Guinness), the filler continued to expand. The masking tape protected the outside of the hull and the tight fit around the form held the pressure. Toxic fumes were the only real problem. Next time I will keep the shop temperature down, use a slow hardener, keep the resin content of the filler low, and fill in two or three steps about six hours apart.

6-65

Since the purpose of the fillet is to ease the transition from one plank to another along the centerline, it will not run continuously from bow to stern. The center of the boat is relatively flat, so there is no need for a fillet in this area. Note that only the stems and keel line received the fillet. The glass will not have a great problem fitting into the joints between the hull panels.

The bow stem is a continuation of the centerline fillet (6-66). I used a 1-inch-wide stick shaped like a tongue depressor to shape the stem fillet until the narrow squeegee could take over. The cake decorator trick worked well for getting filler into the confined space of the stem. Once there was room to move, the putty knife was used to transfer blobs of filler to the centerline to be drawn out and shaped with the squeegee.

Begin the stern fillet at the dam (6-67). If you are using a temporary dam, let the stem cure and remove the dam before making the fillet.

Since the stern is a tight V, I used the tongue depressor to shape from the end back to where the squeegee became useful. Again the cake decorator bag trick was effective for getting filler into the joint and not down the side of the hull. Although the filler is quite deep at the stern, there was no problem with it overheating.

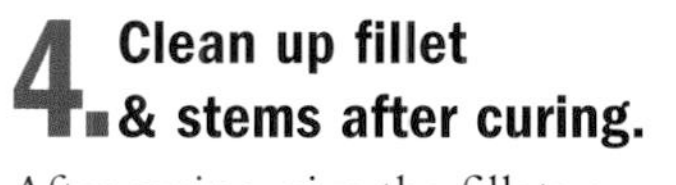

4. Clean up fillet & stems after curing.

After curing, give the fillets a quick sand with 120 grit sandpaper. This is the last smoothing step before the inside is covered. Take the time to vacuum out the dust and check for rough spots by running your hand over the surface. Try shutting your eyes to help you focus on what you are feeling – assuming it is past the sliver stage.

Vacuum out the hull again and wipe down with a rag dampened with lacquer thinner. (If water is used at this point, it will cause the grain to raise.)

5. Fiberglass inside of hull (→ page 91).

6-66

6-67

DAYS 20-21
Join Hull and Deck

To Do
- ○ Position deck on hull and secure.
- ○ Tack joint between hull and deck between fasteners.*
- ○ Clean up edge and complete filling seam.*

Tools & Materials
- ○ clamps
- ○ clamp blocks
- ○ drill/driver
- ○ epoxy resin and hardener
- ○ fiber tape
- ○ filler and coloring agents
- ○ linesman pliers
- ○ masking tape
- ○ pushpins
- ○ putty knife
- ○ rags
- ○ sanding blocks
- ○ 120 grit sandpaper
- ○ scissors
- ○ stir sticks
- ○ utility knife
- ○ wire

Safety
- ○ dust mask
- ○ eye protection
- ○ gloves
- ○ good ventilation
- ○ care with cutting tools

Joining the hull and deck will be quite exciting. You will no longer be looking at components, panels and wires but at a single unit, your kayak. Positioning and securing the deck and putting in the first round of filler will take a full day. Completing the filler on the second day should not take more than two or three hours.

1. Position deck on hull & secure.

After the deck was taped to the hull, I realized I had forgotten to fill in the bow with another end pour. Oh well, I had always wanted to try that stand-it-in-the-tree trip-bucket trick, so here was my chance (→ page 79).

How you position the deck on the hull and secure it will have a lot to do with how the finished kayak will look. If these components do not come together with a clean line, it will be obvious, and disappointing. Take your time; it took me a good two hours to attach and adjust the deck before it was ready for the filler (6-68).

6-68

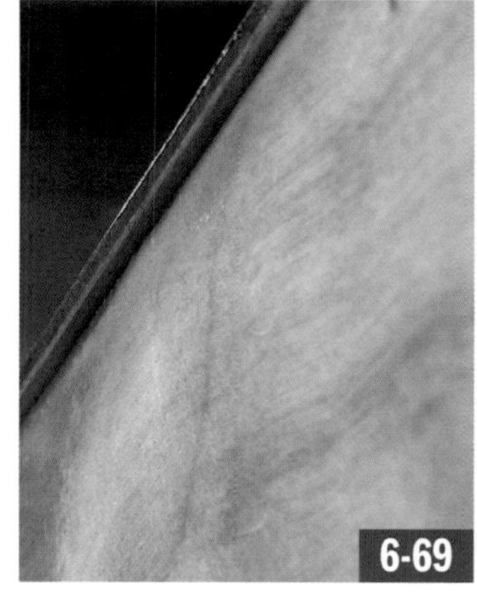
6-69

6-70

Here was another learning opportunity concerning how good is good enough. When the deck panels were taped to the hull for tacking the joints, the edges of the deck were hanging over "just a little bit." Given how flexible 4 mm (5/32-inch) plywood is, I assumed this tolerance would be easy to adjust when the deck and hull were attached. Wrong! The deck was flush to the hull on the other side, but this side extended over the hull up to 1/4 inch in some areas (6-69). This is a good reminder that errors do accumulate. Had the hull been wider than the deck, it would have been easier to correct, as the tape does a better job of holding in than pulling out.

The problem is how to pull the hull out and hold it in position long enough to tack with filler. Planing the edge back to fit the hull was out of the question because the edge of the deck is our guide to a fair joint. Although it would have been possible to get some wires in by drilling at an angle through both hull and deck, the bright finish of this kayak meant that I needed to find a less destructive solution (6-70).

In an area where the hull was being pulled out to meet the deck and there was too much tension for the hot glue on the stick to hold it, I tried a couple of Pygmy's bonus pushpins (6-71). The pins worked fine and I can live with the hole. Tap them in with a small hammer; twist to remove.

Near the bow, the hull spread

6-71

slightly wider than the deck and the tape would not hold it in. I used beveled clamp blocks with coarse sandpaper glued on the face of each one to keep them from sliding down. As it was right in the bow, it was easy to get a clamp on coming up from the bottom and leave space to fill the joint (6-72).

Do what you must with what you have to work with to make sure everything stays in position long enough to be tacked with the filler.

2. Tack joint between hull & deck between fasteners.

Tape off the joint to keep the filler where it will do some good.

There was no simple way of matching the green deck, so the filler I used was color matched to the natural color of the deck edge. Since the hull-deck joint is under a certain amount of tension, I thought it wise to add

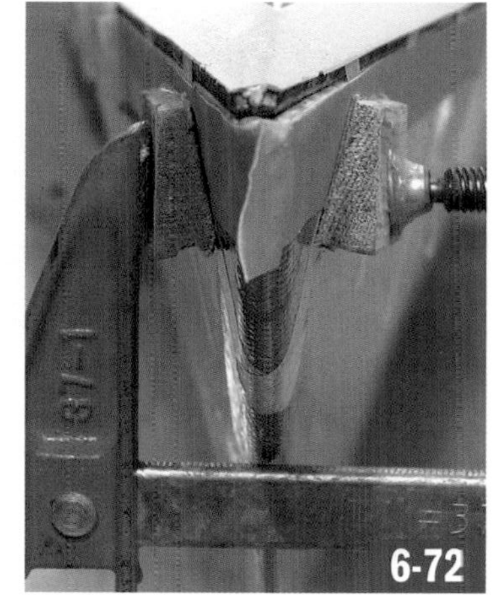
6-72

a structural component to the filler. The filler is a mixture of cotton fiber, a tan cellulose filler for color, and a bit of Microlite to make it creamy enough to work into the narrow cracks and thick enough to fill the larger spaces (6-73).

The joint between the hull and deck is very tight in the ends, with a slight overhang. Trying to work filler into this crack from the outside is difficult at best. I wedged up the end of the deck slightly with a tongue depressor to work the filler into the joint before taping it back into position (6-74).

Remove the masking tape after filling, then let the filler cure until it is hard enough to sand.

6-73

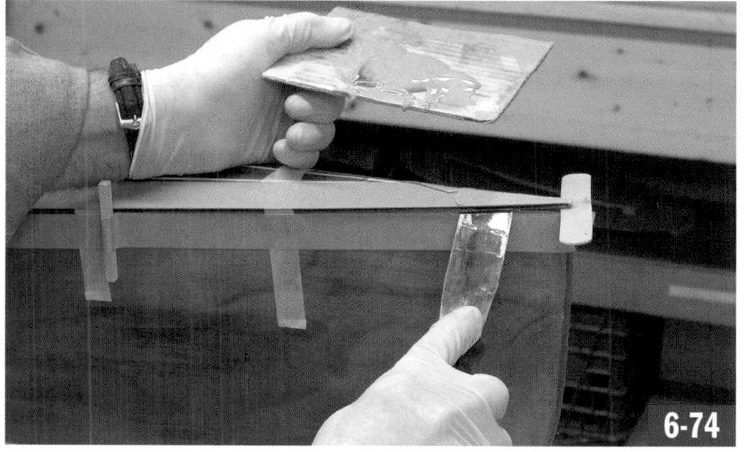
6-74

3. Clean up edge & complete filling seam.

The purpose of the cleanup step is to trim the deck and the filler flush to the hull in a line that projects straight up the side of the hull. Holding off rounding the edge until the joint has been completely filled will help keep the shape of the edge consistent.

If the deck is overhanging the hull, use a block plane to bring the deck edge down almost to the hull, then finish with a firm sanding block.

Since the epoxy surface on the hull needs to be sanded before the deck is glassed, begin by sanding (→ page 96) the first strake. Don't try to get it all at this point;

6-75

6-76

leave some of the sanding for when the deck glass is feathered into the hull. Sanding the whole hull would be unwise, as turning over the kayak in this fragile condition could break something.

This close-up (6-75) shows the edge of the deck trimmed and the top plank sanded.

After cleaning up the dust, fill the remainder of the joint. The trick here is to match the color of this batch of filler with the filler from the first time around.

I didn't want to mess up the hull-deck joint, so I taped it off again before putting in the remainder of the filler.

When the last application of filler has cured, clean it up with a firm sanding block, then round over the edge of the deck (6-76). Use long strokes to reduce the chance of sanding waves along the sheer of the deck. The instructions call for a ¼-inch radius – enough to soften the edge so that the glass will wrap around it, but not so much that the filler holding the hull and deck together will let go.

Because rounding the edge would cut into the green top ply of the deck, I used the line between the two colors as a guide for a consistent and pleasing transition between hull and deck.

Clean up and prep for glassing the deck.

DAYS 22-24

Glass the Deck

To Do
- O Apply fiberglass cloth and first coat of epoxy.*
- O Apply second coat of epoxy.*
- O Apply third coat of epoxy.*

Tools & Materials
- O acid brush
- O 2-inch bristle brush
- O chisel
- O epoxy resin and hardener
- O fiberglass cloth
- O lacquer thinner
- O 2-inch masking tape
- O mixing pots, grunge can
- O rags
- O sanding blocks
- O 120 grit sandpaper
- O scissors
- O squeegee
- O stir sticks
- O tape
- O utility knife
- O vacuum cleaner

Safety
- O dust mask
- O eye protection
- O gloves
- O long sleeves
- O good ventilation

Having glassed the hull and inside the deck, you are now experienced in working with epoxy and glass cloth. But don't relax yet. The deck is not a good place to upset the resin-to-hardener ratio or forget to stir long enough. Nevertheless, these will be easy days of about two hours each.

6-78

6-77

6-79

1. Apply fiberglass cloth & first coat of epoxy.

Before positioning the glass, mask off the hull about 1½ inches below the deck as a guide. Position the glass over the deck and straighten the fibers down the middle by tugging from both ends (6-77). Be generous when you trim the glass because the excess will help keep epoxy from running down the side of the hull. Save the offcuts for other uses.

This was my last chance to use the roller covers I had bought for this project, but I couldn't see where a roller would help much here either. There were too many corners to follow and too many places that needed the precise control of a brush.

The only new trick is working around the edge and smoothing the glass to the side of the hull. To wet out the glass on the side of the hull, use a brush that has most of the epoxy brushed out, lay the brush over the edge of the cloth and gently press it onto the hull between the edge and the tape (6-78). If the brush is loaded, the epoxy will run over the tape. Control the amount deposited by watching how much pressure is required to squeeze the epoxy out of the brush. Try not to get more epoxy on the glass than is needed (6-79). Keep in mind that the surface of the hull has been

6-80

sealed with epoxy, so it will not take as much as the raw plywood deck did.

Try to keep to a minimum the amount of epoxy to be cleaned up along the edge. If it runs over the tape, the saturated glass could become stuck to the hull. Check that the cloth has not lifted along the edge of the tape. If it has, carefully work it down with the squeegee, but not so far that the wet glass gets stuck back down again.

After applying the epoxy, scrape off the excess with the squeegee. If the squeegee is loaded, don't drag it over the edge, causing epoxy to run down the side. When the squeegee has picked up as much as it will hold without dripping off, scrape the grunge into the grunge can and keep working the area until very little is being picked up. At this point continue over the edge, making an effort to pick up the excess before it runs over the tape. If it does, pick up what you can with the squeegee and wipe the surface clean with a small amount of thinner on a clean rag.

When squeegeeing toward the tape, continue up onto the tape. Stopping short will leave excess epoxy in the glass that will require extra work to feather in later.

SAFETY TIP

When sanding this early in the cure stage, remember that uncured epoxy is a chemical hazard. Wear a dust mask and wash well afterward.

My standard squeegee was too large to be of any use around the deck recess. The narrow squeegee worked great there, as well as along the edge of the tape when I was checking for epoxy buildup.

Fitting the glass into the deck recess required cutting across the cockpit opening. Notice that the cut stopped short of the edge, far enough in that the fragile cut edge of the cloth did not have to be worked (6-80). It is a good idea to keep the rest of the cloth in place as long as possible; here it was adding some tension along the side of the cockpit as well as keeping drips of epoxy out of the interior.

Trim the glass around the outside of the deck and remove the tape when the epoxy has reached the green stage – with System Three epoxy, about 12 hours after application.

Complete feathering the cut edge into the hull surface, using a firm sanding block with 120 grit paper (6-82). If you concentrate on keeping the sanding pressure at the cloth edge, most of the rest should take care of itself. However, go easy sanding up to the joint between hull and deck. The glass wrapping around the edge ties this joint together; cutting it now would defeat the whole exercise.

Give the glass a quick hand sanding with the soft block and 120 grit paper – zip, zip – 10 minutes. The object is to cut the tooth, or rough points, but not so much that you get close to the glass fiber. When finished,

CHEAP TRICK

6-81

Cut it cleanly

To slice through the glass at the edge of the tape, use a sharp chisel held at a very low angle (almost flat to the hull). As you cut, peel off the excess glass and tape together (6-81). This will take everything off cleanly, leaving the edge of the glass cut on a bevel; the bevel is the beginning of the feathered edge you want to end up with. At this stage the System Three epoxy was too rubbery to sand clean, so I gave it another day before feathering the edge.

6-82

6-83

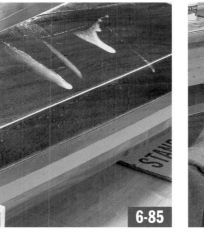

6-85

6-86

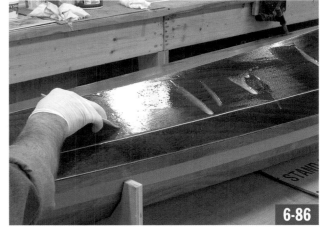

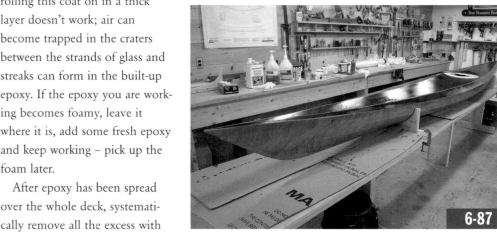

vacuum up the dust (6-83). Pick up the last of the dust with a rag dampened with water or lacquer thinner.

2. Apply second coat of epoxy.

Gracefully applying the second and third coats of epoxy along the hull will be tricky. The challenge is to control the epoxy that wants to run down the vertical surface. Use 2-inch masking tape to corral it. Position the tape about 2½ inches below the edge of the deck (6-84) so that the next two coats of epoxy will continue feathering the edge of the glass down the flat surface of the hull.

The object of the second coat is to fill the weave of the cloth and level the epoxy with the high points.

Along the side, use a minimum amount of epoxy and brush it out thinly down to the tape. It doesn't take much to overwork System Three epoxy on the rough texture of the glass and turn it into foam (6-85). That is why rolling this coat on in a thick layer doesn't work; air can become trapped in the craters between the strands of glass and streaks can form in the built-up epoxy. If the epoxy you are working becomes foamy, leave it where it is, add some fresh epoxy and keep working – pick up the foam later.

After epoxy has been spread over the whole deck, systematically remove all the excess with the squeegee (6-86). When cleaning up along the sides, let the corner of the squeegee ride on the tape. Try holding the squeegee at an angle that will clean the tape and move the grunge onto the hull, where it can be easily collected.

Although the squeegee is ideal on flat surfaces, I suggest finishing

6-84

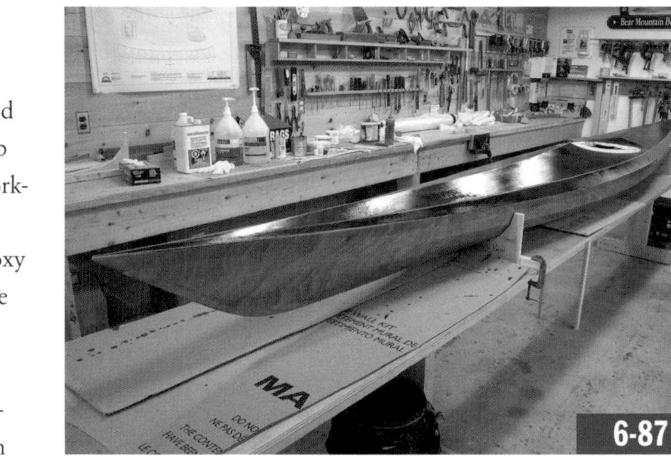
6-87

6-88

along the edge with a dry brush.

After the tape had been removed (6-87), there were a few spots where epoxy had run past the tape; these were wiped off with a rag dampened with lacquer thinner.

Until the epoxy has firmed up, check along the edge for runs. I had occasional drips for about four hours. Even though the epoxy was getting thick by that time, I had no problem picking it up with the squeegee.

3. Apply third coat of epoxy.

The third coat is applied with a brush, using the same routine as for the last coat on the outside of the hull. Apply the third coat to the deck surface only. The edge of the hull was coated well by the second coat, and epoxy from the deck that sneaks over the side will be enough to complete the coating.

After about 30 minutes the epoxy will begin to flow over the edge. Carefully pick up the runs with the squeegee (6-88). Hold it at an angle that will move the epoxy down the hull, away from the edge. This will avoid a further buildup of epoxy along the hull-deck joint and will continue feathering the glass into the hull.

Don't scrape the epoxy off the corner between the hull and deck, because the buildup there will be useful later.

Keep checking this area until you are sure that the epoxy is stiff enough to stop coming over the edge.

Beautiful! Note the grain pattern coming through the green dye and the way the light filler outlines the deck panels (6-89).

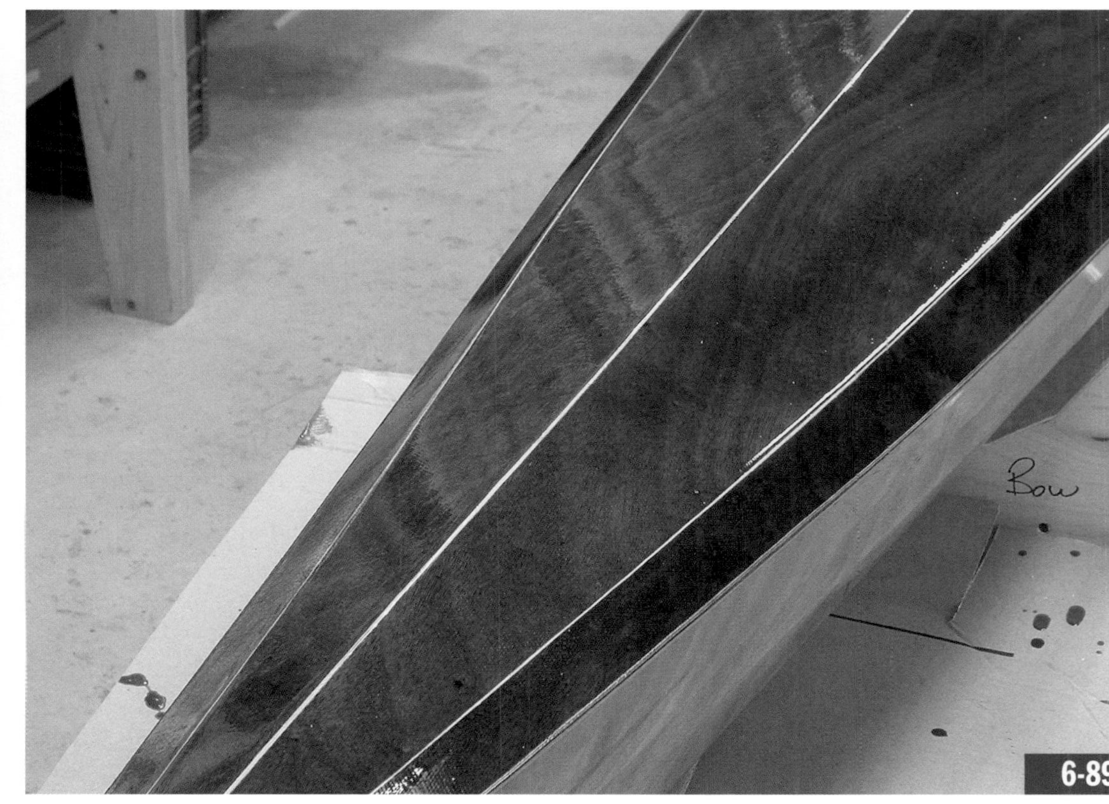

6-89

DAYS 25-29

Trim the Deck

To Do
- O Reinforce inside hull-deck joint.*
- O Install cockpit coaming.**
- O Install hatches.**
- O Install hip braces.
- O Install foot pegs.
- O Install bulkhead.
- O Dry-fit deck rigging.
- O Install seat.

Tools & Materials
- O acid brush
- O clamps (minimum 16)
- O clamp pads
- O cotton fibers for glue
- O drill and 1/16-inch bit
- O duct tape
- O epoxy resin and hardener
- O glue syringe
- O 4-ounce or 6-ounce cloth
- O jigsaw and fine hollow-ground up-cutting blade (12 teeth per inch)
- O lacquer thinner or epoxy solvent
- O masking tape
- O mixing pots
- O plastic tape
- O pull saw
- O putty knife
- O rags
- O rasp and/or hard sanding block
- O router with 1/2-inch round-over bit (optional)
- O firm and soft sanding blocks
- O 80, 120 and 180 grit sandpaper

Continued on next page

Trimming the deck and installing seat and foot pegs will bring our kayak-shaped structure to life. These components are the creature comforts and safety features that customize the kayak.

The many glue-and-let-cure steps will slow things down. To complete everything in five days, the cockpit coaming and hatches will need to be worked on at the same time, requiring many clamps. If you are working with a minimum of clamps, these trim steps are best spread over a number of days, working a few hours each day. Also consider doing some of the prep work beforehand, for example, glassing the bottom of the cockpit rim. Fast hardener, if available, will shorten the cure cycles. A few other shortcuts mentioned will reduce the number of cure cycles, but they add to cleanup time and compromise the quality of the results. Keep in mind that all of these components matter in terms of both safety and comfort, as well as making the builder look good.

1. Reinforce inside hull-deck joint.

This step may be done anytime after the deck has been glassed to the hull and before the hip braces are attached. I left it as long as possible, mainly because it didn't look like a fun job. In reality it was not as awkward as anticipated. Prop up the kayak on its side and let gravity keep the epoxy and filler in the joint. Using a head lamp (if there is room) or a flashlight will give you a reasonable view of what you are doing inside.

The filler is mixed epoxy thickened with Microlite to a mayonnaise consistency. Look for enough body to make a fillet but have it thin enough to dispense from a dental syringe. If a closer color match is desired, a small amount of very fine sanding dust could be used to tint the filler, or choose a different lightweight synthetic filler.

Before filling the syringe, cut its tip back to enlarge the hole. Load up the syringe with filler. Right! If you have some good tricks for getting toothpaste back into the tube, try them here. The trick is to get the filler to the bottom of the syringe without trapping air. The best I came up with was a narrow spatula, patience and a rag.

First run a bead of filler down the joint (called the inside of the sheer seam in the manual) with the syringe (6-90). Press the 4-ounce tape into the filler and shape it into a small fillet, then finish by wetting out the tape (→ page 77). Most of this worked, but the epoxy was slow to saturate the dry tape enough to stick it well to the dry surface. On the opposite side I brushed a thin coat of mixed epoxy on the area to be covered by the tape, placed the filler, then set the tape into it. The tape wetted out much better with the epoxy coming at it from both directions.

To make a consistent bead, dispense the filler with firm, even pressure and move along at a steady rate. There is a limit to

SAFETY TIP

Air quality

Give some thought to the quality of the air in the cavity before you work with your head inside. Solvent fumes will be potent after you have cleaned the joint with thinner. Wait until the air inside has cleared before sticking your head back in. If a small fan is handy, stick it in a hatch hole to speed up replacing the air and keep it moving while you are working. If you have been using a charcoal filter mask for working with epoxy, this is a very good time to wear it.

6-90

Tools & Materials
From previous page
- O small squeegee
- O spokeshave
- O stir sticks
- O straightedge
- O utility knife
- O vacuum cleaner

Safety
- O dust mask
- O gloves
- O good ventilation
- O care with cutting tools

6-91

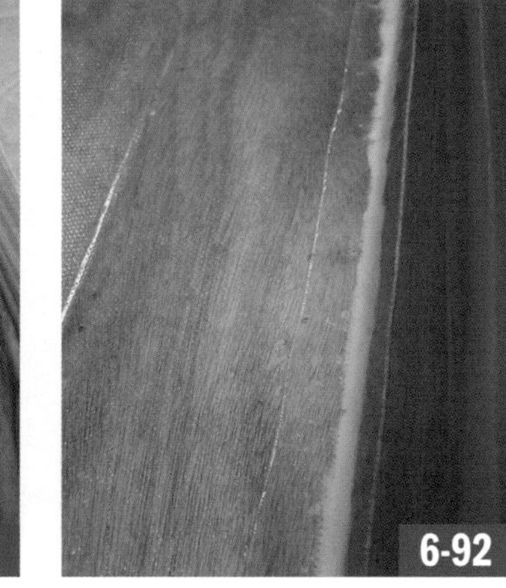
6-92

how far the tape can be worked, but try to run the bead as far as you can reach in both directions. Having access through hatches on both ends would cover most of the length. The instructions suggest taping the syringe to a long stick to reach all the way into the ends. Pressure is transferred to the plunger through a 1/4-inch dowel guided by two eyescrews.

Brush an even coat of mixed epoxy over the area to be covered by the tape, then apply the filler. Center the tape over the joint and press it into the wet epoxy and filler (6-91). Try to place the tape in a straight line centered on the joint. Avoid moving it once it has been stuck into the filler – it will pull the filler with it. With a gloved finger, carefully shape the filler into a smooth cove.

The tape will begin to saturate from the bottom; complete wetting it out by applying more epoxy as needed. Keep it tidy by applying the optimum amount of epoxy and brushing it out thinly along the edge (6-92). This is an awkward place to sand, so this attention to detail is well invested.

When the epoxy is firm enough to stay in place, fillet and tape the other side.

After the epoxy has cured, feather the edges to your standard of perfection.

2. Install cockpit coaming **(→ page 102).**

3. Install hatches **(→ page 110).**

4. Install hip braces **(→ page 126).**

5. Install foot pegs **(→ page 124).**

6. Install bulkhead **(→ page 100).**

7. Dry-fit deck rigging **(→ page 131).**

8. Install seat **(→ page 121).**

DAYS 30-37

Varnish or Paint and Install Fittings

To Do
- ○ Complete sanding epoxy and seal trim.
- ○ Prepare surface and apply varnish or paint to all exposed surfaces.
- ○ Install fittings and bulkhead.

Tools & Materials
- ○ brush
- ○ brush cleaner
- ○ 1-inch masking tape
- ○ paint filters
- ○ paint thinner
- ○ paint pots
- ○ recycled clean cans, plastic tubs
- ○ rags
- ○ tack cloth
- ○ 220 or 280 grit sandpaper
- ○ stir sticks
- ○ varnish or paint

Safety
- ○ dust mask
- ○ gloves
- ○ good ventilation

Completing the sanding will mean the end of the dust and noise. It will take a minimum of six days to apply at least three coats of finish to both hull and deck. The days will be short and will consist of sanding the previous coat, cleaning up and applying the next one. Use the buildup coats to practice for the final one – it is the one that counts. It will take another day after the finish has hardened to replace the rigging.

1. Complete sanding epoxy & seal trim (→ page 97).

2. Prepare surface & apply varnish or paint to all exposed surfaces (→ page 134).

3. Install fittings & bulkhead.

Well, how did you do with all those little pieces of plywood? She is a beautiful kayak, isn't she?

The deck's dark green color with white pin-striping did not take much time and it added another dimension to the okume plywood. Making cradle forms was a small step that went a long way toward keeping the planks under control, as well as keeping the kayak stabilized for all the finishing and rigging work. There were no mysteries to building this kayak. It was a combination of a well-conceived kit, a few rolls of masking tape and satisfaction about each step.

The Mill Creek 13

BUILDING THE MILL CREEK KAYAK is quite different from working on the Coho. Chesapeake Light Craft's method is to assemble the hull in an upright position and secure the panels together on the inside with glass tape. Hull panels are assembled with wire sutures going through predrilled holes and twisted on the outside. Before filleting, the wire on the inside is pressed into the joint and the filler is shaped over the wire.

This is a very fast way to build because the glass tape is positioned over the wet fillet and wetted out along with all of the interior surfaces. Fast, but this kind of speed has given plywood kayak building a reputation for involving endless sanding. The instruction manual says, "You'll spend more time sanding your wood-epoxy kayak than in doing anything else during construction. Is sanding drudgery or is it sculpture?" Since one of our objectives is to find the shortest and healthiest route to the best results, we explored a few detours from the instructions to reduce the "drudgery" and eliminate the "sculpture."

DAY 1

Get Organized

To Do
- ○ Construct worktable or horses.
- ○ Unpack shipping cartons and check contents.
- ○ Organize tools and materials.
- ○ Read instructions.

Tools & Materials
- ○ clamps
- ○ drill/driver
- ○ drywall screws
- ○ level
- ○ material for worktable
- ○ material for legs or horses
- ○ saw
- ○ straightedge
- ○ square
- ○ string line
- ○ tape measure
- ○ utility knife

Safety
- ○ eye protection
- ○ good ventilation
- ○ caution with cutting tools

Getting organized is about all the things you have been thinking about since deciding to build a kayak. The images in your mind and how you feel about the project are major components. Your boat can be everything you want it to be; work clean and keep the steps in order, and you will be dazzled.

1. Construct worktable or horses (→ page 23).

2. Unpack shipping cartons & check contents.

The Mill Creek kit arrived with all the components taped to the inside of a 4- x 8-foot cardboard package. The scarfs on a pair of sheer clamps had broken, but that wasn't a hardship; the sheer clamps were long enough to recut. That was the only damage. The fragile ends of the factory-cut scarfs on the panels were packed in Styrofoam.

The packing slip was a nice touch; it was used to check off the parts as they were removed from the package (6-93).

An impressive spiral-bound construction manual and a full set of plans are included. This is the package that a plans-builder would receive, but is a very helpful reference for the kit-builder as well. CLC combines information for the plans-builder and the kit-builder in one manual. Although the manual is well illustrated and easy to follow, what impressed me most was the effort to draw attention to safety and quality.

6-93

3. Organize tools & materials.

4. Read instructions.

Try to get an understanding of the building technique and how the pieces fit together.

DAYS 2-4

Join Plank Components

To Do
- O Identify and sort components into sets.
- O Join components into planks.**
- O Join sheer clamp to sheer panel.*
- O Construct cradle forms.

Tools & Materials
- O clamp blocks
- O clamps or weights
- O cotton fibers
- O epoxy resin and hardener
- O glue or acid brush
- O heavy plastic film
- O lacquer thinner
- O mixing pots
- O putty knife
- O rags
- O firm sanding block
- O 120 grit sandpaper
- O scissors
- O stir sticks
- O straightedge
- O string line
- O wedges

Safety
- O dust mask
- O eye protection
- O gloves
- O good ventilation
- O caution with cutting tools

The time it takes to glue the scarf joints will depend on how much flat space you have to work on and the number of clamps available. The cure time for the epoxy being used will also affect how long it will take; plan on a cycle time of 4 to 21 hours, depending on brand and hardener used. Expect the first day to be a full one – it takes a while to get everything organized and the first set glued. Joining the balance of the planks will take small blocks of time regulated by the time it takes for the epoxy to kick.

1. Identify & sort components into sets (→ page 58).

2. Join components into planks (→ page 58).

The first step is to join the components into full-length planks or panels by gluing the factory-cut scarf joints.

The construction manual supplies a reference measurement from a straight line to the joint, so having a flat table with reliable edges and a centerline makes lining up these planks a breeze.

This is an excellent reference system if the numbers are correct, but our sheer panel reference was off almost ½ inch, making an obvious hook in the plank that was easy to spot. If you're a first-time builder, it will be the small errors like this one that could get you into trouble; have a good look at the plank from both ends and spring a batten around it to be sure. If you are not working on a table with a centerline, a tight string line will give you the same information. Shim up the ends of the string enough to clear the surface.

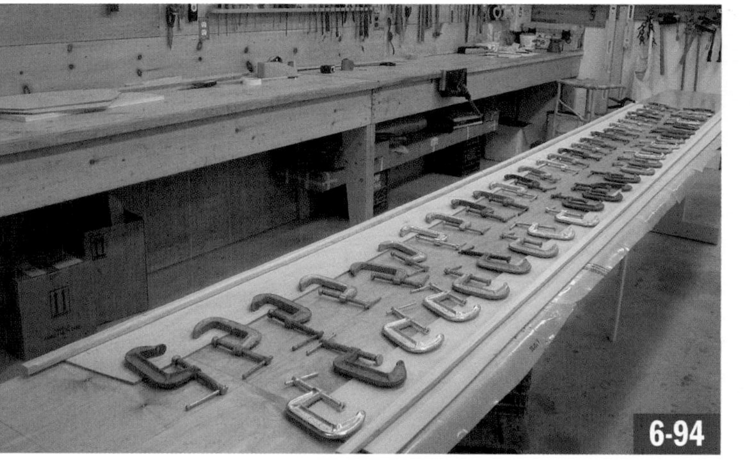

6-94

3. Join sheer clamp to sheer panel.

Sheer clamps make the joint between the hull and deck. The method used on the Mill Creek is to glue the clamps to the inside upper edge of both sheer planks before assembling the hull.

Take time to soften the corner of the sheer clamp that you will see from the inside, using a router or block plane and a firm sanding block (120 and 180 grit) before assembling. It is much easier to get at on the worktable than it will be when glued into the boat.

You may have to put an ad in the paper – "Wanted to borrow: clamps to clamp clamps" – for this step. Given the stiffness of the sheer clamp, two clamps per foot of length is the minimum (6-94).

It is very important to identify the edge of the hull panel that will receive the sheer clamp and to mark it to avoid future confusion. Consider putting the most attractive face of each plank to the outside. Keep in mind that one plank is for the starboard side and the other for port; both sheer clamps must face into the hull.

Do a dry run to set up the clamps; this is a lot of clamps to adjust with glue on your gloves.

It is common practice to glue both planks at one time. While that will save one cure cycle, the glue on the bottom will be impossible to clean up wet. If you clean up the side you can reach, it will be a long haul to make the other side look similar. Gluing the planks individually

6-95

eliminates 95 percent of the sanding and scraping normally involved in this step.

I used mixed epoxy reinforced with cotton fibers (→ page 41) to a consistency thin enough to brush on the mating surfaces (6-95).

An extra pair of hands would help to get the sheer clamp turned over and positioned without making a mess (6-96). Pick up the squeezed-out glue with a putty knife and wipe the surface clean with a rag dampened with lacquer thinner.

4. Construct cradle forms (→ page 25).

6-96

DAY 5

Assemble Hull

To Do
- O Drill suture holes.
- O Set up cradle forms.
- O Make wire sutures.
- O Loosely assemble hull panels.
- O Attach bulkheads.
- O Tune up sutures.
- O Miter sheer clamps.
- O True up ends.

Tools & Materials
- O bevel gauge
- O block plane
- O clamp blocks
- O clamps
- O drill and 1/16-inch bit
- O drywall screws
- O level
- O linesman pliers
- O saw
- O square
- O straightedge
- O string line
- O tape measure
- O wire

Safety
- O caution with cutting tools
- O eye protection

This will be a very busy day but most rewarding. Take all the time you need to fit all the pieces together accurately.

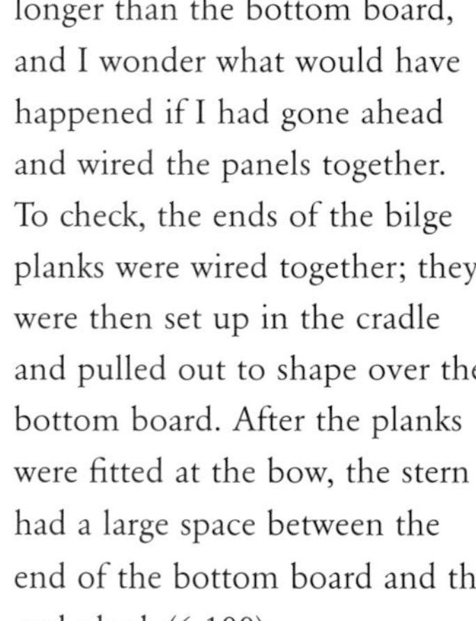
6-97

1. Drill suture holes.

Clamp the sheer planks together and drill on 4- to 6-inch centers (6-97). Scribe a line to guide the holes or avoid having to clean up pencil marks by using a jig (→ page 70).

Drill around the perimeter of the bottom board.

To locate the positions of the holes in the bilge plank, fit the sheer plank to the plank beginning at the bow. Notice that they will not come together for their full length until sprung into the kayak shape (6-98). Use a straightedge to project a line directly across from the hole in the sheer plank to the bilge plank (6-99). Make the mark dark enough to see but not so dark that it will be hard to remove.

Drill along as far as the planks are touching, then pull the planks together around the curve enough to continue walking them to the end. When you get to the end, the ends of the planks should line up; if not, figure out why.

Clamp up the marked plank with its mate and drill. Use the jig to control the distance from the edge; look through the hole to find the spacing line.

Fit the lower edge of the bilge plank to the bottom board using the same routine. A diagram in the manual shows where to begin as the point where the bow curve flattens out into the bottom. When you walk the plank around to the other end, these two points should also line up at the stern.

6-98

6-99

Damage control: After checking, the bilge planks appeared to be longer than the bottom board, and I wonder what would have happened if I had gone ahead and wired the panels together. To check, the ends of the bilge planks were wired together; they were then set up in the cradle and pulled out to shape over the bottom board. After the planks were fitted at the bow, the stern had a large space between the end of the bottom board and the end plank (6-100).

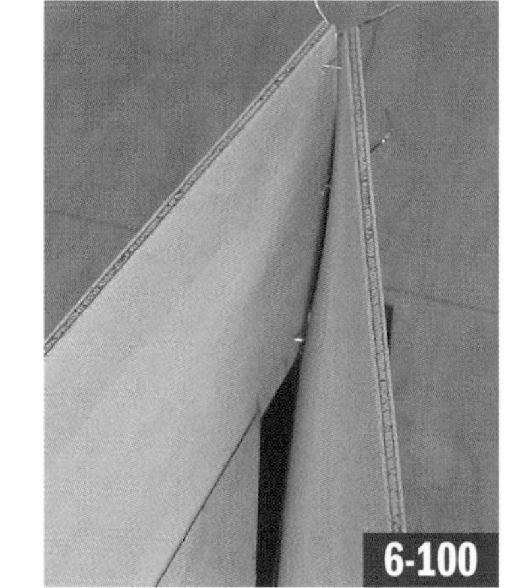
6-100

This is another reminder that we cannot assume that someone else has taken care of all the details. To compensate for this discrepancy the choices are to center the plank on the bottom to split the difference, to leave it where it is and keep all the damage control at one end, or to cut the plank down to fit the bottom. I chose to shorten both of the planks rather than deal with trying to squeeze a blob of filler into the open space, shape and clean it up and then have to look at it forever. I marked the new length from the bottom onto the bilge plank. Then I made a paper template to transfer the original stern shape on the

6-101

bilge plank to the new length mark.

After I trimmed the bilge plank to length, all three components came together tightly (6-101). The bilge plank was then used to transfer the true length to the sheer plank for trimming.

2. Set up cradle forms.

The cradle forms will be set up in the same position as the bulkheads. Find the dimensions on the plans and transfer them to the bottom board. These lines must be perpendicular to the centerline, as they will be the guide for positioning the bulkheads. Put the bottom board in the cradles and position it on the bulkhead lines. Center the cradles on the centerline and fasten them to the table.

Damage control: When I set the bottom board in the cradles on the bulkhead lines, it didn't fit. A quick check with the bulkhead positioned to the line made it obvious that the numbers on the plans were not a reliable reference. It was easy to fix. The

6-102

6-103

bottom of the bulkhead needs to fit the width of the bottom board; once that position was determined, new reference lines were drawn.

3. Make wire sutures (→ page 70).

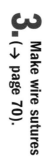

4. Loosely assemble hull panels.

The instructions suggest positioning the bilge plank at the bow, drilling three or four holes, wiring, then repeating on the other side. The planks are gradually pulled into position as the wires progress toward the stern. To help hold the plank more or less upright, the manual suggests tying ropes around the hull as the wires progress.

The cradle will do away with some of the gymnastics and bring the components together accurately in a controlled and relaxed manner, without ropes.

Stack the planks, drill three holes in each end and loosely wire the ends together. Position the planks in the cradle, spread the sides out and clamp them to the cradle with L-shaped clamp blocks.

I decided to take another detour from the instructions by removing the sutures rather than leaving them in and filleting over the wire. Since the wires did not have to be twisted on the outside, I twisted them on whatever side was most convenient. Since the holes are already drilled, it probably does not make a big difference where we start wiring the components. To be sure the ends were flush, I started at both ends and worked into the middle (6-102).

5. Attach bulkheads.

The instructions suggest wiring everything together before inserting the bulkheads. However, there is much to be said for attaching the bulkheads at this point, as it will stabilize the shape of the bilge plank and give us something to bend the sheer plank around.

Put the bulkhead in position and plumb it. Since the bottom of this kayak is flat, I was able to use a combination square off the bottom to find plumb. Note that the L-brackets holding the first planks were also convenient to locate the bulkhead and hold it in position (6-103).

Three sutures are enough to hold the bulkhead in position, one on the centerline and one at the top edge of each bilge plank.

6. Tune up sutures.

When all the sutures are in, begin at the middle and snug up the wires just enough to pull the edges together; overtightening will put a wave in the chine.

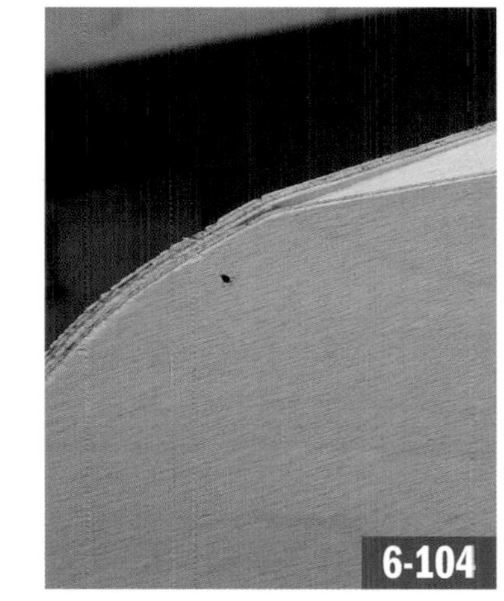
6-104

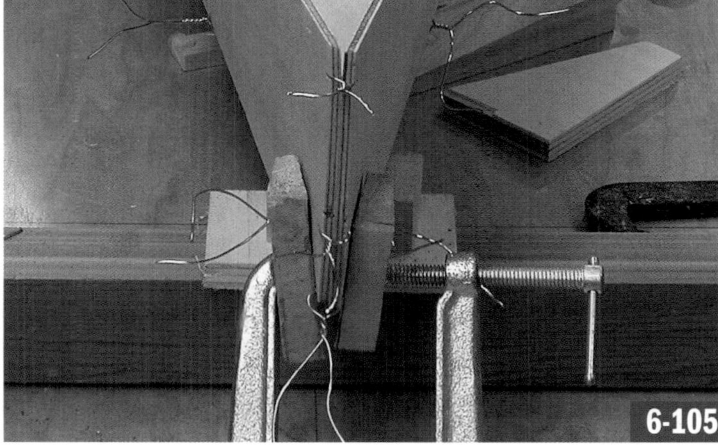
6-105

Keeping the inside corners balanced on one another is always tricky. Approaching the ends, the sides meet the bottom at close to a 90-degree angle, so you may have to play with the joint.

I tried planing a small bevel on the edge of the bottom board to give the side something to sit on, and it seemed to help. A trick I have heard of but not tried is to place a small piece of dowel in the open part of the joint and tighten the wire over it. The dowel will balance the pressure applied to both planks and should keep the corners together. The final 8 or 10 inches of the bottom were fit down between the sides to soften the transition where the bottom becomes the stem (6-104).

These beveled clamp blocks (6-105) give excellent control over the ends of the planks as well as holding them up against the bottom. To reduce the chance of the blocks sliding off, 80 grit sandpaper was glued to the boat side of each block.

In theory, if the plank pairs are the same length they should be flush at both ends. If the planks are off by the same amount at both ends, one of the planks has shifted. If a major amount of work is needed to correct this, trim the ends flush with one another A more important concern is when one end is flush and at the other end one side runs past its mate. This indicates that one side of the hull is longer than the other, or at least that one plank is misaligned and should be investigated.

Before installing the next round of planks, check that the stems are vertical and over the centerline; use a level or a square off the table at the centerline. If you confirm each step as you build it, the boat will come out straight without a lot of frustrating backtracking.

7. Miter sheer clamps.

Loosely wire the ends of the sheer planks together and spring the planks around the bulkheads. Line up the ends and wire them into place.

Miter the sheer clamps and join them before tuning up the wires. Clamp the ends enough to bring the sheer clamps together at

6-106

both ends. Stretch a string line from the point on the stern where the clamp meets the plank to the same point on the bow. The string will run parallel to the centerline and will give the exact angle to cut. Set a sliding T-bevel up to the line for marking both sides (6-106). Unless the hull is symmetrical, you will have to reset the bevel gauge to mark the stern.

Cut the miters with a fine saw, following the line on top and the edge of the plank. Remove the wires in the ends and use a block plane to touch up the joint.

8. True up ends.

This is a very important step and now is the time to do it. When the ends are fastened together, the shape of the hull will be locked. To change the shape after that, something has to be stretched and the hull has to be held under tension while filler is applied to try to correct it.

When you think the fit is pretty close, clamp the ends together and true up the stems. There are several ways to do this and I suggest using one to prove the other. Stretch the string line from bow to stern on the centerline. It should pass directly over the centerlines on the bulkheads. If you are working on a table, plumb the ends to the centerline also.

The instructions describe another method called "winding" for truing up the hull. The hull is set on a level base and straightedges are laid across the hull 4 feet from each end. Get down level with the boat and, while squinting, line one stick up above the other. If they are parallel, the hull should be straight. If the hull is sitting level, you can use a level to check the sticks instead of eyeballing them. To be on the safe side, try a couple of different methods to confirm the shape.

When the ends are where they should be, draw a reference line across the sheer clamp miters. As long as these marks are lined up, the hull will continue to be the shape it is now.

Fasten the ends together with a screw (→ 6-108) for clamping pressure while the glue cures. This could be a nonferrous screw that stays in or a waxed steel screw that will be removed later. It is very important to drill an adequate pilot hole if splitting the sheer clamp is to be avoided.

DAYS 6–9

Join Planks

To Do
- ○ Secure planks at bow and stern.
- ○ Tack planks with filler.*
- ○ Remove sutures.
- ○ Fill joints on outside.*
- ○ Fill wire holes.*
- ○ Clean up filler inside.*
- ○ Apply fillet.

Tools & Materials
- ○ acid brush
- ○ epoxy resin and hardener
- ○ epoxy dispensing pumps
- ○ filler
- ○ gloves
- ○ grunge can
- ○ lacquer thinner
- ○ 1-inch masking tape
- ○ mixing pots
- ○ putty knife
- ○ rags
- ○ firm sanding block
- ○ 120 grit sandpaper
- ○ scraper
- ○ spatula
- ○ squeegee
- ○ stir sticks
- ○ vacuum cleaner
- ○ wire cutters

Safety
- ○ dust mask
- ○ eye protection
- ○ gloves
- ○ good ventilation
- ○ caution with cutting tools

The usual method of joining the planks is to get it over with in one frantic session, then try to recover by doing substantial damage control. If you don't try to do everything at once, you will be able to make each step do its job properly, as well as prepare the stage for the next performance.

I spread this operation over four days to allow the epoxy to cure between steps. This time can be cut in half if a fast hardener is used. None of these days will be full or strenuous, making them ideal for an evening work schedule.

1. Secure planks at bow & stern.

For glue I used a peanut-butter-thick mixture of epoxy reinforced with cotton fibers, with some sanding dust to give it color (→ page 41).

Begin tacking the planks together by gluing the bow and stern. This space is very narrow on our little kayak, but would be more so on a long, skinny hull. Other than using a syringe to place the glue, I could not think of a graceful way of getting it up into the end without making a mess.

Continuing with our theme of thinking lazy, I simply cut the wires, removed the screw and opened up the end to apply the glue (6-107). Since we have a reference mark across the sheer clamp and the screw to pinpoint the position, at this stage there is no danger of losing control of the shape by opening up the ends.

6-107

Clamp the stem back together and replace the screw in the original hole. Since we have removed the wires, the beveled clamp blocks are used to hold the ends together. It is important to place one set of blocks across the joint between the planks to keep them in line (6-108). Keep the clamping pressure at the end to avoid developing a hollow in the plank behind the stem.

I was able to add more glue to the inside with the acid brush and smooth it into a tidy fillet. There will be a larger fillet going over it later; the idea now is simply to hold the ends together and not make a mess that interferes with the fillet.

6-108

This is your last chance – confirm that the stems are still plumb.

2. Tack planks with filler (→ page 70).

This routine can be used to tack any long panel-to-panel joint on the inside that will be filleted to accommodate the fiberglass cloth. The joint between the sheer plank and the bilge plank is gentle enough that glass cloth will follow it. If you are going to use glass tape, a small fillet inside this joint is advisable.

Our objective here is to place just enough filler in the joint to tack the planks, then shape it so that a conservative fillet can be added over top without interference or damage control.

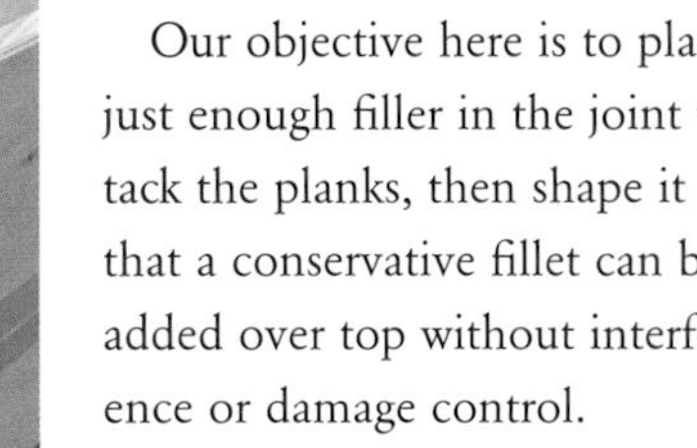
6-109

The lightweight filleting mixture is a combination of Microlite and a microballoon-based compound to add a reddish brown color (6-109). It is a very smooth mixture that is easy to

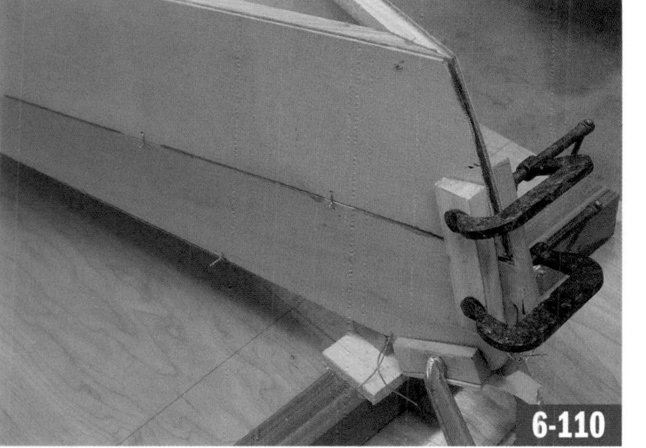
6-110

dispense from a syringe, once it is filled.

The joint on the outside is open and must be filled anyway, so I used filler to tack the planks on the outside anywhere a fillet was not needed on the inside. The time it takes to tape the joint is a better choice than sanding the mess off later. Use a flexible putty knife to pack the wet filler into the joint, especially at the ends where the joint is small; scrape it flush to the tape. Remove the tape after applying the filler (6-110).

6-111

6-112

3. Remove sutures.

One advantage of burying the sutures under the fillet on the inside is that the holes do not have to be filled. On the other hand, removing the sutures before the fillet (6-111) is much quicker than cutting the wire on the outside, then filing the ends of the wires flush to the plywood. We have seen a number of kayaks on which a random orbital sander was used to remove the ends of the wires. The wood was ground down to the plywood glue line and the wire was still higher than the wood; the glass was laid up over this. Later, when the epoxy was sanded, the sander cut through the glass and exposed the ends of each wire again.

If you choose to leave the sutures in, snip the wires and use a mill file to make each wire flush with the plywood before sanding. Keep in mind that the wire is much harder than the wood. A sander will eat through the wood much faster than the wire. Any sanding over the wire ends should be by hand with a hard sanding block.

4. Fill joints on outside.

This is as good a time as any to fill the remaining joints on the outside and to get a look at the kayak from the bottom (6-112). Be careful when turning the hull over as it is only tacked together; set it up securely on a level support.

I used the same filler as on the inside, but mixed to a drier consistency.

The last 10 or 12 inches of the bottom board have been sprung up between the planks to give the bottom a little rocker (6-113). Shape the plank down to meet the bottom and make a pleasing curve between the bottom and the stems (6-114). Try not to cut into the plywood bottom; keep in mind just how thick the layers of wood are.

Mask the joint and apply the filler with a putty knife (6-115). Press the filler in firmly enough to force the air out. Make sure there is enough buildup to round over later. Remove the tape after applying the filler.

When this filler has cured, remove the sutures and give the joint a quick sand with a firm sanding block, using 120 grit. The objective is to bring the filler flush with the plank surface.

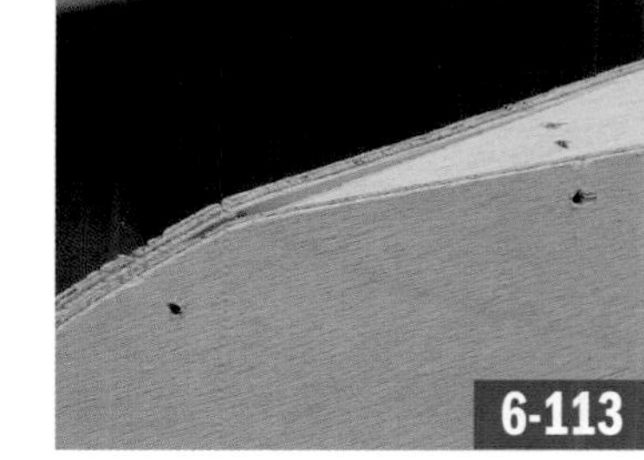
6-113

6-114

6-115

Resist the urge to round over the corner until all the filler is in. Mask and put in the remaining filler.

When the filler has kicked, turn the hull over and set it up in the cradles.

5. Fill wire holes (→ page 73).

The mixture used on the outside is ideal for filling the holes. Force the mixture into the hole and it will come out the other side like fresh pasta.

6. Clean up filler inside.

If care has been taken with the filler, it will be a quick step just to level the filler with the plywood. A sharp scraper will bring the soft filler down without damaging the wood (6-116). Use 120 grit sandpaper on a firm block to finish.

Vacuum the dust and prepare for making the fillet.

7. Apply fillet.

Decision time again. The instruction manual directs us to apply the fillets to the plank joints and bulkheads, place the 3-inch glass tape in the wet filler, wet out the tape and then saturate all the interior surface. This will take 16 separate fillets, 24 pieces of tape to go over them and 48 tape edges to feather later. Then there will be the rough plywood to sand flat. Expect a reasonable cleanup job to take a good day's work and it will still be obvious that it was taped. It is hard to get excited about this much damage control, especially if it can be avoided.

Since glass cloth is used on the outside of the plywood anyway, we are most of the way toward having a monocoque structure; glassing the inside will make it complete. This balanced structure will allow us to eliminate the bulky fillets and heavy tape and make a lighter, stronger hull with a fraction of the unhealthy work.

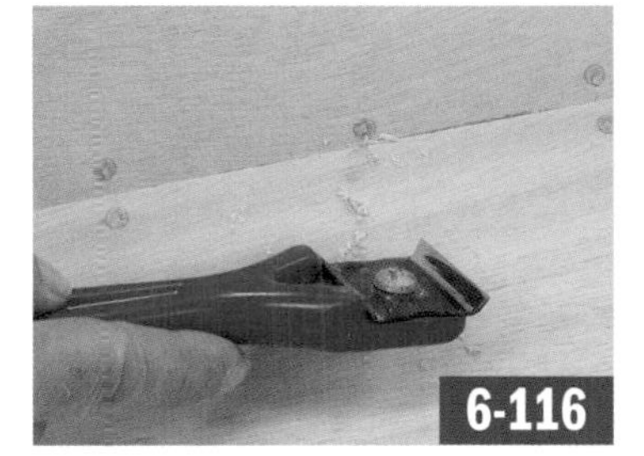
6-116

Removing the bulkheads temporarily will open up the space and you can make the fillets and glass run from end to end rather than working in short sections. By using a sheet of 4- or 6-ounce glass cloth, the number of pieces of glass drops from sixteen to one, greatly reducing epoxy handling and exposure time and 95 percent of the sanding. It also means that the reinforcement does not end at the bulkheads, a theoretical weak point. The bonus is a smooth surface that is uninterrupted by wide fillets and tape lines and that will take only about 20 minutes to prep for varnish or paint.

If the bulkheads are removed, replace them with spreaders to maintain the width (6-117). I noticed that one spreader in the middle produced a different shape than when the two bulkheads were in position. Assuming that the shape developed with the bulkheads is what the designer had in mind, keep them as your reference and use two spreaders. Notice how the rocker changes as the sides are pulled in or spread out.

6-117

6-118

Mask off the area covered by the fillet. My holes were drilled with the jig and their consistent positioning was used as a guide for placing the tape. The tape was placed just outside the holes to hide them under the fillet (6-118).

Place the filler and shape the fillet (→ page 75).

DAYS 10-11

Glass Inside of Hull

To Do
- O Sand inside.
- O Apply first coat of epoxy.*
- O Sand epoxy.
- O Apply second coat of epoxy.*

Tools & Materials
- O epoxy resin and hardener
- O epoxy dispensing pumps
- O filler
- O glass cloth
- O grunge can
- O lacquer thinner
- O mixing pots
- O putty knife
- O rags
- O firm sanding block
- O 120 grit sandpaper
- O spatula
- O squeegee
- O stir sticks
- O vacuum cleaner

Safety
- O dust mask
- O eye protection
- O gloves
- O good ventilation
- O caution with cutting tools

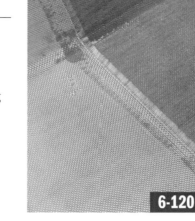

Expect to spend about one hour sanding and cleaning up the inside. Glassing will take one or two days, depending on the epoxy system used. If you can wait for the first coat to get hard enough to feather the edges and give the glass a quick scuff, the second coat will be almost ready for varnish.

1. Sand inside (→ page 96).

Sand the inside by hand using 120 grit sandpaper on a firm block. The objective here is to feather the edge of the fillet and clean and smooth the plywood.

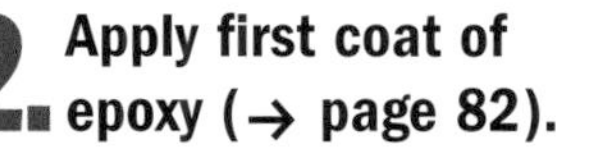

2. Apply first coat of epoxy (→ page 82).

To wet out the cloth, pour a puddle of epoxy in the bottom and use the squeegee to draw the epoxy up the side. Be sure to work the epoxy all the way to the underside of the sheer clamp (6-119).

After picking up all the excess epoxy with the squeegee, trim the glass to just below the sheer clamp. I started off using the squeegee to hold the glass while cutting, but realized that the squeegee was getting nicked. Simply cutting in the corner with a sharp blade worked fine; holding the knife at a low angle helped to keep it from dragging the cloth. Use the squeegee to smooth the cloth after cutting and to scrape the bottom of the clamp clean.

Overlap the next piece about one inch. Anchor the cloth into the wet epoxy and smooth the cloth out to the end and up the sheer (6-120).

When the next section has

6-120

6-121

6-119

6-122

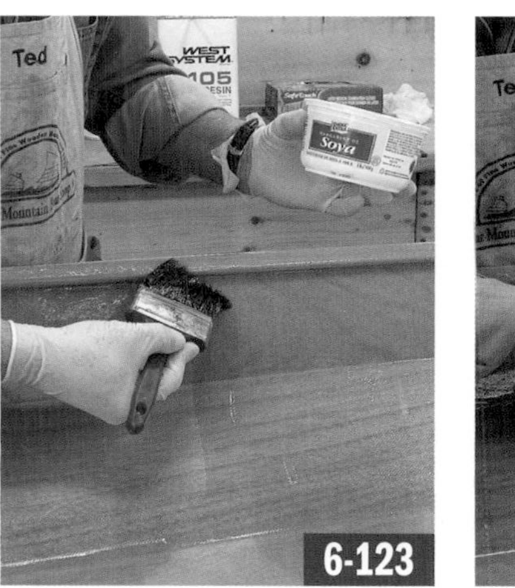

6-123

6-124

been wet out and squeegeed (6-121), use a narrow squeegee to work the epoxy out of the joint and to straighten the threads on the selvage edge.

3. Sand epoxy.

When the epoxy has cured enough to sand, feather the edge under the sheer clamp, the joints in the cloth and the ends of the glass. A firm sanding block with paper covering both sides will feather the glass and clean up the sheer clamp at the same time (6-122).

Give the glass a quick scuff to soften the texture. Vacuum up the dust and wipe surfaces clean with a rag dampened with lacquer thinner or water.

4. Apply second coat of epoxy (→ page 87).

With a brush, coat the sheer clamp and spread epoxy partway down the side (6-123). Use enough epoxy to draw down the side and out into the bottom with the squeegee.

Spread the epoxy around with the squeegee to pack the weave full and force out any air; scrape off the excess and discard. Check the underside of the clamp with the squeegee to pick up any stray drips (6-124). For a first-rate job, finish by dry-brushing the clamp as well as the interior.

DAYS 12-13
Complete Interior

To Do
- ○ Do end pour.*
- ○ Install bulkheads.*
- ○ Install foot pegs.

Tools & Materials
- ○ chisel
- ○ drill
- ○ epoxy resin and hardener
- ○ epoxy dispensing pumps
- ○ filler
- ○ grunge can
- ○ lacquer thinner
- ○ mixing pots
- ○ putty knife
- ○ rags
- ○ firm sanding block
- ○ 120 grit sandpaper
- ○ screws
- ○ spatula
- ○ square
- ○ squeegee
- ○ stir sticks
- ○ vacuum cleaner
- ○ weights

Safety
- ○ dust mask
- ○ gloves
- ○ eye protection
- ○ good ventilation
- ○ caution with cutting tools

Installing these components will be spread over two days to accommodate the cure cycles between steps. The actual time will depend on the brand of epoxy used.

6-125

1. Do end pour (→ page 78).

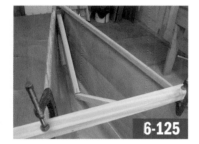

The end pour may be done before or after the inside has been glassed. I chose to do it afterward to avoid staining the bare wood and to simplify cleanup if the filler happened to get out of control.

There are two parts to this step: casting a stem to tie the sides together and doing an end pour to build up enough filler in the ends to take holes for grab handles and for a rudder in the stern. Organize everything needed for the end-pour dam and do a dry run to be sure it works. The stem fillet is an extension of the keel line fillet and should run up far enough to be inside the end pour. To keep the vertical part of the stem fillet from sagging, try propping one end of the hull up high. When the stem fillet is firm, fit the dam and do the end pour.

Stabilizing the dam was a bit of a head-scratcher. This jury rig (6-125) is the best I could come up with.

Curious to see if supporting the dam was really necessary, I simply taped the stern dam in place with duct tape. This is what it looks like when the dam does not do its job (6-126). I allowed the filler to run on its own rather than smear it around trying to pick it up wet. When it kicked, a sharp chisel was used to shave it down.

Both ends took a second pour to top them up.

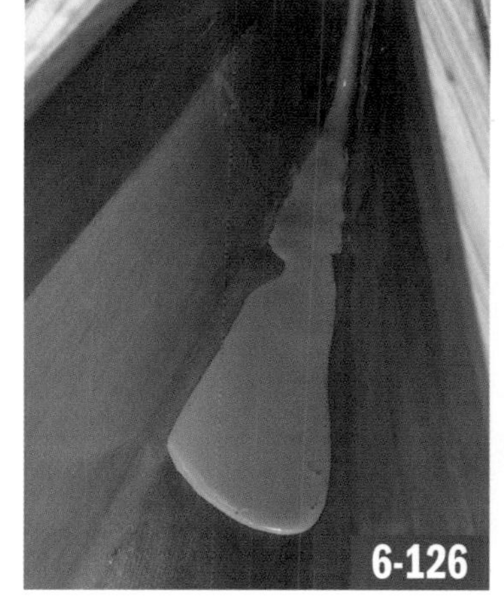

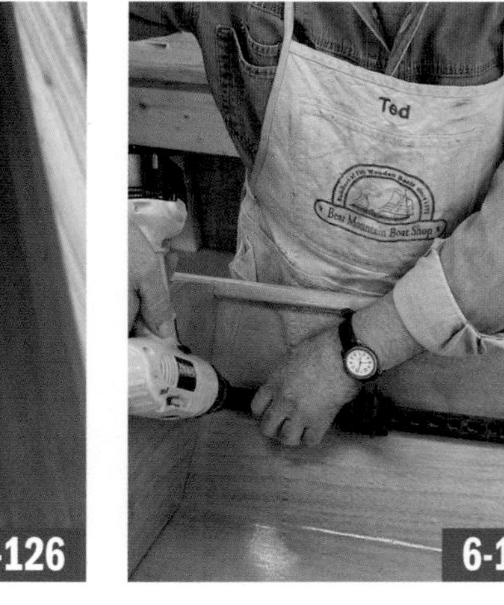

2. Install bulkheads (→ page 100).

3. Install foot pegs (→ page 124).

The position given for the Mill Creek foot pegs is just aft of the bulkhead. Position the track and drill the first hole; insert the screw, then drill the second hole (6-127). Note that the hole in the track is smaller than the screw to allow it to cut its own threads. A smaller bit is used to drill through the track to mark the position, then a larger one is used to ream out the hole in the hull to fit the screw.

To position the mate, use a square to project the end of the track up to the sheer line (6-128), then use a tape measure to measure from this point to the tip of the bow. Swing the tape and transfer this measurement over to the other side and back down to the position of the track.

DAYS 14-18

Glass Outside of Hull

To Do

- O Sand outside.
- O Apply glass and first coat of epoxy.*
- O Reinforce stems.*
- O Feather patches and sand.
- O Install keel (optional).*
- O Apply second coat of epoxy.*
- O Apply third coat of epoxy.*

Tools & Materials

- O 2-inch natural bristle brush
- O drill and bits
- O duct tape
- O epoxy resin and hardener
- O epoxy dispensing pumps
- O fiber tape
- O file
- O file board
- O filler
- O fiberglass cloth
- O grunge can
- O lacquer thinner
- O masking tape
- O mixing pots
- O putty knife
- O rags
- O random orbital sander
- O firm sanding block
- O 120 grit sandpaper
- O spatula
- O squeegee
- O stir sticks
- O screws and driver
- O weights

Safety

- O dust mask
- O eye protection
- O gloves
- O good ventilation

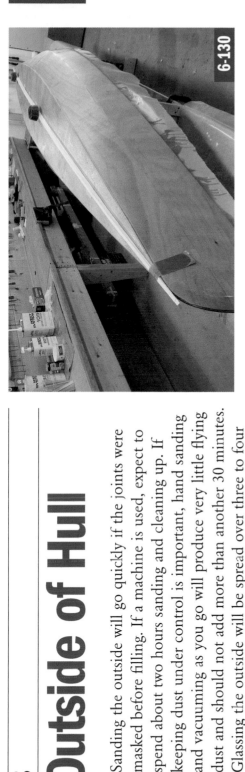

Sanding the outside will go quickly if the joints were masked before filling. If a machine is used, expect to spend about two hours sanding and cleaning up. If keeping dust under control is important, hand sanding and vacuuming as you go will produce very little flying dust and should not add more than another 30 minutes. Glassing the outside will be spread over three to four days, depending on the brand of epoxy used. Patching the stems will slow things down a bit because they should be feathered between the first and second coats of epoxy.

6-129

1. Sand outside.

A half- or quarter-sheet sander is reasonably safe for cleaning up the flat surface of the planks.

Don't try to get it all with the machine; save the corners and tricky spots for the sanding block.

After completing the flat surfaces, round the corners by hand. A long file board or Speed File provides excellent control for keeping the chines straight as you round over the corners (6-129).

2. Apply glass and first coat of epoxy (→ page 81).

3. Reinforce stems (→ page 86).

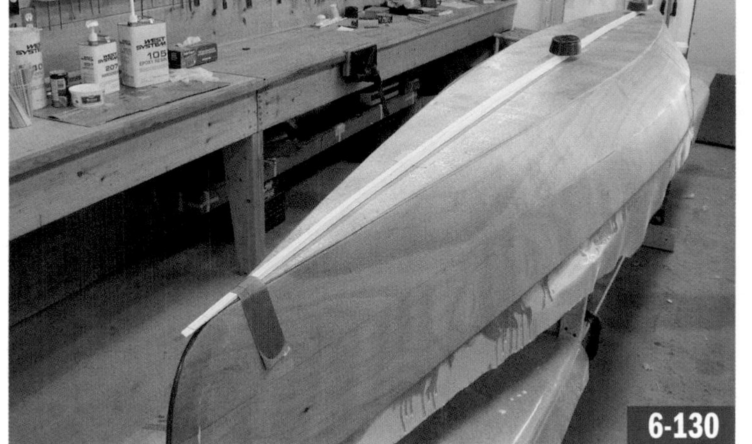

6-130

4. Feather patches & sand.

5. Install keel (optional).

Although external keels are not often seen on modern kayaks, the Mill Creek 13 is more of a Rob Roy-style double-paddle canoe than a kayak. Given its flat bottom and short length, I took the liberty of adding a keel to the Mill Creek 13. It helps the boat's directional stability as well as stiffening up the flat bottom. Save some time by fitting the keel beforehand (6-130) and then installing it after the first coat of epoxy. The next two coats will protect the keel without additional epoxy steps.

The keel is ash, a reasonably dense hardwood, 3/4 x 3/4 x 3/8 inch in section, and has been tapered back about 18 inches on both ends. I used #4 x 3/4-inch steel screws in the ends as temporary fasteners and permanent #4 x 1/2-inch brass screws from the inside to hold the position and provide some clamping pressure.

Begin by positioning the keel on the centerline. Drill a loose pilot hole (5/64 inch) in the ends of the keel for a #4 x 3/4-inch steel screw and washer. After drilling a smaller pilot hole (1/16 inch) through the plywood into the filler inside, fasten the keel with the screw. The hold on the plywood and soft filler will be enough to keep the keel on the centerline if the screw is not over-tightened. Confirm that the keel is straight. Mark the position every 12 inches with short pieces

6-131

6-132

6-133

of masking tape on both sides of the keel. Remove the keel and drill pilot holes between the pieces of tape on 12-inch centers; countersink them on the inside so that the screw heads will be flush.

Wax the threads on the steel screws before gluing so that they can be removed and the holes plugged later. Apply enough glue that it will squeeze out to confirm that the joint is full. Fasten the ends of the keel first and position it between the pieces of tape, drill pilot holes into the keel from the bottom, then drive the #4 screws. An extra pair of hands and eyes is a big help when working on both sides of the hull at one time.

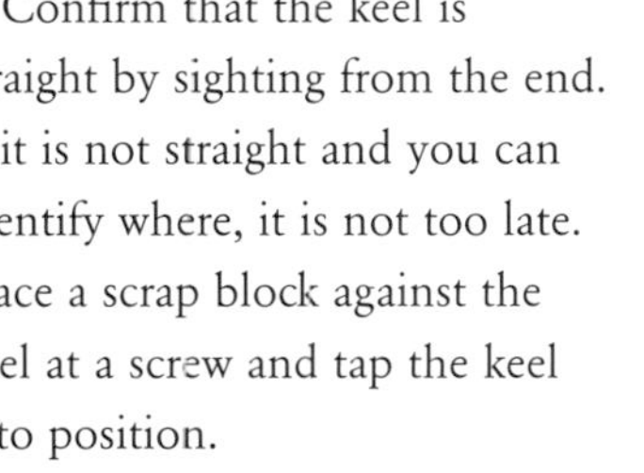

Confirm that the keel is straight by sighting from the end. If it is not straight and you can identify where, it is not too late. Place a scrap block against the keel at a screw and tap the keel into position.

Clean up the squeezed-out glue and add whatever additional clamping pressure is necessary to draw the keel up to the bottom. I used a combination of fiber tape and weights (6-131).

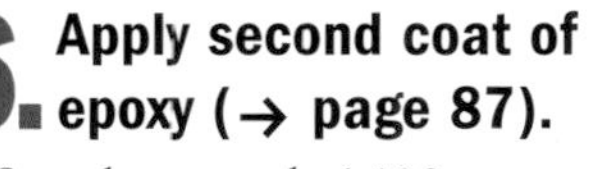

6. Apply second coat of epoxy (→ page 87).

See photograph 6-132.

7. Apply third coat of epoxy (→ page 88).

See photograph 6-133.

DAYS 19-21

Install Bulkheads, Knees and Carlins

To Do
- O Install bulkheads.*
- O Install hanging knees.*
- O Install carlins.*

Tools & Materials
- O block plane
- O clamps
- O drill and bits
- O duct tape
- O epoxy resin and hardener
- O epoxy dispensing pumps
- O fiber tape
- O fiberglass cloth or tape
- O filler
- O grunge can
- O jigsaw
- O lacquer thinner
- O masking tape
- O mixing pots
- O putty knife
- O rags
- O sanding block
- O 120 grit sandpaper
- O screws
- O sliding bevel gauge
- O spatula
- O squeegee
- O stir sticks
- O vacuum cleaner

Safety
- O dust mask
- O eye protection
- O gloves
- O good ventilation
- O caution with cutting tools

A convenient time to install the bulkheads is after the inside has been glassed. If wire is used to clamp the hanging knees, the holes may be filled before glassing the outside. Some of the steps may be combined with other operations to compress the epoxy cure cycles – if you don't mind the accompanying damage control. The choice is between waiting for the epoxy to cure and sanding off a mess later.

If the pieces fit, many of the steps are small and will fit into a leisurely evening work schedule. Save some time by epoxy-coating and sanding the plywood components beforehand.

Note: I got out of sequence while waiting for a pair of deck plates to arrive, but that wasn't a problem.

SAFETY TIP

When cutting epoxy-coated plywood, the safety hazards are similar to when sanding epoxy.

6-134

1. Install bulkheads (→ page 100).

Since the Mill Creek 13 is not a serious expedition kayak, convenient access to the space under the deck is not a priority. Rather than cut hatches in the deck, I used 6-inch ABS screw-out deck plates for access through the rigid bulkheads. They are easy to install and should be watertight.

Before installing each bulkhead, it is a good idea to cut the hole for the deck plate, as it will be awkward to cut from inside the boat.

Find the center of the bulkhead and mark the hole. Cut with a jigsaw, circle cutter or router with a compass jig (6-134). The edge of the cut should be sealed with epoxy at some point; watch for a convenient time when you have epoxy on the go for something else.

6-135

2. Install hanging knees.

Occasionally you may run into a piece in a kit that, for whatever reason, just doesn't fit. Although momentarily disconcerting, this is an opportunity to hone your old-time problem detection and solution skills. A case in point: the hanging knees included in my kit did not come close to fitting the hull at the position given on the plans, or anywhere else for that matter (6-135). If you're faced with something similar, calling

6-136

the manufacturers is a good place to start; they will want to know about the problem and can help with the solution. I decided to treat it as an exercise in problem-solving.

There were a few questions to consider before deciding what to do next. If the hanging knee were installed as is, could I trust that the top edge would support the deck in a fair curve between the bulkheads? Was this the accepted tolerance or should I think about filling the gap and supporting it with glass tape? The bottom of the knee could be shaped to fit the bilge plank a little better, but what would that do to the position of the top?

So, where to begin? The purpose of the knee is to support the deck, so the angle between the sheer plank and the deck is the reference that matters. Start by using a sliding bevel gauge (or make a template) to pick up this angle from the plans; record it for future reference.

After locating the positions of the knees at the sheer, clamp a stick across the hull on the marks as a guide. This reference stick, or stop, will help in positioning the knee perpendicular to the centerline for fitting, as well as make a convenient anchor for gluing.

Clamp the knee into position and adjust the top edge to the angle taken from the plans (6-136). Check the position with a long batten, looking for a fair curve between the bulkheads, the knees and the ends of the kayak.

This is a tricky shape to fit because of the changing angles, so making a pattern is the quickest way to finding the correct shape without confusion (→ Making the Template, page 101). Use a small block slightly wider than the offending gap and a pencil to scribe the shape of the hull onto the knee. Place the knee on the pattern material and transfer the shape from the scribe line to the pattern. Keep in mind that an accurate pattern will save much fitting later and will make you look good.

Line up the top edges of the pattern and knee and transfer the new shape to the knee; mark and cut. Fit the first knee to the hull, then check it on the other side. If it fits better than the pattern, use it to mark the other knee.

In attaching the knee, we are looking for adequate strength to do the job while hiding the reinforcement and minimizing epoxy exposure time. Under normal conditions, the knee is in compression because it supports the deck off the side of the hull. That much is easy, but what if the loaded craft is lifted from the side of the cockpit, directing all the weight through the knee?

I began by edge-gluing the knee to the hull to tack it. The top was clamped to the guide, then a stick was placed across to press the bottom end of both knees down to the hull. This joint is probably strong enough to hold under normal use, but since this is a boat, we must build for the worst-case scenario.

To reinforce yet hide the joint, fillet the aft side of the knee to the sheer plank and finish with glass tape (→ page 78). One healthy tab should be enough to hold without doing all the edges that show. Color match the filler. I didn't think it would show from the back of the boat, but it did. Oh well, wait until you see the next one. (This is a symptom of the disease that drives us to keep building boats.)

3. Install carlins.

Carlins are the curved deck beams that support the edge of the deck and form a base for the coaming.

Begin by clamping a guide block to the fore bulkhead to support the carlin flush to the top edge (6-137). This reference will save a lot of fumbling and simplify fitting; later it will position the carlins for gluing. The aft ends are glued and wedged into slots in the aft bulkhead.

6-137

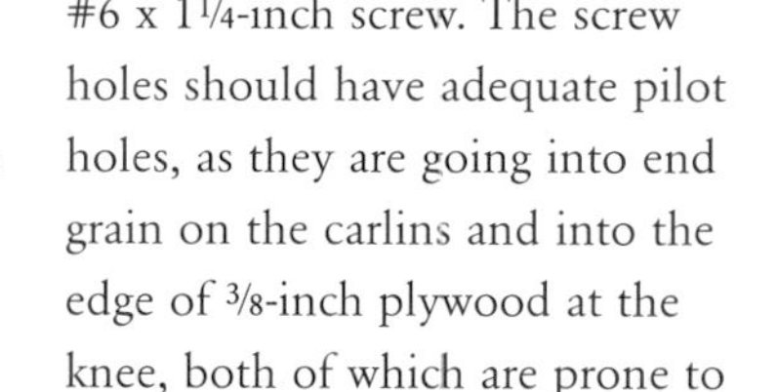
6-139

6-140

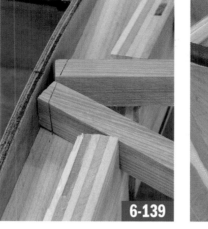

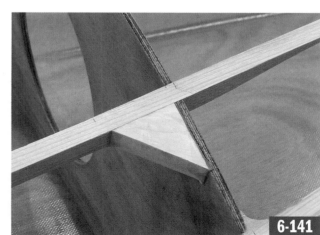

Notice that the carlins must be twisted to make the top surfaces flush to the bulkhead (6-138). Use clamp blocks on both sides to hold the twist for marking, fitting and gluing.

Clamp the carlins into position with the forward ends at the bulkhead centerline. Use a small block to transfer the bulkhead position onto the carlins (6-139). Cut to the line and refine the fit. Check the fit at the knees and the aft bulkhead; they should be flush on top.

Before mixing the glue (→ page 60), it is a good idea to do a dry run with screws and clamps.

The fore end of each carlin is fastened to the bulkhead with a #6 x 1¼-inch screw. The screw holes should have adequate pilot holes, as they are going into end grain on the carlins and into the edge of ⅜-inch plywood at the knee, both of which are prone to splitting.

The effectiveness of a carlin-to-bulkhead butt joint with one screw into end grain is marginal at best. To increase the attached surface area, I glued a quarter knee between each carlin and the bulkhead (6-140). Cut the quarter-knee stock thicker than the carlin (to allow the top side to be shaped later), then glue it flush to the bottom of the carlin.

After the glue has cured, use a block plane to trim (or fair) the quarter knee down to the level of the carlin and bulkhead (6-141).

Sand the raw wood components and seal them with epoxy in preparation for installing the deck.

6-138

6-141

DAYS 22-26

Install and Glass Deck

To Do

- O Complete interior.
- O Bevel sheer clamp.
- O Dry-fit foredeck.
- O Install foredeck.*
- O Install aft deck.*
- O Finish edge of deck.
- O Glass deck.***

Tools & Materials

- O acid brush
- O block plane
- O clamps
- O drill and bits
- O duct tape
- O epoxy resin and hardener
- O epoxy dispensing pumps
- O cotton fiber filler
- O fiber tape
- O jigsaw
- O lacquer thinner
- O laminate trimmer or router (optional)
- O masking tape
- O mixing pots
- O pull saw
- O putty knife
- O rags
- O rope or straps
- O firm and hard sanding blocks
- O 120 and 180 grit sandpaper
- O stir sticks
- O screws and driver
- O utility knife
- O vacuum cleaner

Safety

- O dust mask
- O eye protection
- O gloves
- O good ventilation
- O caution with cutting tools

Installing the deck could get messy because the underside must be sealed with epoxy, then bent to shape and fastened while it is still wet. If the sealer coat is allowed to cure before bending, the increased stiffness could make it difficult to force the panel into shape.

Glassing the deck will be routine after working on the hull, but don't relax; make sure the ratio is correct and each batch well stirred. Time is based on a 12-hour cure cycle, but using a faster-setting, low-blush epoxy could save some time.

1. Complete interior.

Before you install the deck, the interior should be as complete as possible (6-142). It is much easier to do good work when you can see and reach what needs to be done. Ships are built inside whisky bottles, but they too have a system that keeps most of the work on the bench.

6-142

Consider varnishing the cavity enclosed by the bulkheads. Although the epoxy surface is protected from UV, it is exposed to physical damage. If you varnish, mask the surfaces that will be glued to the deck.

I installed the deck plates dry in order to position the screw holes and see what the #6 x ½-inch oval-head screws were doing on the inside. This turned out to be a good idea, because the tips of the screws came through enough to be a hazard.

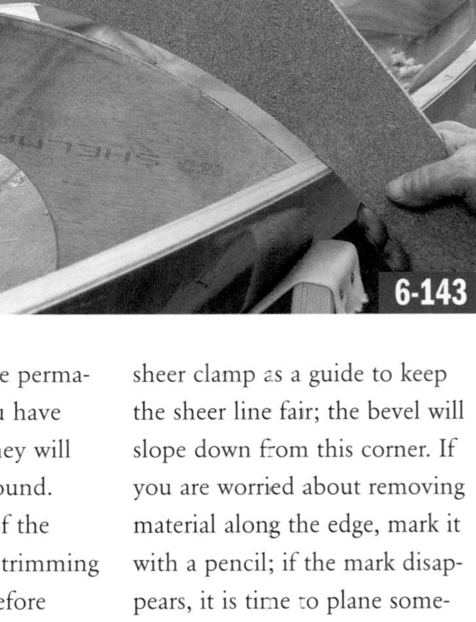

6-143

When the deck pieces are permanently installed after you have varnished the cockpit, they will be set in bedding compound. This will take up some of the space, but I also suggest trimming the ends of the screws before putting them in.

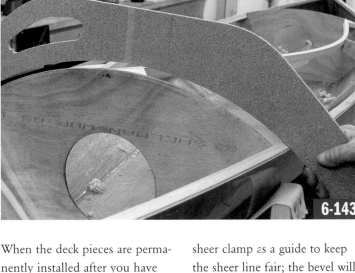

2. Bevel sheer clamp.

Two templates (called planing guides in the manual) are included in the kit to aid in shaping the bevel on the sheer clamp (6-143). They give the bevel at the bulkheads and for some distance on either side. Shape the known areas first, then use your eye and block plane to blend the rolling, or compound, bevel from one area into the other.

Use the inside edge of the sheer clamp as a guide to keep the sheer line fair; the bevel will slope down from this corner. If you are worried about removing material along the edge, mark it with a pencil; if the mark disappears, it is time to plane somewhere else.

A sharp block plane is the ideal tool to shape the bevel, but don't expect the edge to last long when you're cutting glass. Don't even think about the belt sander unless you have a master belt-sander operator's license and x-ray vision – and are very lucky.

Check often by sighting along the outside edge looking for a fair line, as well as by confirming the angle with the template.

CAUTION

If you elect to trim the excess plywood after the deck has been glued to the hull, be very conscious of what the sawblade is doing under the plywood. The angle of the hull to the deck is not consistent, so the blade may clear the hull safely in one place and damage it a little farther along.

3. Dry-fit foredeck.

Begin by dry-fitting the foredeck. A dry run is always a good idea, but very important here because we are making a complex shape from a flat panel; torturing it into submission could introduce unanticipated surprises.

Since it is the shape of the bulkhead that creates the deck camber, clamp the deck there first. Use rope and wedges or a setup like a Spanish windlass to pull the deck down to the bulkhead. I happened to have some ratchet tie-down straps that were as handy as it gets (6-144). The kayak was sitting in sling cradles, so the ends were blocked up and the straps were hooked to the worktable. If your boat is not well supported, there is no reason why the strap or rope could not simply go around the hull and deck.

At this point a generous amount of plywood was overhanging the sides, which made it awkward to check the joint and would make it difficult to clean up the glue later. Trimming it on the bench before attaching the deck avoids possible damage to the hull by the jigsaw if the deck is trimmed after installation. To trim, start by tracing the hull shape onto the bottom of the deck. As insurance, mark it oversized, with a 3/8-inch spacer. It will be trimmed flush when the glue has cured. Remove the panel and trim it to the line. After replacing the deck I checked the fit between deck and sheer clamp and marked the places that needed more trimming.

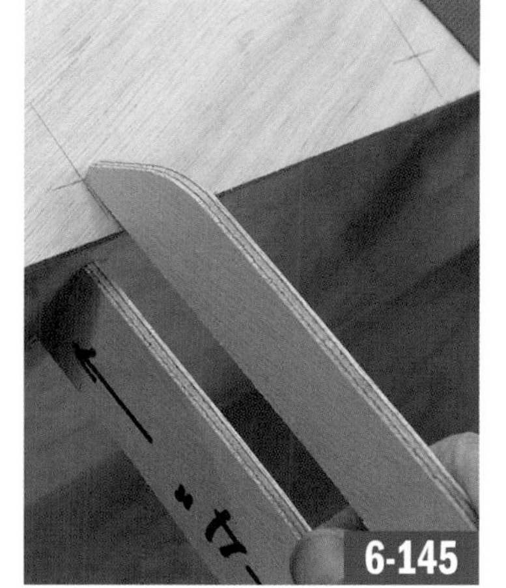
6-144

Gluing and clamping the deck to the carlin is safer than nailing, because the light cross-sectional dimension and long span of the carlin will not take much abuse. If you don't have enough clamps or decide to nail it anyway, there are several things that will help. Use 3/4-inch brass finishing nails, drill pilot holes and support the carlin with a weight opposite the nail being driven.

The deck is usually glued, then nailed to the sheer clamp with bronze ring nails. These nails hold the wood tenaciously and are a good choice for plywood-and-stringer construction. However, it is difficult to hit them hard enough to set the large heads flush with the surface without cracking the softwood sheer clamp. Drilling an adequate pilot hole for each nail will help, as well as tapping the nail down flush rather than using a few bold strokes.

6-145

In an effort to reinforce the traditional feel of the Mill Creek, I used #4 x 1/2-inch brass screws with reasonable success. The trick is to keep the depth of the countersink consistent and the hole perpendicular. Several of my holes were on the deep side of perfect; the result was an obvious buildup of epoxy over the screw head.

Some kits include a handy nailing guide (6-145) to transfer the center of the sheer clamp to the top of the deck. The lower part of the jig rests against the hull and the finger on top extends over the deck. Adjust the length of the finger by finding the center of the combined width of the sheer clamp and hull and cutting the finger off at this point. Note that the lower portion must be tight to the hull to make a useful mark.

Marking the fastener position before mixing the glue means one less thing to do after you get gloved up. We marked the spacing as well as the distance from the edge while the deck was clamped up dry. In practice the spacing lines were very useful, but since the deck did not end up exactly (plus or minus 1/32 inch) in the same place, it was easier to re-mark the distance from the edge than try to shift the panel. It makes more sense to mark the spacing between the nails before gluing, then mark the distance in from the edge of the hull after it has been clamped into the glue.

4. Install foredeck.

Unless the deck camber is fairly flat, the tortured plywood deck must be installed with the inside unreinforced. In order to get some protection onto the underside, it is coated with mixed epoxy just before being glued in place.

There's no need for a brush or roller here, as pouring on a puddle of mixed epoxy and moving it around with the squeegee (6-147) is quite effective (→ page 89). Let the mixed epoxy soak in for 15 or 20 minutes, then scrape off the excess. A buildup of wet epoxy at this point is going to make a mess by the time the foredeck is positioned and fastened, plus it will be sloppy to handle.

6-147

While the epoxy is soaking into the plywood, mix up a batch of glue (mixed epoxy reinforced with cotton fibers) and apply it to the top of the bulkhead and carlins. Hold off applying the glue to the sheer clamp until the deck is positioned and the straps or ropes are set up.

Try to work clean when moving the deck panel and positioning it. If epoxy gets on your gloves, wipe it off with a dry rag. If you remove wet glove-prints from the deck as soon as possible with a rag dampened with lacquer thinner, there will be nothing to sand off later. I was surprised at how easy the deck was to install cleanly. When the butt joint also came out clean, there was no reason not to add some color to the deck.

Be careful not to scrape the glue off the carlins and bulkheads while positioning the deck panel and setting up the straps or ropes (6-148). Leave enough space around the edge to apply the optimum amount of glue to the sheer clamp. When the ropes are tightened, the joint will close without sliding around and the glue will stay where it should be.

Clamp the deck to the carlins before fastening it at the sheer. I noticed that clamping to the carlin raised the deck off the sheer. Once the deck was clamped to the carlin, bending it back down put a pleasing twist in the carlin that followed the natural bend of the plywood. If the deck had been fastened at the sheer first, I don't think the clamps would have pulled the carlin into this pleasing compound curve.

Apply the glue to the sheer

CHEAP TRICK

Nailing jig

If your kit does not include a nailing guide or if you just need to project a position around a corner, you can easily make one out of stiff cardboard or light plywood (6-146).

Consistent fastener spacing is a cheap trick that adds a professional touch. To simplify this, we have added another feature to the nailing jig to lay out the distance between nails. Four-inch spacing will keep waves from developing between the fasteners, so a notch was cut this distance from the end of the jig. When the notch is lined up with the last hole, the end of the jig is positioned to mark the next hole. Another way to get the spacing is to "walk off" the distance with pointed drafting dividers.

6-146

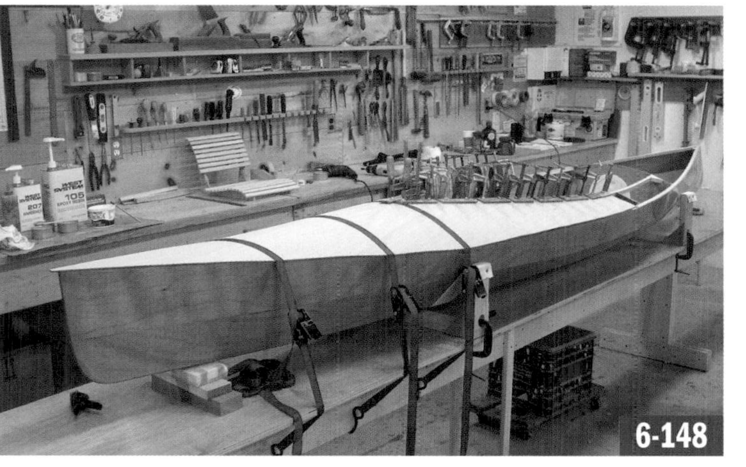
6-148

clamp, then tighten up the straps or ropes. Begin fastening where the deck is tied down to the sheer clamp. Outside this secured area, the plywood is forced down to the sheer by hand as the fasteners are added. Work on alternating sides to draw both sides down evenly.

Pick up all the excess glue you can reach with the putty knife and wipe surfaces clean with a rag dampened with lacquer thinner.

5. Install aft deck.

Installing the aft deck uses the same routine as the foredeck, aside from making a neat joint between the two panels (6-149).

One way to fit the panels is to bend the panel over the aft bulkhead and secure it with the centerline joints on both sides of the cockpit opening slightly overlapped.

The aft panel is now positioned over the fore panel as a guide to cut through the bottom piece with a sharp utility knife. Trimming to length on the first panel works only if enough clamps are available to install both panels while the glue on the first panel is still wet.

Since the glue on the foredeck had cured when I fitted the panels together, it was easier to trim the aft deck than disturb the glued pieces.

The joint is backed up with a plywood butt block that fits between the carlin and the sheer clamp (6-150). To avoid the awkward task of working from underneath, consider fitting and applying an epoxy sealer to the bottom of the blocks before they are installed.

When the glue on the deck has cured, trim the edge of the deck flush to the side of the hull. If you have a router or laminate trimmer and a straight bit with a pilot bearing on the bottom, it is the ideal tool for the job (6-151). Trimming by hand is no problem if a power tool is not available.

Finish with a hard sanding block to refine the bevel for a clean joint between the deck and the guard. Prepare for the guard by sanding the epoxy on the outside of the hull, or at least a strip around the sheer. Once the guard is attached, sanding up to it will be fussy, time-consuming and a setup for damage control.

The instructions show the aft deck trimmed at the bulkhead. To my eye the deck ends too abruptly, and that much bulkhead showing takes away from the traditional feel of the rest of the kayak. Also, this joint will have to be reinforced in some way; ending like this, it leaves the reinforcement visible. Since there was lots of plywood to play with,

6-149

6-150

6-151

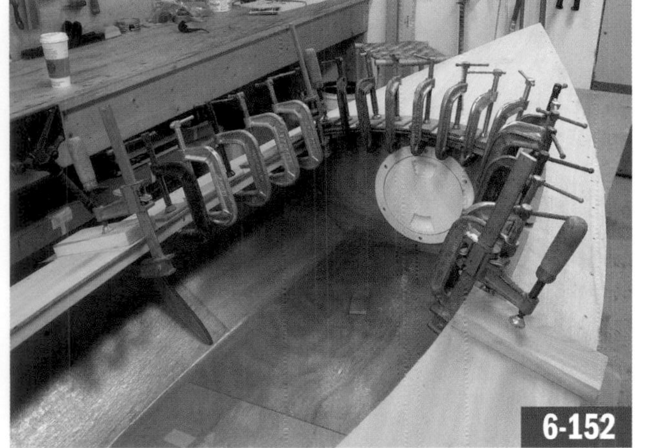
6-152

I took the liberty of letting the deck overhang the bulkhead.

To strengthen the overhang, I ripped a piece of prefinished 4-mm (5/32-inch) ply to 2 3/4 inches wide and fitted it to the bulkhead and between the carlins (6-152). Fit this piece when the deck is clamped on dry, as it must be sprung into the camber of the deck to fit the ends. Glue the backer into place after attaching the deck to the sheer clamp and cleaning up.

Besides strengthening the deck, the backer will seal the joint between the bulkhead and deck between the carlins without having to fillet or tape. Increasing the thickness of the edge of the deck will make a good base for the trim that will come later. Also, because the piece is ripped parallel and fitted to the bulkhead, which we know is perpendicular to the centerline, it is a convenient guide for trimming the aft edge of the deck.

6. Finish edge of deck.

After trimming the deck flush (6-154) it's time to decide how the edge of the deck will be finished. The plans show the top of the guard (rubrail) shaped as a pleasing extension of the deck, while the instructions suggest the additional steps of putting a radius on the edge of the deck and bringing the cloth around the corner and down the side of the hull. The guard is then fastened below the rounded edge, a step that is difficult to do consistently and make fair.

When building the Coho, I learned some tricks for gracefully bringing the glass around the edge of the deck and down the side of the hull. I also learned that it is not a simple or quick joint to make, but it was necessary on the Coho because it did not have a sheer clamp to tie the hull and deck together.

This is another case of eliminating steps to save time and health and to achieve professional-looking results. Given that we do have a sheer clamp joining the hull and deck on the inside, if we position the guard to bridge both hull and deck, the joint will be locked together without all the unhealthy steps and the visual distraction of the deck glass feathered into the hull.

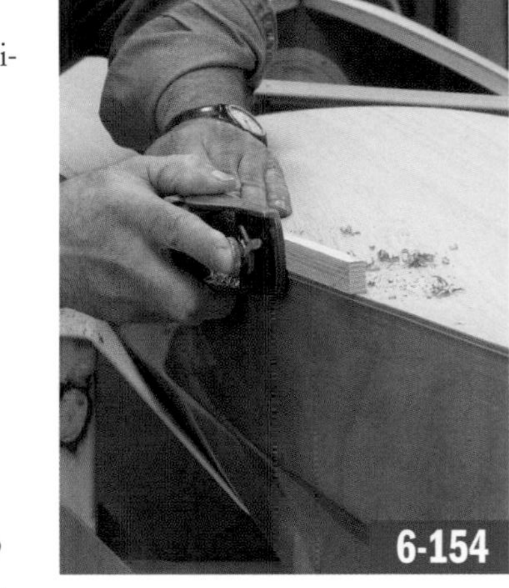
6-154

7. Glass deck

Although we could leave the deck with a natural finish and it would look great, I thought it would be interesting to see if I could make okume plywood look like mahogany. I used a premixed rosewood-colored dye, which was the closest match I could find to a red-brown mahogany color. Counting the extra sanding time, adding a rich color to the deck

CHEAP TRICK

Plane fence guide

When a block plane is used to trim the edge of the deck, watch out for two things. Remember that the plywood edge of the deck must be shaped as an extension of the side of the hull for the guard to make a clean joint with the deck. More importantly, the blade of the plane will bite into the epoxy-and-glass coating on the hull if the blade extends too far down the side.

Using this simple accessory for the plane will help control both situations (6-153). Fasten a wooden guide (about 1/2 x 3/4 x 10 inches) to the bottom of the plane with two-sided tape to limit the amount of blade exposed. (Clean the wax off the bottom of the plane with lacquer thinner in order for the tape to stick.) If the jig is centered, the plane will work in both directions.

6-153

(→ page 140) took about two hours.

Installing the guards before the deck is glassed is worth considering. The cloth will extend over the top of the guard and disappear into the curve on its edge. Consider trimming the glass after the first coat has kicked and bringing the next two coats of epoxy over the guard. Protect the hull by masking just below the guard.

I had to make some decisions because of the dye. If the guards are installed before the dye, the guards and the deck will change color together. On the other hand, a contrast between the deck and the guard can be a nice detail. I chose to go for the contrast. Trying to dye the deck, then fit the guard without making a mess is not going to happen. One choice is to seal the deck after it is dyed, then fit the guard – an extra epoxy step, and the surface is still exposed when you fit the guard. The alternative is to glass the deck with all three coats of epoxy, then fit the guard and shape it before sanding the deck. The important thing to watch for is keeping the epoxy a consistent thickness out to the edge.

Mask the edge of the hull and deck in case the epoxy runs down over the edge. A generous amount of glass hanging over the edge will soak up most of the excess epoxy so it won't run down the side of the hull (6-155). This wicking action will also keep the film thickness consistent up to the edge. Avoid working along the edge with a large amount of epoxy; sneak up on the edge a bit at a time.

The deck is covered with 50-inch-wide 4-ounce fiberglass cloth. This light cloth is a good choice because its purpose is to add durability rather than strength.

Covering the wedge-shaped fore and aft decks with one sheet of fiberglass would waste a lot of cloth, so the plan is to split the 3-yard by 50-inch cloth on the

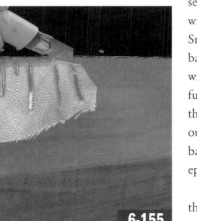

6-155

diagonal and join it in the middle to cover the full length of the deck.

I began by positioning the cloth on the foredeck with 4 to 6 inches hanging over one side. This put the offcut where it could be trimmed conveniently. If it looks like the amount of available cloth will be tight, reduce the overhang and do some measuring to be sure before cutting. Handle the cloth carefully, as it is easy to snag it on the edge of the deck.

On our little kayak the cloth reached to the aft end of the cockpit, which worked out well (6-156). This is the most inconspicuous place to make the joint because there is competing visual activity at the end of the cockpit coaming.

When the first piece of glass is settled, position the other piece with about a 1-inch overlap. Smooth it out, then fold the edge back out of the way (6-157); this will save trying to position the full piece with sticky gloves. After the forward piece has been wet out and squeegeed, fold the cloth back and smooth it into the wet epoxy to anchor it.

The epoxy is applied with the three-step method used on the outside of the hull (→ page 82).

6-156

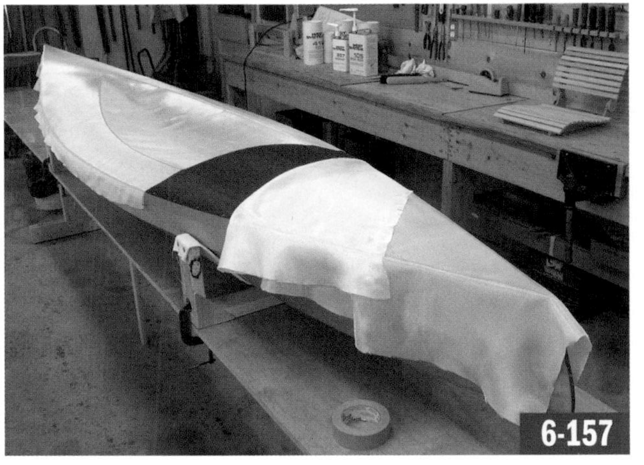

6-157

When the third coat of epoxy has cured, trim the glass and finish with a firm or hard sanding block. Make an effort not to round over the edge if a clean joint between deck and trim components is expected. Clean up in preparation for installing the trim.

DAYS 27-30
Install Trim

To Do
- O Install guard.
- O Make seat.
- O Sand deck.
- O Install coaming.**
- O Install seat.
- O Install floorboards.

Tools & Materials
- O acid brush
- O block plane
- O clamps
- O cotton fiber as filler
- O drill and bits
- O duct tape
- O epoxy dispensing pumps
- O epoxy resin and hardener
- O fiber tape
- O jigsaw
- O lacquer thinner
- O masking tape
- O mixing pots
- O pull saw
- O putty knife
- O rags
- O firm and hard sanding blocks
- O 120 and 180 grit sandpaper
- O screws and driver
- O stir sticks
- O vacuum cleaner

Safety
- O dust mask
- O eye protection
- O gloves
- O good ventilation
- O caution with cutting tools

Installing the trim could be the high point of the project because it is the details that give this little boat character. These components are going to be noticed, so work to a standard that will make you proud of them. I assembled the seat as a fill-in job while working on the deck, but if you haven't got to it yet, it will fit in well between installing the guard and the coaming.

1. Install guard (→ page 116).

2. Make seat (→ page 122).

3. Sand deck (→ page 96).

4. Install coaming.

6-158

The coaming components are fitted and installed in this order: fit the snout to the deck; fit the sides between the snout and the aft end of the cockpit; install the trim across the back of the cockpit; install the moldings around the cockpit.

Our instructions suggest shaping the forward end of the snout to fit the narrow V where the cockpit sides come together. This is fine if the deck has been trimmed with a router bit and pilot bearing, but if it has been shaped by hand, it may not be neat enough to use for the shape of the snout.

To address this concern, consider shaping only the portion of the snout that will be below the surface of the deck (6-158). This will also allow the forward portion of the snout to extend over the deck, making a tidy joint.

6-159

The sides of the coaming will fit between the snout rabbet and the aft end of the cockpit. To find the forward position, hold the snout in place and mark at the end of the rabbet (6-159). Use a sharp pencil to take the guesswork out of where to cut.

Position each side just far enough down the carlin to clamp and extending over the deck on the forward end. Use a combination square to project the line on the deck up the side, mark and cut.

Fit the side into the cockpit and flush to the bottom of the carlin. The aft end of the coaming has a traditional-looking tail that flows out over the deck (6-160). Use a sharp pencil on its side to scribe a line parallel to the deck onto the coaming.

Cut to the line on the bench, then clamp the coaming back into position. Expect the fit to be less than perfect. It's tricky to pick up the subtle deck camber the first time.

For a perfect joint, position a piece of 120 grit sandpaper (grit side up) between the deck and

6-160

6-161

6-162

6-163

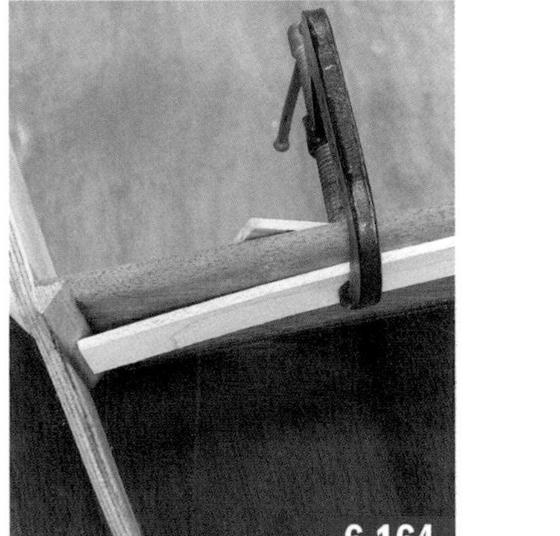
6-164

the coaming (6-161). Clamp snug to the paper. Work the sandpaper until the shape of the deck has been transferred to the lower edge of the coaming.

With the sides looking good at the stern and clamped into position, do a final dry fit with the snout. My gluing strategy was to make the snout a slip fit so that it could be installed after both sides had been secured. Before gluing into place, consider sanding the components up to the 180 grit stage. Hold off shaping the top edge until after the moldings have been installed.

Use a structural mix of mixed epoxy and cotton fiber for the glue. Adjust the color to suit your kayak.

For a tight joint, clamp on no less than 4-inch centers. Clean up the squeezed-out glue, paying particular attention to the outside edge. Wipe clean with a rag dampened with lacquer thinner.

After the ends of the trim across the back of the cockpit have been cut roughly to fit, clamp guide blocks on either end to help position the trim at the intended angle and tight to the deck (6-162). Before gluing the trim into place, sand it up to the 180 grit stage and round over the bottom edge.

The guide blocks need to be removed before you place the trim into the glue, but they will be used again for holding the trim in place while the ends are being nailed. Draw a light pencil line along the edge of each block as a reference mark for replacing it.

Pre-coat the end grain of the trim and the edge of the plywood deck with mixed epoxy until they stay shiny. Also coat the portion of the trim that will be under the deck; it will save standing on your head to coat it later.

Thicken the remainder of the epoxy with a structural mix of cotton fiber and a bit of sanding dust for color. Apply along the edge of the deck and to the ends of the trim. Press the trim straight into the glue and secure it with the guide blocks. Before the glue has had a chance to run, shape the fillet with a gloved finger into a tidy cove.

The ends are fastened with $3/4$-inch brass finishing nails in $1/16$-inch pilot holes (6-163). After nailing, remove the guide blocks and clean up the joint.

This joint as it stands is marginal. Epoxy is a good waterproof glue but it does not take the place of an engineered joint. To increase the surface area, I have shaped the offcut from the molding to make a corner block (6-164). In addition to tying the joint together, the corner block fills in a corner that would first fill up with a puddle of varnish and later with dirt.

The molding supplied in the kit is a $1/4$ x $1/2$-inch piece of soft tropical hardwood that fits along

6-165

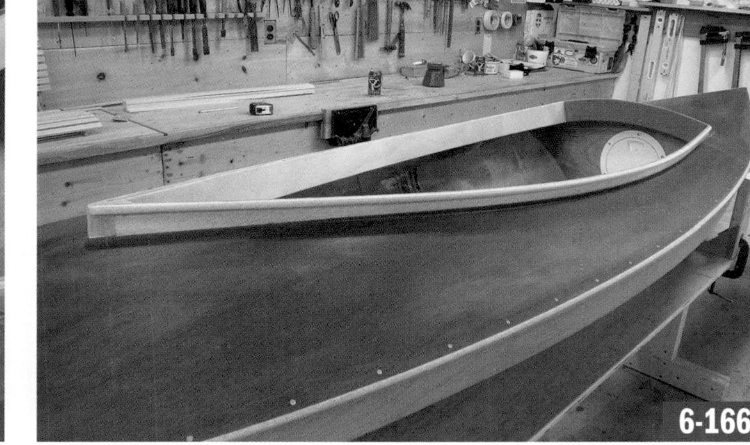

6-166

6-167

the top edge of the coaming. It will strengthen the edge and give the coaming a traditional appearance.

Do a dry fit to set up the clamps and confirm the fit. The snout may need a little work to get the molding to lie flush against it. Coat both surfaces with a structural glue mix but go easy on the amount of glue. It is important to clean up all the excess on the underside of the molding as scraping and sanding will be difficult later.

When the glue has cured, work the top edge flush with a rasp or hard sanding block. To trim the snout, lay the saw along the top of the coaming as a guide and cut halfway from each side (6-165). Cut slightly upward; it is easy to file a raised area down later but hard to replace a hollow.

A sanding block won't fit into the confined space under the molding's bottom edge, so try a piece of 80 grit paper wrapped around the edge. To shape the top edge, use a sanding block with 120 grit and long strokes. Dampen the surface to raise the grain and sand to the 180 grit stage, dampen again and sand to the 220 to 280 grit stage (6-166).

5. Install seat (→ page 124).

6. Install floorboards.

I have taken the liberty of installing floorboards in the Mill Creek because it is more of a Rob Roy-style double-paddle canoe than a kayak. Besides complementing the traditional feel of the craft, it will also keep your pant legs from soaking up the water that will inevitably find its way into this large open cockpit.

To keep the weight to a minimum, I have used 1/4-inch white cedar for the floorboards and 3/16-inch ash for the cleats that tie them together.

Floorboards (6-167) should be easy to remove from time to time for cleaning. Turn buttons may be made from wood, plastic or a nonferrous metal. I used a piece of 3/16-inch half-oval brass drilled and countersunk for a #4 x 1/2-inch brass screw.

An oil finish is a good choice for floorboards. It is less slippery than varnish and much easier to maintain.

DAYS 31-36

Varnish or Paint, Install Fittings

To Do
- O Complete sanding epoxy.
- O Seal trim.
- O Prepare surface.
- O Varnish or paint.
- O Install fittings.

Tools & Materials
- O brush
- O brush cleaner
- O 1-inch masking tape
- O paint filters
- O paint thinner
- O paint pots
- O recycled clean cans, plastic tubs
- O rags
- O tack cloth
- O 220 or 280 grit sandpaper
- O stir sticks
- O varnish or paint

Safety
- O dusk mask
- O gloves
- O good ventilation

These will be short days, ideal for part-time work. Good luck with the last coat of finish – make each coat a practice for the finale.

1. Complete sanding epoxy (→ page 97).

2. Seal trim (→ page 135).

3. Prepare surface (→ page 134).

4. Varnish or paint (→ page 136).

5. Install fittings.

Building the Mill Creek 13 was a pleasure. Traditional double-paddle solo canoes have always caught my attention, so it was fun to explore developing traditional features using plywood. Given its Rubenesque proportions, I had not expected this little boat to grow on me the way it did. As the traditional details began to develop, it started to come alive. And painting the bottom pulled it all together.

The Enterprise

HISTORICALLY, MOST BOAT DESIGNS draw on a combination of tradition, proven technology and innovation. Such is the case with our third design, Bear Mountain's 17'4" Enterprise. The Enterprise combines a stitch-and-glue hard-chined hull with the fluid curves and natural color combinations possible with a strip-planked deck.

Drawing on Steve Killing's very successful Endeavour, a soft-chine sea kayak designed for strip-planking, the Enterprise combines straightforward stitch-and-glue building methods and a few traditional boatbuilding components, with some Bear Mountain innovations thrown in. Using forms to build the hull upside down is a well-proven system adapted from wood-strip-and-epoxy building methods. A traditional feature is the use of stems to control the ends of the planks and to add integrity to the ends of the hull. Although stems are unheard-of in light stitched-seam construction, the effort to make them is more than compensated for by the time they save, as well as the help they provide to make the shape of the kayak predictable.

An important Bear Mountain innovation is bonding of the deck to the sheer clamp. This allows us to join the hull and deck from the outside rather than enduring the ungraceful exercise of glassing the joint from the inside and doing an end pour.

That said, let's put an Enterprise together.

DAY 1

Get Organized

To Do
- ○ Construct worktable.
- ○ Check parts against packing slip.
- ○ Organize tools and materials.
- ○ Read instructions.

Tools & Materials
- ○ clamps
- ○ drill/driver
- ○ drywall screws
- ○ level
- ○ material for worktable
- ○ saw
- ○ straightedge
- ○ string line
- ○ square
- ○ tape measure
- ○ utility knife

Safety
- ○ eye protection
- ○ good ventilation
- ○ caution with cutting tools

Building the Enterprise will be an exercise in building fast by putting our time and effort into preparation rather than damage control. Our objective is a beautiful kayak that is also quick to build.

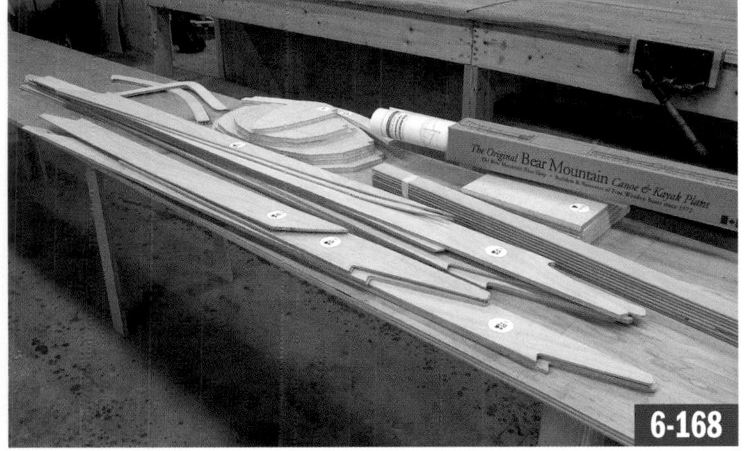

6-168

1. Construct worktable (→ page 23).

2. Check parts against packing slip.

As well as confirming that you have received a complete kit, checking the parts against the illustrated packing slip will introduce you to the pieces of your kayak, what they are called and what they look like (6-168).

3. Organize tools & materials.

4. Read instructions.

Looking over the instructions will give you a good overview of how the pieces will come together.

DAYS 2–3

Join Plank Components

To Do
- O Identify and sort components into sets.
- O Join components into planks.**
- O Assemble building forms.

Tools & Materials
- O fine ballpoint pen
- O blocks for station forms
- O clamp blocks
- O clamps and/or weights
- O drill/driver and bits
- O epoxy resin and hardener
- O fiberglass tape or cloth
- O glue brush or acid brush
- O heavy plastic film
- O lacquer thinner
- O mixing pots
- O plastic packing tape
- O putty knife
- O rags
- O firm sanding block
- O 120 or 180 grit sandpaper
- O scissors
- O screws
- O square
- O squeegee
- O stir sticks
- O straightedge
- O string line
- O tape measure
- O utility knife

Safety
- O dust mask
- O eye protection
- O gloves
- O good ventilation
- O caution with cutting tools

I was able to assemble the hull plank components in two days by using a slow hardener that cured in about eight hours. One pair was glued in the morning and the other after dinner. Using a fast hardener could shorten the day as well as speed up the filling jobs, but buying an extra can of hardener for one project is hardly justified if you are building in short blocks of time. Assembling the six building forms is a good fill-in job while the epoxy cures.

1. Identify & sort components into sets.

The plank components are identified by numbers on the inside surface of the plywood; the forward end of the kayak is indicated with an arrow. Organize the components into sets of port and starboard planks.

To make up the planks, the components in the kit are joined with a butt joint in the shape of a common scarf. Although a straight butt joint is adequate and appropriate for the plans-builder, CNC technology allows us to design a shape that will look good as well as work for us. This style of scarf joint is a familiar nautical sight, often seen in the covering boards of quality sail and power yachts. The ends of the scarf are trimmed back to eliminate a fragile tip, and the angle is such that the components are drawn into alignment when the parts are pressed together. Taking the nautical image one step further, all the plank joints are staggered in a pattern appropriate for a traditionally planked hull. While the plywood is simply a core material, the joints will show, so they might as well contribute to the overall "rightness" of the finished kayak.

2. Join components into planks.

Using the distances from the baseline given on the plans, lining up the plank components was straightforward and accurate. While the joint is designed to pull the planks into line, the accuracy we need must be confirmed from a reliable baseline. Having a flat surface to work on, with straight sides and a centerline, was worth all the effort of building the table.

Before laying out the planks, remove any fuzz on the edges of the components using 180 grit sandpaper. Do not round over the edges, as that will cause a wider than necessary glue line. Be careful working along the edges of the planks – okume plywood can be splintery.

Select the components to make up a pair of planks. The number label should be on the inside surface of the plank (it's removed when the inside of the plank is sanded). Since a glass-cloth butt block is used on the inside only, it is important to identify the side you are working on to make sure that everything comes together correctly. Take a good look at both sides of the plywood before committing to the glue. If you find that another arrangement of the components looks better to you, go for it. The most important point to remember is that you are making planks for both port and starboard sides of the hull. Also keep in mind that the veneer on the inside surface is often of a lesser quality than the face ply and will require a little more attention to sanding if a clear finish is anticipated. Be sure to mark new inside surfaces to avoid confusion later.

One side of each pair is set up to a baseline after gluing and will then become the pattern for assembling its mate.

Masking the outside surface is an optional step, but worth considering if you want to cut down on cleanup or if a bright finish is desired.

Begin by fitting the components together with the outside face of the plank facing up. Position the plank so that the joints are close enough to the edge of the table for your clamps to reach. Clamp the middle component first, then press the end sections firmly into place and clamp. A clamping block under the clamp will avoid having to deal with a bruise later.

Use plastic packing tape to

6-169

mask the joint (6-169). I used pieces about 12 inches long stretched tight and flat across the joint, to protect as well as to draw and hold the components together. Press the tape down tightly along the joint. Remove the clamps and gently turn the assembled plank over.

Position the plank, which is now inside face up along a baseline, and secure. Using dimensions taken from the plans, confirm that the shape is correct (6-170). Clamp the components to the table, keeping the clamps clear of the joints.

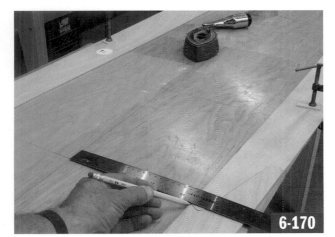

6-170

This is a good time for a final check that the curve along the edge of the plank is fair; it will be harder to see when the joints are cluttered with clamps. Stand at the end of the table and squint so that all you are seeing is the edge. If it looks right, there is a good chance that it is.

If an even color density is desirable, consider lightly sanding the area covered by the glass butt block before applying it. Unsanded, the raw surface of the plywood will absorb more resin and appear darker. This is the safest time to sand because, with the components clamped together, there is no chance of rounding the edges along the joint.

Protect the table and mold from epoxy that will squeeze through the joint by sliding a patch of 6-mil plastic film under each joint. Make it large enough to extend a safe distance around the joint.

I used 3-inch-wide tape made from fiberglass cloth cut on the bias to form a smooth, flat joint. Using an acid brush, apply mixed epoxy to the area to be covered by the glass and place the cloth in the epoxy. Use just enough epoxy to saturate the surface of the plywood and the glass cloth (6-171); any more will result in a lumpy joint and/or excess epoxy to be cleaned up later.

6-171

To mold the joint, place a piece of heavy plastic film over the wet glass and work the air out with a gloved finger. I found that a small squeegee worked well to move any excess epoxy out to the edge of the plank (6-172). This step can be helpful when weights are to be used as a clamping device and they may not provide sufficient pressure to force the excess epoxy and air out.

6-172

I used a smooth clamp block about 6 inches wide by a safe distance longer than the joint (1 or 2 inches) to mold the glass and epoxy into a thin, flat surface (6-173). C-clamps are recommended for controlled pressure,

6-173

6-174

but a weight of 10 pounds or more should be enough to hold the plywood flat and exclude the air.

When the epoxy has kicked, remove the clamps and trim the glass and excess epoxy from the edges. By catching the epoxy at the rubbery stage, you can use a sharp chisel to slice cleanly through the glass and epoxy (6-174). Once the epoxy has become hard, a rasp or hard sanding block is the best cleanup tool. It is important to maintain the shape of the plank by not removing wood along with the epoxy and glass.

After being clamped up tight, the plastic tape protecting the outside of the plank will be well bonded to the wood and will take some wood with it if simply peeled off. A little heat from a hair drier or heat gun will soften the glue's grip on the wood, allowing it to be removed more easily.

6-175

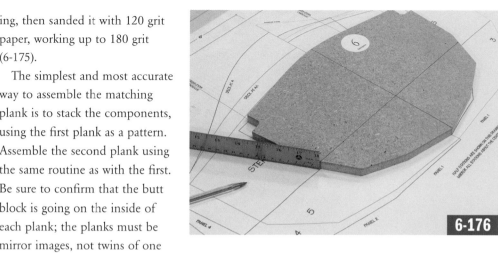

As it stands, the joint is finished; no cleanup is necessary. The next attention it gets will be when the little bit of epoxy showing gets scuffed up during sanding in preparation for the glass and epoxy. I was considering dyeing the hull before glassing, so I gave the joint a light scraping, then sanded it with 120 grit paper, working up to 180 grit (6-175).

THINK LAZY

Accurate reference marks will eliminate many problems before they happen. This is one of the keys to professional results without the apprenticeship.

The simplest and most accurate way to assemble the matching plank is to stack the components, using the first plank as a pattern. Assemble the second plank using the same routine as with the first. Be sure to confirm that the butt block is going on the inside of each plank; the planks must be mirror images, not twins of one another.

3. Assemble building forms.

There are six forms positioned on 30-inch centers in this kit. Although two or three forms are the norm for stitch-and-glue kayaks, for strip-planking, a 30-inch span is pushing the limit. The bonus for setting up a couple of extra forms is absolute control over the shape and the ability to eliminate many sutures.

I began assembling the forms by drawing centerlines and a design waterline on the precut forms and extensions. The centerlines are used in assembling and setting up the forms; the design waterline is the reference for attaching the extensions.

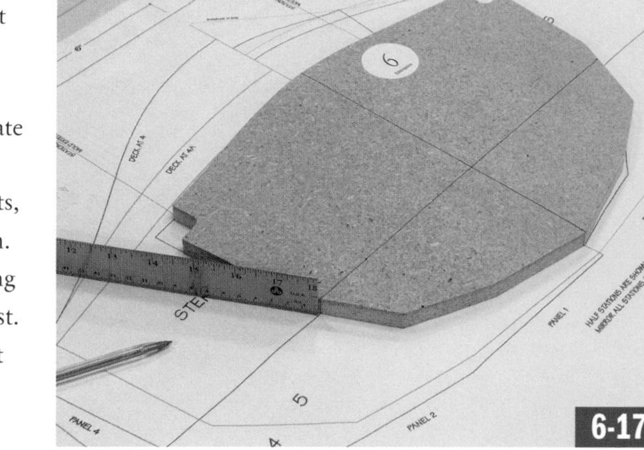
6-176

To find the position of the lines, I positioned the form over the appropriate lines on the plan. Then, with a ruler used as a small square, the line was projected up and drawn on the side of the form (6-176). From there it was straightforward to join these lines on both faces of the board. Use a fine ballpoint pen to make accurate, easy-to-see reference lines. For a quick confirmation of the centerline, measure the length of the waterline; divided by two it

CHEAP TRICK

Removing ink line

If by chance that line in permanent ballpoint ink needs to be moved over 1/16 inch, erasing or sanding it off will take forever, and leaving it will be confusing. I once drew a line in the wrong place and found that a paint scraper with the blade sharpened in a low arc sliced it off before I could feel dumb.

6-177

6-179

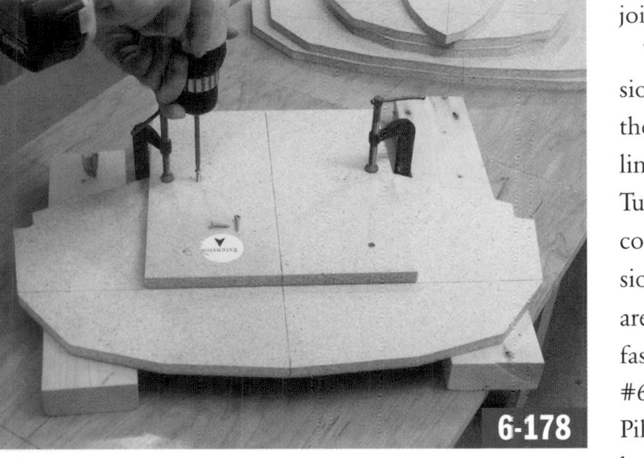

6-178

should agree with your centerline.

Prepare the extensions by finding the center of the 10-inch width and drawing a vertical line with the square (6-177). Confirm by measuring the width at the other end. When satisfied with the position, project the lines down the side of the board and join on the other side.

To join the form and the extension, position the extension at the waterline and over the centerline and clamp them together. Turning the form over will confirm that the form and extension centerlines on the other side are in line. The extension is fastened to the form with four #6 x 3/4-inch flat-head screws. Pilot holes are a good idea because they allow the screws to pull the pieces together without binding in the hole, as well as making it much easier to remove the screws later (6-178). The ideal is to have the threads just holding in the bottom piece, allowing the screw's head to act as a clamp.

If you can find another flat surface to work on, laminating the two layers of 4 mm (5/32-inch) ply that make up the stems is another fill-in job to keep you occupied while waiting for the glue on the planks to cure (6-179). The stems are made up of two layers of 4 mm plywood. While we could use one layer of 6 mm (15/64-inch), you can't control one warped piece of plywood. With two pieces, the warped pieces can be arranged to work against each other and, if glued together on a flat surface, should remain flat.

DAY 4

Set Up Forms

To Do
- ○ Set up blocks for forms.
- ○ Set up forms.
- ○ Make jigs.

Tools & Materials
- ○ clamps
- ○ clamp blocks
- ○ drill/driver
- ○ 1⅝-inch drywall screws
- ○ level
- ○ saw
- ○ square
- ○ straightedge
- ○ string line
- ○ tape measure

Safety
- ○ eye protection

This could be a short day, but take all the time you need to get set up right. Enjoy the process; it is a taste of traditional boatbuilding.

1. Set up blocks for forms.

Since forms are used to control the shape of the kayak, it is important to have confidence in that shape before you start to build. Once the forms are set up to your satisfaction, the shape of the kayak is taken care of and you can concentrate on making the skin fit.

Assuming the table already has a centerline drawn on it, begin by laying out and drawing the perpendicular station lines. Our centers here are 30 inches, but these kinds of numbers should always be confirmed from the plans. Because I know that the sides of my table are parallel, I marked the lines from the side of the table with a framing square. If the edges of your table are not straight and parallel, working from the centerline would be more accurate.

Attach 1½ x 1½-inch blocks to the table on the specified centers. I used blocks cut the width of the table to facilitate clamping at the ends (6-180). If you are short on material and can devise a way to clamp in the middle of the table, the 10-inch width of the extension is all that is really necessary. A bonus here is a 7-inch-wide clear bench space on each side of the boat.

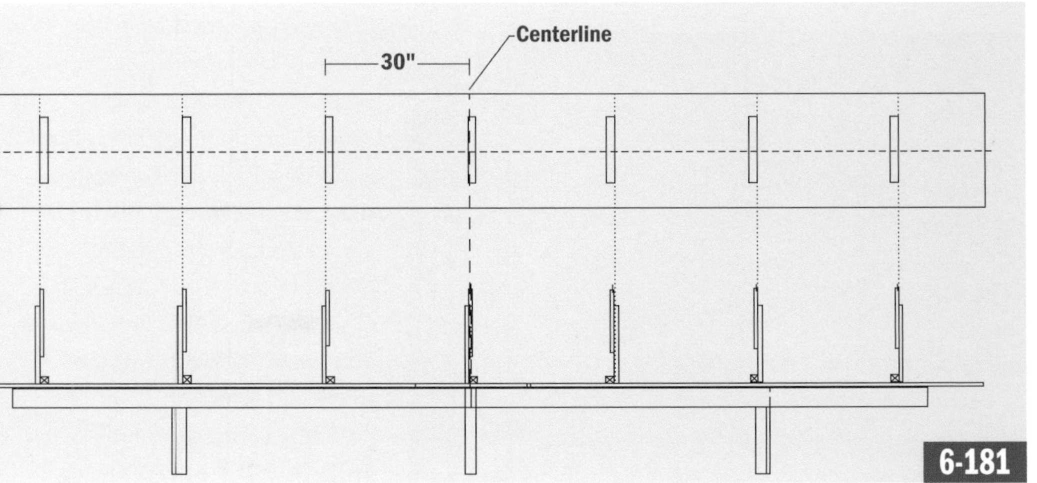

6-180

The sides of the blocks should be square in order to hold the forms perpendicular. Finding square construction-grade 2 x 2 stock at the lumberyard could be a problem. Consider a cabinet-grade softwood if you can afford it or, if you have access to a table saw, the best construction-grade 2 x 4 in the pile ripped in half. If a jointer is available, you might as well go all the way and make it perfect.

A very important consideration when attaching the blocks is figuring out which side of the line to put the block on (6-181). The objective is to have the edge of

6-181

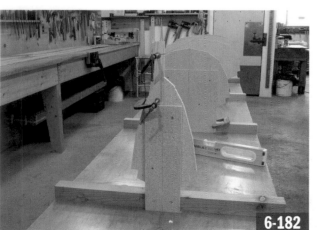

the form that the plank will rest on in line with the station line. Assuming that the hull has its maximum beam in the center, the middle form will be centered over the station line and the plank will lie flat across the entire edge. As the planks converge to a point at the bow or stern, the plank will no longer touch the entire edge of the form but will rest on the side of the form closest to the station line. This means that the blocks should be on opposite sides of the line as they move out from the middle of the hull. With this in mind, I fastened the blocks on the side of the line facing the middle. This put the extension on the side of the block facing the end, with the form suspended over the block.

The blocks are fastened to the table with screws coming up from under the table. It is a good idea to clamp the ends in place first, then make any fine adjustments necessary. Clamping also guarantees that the block will not slide around when the screw hits it, as well as drawing the pieces tightly together.

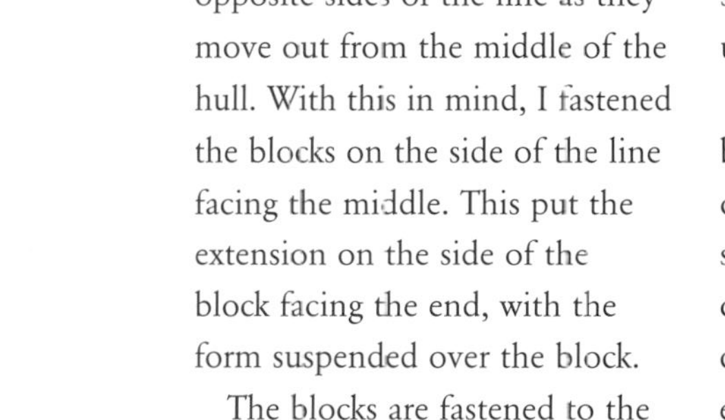
6-182

2. Set up forms.

The two end forms are set up first and become an anchor for a string line that will guide setting up the remainder of the forms.

Clamp the extension to the block and confirm that the centerline is exactly plumb, then screw the extension to the block; check again. The table with its centerline is the horizontal reference; now these two forms become the vertical reference. They are key reference points, so accuracy is very important.

To attach the string line, clamp a short straight-edged stick along the centerline of each end form and projecting above the top of the form so that the string will clear the highest middle form. Pull the string tight enough to twang and clamp it.

Setting up the remainder of the forms (6-182) is a simple matter of clamping the extension centerline over the table centerline and directly under the string line. Stand on something so that you can look directly down the form centerline. If the form is correctly positioned, the string line should mask the lines on the form and on the table.

6-183

The forward end of the stem is fastened to a cleat on the table to hold it over the centerline; the other end sits in a slot in the form.

The stem keeps the hull straight and the planks in line. This is the time to confirm that the stem is positioned correctly. We know that the ends of the stem are where they should be, so the place to check is in the middle. Use a level to plumb from the side of the stem down to the table centerline. If the level is showing plumb, the bottom of the level should be 4 mm (5/32 inch), or half the width of the stem, off the line.

If the stem is not showing plumb in the middle, the place to adjust it is the block on the table (6-183). I initially installed the block with one screw, which allowed it to pivot slightly to correct any hook in the stem. After confirming the position, a second screw was added.

The next step is a boatbuilding step. The objective is to make a narrow flat face on the side of the stem for the plank to land on. A good place to start is at the end that is over the form. When the sides of the form are projected through the stem up to the centerline, they should come to a point

6-184

in the middle of the stem. Check this first and adjust the stem in the notch if necessary (6-184).

Use the angle on the form as a reference to begin shaping with the block plane (6-185). Keep in mind that this is a rolling bevel that will change as it progresses around the curve. The stern stem is tricky because the bevel changes quickly as it goes around the tight bend from horizontal to vertical.

Keep track of the bevel by springing a light batten around several forms and checking the fit at the stem (6-186).

Somewhere between the defined V at the form end and the leading edge of the stem, the leading edge of the stem will go from a point to something wider. This is determined by eye, the consideration being how wide you want the stem to be. As the stem was reaching vertical I took off the first two layers of veneer, which left a face (with the planks installed) of just over ½ inch. This was about right for my kayak because I planned to use an outside stem, which would add to the length and decrease the width. If the end is going to be finished with a fillet or if a narrower shape is desired for the bow, consider bringing the leading edge closer to a point.

6-185

Try for a nice flat landing surface. Fortunately for some of you, this is not traditional wooden boat construction, where a tight wood-to-wood joint is what keeps the water out. The planks will be tacked to the stem with thick glue, so sins are hidden so fast we won't even call them sins.

With the exception of the rapidly changing bevel, preparing the stern stem involves the same routine as setting up the bow (6-187).

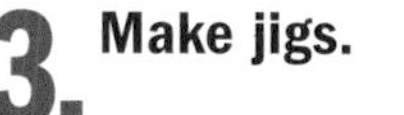

3. Make jigs.

The last little detail to take care of before building our kayak is to prepare L-shaped clamp blocks that will hold the plank in position on the form (→ 6-188). The jigs are made out of ½-inch plywood, but a lighter material would work as well. The two legs of the L are 4 inches and 2½ inches, measured on the outside of the L.

6-186

6-187

DAYS 5-7

Assemble Hull

To Do

- ○ Sand inside surface of planks (optional).
- ○ Make wire sutures.
- ○ Fit garboards.
- ○ Wire and glue first two pairs of planks to stem.
- ○ Tack planks with filler.*
- ○ Remove sutures and clean up filler.
- ○ Install third and fourth planks.
- ○ Tack joints and glue planks to stems.*
- ○ Clean up filler and complete tacking stems.*
- ○ Install outside stems (optional).
- ○ Prepare hull for fiberglass.

Tools & Materials

- ○ block plane or spokeshave
- ○ clamps
- ○ drill or driver
- ○ 1/16-inch drill bit
- ○ epoxy resin and hardener
- ○ epoxy dispensing pumps
- ○ fiber tape
- ○ filler
- ○ 1-inch masking tape
- ○ mixing pots
- ○ grunge can
- ○ lacquer thinner
- ○ level
- ○ linesman pliers
- ○ putty knife
- ○ rags
- ○ firm sanding block
- ○ 180, 220 and 280 grit sandpaper

Continued on next page

Looking at the forms and stems set up, you can begin to visualize what the kayak is going to look like. This is the time to start putting a skin on your dream. It's an exciting part of the process, but over before you know it, so don't forget to pause now and again to take some photos.

I was able to do this step in two days by using a fast hardener, but for the first-time builder using a hardener with up to a 12-hour cure time, three days will be comfortable. Expect the first day to be full and intense, followed by a break with shorter days and routine tasks.

Assembling and tacking the planks has been broken into two steps for several reasons. Pulling the planks together at the ends is tough to control and check using the free-form method, a big reason why the stems have been added. Unless we have access to the flimsy stem to confirm that the kayak is straight, we are no better off than if we pull all the planks together by eye. The second plank from the keel line will have a lot of influence on the position of the stem. For this reason it will be fastened to the stem first, while there is access to the stem and centerline for confirmation. Once the first two rows of planks are glued into place, the stem is stabilized for attaching the third and fourth rows.

THINK LAZY

Sand the inside now

Since the inside of the hull is not going to get messed up between now and when the glass goes on, the time to sand is before the pieces are put together. It is so much more efficient, healthy and comfortable to sand on the bench, where you can see what you are doing.

6-188

1. Sand inside surface of planks (optional).

Although sanding the interior isn't a requirement, if you want a respectable finish inside, the plywood will have to be sanded at some point.

2. Make wire sutures (→ page 70).

CHEAP TRICK

Hot glue plank control

Handling a bunch of floppy planks is not a problem for the traditional boatbuilder because each plank is fastened to a rib or frame before the next one is added. Our forms and hot glue can do the same for us.

3. Fit garboards.

Lay the first plank on the form and position it fore and aft and along the centerline; secure it to each form with the L-shaped clamp blocks. Let the ends of the planks fly for now, as they will be easier to control when the second pair of planks is installed. Position the mate and secure. To help maintain this position, draw a light pencil line reference across the two planks somewhere around the middle of the kayak.

Begin by masking the surface of the plank where it will be hot-glued to the form. With the planks in position, make a light pencil line on the inside of the plank on each side of each form. (Make it light because it will have to come off later). Turn the plank over and place masking tape over the marked area; press the tape down firmly (6-188). Replace the plank, line it up with the reference mark and clamp in position. Remove its mate and repeat the above routine.

Loosen a few of the clamp blocks and lift the plank enough to lay a bead of hot glue along the edge of the form (6-189). Press the plank into the glue and hold it until the glue grabs; then replace the clamp.

6-190

4. Wire and glue first two pairs of planks to stem.

Fasten the second pair of planks to the stem first (6-190). They have the most influence on the stem position, and the garboard has a nasty twist in the end that needs something to hang on to.

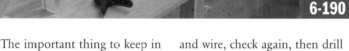

6-189

The important thing to keep in mind when clamping the plank to the stem is keeping the stem on the centerline. Attaching the planks as a pair will balance the pressure on the stem, but keep the level handy. Bring the planks together over the stem and fasten them temporarily with a spring clamp. Twist the garboards into position to confirm that they will fit if the second plank is fastened in this position.

Also check the joint where the angle between the planks is greatest. Consider planing a small flat landing area on the inside edges of the planks to close up the joint a bit, as well as to help keep the plank edges in line.

Using the level, confirm that the stem is still on center; adjust if necessary. Drill the first hole and wire, check again, then drill and insert the second wire (6-191). Check again before committing to the glue.

Draw the ends of the garboard into position and, using fiber tape, secure it to the second plank. This is a good time to confirm the fit to the stems. If the plank does not seem to be sitting comfortably on the stem, find the high spot and take a little more off with a sharp chisel.

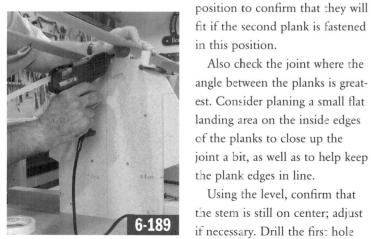

6-191

Having the planks hot-glued to the forms did a good job of holding the plank edges in line. This allowed me to use sutures only where they were needed (6-192). Not knowing in advance where the holes would be, I drilled them in place using the spacer jig (→ page 70) for consistency.

This step went fast because some of the sutures in the bottom were up to 12 inches apart, but mostly because, once the wire was tightened, the joint very seldom moved. Anyone who has built using the free-form method will understand the frustration of getting one area settled and then having it move while adjusting another part of the hull.

6-192

Tools & Materials
From previous page
- O square
- O stir sticks
- O tape measure

Safety
- O dust mask
- O gloves
- O eye protection
- O good ventilation
- O caution with cutting tools

6-193

6-194

6-195

When all the sutures were in and adjusted and I was sure that everything was going to fit, the sutures in the stems were cut and the planks allowed to spring back from the stem (6-193). This gives you plenty of access to the stem for applying the glue.

For glue (6-194) I used a thick structural mixture of epoxy blended with cotton fiber and a little sanding dust (→ page 41).

Draw the planks back together and replace the fiber tape and the wires. If the wire goes into the original hole, there is a good chance the stem is still straight, but don't leave it to chance. Check again.

To hold the garboards to the bow stem, holes are drilled on either side of the stem. A long wire goes through this hole, under the stem and up the other side to be twisted on top. This effectively draws the ends of the garboards together and down to the stem.

The garboards at the stern are under a lot of tension and would have taken a number of sutures to subdue them. I used the beveled-clamp-blocks-with-sandpaper trick (→ page 169) for better distribution of the pressure and to avoid having more holes to deal with later (6-195).

5. Tack planks with filler (→ page 70).

Masking the joints before applying the filler (6-196) is about looking good, but it is also about staying healthy while thinking lazy. It probably takes less time to put the tape on than to sand the mess off later, so you know what I did.

Check that the inside plank edges are in line before applying the tape (6-197). Because they were stabilized by the forms, mine stayed in place, but do keep this in mind during the masking and filling. If while masking and filling you happen to mess anything up, fix it before you forget or can't find it again.

6-196

It is important to take time to pack the filler down to the bottom of the void. If filler is forced through a crack, it is best not to try to clean it up at this point. The contained extrusion can be scraped and sanded clean more easily after it is hard. At this point you will only succeed in smearing it around with a rag.

If you have accomplished all of this step in one day, this is a good time to take a break. When the filler has cured, the bottom and the stems will be stabilized, and work on the remaining planks can go forward without worrying about bumping something out of position.

6. Remove sutures & clean up filler.

This is a nice little job to get the day going. Cut the sutures and carefully remove them. Clean up the filler by hand with a firm sanding block. The outside of the hull will be sanded after all the filler is in, so don't take off any more wood than necessary at this stage. Work the filler down to the flat surface of the plank, but don't round over the edges yet.

Clean up and mask the joints around the sutures, which haven't been filled yet. Short pieces of tape are economical and fast to apply using a tape dispenser, but very time-consuming to remove. Consider a continuous piece of tape to save a little time.

6-197

7. Install third & fourth planks.

The third and fourth planks are a little easier to hang than the first two, as there is very little twist in the ends. One thing to keep an eye on is the width of the joint where the angle between planks is acute. If it looks too wide, do not hesitate to plane a small flat surface on the inside edge to close it up and help keep the edges in line (6-198).

Another place to check is the joint on the inside of the plank over the forms. If the next flat face on the form is high, it will put a step in the joint and a hump in the hull. To check, lay a short straightedge on the form and check where it meets the last plank (6-199). It should touch the bottom corner or be slightly below the inside face of the last plank. If it is high, work the form down with a rasp and check again.

One last detail to check is how the planks land on the stems. Adjust them if necessary.

When I was happy with the dry fit, the third pair of planks was tacked to the forms with hot glue and the joints were sewn together. The last row of planks was hung using the same routine.

8. Tack joints & glue planks to stems.

To save a little time, I glued the ends of the planks to the stems and filled the joints between the planks in one epoxy session. Prepare for the filler by masking the joints between the last two planks as well as any joints missing filler in the first set of planks. The suture holes in the first two planks are also masked. Whether you mask around the holes will depend on your expectations, but filling them is well worth the effort. The alternative is to have epoxy wick through the hole and make a hard-to-remove mess on the inside.

After masking, I cut the sutures. Then I opened up the ends, applied the glue and refastened them (6-200).

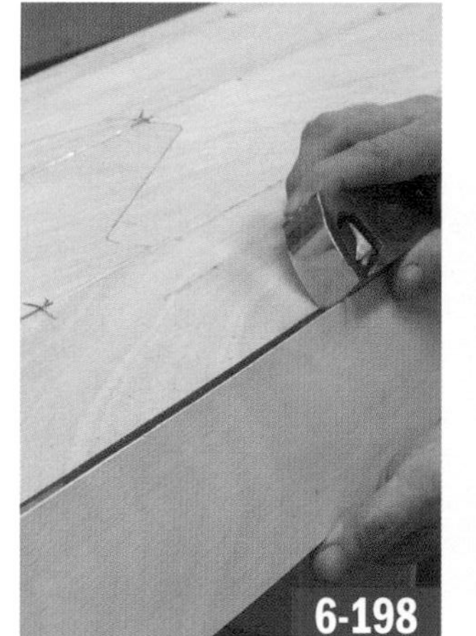

6-198

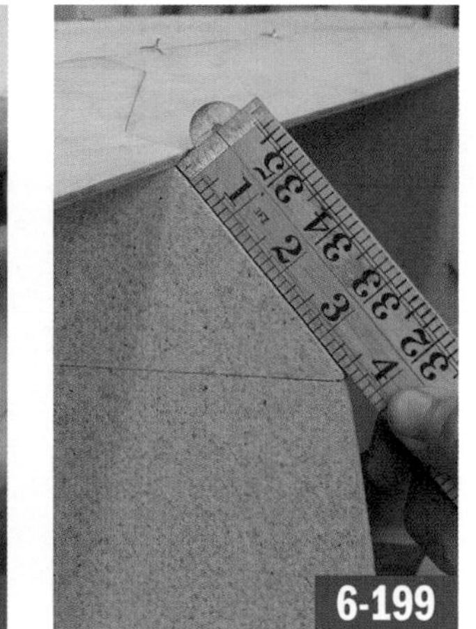

6-199

6-200

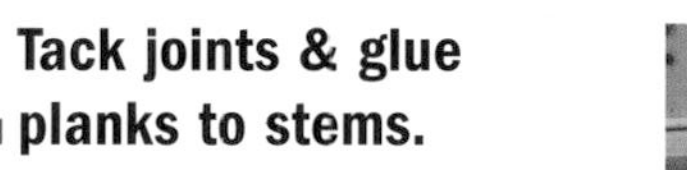

The sutures do a reasonable job of holding the planks up to the stem but are not strong enough to ensure consistent clamping pressure along the edge. To distribute the pressure, beveled clamp blocks were positioned just behind the sutures. Avoid clamping over the wire, because it will leave a deep bruise

6-201

in the wood. Watch the pressure on the clamps; it should be just enough to draw the plank up to the stem but not so much that it is forced into an unnatural curve behind the stem (6-201).

Fill the joints between the planks and carefully remove the tape.

9. Clean up filler & complete tacking stems.

10. Install outside stems (optional).

Preparing and installing outside stems is a nice little project to keep us busy while the filler cures. If you are at all curious about steam bending (6-202), this is an opportunity to experience wood in its plastic state. Should the bend not be successful, it won't be too late to cast the stem with filler.

Aside from giving this kayak a more traditional wooden-boat look, there is another reason for installing outside stems. The continuous fiber of the stem will absorb and distribute an impact more effectively than molded filler. It also allows us to increase the width of the leading edge of the stem as it rises above the waterline. In theory, when you run out of water the blunt stem should help protect the vulnerable end of your kayak.

In terms of working time, the time needed to install outside stems is traded off against interrupting the layup to wrap the ends with glass tape, waiting for the epoxy to cure, then feathering the edges, sanding the hull and cleaning up before proceeding with the second and third coats of epoxy.

The outside stems are prepared and installed in three steps: steaming and bending to shape (→ page 115), laminating (→ page 116) and installing.

Installing the outside stem may seem a confusing process; just keep in mind that the outside stem was glued up to fit the inside stem, and installing is simply fitting them back together.

6-202

Along most of the length of the stem, the inside stem is exposed between the planks. As the stem begins to flatten out into the bottom, the planks will be over the stem. In order to fit the inside and outside stem back together, a mortise must be cut through the planking down to the level of the inside stem.

Rather than cut the mortise, then try to fit the outside stem into it, I shaped the stem first, then used it as a pattern to lay out the mortise.

Begin by cleaning up along the exposed part of the inside stem and planking to make a flat surface for the outside stem to land on. It is important to keep the end of the hull perpendicular to the centerline and not to remove any of the inside stem. If the inside stem is reshaped, the outside stem – too stiff to bend into a new shape – will leave a void. Use a rasp or hard sanding block to shape the ends of the plank down to meet the stem perpendicular to the centerline. If one side is cut lower than the stem, you will have to live with the gap, because cutting into the stem to flatten it will only make it worse. While less than perfect, this is not the end of the world, because the glue will be thick and, if color-matched, it could be inconspicuous. Stop shaping where the plank begins to cover the stem.

To prepare the outside stem, trim the end that will be in the bottom of the boat so that it is

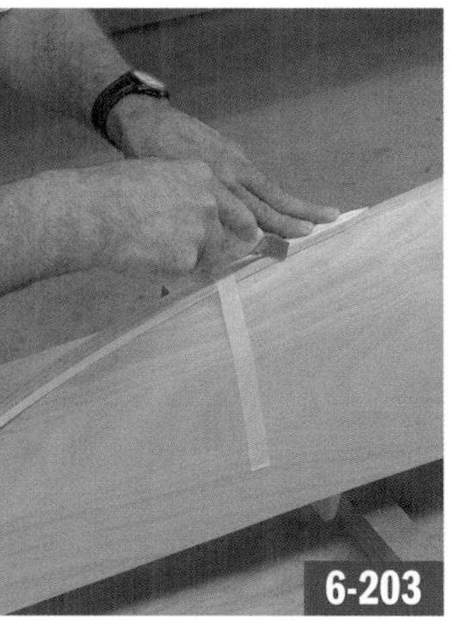
6-203

6-204

about 1 inch shorter than the inside stem (6-203). The purpose of this is to be sure that the mortise will be backed up by the inside stem. Also taper the end, beginning back about 12 inches, down to about 1/4 inch wide at the end. This will reduce the width of the stem and avoid cutting through the bond between the planks and the inside stem.

After shaping the taper, hold the stem in position, check that it is centered and mark the shape of the mortise with a sharp knife. The knife will make a very accurate mark as well as beginning the cut along the edge of the mortise. Remove the stem and finish making the vertical cuts with the knife. Clean out the bottom of the mortise with a 1/4-inch chisel (6-204). To check the fit, slide the stem into the mortise from the end, watching for the first place it gets hung up. Work this area a little more, then try again. It is important not to force the stem into the mortise. You don't want to break the planks away from the stem.

Clamping pressure for gluing the stem is provided by #4 x 1-inch screws on 6- to 8-inch centers. When the stem fits into the mortise, do a dry run with the screws to be sure the stem fits to your satisfaction (6-205). The pilot holes (7/64-inch) in the outside stem should be loose enough that the screw does not bind in the hole. The edge of the plywood inner stem does not give us much to hang on to, as well as being prone to split if the screw is too big for the hole. For these pilot holes use a 5/64-inch bit.

For glue I used mixed epoxy reinforced with cotton fibers, with a little sanding dust for color. The light color of the stem defines the shape, so I matched the color of the plywood to keep the line of the stem crisp. Consider masking the hull to save some cleanup time and keep the wood clean (6-206).

One more detail to take care of

SAFETY TIP

Remember that the utility knife is the most dangerous tool in your shop. Always keep your free hand away from the cutting direction of the blade.

CHEAP TRICK

Drilling a pilot hole

It is important that the screw go into the middle of the stem, but it is not a big target at only 8 mm wide. To be sure that the hole in the outside stem is centered, drill the pilot hole from the inside to the outside. If the hole is not drilled perpendicularly, the variation is on the outside, where it does not really matter.

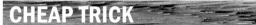

6-205

6-206

6-207

6-208

is to wax the screws so they can be removed more easily after the glue has cured. Rub the screw on a piece of paraffin wax (or paste wax), then heat it slightly with a hair dryer to melt the wax.

Mix up a small batch of epoxy and coat the end of the stem with the unthickened mixture. Then brush one coat onto the mating surface of the outside stem. When it stops soaking in, thicken the remainder of the epoxy to a peanut butter consistency. Apply the thick glue liberally; it is easier to pick it up after it squeezes out than to force it in if there is a void. Carefully position the stem in the glue and replace the screws.

If the screws are overtightened, the threads in the wood will be stripped and the screws will lose their holding power. Always put these screws in by hand and concentrate on what you can feel through the screwdriver (6-207). A clue that tells you when to stop turning is the glue as it squeezes out; when the glue stops moving, there is a good chance that the screw has been tightened enough.

When you pick up the excess glue, scrape it clean but check that the epoxy fills the joint or is slightly above the surface of the plywood. Another advantage of the masking tape is that the glue can be scraped off flush, leaving it slightly higher than the wood when the tape is removed. If the joint is not full, that will mean another epoxy filler application and cure cycle.

After the glue has cured, carefully remove the screws. Do not use a power driver, as sudden application of torque will often break the screw. Gradually build up the pressure on the screwdriver and the screw should break loose. If you feel the screw begin to stretch, whacking the screwdriver on the head with a hammer while applying turning pressure should do the trick.

Fill the screw holes with wooden plugs whittled to fit the holes. Put a dab of glue on the plug and drive it into the hole. Don't drive it farther than it wants to go, because the wedging action can split the stem. Cut the plug off flush and sand the end smooth.

The stems are shaped in three steps. The first step is to shape the stem in profile. The objective is to reestablish a fair line along the bottom of the hull that blends into the stem. Have a good look at the profile drawing before beginning to plane the stem down, so you know when to stop. Sneak up on the shape; stand back often to look directly into the side of the hull for the best view. Placing a batten along the hull centerline is also helpful for relating the shape of the bottom to the stem (6-208).

6-209

The next step is to dress the sides of the stem so that they become an extension of the planks. Most of this can be done with a sharp block plane; a spokeshave will be handy in a few places but is not imperative. Finish with a scraper (6-209) or hard sanding block to bring the sides of the stem flush with the plywood.

While shaping the stem, it is tricky to avoid damaging the plywood, because the grain on the stem is running in a different direction. I started off with masking tape on the hull for most of the shaping, then removed it for scraping. If the scraper is worked in a direction that favors the plank, it will avoid damaging the plywood but leave scratches across the stem. Remove the scratches after shaping with a hard sanding block loaded with 220 grit sandpaper. Work at an angle that will split the difference between the grain directions of the plank and the stem. The 220 grit scratches are fine enough that they are not going to be obvious on either the plank or the stem.

The last step is to round over the corners. I shaped the stem into a half-round at the waterline that gradually becomes a half-oval at the sheer line. Rough out the shape with the plane or spokeshave, then finish with a firm sanding block with 120 grit sandpaper. Be careful not to sand across the grain on the plywood with the 120 grit because it will scratch more deeply than you want to sand to clean it up. Finish with 220 grit sandpaper.

11. Prepare hull for fiberglass.

This is a good time to soften the joints between the planks. Our objective is to create a durable edge and a shape that the glass cloth will follow. Don't push the curve too far. The lines should be crisp, and cutting into the plywood too deeply will expose a dark glue line. To keep the shape consistent, use long strokes with a firm sanding block loaded with 120 grit sandpaper.

I was able to get to this stage without messing up the plywood, so sanding took no time at all. Very little wood should be removed. The objective is to clean up the surface and remove the fuzz. I used a half-sheet sander with 180 grit sandpaper and was careful not to let it wrap over the edges. It went so quickly that I think there is no reason for not sanding by hand if dust is an issue, or if you want better control of what is happening under the sandpaper.

Dampening the surface with water at least once to raise the grain is a good idea even if a clear finish is not important. The veneer is so stressed from the manufacturing process that the first application of any finishing material will swell it up into a very rough surface. Although the glass and epoxy will level it out, there seems to be more of a problem with air bubbles lifting the cloth on an unsanded surface than on a cleanly sanded surface.

With a clear finish in mind, I put the plywood through three grain-raising and sanding cycles and some fuzz was still coming up. Each cycle went to a finer grit size – 180, 220 and 280. Using the 280 grit could be considered obsessive, but the grain was visibly cleaner. There is no need to use a power sander here, as all we are doing is cutting off the fuzz. Use a firm block and work at a slight angle to the direction of the grain; this will cut the fibers off rather than push them back down below the surface.

After completing the sanding step, clean up the hull and your shop in preparation for a big day tomorrow.

DAY 8

Glass Outside of Hull

To Do
- O Assemble epoxy application materials and equipment.
- O Position glass cloth.
- O Apply first coat of epoxy.
- O Apply second coat of epoxy.
- O Apply third coat of epoxy.*

Tools & Materials
- O 2-inch low-end bristle brush
- O epoxy dispensing pumps
- O epoxy resin and hardener
- O fiberglass cloth
- O grunge cans
- O lacquer thinner
- O mixing pots
- O rags
- O scissors
- O squeegee
- O stir sticks
- O utility knife
- O vacuum cleaner

Safety
- O eye protection
- O gloves
- O good ventilation

I was able to complete all three coats of epoxy in one day by using WEST 207 slow hardener and because I didn't have to stop to reinforce the stems and wait for the patch to get hard enough to feather. This resin and hardener combination kicks in about four hours, allowing me to apply the first coat in the morning, one after lunch and the last one after dinner. Completing this step in one day reduces epoxy exposure time and the possibility of surface contamination.

1. Assemble epoxy application materials & equipment.

Once the first batch of epoxy has been mixed (→ page 59), there is no turning back. Prepare everything you will need beforehand and put it where you can find it. A good understanding of what each step will accomplish will keep you on track.

2. Position glass cloth (→ page 81).

Before spreading the cloth over the hull, I vacuumed the hull and gave it one last wipedown with lacquer thinner on a clean white cotton rag. Wipe until a clean portion of the rag stays clean.

Carefully roll the cloth out over the hull and straighten it by pulling on the ends (6-210). To reinforce the centerline and bow stem, a 4-inch-wide strip was cut off the side of the cloth and positioned down the centerline under the full sheet.

6-210

The cloth may be worked around the bow stem for added durability and to save having to trim the glass. The plumb stern stem changes direction quickly, so there is a limit to how far around the curve the cloth can be worked. After wetting out the cloth, trim it to about 1 inch past the stem. When the epoxy has kicked, the cloth will be trimmed flush.

3. Apply first coat of epoxy (→ page 82).

The important point to remember when applying the first coat of epoxy is to spread it quickly over the cloth and allow it to soak into the cloth and saturate the surface of the wood under it. Any effort to work the epoxy into the cloth will be counterproductive and will result in a less-than-clear finish.

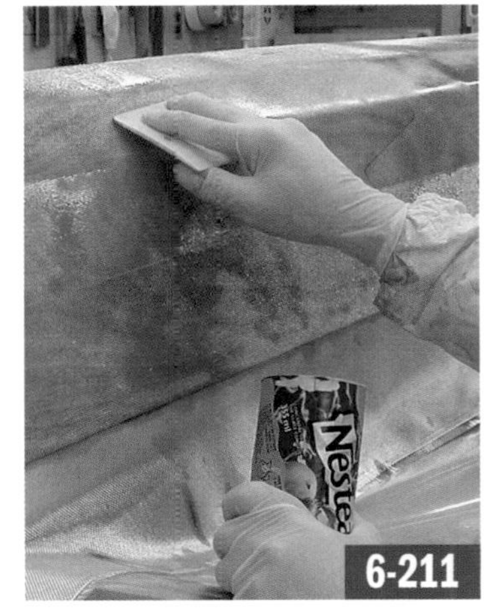

6-211

When all the epoxy has been applied or when you run out of working time on the first batch, remove the excess epoxy and bubbles with the squeegee (6-211). This step will give you the clearest finish with the least amount of sanding, so take the time to get it right. After squeegeeing, the cloth should look saturated with epoxy but there shouldn't be any shiny puddles.

Since it was a comfortably warm day, I was able to trim the glass at the stern after four hours without it sticking to the knife (6-212).

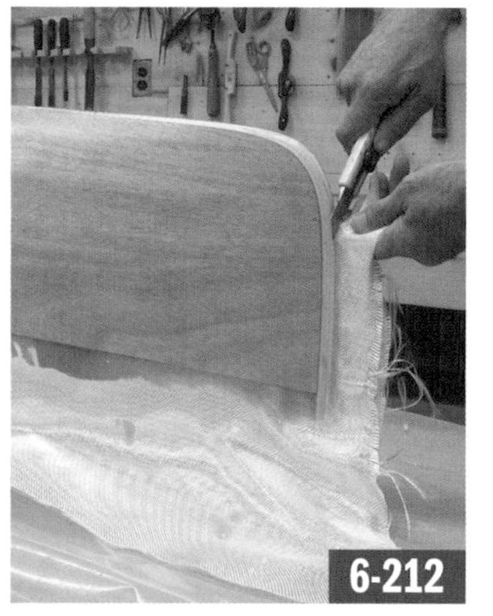
6-212

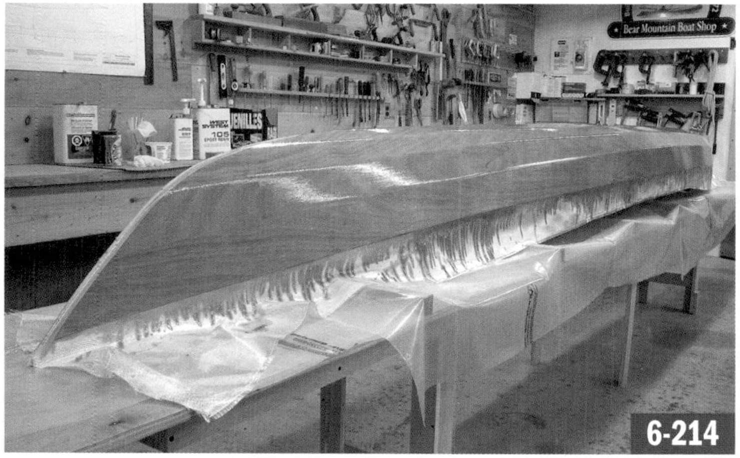

6-214

4. Apply second coat of epoxy (→ page 87).

(→ page 87)

Although you could simply pour out a puddle of epoxy and move it around with the squeegee, moving epoxy down a vertical surface is awkward. I used a brush to move it from the pot to the boat (6-213). Since the lower edge and around the stems often get missed, I transferred the epoxy to these areas with the brush, then used the squeegee to draw it up from the bottom.

Pack the epoxy into the weave, then go over the whole surface and systematically remove the excess. Look for an even texture over the whole surface.

5. Apply third coat of epoxy (→ page 88).

It was good to get this major step over in one day with only four to five hours of epoxy exposure time. If your layup goes as well as mine did, the hull is about two hours of sanding away from varnish (6-214).

6-213

DAYS 9-11
Plank the Deck

To Do
- O Remove hull.
- O Set up cradle forms.
- O Install sheer clamps.
- O Shape sheer clamps.
- O Install covering boards.*
- O Install remaining planks.*
- O Shape and sand deck.*

Tools & Materials
- O batten
- O block plane
- O chisel
- O clamps
- O drill and 5/64-inch bits
- O file
- O carpenter's glue
- O dividers
- O fiber tape
- O glue syringe
- O masking tape
- O plastic film
- O pull saw
- O putty knife
- O rags and bucket of water
- O firm and hard sanding blocks
- O random orbital sander
- O ruler
- O 120 and 180 grit sandpaper
- O scraper
- O screws
- O #4 screwdriver
- O spokeshave
- O staple gun and staples
- O staple puller
- O utility knife
- O vacuum cleaner

Safety
- O eye protection
- O good ventilation

The two days it will take to plank the deck will be busy but rewarding. Take time to look at the color and grain pattern of the planking you have and arrange the pieces in an order that looks right to you. It is a small step, but it will make you and your kayak look good. The shaping and sanding step won't take much time because the deck area is small. This is the part of your kayak that you will be looking at, so make an effort to keep the surface fair.

1. Remove hull.

Unfasten the forms from the blocks and carefully remove the hull and forms from the table. The hull will want to spread when it is turned over because of the weight of the forms inside. To avoid breaking the bond between the hull and the forms, tie the sides together with fiber tape or rope before turning (6-215).

2. Set up cradle forms.

The supplied cradle forms use the same numbering system as the building forms and are positioned on the same side of the corresponding blocks. Prepare the forms by drawing a centerline on each and position them on the table centerline (6-216).

3. Install sheer clamps.

Prepare the sheer clamps by gluing the precut scarf joints together to make up the full-length members. I assembled the sheer clamps as a little fill-in job while the epoxy on the outside was curing.

Fit the sheer clamp into the notch in the forms, with some extra length hanging over both ends, and secure (6-217). Check the fit between the top inside edge of the sheer clamp and the deck portion of the form. The corner should be flush with the deck form; if it is not, adjust as necessary.

6-215

Since the bow will be trickier to fit than the stern, it is a good idea to get it settled first. The extra length at the stern will give us lots to play with if a second cut is necessary.

The trick here is to find the point on the sheer clamp that will be up against the stem when the sheer clamp drops down into position. Eyeballing it will not work, so the idea is to find a place where the sheer clamp and the edge of the hull will fit together to establish a common reference point and then work from there. The sheer clamp will

6-216

6-217

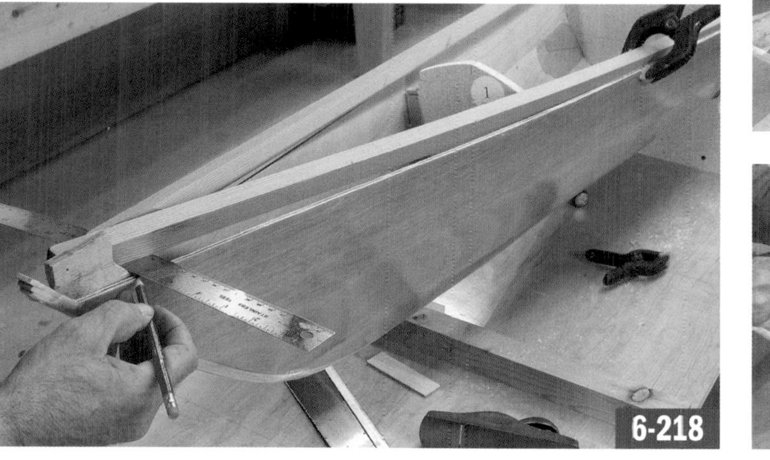

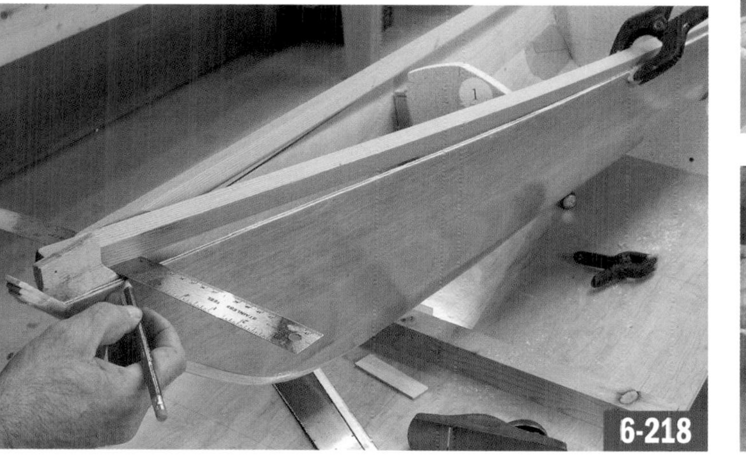

6-218

6-219

6-220

6-221

6-222

6-223

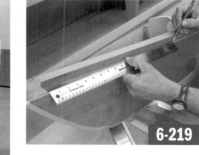

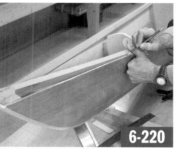

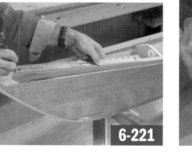

butt up to the backside of the stem, so begin by projecting this point out to the edge of the hull (6-218). From this point we can measure back along the edge of the hull to the common reference point.

On this boat I was able to press the sheer clamp into position the length of my ruler back from the stem (6-219). The actual distance does not matter as long as it is the same in both directions.

Press the sheer clamp into position and transfer the mark to the top outside corner of the sheer clamp (6-220).

Now measure the same distance back along the outside edge of the sheer clamp and make a mark (6-221).

Now that you know where the end will be, it is straightforward to pick up the angle between the stem and the edge of the hull and transfer it to the end of the sheer clamp (6-222). Also make a mark on top of the sheer clamp that is perpendicular to the centerline.

Cut to the lines and the sheer clamp should drop into position (6-223). If the measurements were accurate and the pencil sharp, the sheer clamp should fit as intended. If by chance it doesn't fit, the extra length at the stern will give you room to make adjustments.

The last cut is the miter down

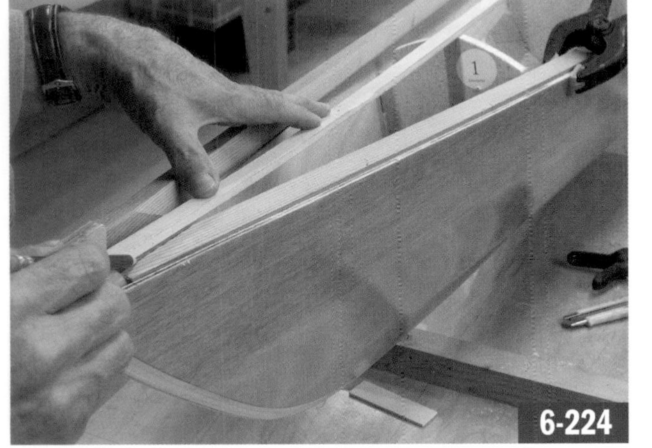

6-224

6-226

6-227

the centerline to make space for the other sheer clamp. To mark this angle, tack a batten along the centerline of several forms with the end centered on the stem (6-224).

Lay the sheer clamp over the edge of the hull and make the cut (6-225). Try to make the cut plumb but plan on some touch-up work when both sides are fitted together.

6-225

Use the same measuring method to mark, cut and fit the sheer clamp at the stern. Because the stern stem is almost plumb, it is tempting to mark and cut by eye. You may get away with it, but if you want to be sure, find a common reference point and get it right the first time.

Mark and cut the other side using the same method, then fit both ends together inside the hull. The block plane is a good tool to make the final fit.

Note that the sheer clamp is positioned above the edge of the hull (6-226). This distance will change as it follows the changing camber of the deck. To determine how much this distance will be at the stems, note the changing distance at the forms and project it smoothly out to the stems.

Fasten the sheer clamps to the hull with #4 x 1/2-inch or 3/4-inch flat-head screws on about 12-inch centers. Drill the pilot hole 1/8 inch below the edge so that the screw heads will eventually be hidden behind the guard. A countersink will also be necessary as the plywood is too dense for the head to draw in flush on its own.

4. Shape sheer clamps.

The objective in shaping the top of the sheer clamp is to make it an extension of the deck shape being developed by the forms. The plank will be glued to this surface, so try to keep it flat and fair.

A sharp block plane is the tool of choice. The base of the plane will help keep the cut fair between the forms yet it is short enough to follow the rolling bevel.

To set up the angle, begin with the back of the plane resting on the form (6-227). Aim for the next form, making a continuous cut that rolls smoothly into the new angle at the next form. Making this cut systematically from form to form is much easier than pecking away at it here and there, then trying to fit everything together later.

Trim the inside stem flush with the top of the sheer clamp to support the deck planking (6-228). If you've added the optional outside stem, it is not trimmed until the deck has been planked and shaped.

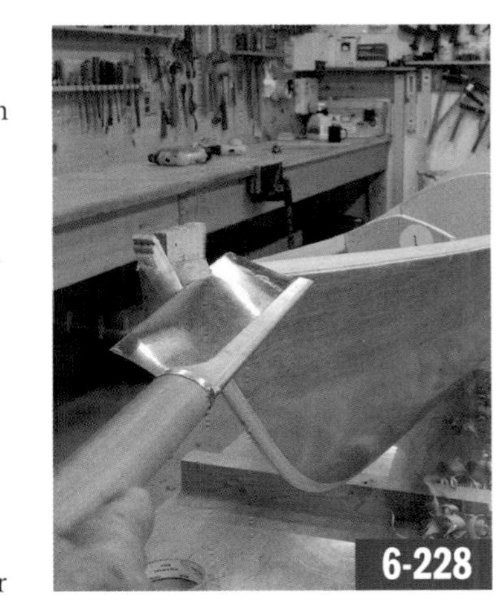

6-228

6-229

Is it fair? A good view is from the end, with your eye level with the sheer line. Focus on the angle at the stem, then slowly move your head away from the hull to allow your eye to follow the changing bevel as it moves around the boat. Keep the forms in the background and try to visualize how the sheer clamp fits into this space between the forms.

For a second opinion, use a fairing batten to check from the top. Look for the little things – a crown in the middle or more work needed to bring the top of the sheer clamp flush with the edge of the hull.

One last detail to take care of before planking is to protect any surface we don't want to become part of the deck. The deck will be glued to the sheer clamp and we want it to come off gracefully when the screws are removed. Cover the forms, the stem and the edge of the hull with plastic packaging tape.

Being in a rush, I covered the edge of the hull with green masking tape (6-229) and wasted some time later because the carpenter's glue stuck to the tape. The lazy way would have been to back off the screws a few at a time and slide a piece of plastic film down between the hull and the sheer clamp, draping it over the edge of the hull.

5. Install covering boards.

If planking the deck is a step you have been looking forward to, I think we are finally ready.

Give some thought to where the planks will begin and the pattern they will create. One of the features of strip-planking is the unlimited visual possibilities it provides for combining various natural wood colors with changing plank lines. In his book, *The Strip-Built Sea Kayak*, Nick Schade explores a free-form method that begins with the first plank, often a narrow plank in a contrasting color that travels around the deck. More free-form planks are added, then the space is filled in with planks running parallel to the centerline. Some very dynamic decks have been created using this method, and if it interests you, check it out.

Ron Frenette, the founder of Canadian Canoes, and his crew have been creating patterns by gluing contrasting sections into a number of planks running in a traditional pattern. I was playing with their idea on the kayak used to illustrate *KayakCraft* and found that the contrasting colors could be butt-glued into a full-length plank before it was fastened to the form. Working with a full-length plank has the advantage of creating a consistent fair curve between the forms, plus it is fast to cut and assemble the pieces in a jig. Individual little pieces are time-consuming to cut and fussy to fit, but the real problem is to keep the pieces in a fair curve. This is less of a problem with forms that are closely spaced, but would be a problem with the widely spaced forms used here.

If you prefer a simple deck pattern, are pushed for time or just don't care, at least keep the deck planks matched. Choose planks in matching pairs and put one on each side of the centerline. It won't take much time or effort but it will make you look good. Personally, I prefer traditional patterns that allow the wood to speak for itself – an understatement that does not overpower the kayak as an entity. The direction of the lines should make the boat look like it is going somewhere.

Another pattern to consider is planking out from the centerline with the ends trimmed at random past the edge of the hull. This method is fast as it does not require any fitting; all the planks are trimmed at one time when the planking is complete. Note that this pattern will not work on the Enterprise because of the flat covering-board area. Another possibility is to spring the planks

6-230

6-233

around the sheer and join them down the centerline. Not my first choice, as there is still a lot of fitting to do and the converging lines make the kayak look short and static.

The Enterprise strip-planked deck is outlined with covering boards, then planked fore and aft parallel to the centerline. This is fast and allows the planks to do their best at creating a fair curve between forms. This flat area around the perimeter corresponds to the flat sheer panel on a plywood-deck model. In a visual sense, the shape identifies with the flat plywood hull panels, easing the contrast of materials while creating a traditional wooden boat feel.

Included in the kit are $1/4$ x $7/8$-inch planks for the covering-board area. The $7/8$-inch width is the maximum that will bend gracefully around the edge of the deck. To simplify fitting the fore and aft planks to the covering boards, one pair of planks is shaped on one edge only; they are the first planks installed, with the square edge facing the centerline (6-230). The balance of the planking is $1/4$ x $1\,3/4$-inch planks to fill in the center. This width was chosen for its greater stiffness and because it reduces the number of planks to fit.

The first plank is positioned at the point on the form where the flat becomes the cambered portion of the deck (6-233). This point will be subtle on some forms, so it is wise to check the plans to confirm.

Although the first plank could

CHEAP TRICK

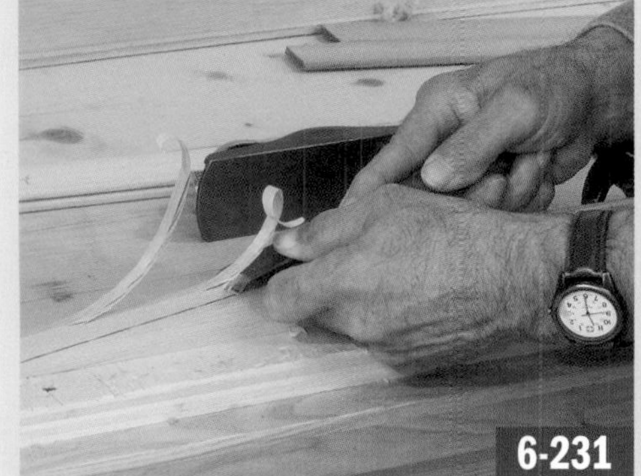

6-231

6-232

Tool skills

Marking, cutting and fitting the planks will go fast once you are comfortable with your tools and have a system. For safety and convenience, make a jig to hold the plank out of $3/4$-inch-thick x $1\,1/2$-inch-wide softwood scrap. The base should be about 20 inches long, with a piece about 6 inches long screwed to the side. Clamp the plank on edge to the short piece, with the end flush with the end of the base. Use a sharp chisel to trim the waste down to the line. Remember to keep both hands behind the blade (6-231).

Clean up this cut with the block plane and bevel the edge to where you think it should be (6-232).

be simply stapled to the forms on the marks, for more control and a chance to adjust the curve, I used those L-shaped jigs used to assemble the hull. They will help position the first plank before you commit to the 9/16-inch staples, but, more importantly, they prevent the plank from being pushed out of line when the next plank is pressed into it. For a planned look, try to keep the staples in line across the width of the deck.

Should the thought of staple holes in the deck bother you, see how to build without staples in *Canoecraft* or *KayakCraft* for the complete system. Our deck will have a minimum number of fasteners if we employ some of those tricks.

Since this kayak has outside stems, the first and second planks are dry-fitted before applying the carpenter's glue (6-234). Trim the ends for a neat fit up to the back of the stems and draw a reference line so that you can find the same position after the glue has been applied. If your kayak has a molded stem, let the planks fly past the end for now and trim them after gluing and fastening.

Before removing the planks, mark on the sheer clamp the area that will be covered by the planks, as a guide for applying the carpenter's glue.

6-234

6-236

Glue is applied to the cove side of the second plank with a glue syringe (6-235). Expect to take a few planks to judge the optimum amount of glue; look for a little bit of squeeze-out so that you are sure there is enough glue in the joint, but not so much that it will be a nuisance to clean up. As a guide, the 12 cc syringe I used was enough for about 18 feet, so at 17 feet there should be about 1/8 inch of glue left in the syringe.

If you are working alone, you may want to make a couple of small jigs to hold the plank over the forms while the glue is being applied. Another possibility is to hold the plank on edge with spring clamps on the bench.

6-235

Spread a thin film of glue over the marked area of the sheer clamp. Position the plank, squeeze the two together, then fasten. The plank also needs to be clamped to the sheer clamp with either a number of staples or some clamps. "Schedule 40" clamps cut from plastic pipe (→ page 35) are a cheap solution for this job if you are short of clamps.

Given the span between forms, the planks cannot be expected to stay consistently tight without some attention. Squeeze the planks together and watch what happens when you let go. If the joint opens up, place softwood clamp blocks across the joint, squeeze the planks back together and snug up the clamp (6-236). The pad will bridge the joint to hold them in line and the friction will hold them together. If you are running out of clamps, fiber tape or packing tape will do the job of holding the planks together, but check that the joint is still flush on both sides.

The covering board is wide in the middle and tapers toward the bow and stern. This shape accents

6-237

6-238

6-239

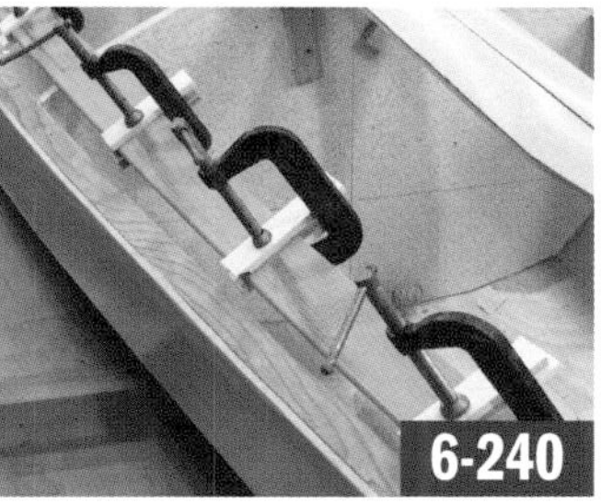
6-240

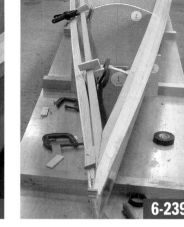

the length of the kayak and draws the eye along it – a nice detail, but it is a bit tricky to maintain the flat panel shape when most of the last short piece is flying over the edge of the hull. Rather than blow it full of staple holes, I used clamp blocks to bridge the joints and keep this piece flat as it extended over the edge of the hull. Use the clamps you have and tape if necessary (6-237).

Using a fast-drying carpenter's glue means we can keep going while the glue sets. By now the ends should be dry enough to cut the miter in the first two planks installed.

Tack a batten along the centerline of a few stations and centered on the stem. The most effective way to mark the centerline on the planking is with a utility knife (6-238). It will project straight down from the batten, make an accurate mark and begin the cut. Make a number of passes with the blade to begin the cut. Remove the batten and trim the plank with a sharp chisel, working from the middle toward the stems. Try to keep the cut plumb and straight; the closer it is to a machined edge, the easier it will be to fit the other side up to it.

Building up the covering board on the other side and fitting it to the centerline may look tricky to some first-time builders, but this is as difficult as planking the deck will get.

Use the L-jigs to clamp the first plank up to the marks, with the ends lying over the centerline (6-239). Having the plank under control and being able to reposition it back in the same place after cutting will simplify this step. Use a straightedge to mark where the plank crosses the centerline, cut to the line on the bench, then replace it to see how it looks. Take note of how close you are on the first try; this information will be helpful for adding some extra length when the other end is trimmed.

Do the final fitting with the block plane, then make a reference mark from the plank to the form in the middle of the kayak. Use this mark for fitting at the stern as well as for positioning the plank after applying the glue.

Mark and trim the aft end and refine the cut until the reference marks in the middle line up. When you are happy with the fit, glue the ends of the planks at the centerline and where they cover the sheer clamp; fasten to the forms with the L-jigs or staples.

Fit the next plank using the same routine, glue and clamp (6-240). The rest of the planks are easier to install because the ends are left to hang over the edge of the hull and are trimmed when dry.

6. Install remaining planks.

Planking the center portion of the deck on this model has been designed to be fast and simple for the first-time builder. The deck line breaks at the cockpit cutout, which means that every plank is essentially in two parts, one forward of the cockpit, the other aft. Instead of having to fit two fine angles on a single plank and get the length exactly right, you just have to fit a single angle on two planks. Plank length is less important because the excess overhangs the opening.

A good start is important because the planks to follow will mirror the first plank. Fitting the first two planks as a pair simplifies positioning the joint over the centerline and bringing the pair to a point on the end.

Begin by setting up the L-jigs to position the first plank on one side of the centerline. A simple way to do this is with another small jig. Cut two short pieces off the end of the plank (there's about a foot extra) and tape the pieces together with one end flush. Bend them enough to make a point and mark the end as the centerline. Place the jig on the form with the centerlines together and clamp the L-jig up to it.

Tape the first pair of planks together, position them on the centerline and mark at the edge of the covering boards where the planks cross the covering boards. Make the cut on the bench for safety and clean it up back in position.

Before taking the tape off to apply the glue, draw a reference mark across the joint so that all the pieces will fit back together as planned. Apply the glue, line up the reference marks and tape the planks back together. Now apply the glue to the miters and staple the pair into position; I found that fiber tape worked well to draw the ends up tight (6-241). Keep an eye on this joint – the top of the plank must be flush with the covering boards. Do the squeeze test between the forms. If the joint opens up when you let it go, do what you can to keep it tight.

To control the color, keep the planking on both ends progressing at the same time. The planks in the kit are full-length, so by cutting them in the middle and finishing with the offcut, we can continue the natural color from bow to stern.

Use the common-reference trick to trim the aft planks at the center form (6-242). After fitting the miter, mark the plank at the next form, measure from this point to where you want the plank to end, then transfer this distance back along the plank edge and cut.

Fitting the last plank might slow you down a little. Use dividers or marks on a stick to transfer the width of the opening to the plank (6-243). Transfer the distance every inch or so, then use a batten to join the points; trim to the line. Slide the plank

6-241

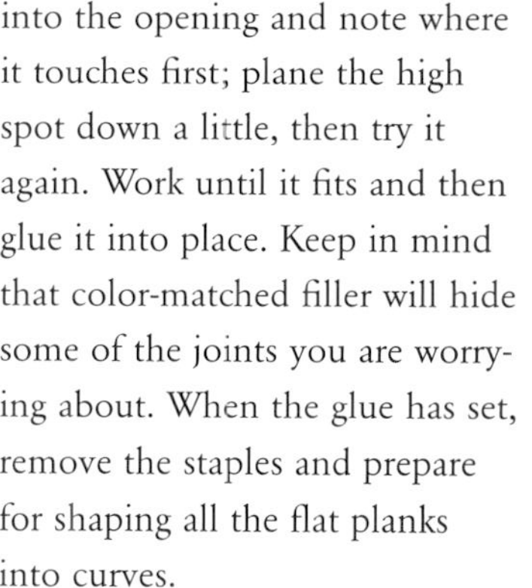

6-242

6-243

into the opening and note where it touches first; plane the high spot down a little, then try it again. Work until it fits and then glue it into place. Keep in mind that color-matched filler will hide some of the joints you are worrying about. When the glue has set, remove the staples and prepare for shaping all the flat planks into curves.

7. Shape and sand deck.

It will help to think of this step as meeting two different objectives. The first is to develop the shape and the second is to smooth any scratches remaining from the shaping step. Confusing these steps can waste a lot of effort and create an unfair surface.

About 85 percent of the shaping can be done with a block plane and a spokeshave. I would much rather be up to my ankles in pleasant-smelling shavings than have my ears ringing, my arms numb and dust everywhere. Use long strokes to keep the lines fair fore and aft and work systematically so that the entire surface

CHEAP TRICK

6-244

6-245

Avoid staple holes

This was such an easy shape to plank that I gave up on using staples after the first pair was anchored. The L-jigs got in the way of placing a staple anyway, so they were left in place until the glue grabbed. As the deck grew, it needed a few spots of hot glue to tack it to the form. To avoid damaging the plank, protect the wood with masking tape and tack only where it needs it. To increase the effectiveness of the jig and to keep from damaging the edge of the plank, a wedge cut from a piece of shaped planking was used between the jig and the plank edge to create controlled pressure (6-244). With four corners to work on and a fast carpenter's glue, there was no waiting to move the wedges and fit the next plank.

Another handy use of this style of wedge is between the plank and the covering board. This is an awkward place to clamp or tape, but the wedge will slip in and do the job (6-245).

6-246

gets the same treatment.

Complete the shaping step with 80 grit sandpaper. For the fairest surface, finish up by hand using a file board, but a respectable surface is possible with a random orbital sander if you keep it moving.

Dampen the surface with water for a preview of the finished color and to raise the bruised grain. If there are places that need to be filled, this is a good time to do it; the smoothing step will clean up the filler.

When dry, smooth the surface with 120 or 180 grit sandpaper, using the same method you chose for the 80 grit step. The reason? Using the machine over a shape developed with a file board could mess up all that careful handwork, and using a file board to remove the inevitable waves caused by a machine would take forever.

Since I planned to add a rudder hung from a custom deck fitting, I made a flat landing spot for it before the deck was glassed (6-246).

The Enterprise deck has a subtle ridge down the centerline as well as a hard line between the deck and the covering boards. To preserve these details, work parallel to the line with both plane and sander; crossing over these edges will eat up the detail. For the cleanest line, soften these edges only after the final sanding.

Another place to keep an eye on is around the edge of the deck. Try to maintain a consistent thickness around the edge for a crisp fit to the guard. Shaping with the block plane here should not be much of a problem, but allowing the pad of the sander to wrap around the edge will cut it down in a flash.

When the sanding is complete, clean up your work space in preparation for glassing the deck.

DAYS 12-14

Glass the Deck

To Do
- O Apply glass and first coat of epoxy.
- O Apply second coat of epoxy.
- O Apply third coat of epoxy.*
- O Remove deck and forms.
- O Shape and sand inside of deck.
- O Fillet sheer clamp.*
- O Glass inside of deck.*

Tools & Materials
- O 2-inch bristle brush
- O epoxy resin and hardener
- O fiberglass cloth
- O file
- O filler
- O grunge cans
- O lacquer thinner
- O mixing pots
- O putty knife
- O rags
- O random orbital sander
- O rasp
- O firm and hard sanding blocks
- O 120 and 180 grit sandpaper
- O scissors
- O scraper
- O squeegee
- O stir sticks
- O utility knife
- O vacuum cleaner

Safety
- O eye protection
- O gloves
- O good ventilation
- O caution with cutting tools

Glassing the outside of the deck will involve the same routine we used on the outside of the hull. By using the WEST 207 hardener, I had an easy day broken into three short periods of activity. If ventilation is a problem, it is a good idea not to hang around watching the epoxy cure. Just check back from time to time. Don't relax yet; make sure the epoxy/hardener ratio is correct and that the material is well combined. Taking the hull and deck apart and preparing the underside of the deck and the fillet between deck and sheer clamp will be a full day. Glassing inside is an easy day, broken into two short epoxy sessions with about five hours between.

1. Apply glass & first coat of epoxy (→ page 82).

The 6-ounce cloth is 60 inches wide. Roll the cloth out on the deck, then cut it in half down the middle, carefully rolling the extra piece back onto the roll for reinforcing the inside of the deck. Tug the cloth from the ends to straighten the threads and adjust it to the shape of the deck (6-247).

Cut the cloth across where the deck line changes, then slit it to overlap the excess width and smooth it over the stern deck (6-248).

Although glassing over strip planking uses the same method as glassing over plywood, there is one important difference. The amount of resin that plywood absorbs is controlled by the relatively even density of the veneer; the first glue line sets a limit as to how deep the epoxy can penetrate. In contrast, solid wood has no limit and each piece has a different appetite. The only way to give each plank as much epoxy as it will absorb is to apply it generously with the brush, allow it to soak in, then squeegee off the excess (6-249). Once the surface has been sealed with the first coat of epoxy, the second and third coats will behave as if they were over plywood.

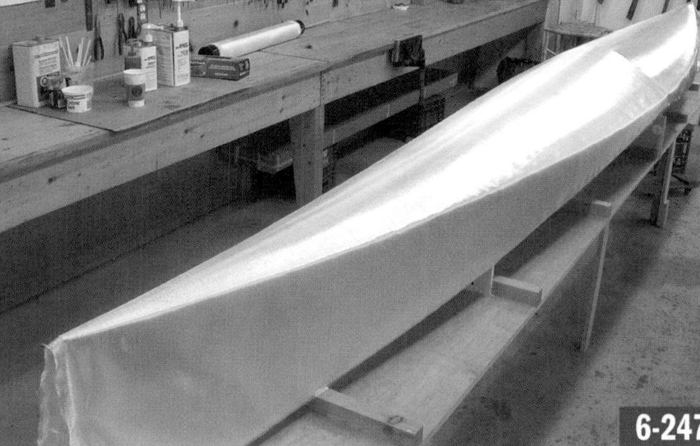
6-247

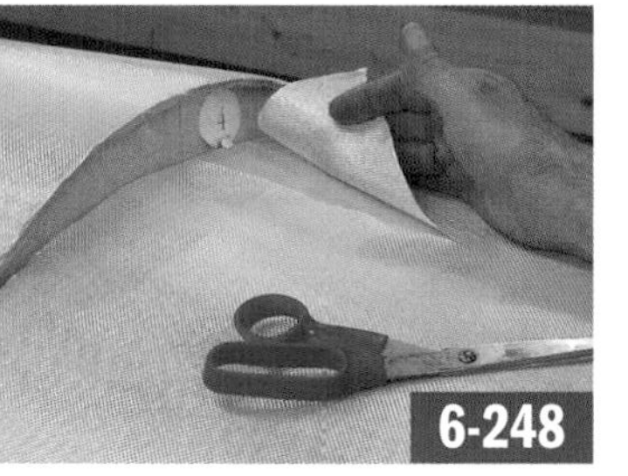
6-248

6-249

2. Apply second coat of epoxy (→ page 87).

My second, weave-filling coat went on after lunch (6-250).

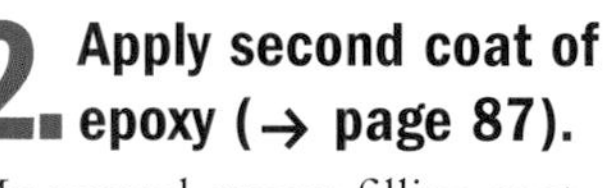

3. Apply third coat of epoxy (→ page 88).

After I had a break for a nap and

6-250

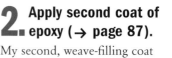

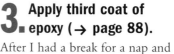

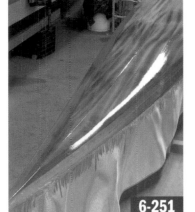

6-251

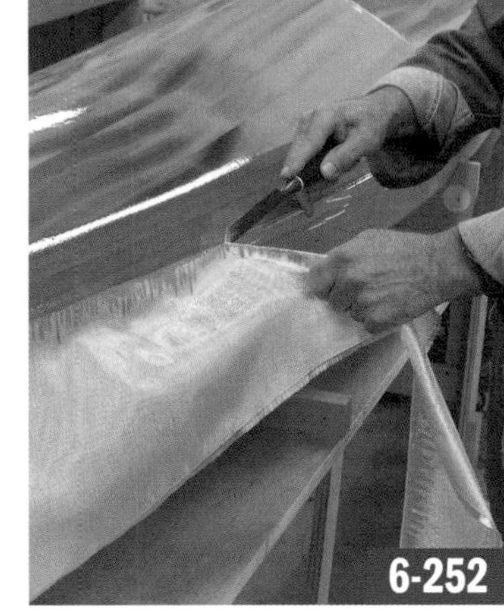

6-252

6-253

dinner, the second coat had reached the green stage and was ready for the final coat (6-251).

4. Remove deck & forms.

Wow! No runs and not too many bugs. The pattern I was trying to create with the supplied planking worked, with only a few surprises.

The epoxy had set up hard overnight, so I started the day by trimming the glass around the deck. Use a utility knife or a sharp chisel (6-252). Remove whatever you have protecting the side of the hull in order to gain access to the screws holding the hull and deck together.

Removing the screws should allow the deck to pop off like the lid of a cookie jar (6-253). On the other hand, it might be more like opening a childproof pill container. If the deck is stuck, find out where it is hung up and work cautiously from there. Keep in mind that prying under the edge of the deck could crack the wood and fold the glass. Gluing the wood back together is just more work, but you will have to live with damage to the glass.

First check that all of the screws have been removed. Stand at the bow and gently shake the kayak up and down; look for areas that are moving and follow along the edge to the place that isn't moving to find out why. My deck was stuck in a number of places by the carpenter's glue and the masking tape. The solution was to slide a thin putty knife carefully along between the tape and the hull to release it.

Removing the forms was no problem, and when the tape was carefully peeled off, my effort to keep the inside clean was rewarded (6-254). There is no reason why you can't go ahead and finish inside the hull at this point. I decided to finish the deck first, just to keep the work on the deck together. The deck is the least stable of the two components, so if you think it might be a while before you find time to finish both, I suggest completing the deck first.

CAUTION

Wear work gloves to handle the deck after trimming the glass cloth; it is glass and it will cut you.

6-254

5. Shape & sand inside of deck.

Set up the deck in the deck cradle forms and secure it with the L-jigs to keep it from sliding around. The first thing to do is use a rasp to work the glass flush to the edge of the deck. The objective is to make the edge safe without removing any wood (6-255). (Did you notice that I'm not wearing protective gloves? I

6-255

6-256

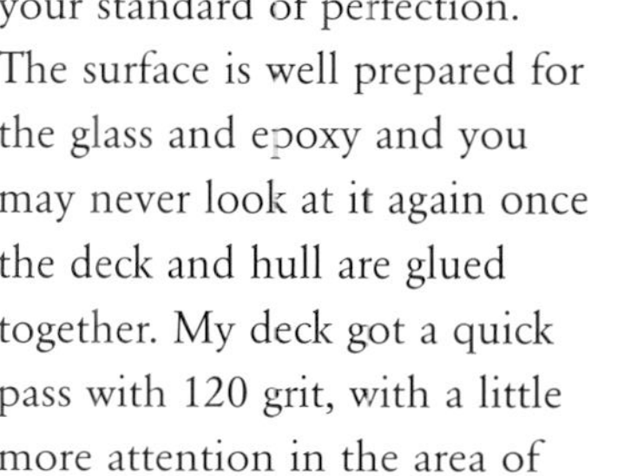

6-257

should be. The uncured epoxy dust is still toxic until it reaches a full cure.)

Tools for shaping concave surfaces are not as common as tools for flat or convex shapes. Since the inside of this deck resembles the inside of a bowl, we have to be creative to get the shape we are after.

My tool of choice is a paint scraper with the blade filed into an arc that fits the shape I am working (6-256). With the blade sharp and held in the right position, it is hard to imagine a better tool for the job. If you are just producing dust, try a different angle or confirm that the edge is sharp. The scraper is quite tolerant of changes in grain direction; you will find a direction that will cut clean.

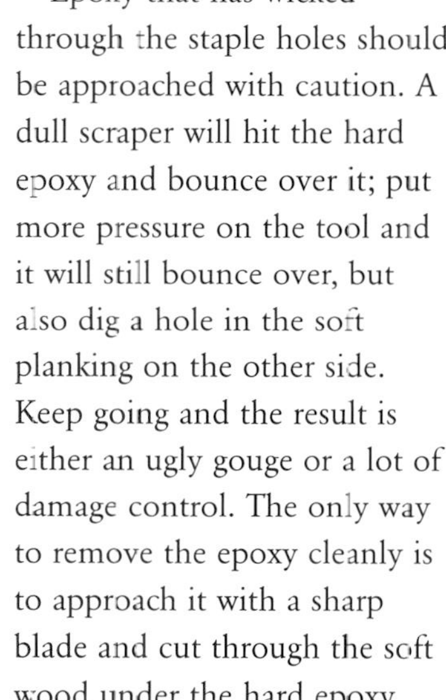

Epoxy that has wicked through the staple holes should be approached with caution. A dull scraper will hit the hard epoxy and bounce over it; put more pressure on the tool and it will still bounce over, but also dig a hole in the soft planking on the other side. Keep going and the result is either an ugly gouge or a lot of damage control. The only way to remove the epoxy cleanly is to approach it with a sharp blade and cut through the soft wood under the hard epoxy.

Complete the shaping step with 80 grit sandpaper on a random orbital sander (6-257). Clean up and check for steps between the plank edges and for stray carpenter's glue. What you do next will depend on your standard of perfection. The surface is well prepared for the glass and epoxy and you may never look at it again once the deck and hull are glued together. My deck got a quick pass with 120 grit, with a little more attention in the area of the hatch cover.

Vacuum up the dust and clean the surface in preparation for the fillet.

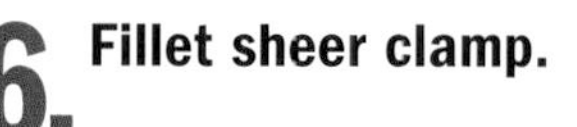

6. Fillet sheer clamp.

The purpose of the fillet between the deck and the sheer clamp is to tie the two components together and to allow the glass to extend gracefully up the side of the sheer clamp (6-258). If this fillet has been put in neatly and cleaned up well, you could go ahead with the glass reinforcement over the uncured fillet. In my case it was the end of the day, so the fillet was left to set up overnight for a fresh start on the epoxy and glass the following morning.

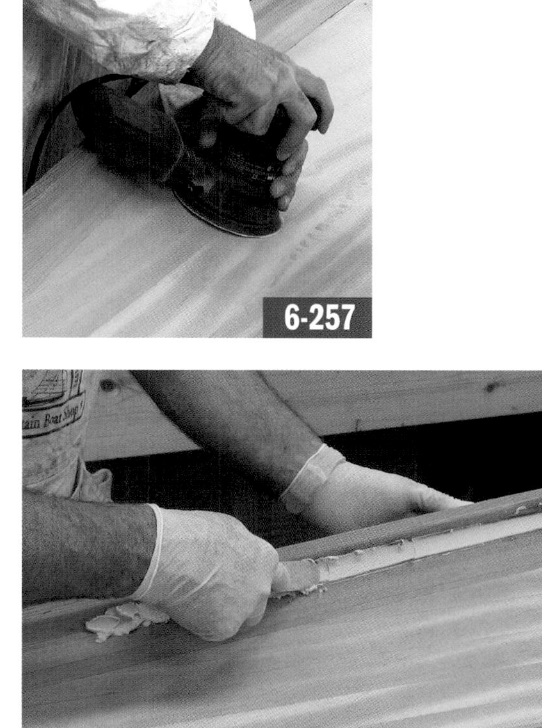

6-258

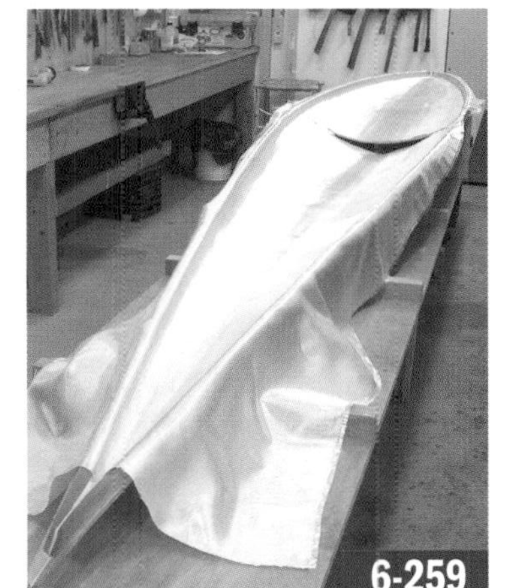
6-259

6-261

7. Glass inside of deck.

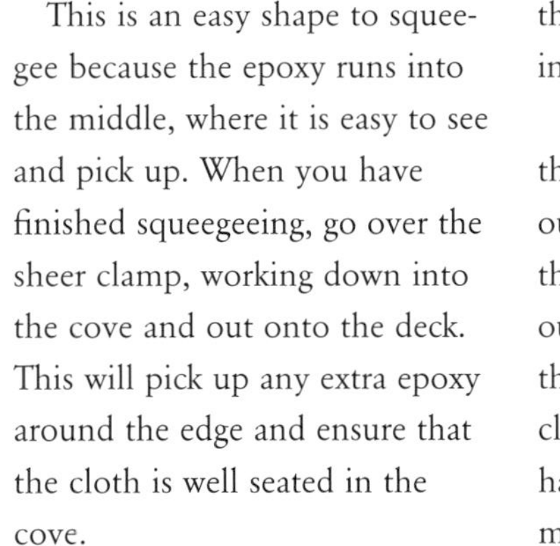

Spread the glass cloth over the deck, then smooth it, working out from the middle. When it is settled, cut the cloth across at the step in the deck and up the middle, enough to get it to lie down. Work the cloth into the cove and up the side of the sheer clamp (6-259).

Use a brush to spread the epoxy over the cloth (6-260) and give it time to saturate the cloth and the surface of the planking. Work from the centerline out to the sheer clamp, then press the cloth down into the cove and let it stand up the side. The cloth will drape over the top of the sheer clamp for now; it will be trimmed off after the first coat has kicked.

This is an easy shape to squeegee because the epoxy runs into the middle, where it is easy to see and pick up. When you have finished squeegeeing, go over the sheer clamp, working down into the cove and out onto the deck. This will pick up any extra epoxy around the edge and ensure that the cloth is well seated in the cove.

Trim the glass along the corner of the sheer clamp after the first coat has kicked, then feather the edge with 120 grit sandpaper. If you don't plan to varnish the underside of the deck, give the surface a quick pass with sandpaper to knock off the sharp points before applying the second coat. That will make sure that nothing catches on your gear. Mask the outside edge of the sheer clamp to catch the inevitable runs over the edge.

Use a brush to apply epoxy to the sheer clamp and a short way out onto the deck (6-261). Use the squeegee to draw the epoxy out onto the deck. This is easier than working it up the sheer clamp with the squeegee, plus the hard-to-see parts won't get missed. This initial application of epoxy is also soaking into the bare wood on the top of the sheer clamp. After all the squeegeeing has been completed, use a dry brush to break the bubbles, then flow on a full coat of epoxy. It won't be as neat as two or three coats that have been sanded in between, but it is adequate for here and faster than more epoxy application and cure cycles.

DAYS 15-16

Glass Inside of Hull

To Do
- O Sand and prep inside of hull.
- O Fillet around stems.*
- O Fiberglass inside of hull.*

Tools & Materials
- O 2-inch bristle brush
- O chisel
- O epoxy resin and hardener
- O fiberglass cloth
- O filler
- O grunge cans
- O lacquer thinner
- O mixing pots
- O putty knife
- O rags
- O firm and hard sanding blocks
- O 120 and 180 grit sandpaper
- O scissors
- O squeegee
- O stir sticks
- O vacuum cleaner

Safety
- O dust mask
- O eye protection
- O glasses
- O gloves
- O good ventilation

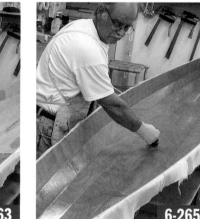

Finishing the inside of the hull brings us to the end of building the hull and deck and to the end of the glass-and-epoxy work. Since there was no reason to mess up the interior, preparing the surface means simply checking it over and knocking off filler that was forced through the suture holes. Glassing the interior is simplified by applying the cloth in 60-inch sections.

1. Sand & prep inside of hull.

Go over the joints with 120 or 180 grit sandpaper on a firm block to flatten any filler that has squeezed through. Vacuum out the hull and check it over.

2. Fillet around stems (→ page 75).

Complete the stems by molding a fillet down both sides of the plywood stem (6-262).

The inside stem allows the mass of filler to be broken up, so it stays in place without a dam being necessary on the vertical portion. It also avoids the problem of dangerous heat buildup that is sometimes seen in large end pours. Bring the filler to the top of the stem so that the end will be solid after the deck is glued on.

3. Fiberglass inside of hull (→ page 91).

Position the first piece of cloth over the cockpit area so that the overlapping glass will be out of sight. On this kayak that's a convenient 60 inches from the stern (6-263). Complete the squeegeeing on each section before putting in the next piece of cloth. Overlap the cloth about 1 inch; for a tidy joint, straighten out the threads on the selvage edge. Wet out the cloth, squeegee off the excess, then cut the glass over the stem and let it stand up the sides of the stem.

When the epoxy has kicked, use a chisel to slice off the glass standing up the sides of the stem (6-264) and sand it smooth. Feather the ends of the glass at the stems and soften up the overlaps between sections of cloth. Give the surface a quick scuff by hand and clean up.

Apply the second and last coat with the squeegee. Use the brush to apply the epoxy up in the ends and around the stem (6-265); where there is more room to move, pour out a puddle and spread it with the squeegee. Scrape it clean and finish by drawing a dry brush aggressively fore and aft.

Trim off the overhanging cloth.

6-262

6-264

6-263

6-265

DAYS 17-22

Complete Deck

To Do

- O Replace deck.
- O Install cockpit coaming.**
- O Install hatch trim.**
- O Sand epoxy.
- O Install foot pegs.
- O Install rudder.*
- O Join hull and deck.*
- O Install guard.
- O Dry-fit seat and deck rigging.

Tools & Materials

- O acid brush
- O block plane
- O clamps (minimum 16)
- O clamp blocks
- O cotton fibers
- O drill and 1/16-inch bits
- O epoxy resin and hardener
- O grunge cans
- O hacksaw blade
- O jigsaw and fine hollow-ground up-cutting blade
- O lacquer thinner
- O masking tape
- O mixing pots
- O plastic tape
- O pull saw
- O putty knife
- O rags
- O rasp and/or hard sanding block
- O router with ½-inch round-over bit (optional)
- O firm and soft sanding blocks
- O 80, 120 and 180 grit sandpaper
- O screwdriver
- O spokeshave
- O 0000 steel wool

Continued on next page

These steps will complete the building process, prepare the kayak for finishing and dry-fit the foot pegs, seat, rudder and deck rigging. Installing the coaming and hatches will make for short days, the amount of time being set by the number of clamps available and the cure time of the epoxy glue.

While the hull and deck are attached, you might as well sand the epoxy. After the deck has been removed, the foot pegs may be installed. If a rudder is to be installed, this is the time to start putting the pieces together. The hull and deck are glued together and the guards installed after all of the interior work has been completed. It is a good idea to do a dry run with all the deck rigging before varnishing. An extra hole in the deck will be easier to fix at this stage than it will be after the finish has been applied.

1. Replace deck.

The deck should slide gracefully back into position, but if it doesn't, don't force it. The ends of the deck that overhang the sheer clamp are fragile and will break if bent back too far. Be sure the deck is centered before pushing down on the ends. Put a few screws in by hand to be sure that the holes line up.

6-266

6-267

6-269

2. Install cockpit coaming (→ page 102).

See photograph 6-266.

3. Install hatch trim (→ page 110).

See photograph 6-267.

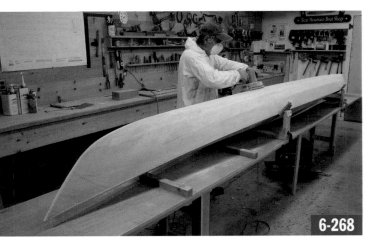

6-268

4. Sand epoxy (→ page 97).

While the hull and deck are attached is a logical time to sand the epoxy on the outside of the hull. All the effort put into building up the epoxy in even layers pays off here. The hull was sanded with 120 grit up to 180 grit and the shop cleaned up in less than two hours (6-268).

5. Install foot pegs (→ page 124).

Attaching the track for the foot pegs with a bolt from the outside is functional and fast. On the other hand, as your kayak begins to shine, the bolt heads may start to look like an afterthought. They do distract me, so I fastened the track to a cleat glued to the inside of the hull (6-269).

6-270

6. Install rudder (→ page 127).

See photograph 6-270.

7. Join hull & deck.

Before making the joint between the hull and deck (6-273) permanent, everything that is easier to do with the deck off should be completed. I would have felt better about varnishing the interior first but could not take the time. Since the varnish was sprayed on, I was able to splash what I could reach through the cockpit and the hatch opening – adequate but awkward.

Assemble the kayak upside down in the deck cradle forms. This will make it easier to apply epoxy glue to the sheer clamp; the bonus is that the glue does not have anywhere to run except to the outside, where it is easy to clean up. Setting the hull on blocks over the deck beforehand will make it easy to position after the glue has been applied.

6-271

Apply a generous amount of epoxy glue to the edge of the sheer clamp and the underside of the deck (6-271). Leave enough glue at the ends to fill up the space between the stem and the deck. Lower the hull and replace the screws in the original holes. Clean up the excess glue and wipe clean. Check: if there are places where the joint is loose, try fiber tape or add more screws. Be sure that the screw heads are below the surface; if they aren't, they will interfere with trimming the deck.

To make a clean line between the deck and the guard, the extra bit of deck we left on will have to be trimmed flush with the hull. Depending on how much is to be removed, use a block plane or a rasp; finish with a hard sanding block. Keep an eye on the screw heads; if they are in the way, try removing them. They will either come out or break off. Try to make the edge of the deck an extension of the hull; rounding it will leave a space between the deck and the guard.

6-272

8. Install guard (→ page 116).

Clean up the kayak and the shop. Mask off the guard and apply sealer (6-272); sand it when dry.

9. Dry-fit seat & deck rigging.

Tools & Materials
From previous page
- O stir stick
- O straightedge
- O utility knife
- O vacuum cleaner

Safety
- O dust mask
- O gloves
- O good ventilation
- O caution with cutting tools

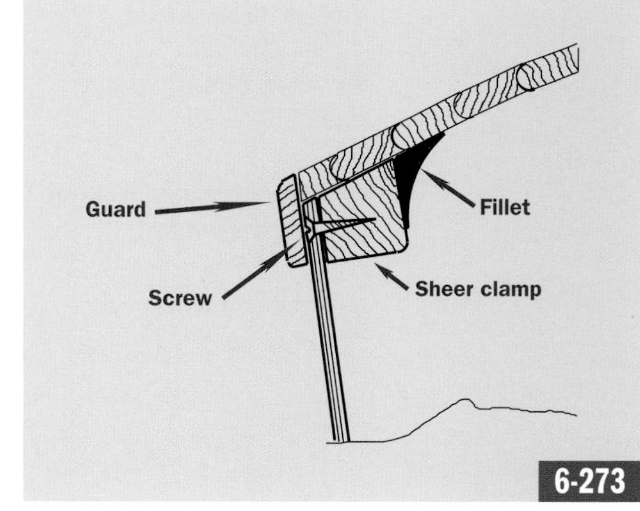

6-273

DAYS 23–28
Varnish

To Do
- ○ Prepare surface.
- ○ Seal trim.
- ○ Apply varnish or paint.
- ○ Install fittings, bulkhead and rigging.

Tools & Materials
- ○ brush
- ○ brush cleaner
- ○ 1-inch masking tape
- ○ paint filters
- ○ paint thinner
- ○ paint pots
- ○ recycled clean cans, plastic tubs
- ○ rags
- ○ 220 or 280 grit sandpaper
- ○ stir sticks
- ○ tack cloth
- ○ varnish or paint

Plan on a minimum of six days to apply at least three coats of finish to both hull and deck. This is good evening work, as the days are short. When the finish has hardened, it will take another day to replace the fittings.

1. Prepare surface **(→ page 134).**

2. Seal trim **(→ page 135).**

3. Apply varnish or paint **(→ page 136).**

4. Install fittings, bulkhead & rigging.

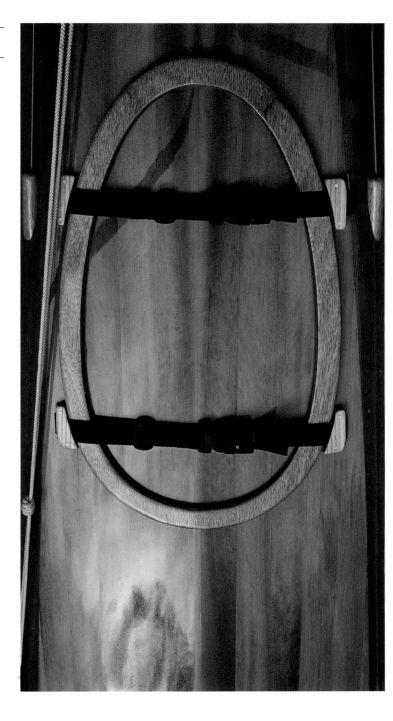

Well, there it is. Two sheets of plywood, a handful of cedar sticks, a couple of gallons of epoxy and some fiberglass cloth. Between a raw beginning and a beautiful, functional craft is the builder. I may have built this one, but there is no reason why I should have all the fun.

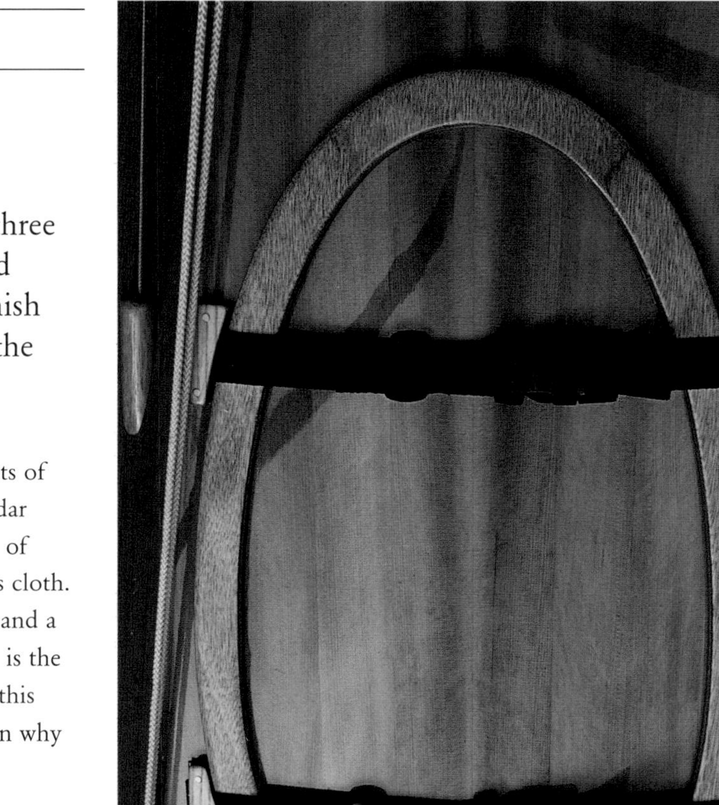

GLOSSARY

A

Aft – the rear end of a boat or behind the cockpit.

Amine blush – a greasy, waxy coating that can develop on the surface of cured epoxy. It is a byproduct of the hardener and is water soluble.

Aniline dye – a powder that is dissolved in water to make a brilliant, non-fading dye for wood.

B

Baseline – a line used as a basis for measurement, calculation or location.

Batten – a thin, flexible length of wood used to create a smooth, fair line.

Beam – the measurement across the greatest width of the hull; a structural member.

Bevel – an angle or slant planed into a piece of wood, usually to facilitate the joining of that piece of wood to another.

Bevel gauge – a gauge used to capture angles.

Bias-cut cloth – fiberglass cloth cut at a 45-degree angle to the selvage to keep the edge from falling apart.

Block plane – a short hand plane used for trimming.

Bore – to drill a cylindrical hole.

Bottom board – the one-piece flat bottom of a boat.

Bow – the forward end of a boat.

Breast-hook – a structural member that ties the end of a small boat together at the sheer line.

Bulkhead – a vertical partition that separates the cockpit from the rest of the boat.

Butt block – a gusset-like block of wood or piece of fiberglass cloth used to back up and reinforce the joint between two pieces of planking.

C

Camber – a convex curve found on a deck, breast-hook or other transverse structural member, such as a deck beam.

Carlins – curved deck beams that support the edge of the deck.

Catalyzed epoxy – epoxy resin that has had the hardener combined with it; mixed epoxy.

Centerline – a line running fore and aft equidistant from the port and starboard sides.

Chine – an angular joint running along the length, fore to aft, of the hull where two planks meet.

Clamp – any device used for temporarily clasping or fastening things together.

Cleat – a piece of wood or metal fastened to something to strengthen or brace it.

Coaming – a ring of wood enclosing and stiffening the top of the cockpit.

Cockpit – the opening in the deck in which the paddler sits.

Collodial silica – a thickening additive used to control the viscosity of the mixed epoxy.

Combination square – a small square with an adjustable arm; used to measure depth and to scribe parallel lines.

Cradle forms – a set of cradles used as a female mold in which to assemble the kayak components.

Cross-spall – a temporary spreader placed sheer to sheer to hold the shape of a hull until permanent interior bracing is installed.

Curtain – a long horizontal run of epoxy, varnish or paint.

D

Dampen – to moisten a wooden surface with water. Dampen means dampen – no puddles.

Deck – in a kayak, the covering of the hull above the sheer.

Dry brush – to work a wet surface with a dry brush to even out the surface without adding more material.

E

End grain – the fiber layers visible on the end of a piece of wood.

End pour – casting a stem or breast-hook with an epoxy-based filler.

Epoxy – often used in this book to mean mixed epoxy, a combination of resin and hardener.

Exothermic – a chemical reaction that liberates heat.

Eye pad – a small looped metal or plastic fitting used to attach lines to the surface of the kayak.

F

Fair – describes a line that is smooth without any unnatural distortions, lumps, hooks or hollows.

Feather – to sand the edges of fiberglass tape or cloth so that they blend smoothly into the surface.

File – a flat steel tool with closely spaced ridges on its surface; used for smoothing, grinding down or cutting through hard material.

File card – a brush with short wire bristles for cleaning and unplugging a file or rasp.

Fillet (*fill*-ett) – a band of thickened epoxy, concave in cross-section, used to ease or smooth the transition between two adjoining planks.

Film thickness – the thickness of a material that has been applied as a liquid.

Finish – varnish, paint or oil.

Fisheyes – round craters (often dry in the middle) on the surface of epoxy coatings or finishes. They are caused by underlying contamination.

Fore - forward end of the boat.

Form – a spacer that the planks are bent around to help develop the kayak's shape.

Freeboard – the vertical distance measured on a boat's side from the waterline to the upper side of the deck.

G

Garboard – the first row of planks on either side of the keel or the bottom board of the hull. On a plywood kayak, the joint between the two planks becomes the keel line.

Graphite – a powder added to mixed epoxy to make a hard slippery surface.

Glass – abbreviation for fiberglass.

Grease pencil – a pencil with a colored compressed grease center used for marking on surfaces that have a glossy finish.

Green stage – epoxy that has been partially cured to a point that it feels firm and dry but is still rubbery; can be cut with a sharp knife without the epoxy sticking to the blade.

Grit – hard particles of sand or manmade particles used to make sandpaper. The higher the number, the finer the paper.

Grunge – excess or unwanted epoxy.

Guard – a thin piece of hardwood covering and protecting the joint between the hull and the deck. Also called a rub rail or outwale.

H

Hatch – an opening in the deck.

Hatch doubler – a ring of plywood under the deck to reinforce the rim of the hatch opening.

Hogged – describes a hull that has been distorted in such a way that the fore and aft ends droop lower than the rest of the keel. When the boat is upside down, it looks as though the bottom is caved in.

Holiday – an area that has been missed when applying a coating or finish.

I

Iron – a flat slab of iron with a beveled cutting edge; used in woodworking tools such as planes or spokeshaves.

Initial stability – a boat's initial resistance to leaning or being tipped from the upright position.

J

Japanese saw – a versatile hand saw with a very thin blade and closely spaced teeth.

Jig – any device, guide or fixture that helps the builder do a task accurately and repeatedly.

Joint – the line where two parts are joined.

K

Keel – the main structural member running fore and aft in a conventional boat. Often used to describe the bottom centerline joint in a plywood kayak.

Kick – mixed epoxy "kicks" at the end of the initial curing step; it turns from a workable mixture into a rubbery mass.

Kiln dried – wood that has been artificially dried to a specific moisture content.

L

Laminate – to glue two or more layers together to make a thicker, stronger structure.

Layup – the application of epoxy to fiberglass cloth on wood or foam.

Level – true horizontal.

LOA – length overall.

Load Waterline (LWL) – the theoretical level at which the hull will float when carrying its design weight.

Lofting – the process of making a full-sized drawing of the lines of a craft; used to produce station molds and patterns for planks.

Lumber marker – a soft wax crayon for making marks on wood.

M

Micro-abrasive sheet – extremely fine abrasives on a Mylar backing; used to put a perfect edge on cutting tools.

Moisture content – for the purpose of this book, the moisture present in wood.

Multi-chined hull – a hull shape developed by using multiple chines running fore and aft.

MSDS – Material Safety Data Sheet.

N

NIOSH/MSHA – National Institute for Occupational Safety and Health/Mine Safety and Health Administration

Nonferrous screws – screws that do not contain iron.

O

Outwale – another name for the guard or rub rail on the outside sheer of a boat.

P

Panel – a longitudinal section of the deck.

Peel strength – the amount of tension necessary to peel fiberglass cloth from the substrata.

Piano finish – a flawless deep gloss finish made by polishing.

Pilot hole – a hole that is drilled in a material to guide the path of a screw as it is being inserted.

Plumb – exactly vertical.

Plywood – a construction panel made of thin layers of wood glued and pressed together.

Port – the left side of a boat when facing forward.

Pot life – the amount of workable time from when the epoxy resin and hardener are mixed to when the epoxy begins to thicken and is no longer usable.

Product Safety Data (PSD) – information on hazardous materials available from a manufacturer.

Profile – the side view of a boat as seen at a right angle to the keel or centerline.

Proud – raised above the surface.

PSA – pressure-sensitive adhesive.

Q

Quartersawn lumber – sometimes called vertical-grained or edge-grained lumber; the grain runs at right angles to the flat side of the board.

R

Rabbet – a groove or step cut along the edge of a piece of wood that is to be joined to another piece of wood.

Rasp – a type of rough file with raised points instead of ridges.

Resin – the substance that is mixed with hardener to make catalyzed epoxy resin, or mixed epoxy.

Respirator – a device worn over the mouth and nose to prevent the inhaling of harmful substances.

Rib – the nautical equivalent to the stud in a wall. Ribs or frames generally run perpendicular to the keel.

Rocker – fore and aft curvature in the keel.

S

Sanding block – a flexible or rigid back-up block for sandpaper.

Sandpaper – strong paper or fabric with sand or other abrasives glued to one side.

Scarf – to join two pieces of wood using a scarf joint.

Scarf joint – a joint made by cutting long bevels into the ends of corresponding pieces of wood and joining them together.

Scraper – a tool with a vertical blade used to peel off a substance from a surface.

Scribe – to pick up and transfer the shape of an opening using either a compass or a block of wood and a pencil; to scratch or etch a line into a piece of wood with a sharp tool.

Scuff – a quick, light sanding.

Selvage edge – the woven edge of a piece of fabric.

Sheer – the long, sweeping line that defines the upper edge of the hull.

Sheer clamp – in plywood kayak construction, a long piece of wood joining the hull and deck.

Shim – to elevate or level something using a thin piece of material.

Skeg – a short stabilizing fin that operates from a box built into the stern of the kayak.

Slump – to slide down slowly.

Small batch – for epoxy glue, one shot from each dispensing pump. For fiberglass application, ½ cup of mixed epoxy.

Solvent – a liquid that can thin or dissolve another substance.

Spline joint – a joint that is made by inserting a narrow key into slots cut in the edges of the pieces being joined.

Spokeshave – a shaving plane used with both hands.

Square – a tool that measures and indicates a true 90-degree angle.

Squeegee – a flat, flexible tool for spreading epoxy.

Starboard – the right side of a boat when facing forward.

Starved glass – fiberglass cloth that has not been saturated completely with epoxy.

Starved joint – a joint that has been robbed of epoxy by absorption or excessive clamping pressure.

Station – a two-dimensional slice at regular intervals through the hull; similar to slices in a loaf of bread.

Stem – the vertical or near vertical ends of a hull onto which the planks are fastened.

Straightedge – a thin piece of wood or metal having a perfectly straight edge; used for drawing lines.

Strake – a continuous run of hull planking from fore to aft; can be either a single piece or several pieces joined together.

String line – a fine, strong string used to establish the centerline and true up the hull.

Strongback – a frame used to support a boat while it is being built.

Sutures – the temporary wire "stitches" that hold the plywood planks and panels together.

Syringe – a disposable plastic syringe used for injecting filler and glue.

T

Template – a pattern made of thin stock, poster board or cardboard.

Thinner – for epoxy, use acetone or lacquer thinner; for oil-based paints and varnish, use paint thinner.

Tongue depressor – a thin hardwood stick with rounded ends; useful for shaping filler or cut into pieces for clamp blocks.

Tooth – a high, sharp point seen after applying the first coat of finish to a raw wood surface.

U

UHML – ultra-high molecular weight.

Up-cutting blade – a fine jigsaw blade that cuts on the upstroke; ideal for cutting openings for hatches and cockpit.

V

Viscosity – a measure of the thickness of a liquid and its resistance to flowing.

VOC – volatile organic compound.

W

Waterline length – the length of the boat in contact with the water.

Weight – any heavy object used to provide holding and clamping pressure.

Wet out – to apply epoxy to fiberglass cloth.

Wetted surface – the amount of boat surface area making contact with the water.

Wood flour – commercial or homemade sanding dust (120 grit or finer) used as a coloring additive for epoxy filler.

SOURCES

Plywood kayak kits, building supplies and accessories

Bear Mountain Boat Shop Inc.
P.O. Box 191
Peterborough, ON K9J 6Y8
Toll-free order line (877) 392-8880
www.bearmountainboats.com

Chesapeake Light Craft, LLC
1805 George Avenue
Annapolis, MD 21401
(410) 267-0137
www.clcboats.com

Newfound Woodworks
67 Danforth Brook Road
Bristol, NH 03222
(603) 744-6872
www.newfound.com

Pygmy Boats Inc.
P.O. Box 1529
Port Townsend, WA 98368
(360) 385-6143
www.pygmyboats.com

Roy Folland Wooden Kayaks
130 Como Gardens
Hudson, QC J0P 1H0
(450) 458-0154
www.royfolland.com

Kayak outfitting equipment (spray skirts, seats, rudders, paddles and accessories)

Cascade Designs
4000 First Ave. S.
Seattle, WA 98134
(206) 505-9500
www.cascadedesigns.com

Cricket Paddles
17530 W. Hwy. 50
Salida, CO 81201
(800) 243-0586
www.cricketdesigns.com

Feathercraft Folding Kayaks and Accessories
4-1244 Cartwright Street
on Granville Island
Vancouver, BC V6H 3R8
(604) 681-8437
www.feathercraft.com

Grey Owl Paddles
62 Cowansview Road
Cambridge, ON N1R 7N3
(519) 622-0001
www.greyowlpaddles.com

Magellan Systems Corporation
960 Overland Court
San Dimas, CA 91773
(909) 394-5000

Mountain Equipment Co-op
130 West Broadway
Vancouver, BC V5Y 1P3
(604) 876-6221
www.mec.ca

Nimbus Paddles
1087 Gordon Drive
Kelowna, BC V1Y 3E3
www.nimbuskayaks.com

Northwater Rescue and Paddling Equipment
52925 Oak Street
Vancouver, BC V6H 2K7
(604) 264-0827
www.northwater.com

Ritchie Navigation
243 Oak Street
Pembroke, MA 02359
www.ritchienavigation.com

Salamander Paddle Gear
(800) 641-0500
www.salamanderpaddlegear.com

Seairsports
2043 Main Street
San Diego, CA 92113
(619) 230-1167
www.seairsports.com

Seaward Kayaks
Box 2026, Ladysmith, BC V9G 1B5
(800) 595-9755
www.seawardkayaks.com

University of Sea Kayaking
P.O. Box 6708
Santa Barbara, CA 93160
(805) 696-6966
www.useakayak.org

Werner Paddles
Northwest Design Works, Inc.
12322 Highway 99 South
Everett, WA 98204
(800) 275-3311

Tool Catalogs

GarrettWade
161 Avenue of the Americas
New York, NY 10013
(800) 221-2942
www.garrettwade.com

Highland Hardware
1045 N. Highland Ave. NE
Atlanta, GA 30306
(404) 872-4466
www.highlandhardware.com

Klingspors Sanding Catalogue
P.O. Box 3737
Hickory, NC 28603-3737
(800) 228-0000
www.sandingcatalogue.com

Lee Valley Tools Ltd.
1090 Morrison Drive
Ottawa, ON K2H 1C2
(800) 267-8767
www.leevalley.com

Epoxy Suppliers

MAS-Phoenix Resins
1501 Sherman Avenue
Pennsauken, NJ 08110
(800) 398-7556
www.masepoxies.com

System Three Resins Inc.
P.O. Box 70426
Seattle, WA 98107
(206) 782-7976
www.systemthree.com

WEST SYSTEM®
Gougeon Brothers Inc.
P.O. Box 908
Bay City, MI 48707
(989) 684-7286
www.westsystem.com

Varnish

Epifanes
58 Fore Street
Portland, ME 04101
(800) 269-0961
www.epifanes.com

Interlux Paint Inc.
2270 Morris Avenue
Union, NJ 07083

Pettit Paint Co.
36 Pine Street
Rockaway, NJ 07866

Woolsey/Z-Spar
36 Pine Street
Rockaway, NJ 07866
(800) 221-4466

Publications

Adventure Kayak
P.O. Box 115
Quadville, ON K0J 2G0
(613) 754-2732
www.adventurekayakmag.com

Canoe and Kayak Magazine
P.O. Box 3146
10526 NE 68th Street, Suite #3
Kirkland, WA 98033-3146
(800) 692-2663
www.canoekayak.com

EPOXYWORKS
P.O. Box 908
Bay City, MI 48707-0908
www.westsystem.com

Kanawa
Box 398
Merrickville, ON K0G 1N0
(970) 879-1450
www.crca.ca

Paddler
P.O. Box 775450
Steamboat Springs, CO 80477
www.paddlermagazine.com

Sea Kayaker Magazine
7001 Seaview Ave. NW
Seattle, WA 98117
(206) 789-9536
www.seakayakermag.com

WaveLength Magazine
2735 North Road
Gabriola Island, BC V0R 1X7
(604) 247-9789
www.WaveLengthMagazine.com

WoodenBoat
P.O. Box 78
Brooklin, ME 04616 USA
(207) 359-4651
www.woodenboat.com

Further Reading

The Aleutian Kayak
by Wolfgang Brinck
Ragged Mountain Press/McGraw-Hill
ISBN 0-07-007893-9

Baidarka
by George Dyson
Alaska Northwest Publishing Company
ISBN 0-88240-315-X

The Bark Canoes and Skin Boats of North America
by Edwin Adney and Howard Chapelle
Smithsonian Institution Press, 1964

Brightwork: The Art of Finishing Wood
by Rebecca J. Wittman
International Marine/McGraw-Hill
ISBN 0-87742-984-7

The Canoe: A Living Tradition
by John Jennings
Firefly Books
ISBN 1-55209-509-6

Canoecraft: An Illustrated Guide to Fine Woodstrip Canoe Construction
by Ted Moores
Firefly Books
ISBN 1-55209-342-5

Canoes and Kayaks for the Backyard Builder
by Skip Snaith
International Marine
ISBN 0-87742-2427

KayakCraft: Fine Woodstrip Kayak Construction
by Ted Moores
WoodenBoat Books
ISBN 0-937822-56-6

The New Kayak Shop
by Chris Kulczycki
Ragged Mountain Press
ISBN 0-87742-367-9

"A retractable skeg: Better performance for your sea kayak"
by Rob Bryan
WoodenBoat Magazine
January/February 1995, Number 122

The Strip-Built Sea Kayak
by Nick Schade
Ragged Mountain Press
ISBN 0-07-057989-X

Wood and Canvas Kayak Building
by George Putz
International Marine
ISBN 0-87742-258-3

ACKNOWLEDGMENTS

WRITING A BOOK and building a boat have much in common. While both begin with the skeleton of someone's dream, it takes the contribution of others and a good crew to put a skin on it. It has been a pleasure working with the many people who have enriched this book by providing information and products. Thank you.

The biggest component of writing a book is time. I owe my partner, Joan Barrett, for the gift of time to focus on this project.

For helping to get the book started, I must thank Charis Cotter, for believing in the project and for her proposal to Firefly Books. When Greg Rössel agreed to come onboard, we needed some time working together and to find a direction for this book. Thank you, Chaa Creek Lodge, Cayo, Belize, for hosting our stay in paradise.

Our three beautiful kayaks were built from kits supplied by Bear Mountain Boats, Chesapeake Light Craft and Pygmy Boats. For some of the bits and pieces, thank you Don Curtis, Ron Frenette and Bill Robbins.

For providing historical and technical information, thank you John Lockwood, Pygmy Boats, and the technical staff at WEST SYSTEM Epoxy.

The most satisfying part of this project has been working with our crew. They are inquisitive, strive for personal excellence in their craft and have fun doing it. I have admired Greg's teaching and writing style for years, so it has been a pleasure to work with him and steal some of his tricks. Our editor, Laurie Coulter (a non-boatbuilder/woodworker), showed a lot of courage jumping into the project with a couple of wooden boatbuilders. Laurie became a natural member of the crew as she is a wizard at her craft and her high editorial standards fit well with our expectations for this book. Thank you for shaping the parts we made into a structure, throwing away the pieces we didn't need and asking all the questions a first-time builder could ever think of. Gareth Lind provided the wonderful book design, John de Visser photographed the "glamor" shots for the book and copyeditor Gillian Watts polished our words. To the crew at Firefly Books – Lionel Koffler, Michael Worek and Brad Wilson – thank you for believing in quality books of substance.

– T.M.

INDEX